A Young Generation Under Pressure?

Joerg Chet Tremmel
Editor

A Young Generation Under Pressure?

The Financial Situation and the "Rush Hour" of the Cohorts 1970–1985 in a Generational Comparison

Springer

Editor
Dr. Joerg Chet Tremmel
CPNSS
London School of Economics and Political Science
Houghton Street
London WC2A 2AE
UK
J.Tremmel@lse.ac.uk

Many articles of this book were originally presented at the symposium "Easing the Rush-Hour of Life" in July 2008 in Berlin. This symposium was financially supported by VolkswagenStiftung, Robert Bosch Stiftung, and Haniel Stiftung.

HANIEL STIFTUNG   Robert Bosch Stiftung   VolkswagenStiftung

ISBN: 978-3-642-03482-4   e-ISBN: 978-3-642-03483-1
DOI 10.1007/978-3-642-03483-1
Springer Heidelberg Dordrecht London New York

Library of Congress Control Number: 2009933606

Cover design: WMXDesign GmbH, Heidelberg, Germany

Printed on acid-free paper

Springer is part of Springer Science+Business Media (www.springer.com)

Preface

Justice between generations is still not as prominent on any agenda as justice between the rich and the poor or between men and women. For the first time, this three part book explores the labour market situation of today's young generation in comparison with that of their predecessors. The first part of the book, *The Financial Situation of the Young Generation in a Generational Comparison*, deals with the financial situation of the young generation and the second part, *The Rush Hour of Life*, with their time restrictions. Both are considered from a life-course perspective. The third part, *On the path to Gerontocracy?*, addresses the demographical shift in favour of the elderly in ageing Western democracies.

Regarding the first part: older employees in the public service – as in many branches of the private industry sector – receive higher salaries, profit from a significantly higher level of dismissals protection, enjoy more days of vacation and work less hours per week than their younger colleagues. As far as distributive justice is concerned, redistributions among age groups are not unjust as such, because everybody ages. After all, in 50 years, today's youth might also benefit from all these nice things.

But will they really? Some of the articles in this anthology show that today's younger generation is at a disadvantage compared to their direct predecessor. The relative level of income of young adults has diminished constantly in recent decades. For continental Europe, several studies show an increasing percentage of graduates partaking in at least one internship after their academic degree; half of them are uncompensated. Because of the difficult situation on the labour market, the young cohorts are forced to enter precarious, temporary jobs or internships to avoid unemployment. These jobs are characterized by working overtime and on weekends, minor holiday entitlement, low or no wages, nor social security. Key questions for the first part of the book are:

- *How can precariousness be defined? What empirical evidence is there for precarious employment for the young generation? In an historical comparison with the youth of the 1970s, is the situation for today's youth worse?*

- *Are young cohorts – with a delayed entry in the labour market – supposed to make up for this in later stages of life, or can we assume there will be "scarring effects" over the course of the lifetime?*
- *Which policies should be implemented to improve this situation? On which level should they be implemented?*
- *How do legal regulations like the seniority principle and age-biased dismissal protection respect the principle of intergenerational justice in the labour market?*
- *Using common typologies of welfare states, which political system is best in coping with the challenge of inter- or intracohort inequalities?*
- *How has globalisation changed the state of affairs? Has it increased the level of job insecurity for young and old workers, for men and women alike?*

Regarding the second part: even though life expectancy continues to rise, many people feel that they do not have the time to combine work, children and leisure. The book focuses on the easing of the so-called "rush hour" of life between 28 and 38 years of age. In this period, people finish their studies, take decisive career steps and have to decide whether or not to start a family. It is important to examine this crucial period of time, in order to understand why the actual birth rate is lower than the desired figure across various industrialised countries. Key questions for the second part of the book are:

- *How can the phenomenon known as "rush hour of life" be defined?*
- *How can motherhood at a later stage in life support easing the rush-hour? With the knowledge that their life expectancy is higher than that of previous generations to what extent should individuals change their life plans?*
- *How can the public sector and/or the private sector support a balance between every domain of life?*

Regarding the third part: Are we on the path to gerontocracy? In numerical terms, the political balance between different age cohorts has shifted in favour of the elderly in ageing Western democracies. For about 15 years, political scientists have considered the possibility that these states are on the path to gerontocracy. That is, they are increasingly likely to reflect elderly power. A correlate of this is that governments which represent ageing populations increase old age related expenditure, for instance for pensions, health and care. Key questions of the third part of the book are:

- *Are we shifting from a democracy to a gerontocracy?*
- *How is the party formation process affected by the ageing of modern welfare states?*
- *How is the political participation process affected by ageing?*

Most of the articles stem from a symposium that the Foundation for the Rights of Future Generations organized on the topic of the "rush hour of life" in Berlin in July 2008. Many thanks go to the sponsors Volkswagen Stiftung, Robert Bosch Stiftung and Haniel Stiftung who supported the symposium financially.

Joerg Chet Tremmel

Contents

Contributors

Prof. Dr. Hans-Peter Blossfeld is director of the Institute of Longitudinal Studies in Education (INBIL) at the University of Bamberg and principal investigator of the National Educational Panel Study (NEPS). Since 2001, he has held a chair of sociology at Bamberg University, and since 2003, he has been the director of the State Institute for Family Research at Bamberg University (ifb). He received his training in sociology, economics, social statistics and computer science at the University of Regensburg (Diplom-Soziologe, 1980), the University of Mannheim (Dr. rer. pol., 1984), and the Free University of Berlin (Habilitation, 1987). Blossfeld is the chairman of the European Consortium of Sociological Research (ECSR). Blossfeld has published 24 books and over 180 articles on globalization, social inequality, youth, family, and educational sociology, labour market research, demography, social stratification and mobility, the modern methods of quantitative social research and statistical methods for longitudinal data analysis.

Prof. Dr. Giuliano Bonoli is professor of social policy at the Swiss Graduate School for Public Administration (IDHEAP), Lausanne. He previously worked at the Universities of Fribourg and Bern in Switzerland, and at the University of Bath in Britain. He has been involved in several national and international research projects on various aspects of social policy. His work has focused on pension reform, labour market and family polices, with particular attention paid to the politics of welfare state transformation. He has published some 40 articles and chapters in edited books, as well as a few books.

Prof. Dr. Louis Chauvel is professor at the Institut d'Études Politiques de Paris (Sciences-Po Paris). He was born in 1967, studied at the École Nationale de la Statistique et de l'Administration Économique (Master 1990), completed a Ph.D. with distinction at the University of Lille (1997) and habilitated at the Institut d'Études Politiques de Paris. His main research interests are analysing social structure and the life chances of generations. His book *Destin des Générations* (1998, PUF) caused a vivid debate in France. Since 2005, Chauvel is General Secretary of the European Sociological Association. He is also a member of the executive committees of the International Sociological association (ISA).

Dr. Achim Goerres is assistant professor (Akademischer Rat) of research methods at the University of Cologne. He studied European studies and comparative politics in Osnabrück (Germany), Leiden (Netherlands) and the London School of Economics and Political Science (LSE, United Kingdom) and obtained his Ph.D. in Government from the LSE in 2006. Before moving to the University of Cologne, he was a postdoctoral research fellow at the Max Planck Institute for the Study of Societies. His research interests include politics and public policies in ageing societies, comparative political behaviour and public opinion and applied research methods. Goerres has published articles in *Electoral Studies*, *Journal of European Social Policy* and *Politische Vierteljahresschrift*. His monograph *The Political Participation of Older People in Europe: the Greying of our Democracies* was published by Palgrave Macmillan in 2009.

Dr. Silja Häusermann is a Max Weber Fellow at the European University Institute in Florence, Italy, and a lecturer (Oberassistentin) in comparative politics at the University of Zurich, Switzerland. Her research interests are in comparative politics, welfare state research and comparative political economy. Most recently, she has done research on welfare policy developments in continental Europe, conflict dimensions and coalition-formation in welfare politics, and the linkages between party system change and welfare policy change.

Silja Häusermann studied political science at the Universities of Geneva, Lausanne, Zurich and Harvard. She holds a Ph.D. from the University of Zurich. Her forthcoming book with Cambridge University Press, entitled *The Politics of Welfare Reform in Continental Europe: Modernization in Hard Times*, explains the adaptation of continental welfare states to post-industrial risk structures. Silja Häusermann has also published in journals such as the *Journal of European Public Policy*, the *Journal of European Social Policy*, *European Societies* and *Socio-Economic Review*.

Dr. Seán Hanley is senior lecturer in politics at the School of Slavonic and East European Studies, University College London, having previously worked in the Department of Government at Brunel University, West London. His research interests principally cover politics and society in Central and Eastern Europe, the formation and organisation of political parties, the comparative politics of the European centre-right the political representation of older people in Central and Eastern Europe. He is co-editor (with Aleks Szczerbiak) of *Centre-Right Parties in Post-Communist East-Central Europe* (Routledge, 2004) and author of the *The New Right in the New Europe: Czech Transformation and Right-Wing Politics 1989–2006* (RoutledgeCurzon, 2007). He has additionally published widely in journals such as *West European Politics*, *Party Politics and Perspectives on European Politics and Societies* and *The Journal of Communist Studies and Transition Politics*.

Dr. Steffen Hillmert is professor of sociology with specialization in research methods and social stratification at the University of Tübingen. He studied sociology in Bamberg, Cambridge, UK and Berlin, was a doctoral research fellow at the Max Planck Institute for Human Development, Berlin, and received his Ph.D. in sociology from Free University Berlin.

Over the last few years, Professor Hillmert's research has focussed on various aspects of social inequality and the life course. He investigated mutual relationships between life-course developments and structural changes in social collectivities, i.e. relationships between micro and macro levels of society on the basis of quantitative empirical data. He is particularly interested in links between education, employment and social stratification (e.g., group-specific chances of education, risks of unemployment, labour–market mobility and long-term changes in transition patterns). Applying and further developing adequate analytical techniques has also been part of this program.

Dr. Ute Klammer is professor of social policy and vice rector at the University of Duisburg-Essen, Germany. She graduated at Cologne University, Germany, in philosophy and literature (1990) as well as in economics (1991) and holds a Ph.D. in economics of Frankfurt University, Germany (1995). She was awarded the *Matthöfer Science Prize* for her Ph.D. thesis on old age security in Italy. Ms. Klammer has worked at several German universities and at the University of Louvain-la-Neuve, Belgium, as a researcher and lecturer before she changed to her current position in 2007. Ute Klammer's main fields of interest and research are social policy, labour–market research, flexicurity, European and comparative social policy research as well as gender research. She acted as a consultant for the Council of Europe, for several political parties in Germany and for the German Trade Unions.

Ms. Klammer's list of publications contains more than 100 titles on different aspects of social security and social protection. She is board member of the section "social policy" within the German Sociological Association and of the Society for Social Progress. She is also co-editor of the scientific journal *German Review of Social Policy*.

Since 2008, Ute Klammer is a member of the German family ministry's "Expert Commission on Gender Equality" and of the German "Council for Sustainable Development".

Prof. Dr. Martin Kohli, born 1942 in Switzerland, is professor of sociology at the European University Institute (Florence) and emeritus at the Free University of Berlin. He is a member of the Berlin-Brandenburg and the Austrian Academy of Sciences, and was president of the European Sociological Association from 1997 to 1999. He was a fellow of the Institute for Advanced Study (Princeton), the Collegium Budapest and the Hanse Wissenschaftskolleg. Moreover, he was a visiting professor at Harvard, Stanford and Columbia University. His research focuses on the life course, aging, generations, work, family and welfare. Currently he is engaged in a MacArthur Foundation Network on the aging society and in an Academy Group on fertility.

Dr. Lefteris Kretsos is research fellow at the Coventry University, Faculty of Business Environment and Society. He is also an associate lecturer in Human Resource Management and Employee Relations at the Robert Gordon University (RGU), Aberdeen Business School. His research interests focus on employees' experience of work and their response to organisational change and restructuring. Recent research projects have addressed the nature of change in a variety of work organisations, how this has impacted on employees, and how industrial relations processes shape the nature of outcomes of restructuring. A large part of his research is also dealing with the issues of union revitalization strategies, migration and labour market segmentation in the framework of flexicurity employment policy guidelines. Before joining the academia he used to work as a researcher and policy advisor for the trade unions in Greece. He was also working as a national correspondent for the European Foundation for the Improvement of Living and Working Conditions in Dublin.

Harald Lothaller is a social psychologist from Graz (Austria). Currently, he is responsible for statistics, data analyses and reporting at the University of Music and Performing Arts Graz as his main job. Aside, he is still engaged in different research activities in the fields of social psychology and medicine. Furthermore, he is lecturer at the Department of Psychology of the University of Graz and at Health Sciences area of the University of Applied Sciences Joanneum Graz. Until 2006, he was research assistant of Prof. Gerold Mikula at the University of Graz and worked in several research projects that focused on the reconciliation of life domains.

Prof. Dr. Melinda Mills is adjunct professor for Sociology of the Life Course at the University of Groningen, a Rosalind Franklin Fellow and editor of the journal *International Sociology*. She received her master of sociology at the University of Alberta in Canada and wrote her Ph.D. thesis on *The Transformation of Partnerships. Canada, the Netherlands, and the Russian Federation in the Age of Modernity* at the University of Groningen. She was associate professor at several Universities in Germany and the Netherlands between 2001 and 2008. Her research field include life course studies, gender studies and demography studies.

Dr. Tomáš Sobotka is research scientist at the Vienna Institute of Demography (Austrian Academy of Sciences) and managing editor of the Vienna Yearbook of Population Research. He received his Ph.D. in demography from the Population Research Centre, University of Groningen (the Netherlands) in 2004.

His research deals mainly with fertility trends in the developed world; his work focuses especially on the postponement of childbearing and very low fertility, changes in family and living arrangements, childlessness, fertility intentions and assisted reproduction. Sobotka's work has been published regularly in major demographic journals and selected monographs; recently he has co-authored a three-volume monograph on *Childbearing Trends and Policies in Europe*.

He has been lecturing at the Max Planck Institute of Demographic Research in Rostock and, together with Joshua Goldstein and Vladimir Shkolnikov, he has initiated a *Human Fertility Database Project* that aims to provide access to detailed and standardised data on births and fertility in countries with high-quality data.

Dr. Joerg Chet Tremmel is a research fellow at the London School of Economics and Political Science. Tremmel studied business administration (MBA, 1998) and politics (MA, 2003), and thereafter finished two Ph.D.s in sociology (2005) and philosophy (2008). In winter semester 2009/10, Tremmel is a visiting lecturer at the Johann-Wolfgang-Goethe-Universität Frankfurt, the Georg-August-Universität Göttingen, the Heinrich-Heine-Universität in Düsseldorf and the University of Stuttgart. A selection of taught courses: Intergenerationally Just

Policies, Normative and Empirical Justice Research, Epistemology, Population Sociology. He has published five monographs (e.g. *A Theory of Intergenerational Justice*, London: Earthscan) and about 70 articles in journals and edited anthologies.

Patrick Wegner is research associate at the Foundation for the Rights of Future Generations and editor for *the new police in Europe* and the *Intergenerational Justice Review* journals. He studied political sciences, sociology and public law at the Justus-Liebig-University in Gießen and the University of Leicester in England. His research fields include generational justice and armed conflicts, the assessment of social and political consequences of climate change as well as state failure and terrorism. Recently he has published a monograph and journal articles on the ideology of Islamist terrorism.

Summary of the Chapters

This interdisciplinary anthology is composed of chapters by sociologists, political scientists, demographers, economists and social psychologists. The contributors come from a number of different European countries, namely Germany, the United Kingdom, Switzerland, Austria, France, the Netherlands and Greece.

Part I The Financial Situation of the Young Generation in a Generational Comparison

Usually, you do not make a mistake if you clearly define your key terms at the beginning of your research, and if you take a look at the history of the issue at hand. Both tasks are undertaken in the first chapter of the first part of the book where Lefteris Kretsos (Coventry University) discusses the issue of precariousness at work for young people in Europe. His chapter, *The Persistent Pandemic of Precariousness: Young People at Work,* aims to show that young workers have become permanent "outsiders" of the labour market in the last 30 years.

The author examines the employment situation of young people using data from Eurostat and OECD for all the "old member-states" of the European Union (EU-15). Rodgers' definition of precarious employment is also used as a disciplinary device in the analysis and the selection of the data. According to his definition, there are four dimensions to establish if a job should be called precarious or not, namely: (i) the degree of certainty of continuing working (temporal dimension), (ii) the control over working conditions, hours, wage and working intensity (organizational dimension), (iii) the absence of trade unions and the employers' control over the labour process (social dimension), (iv) issues of decent salary and pay rises and the level of income (economic dimension).

The chapter first discusses the historical dynamics of precarious employment. As it is argued there, the economic theory considered atypical work two centuries ago as a problem attributed solely to the low morality and the immature work ethos of the unemployed and the temporary workers. Atypical work (nowadays understood as part-time and temporary employment, irregular and unsocial working hours) was synonymous with unemployment and the individual characteristics of the unemployed. Today, fixed-term and other types of flexible contracts are part of the official European Employment Strategy, and instead of constituting a problem, they are actually promoted as the solution to the problem of unemployment.

This development is the result of the abandonment of the target of full employment and the social democratic consensus reached between governments and social actors after the Second World War in Europe. The dominance of neoliberal policies across Europe in the last three decades has promoted the expansion of a typical forms of work and has spread more risk and insecurity among the young workforce. Young people in atypical contracts are asked to be flexible and to always bear in mind that planning their lives in the long-term is not a wise option given the current conditions that prevail in the labour markets.

Such conditions indicate that precarious employment is a structural characteristic of European labour markets for young people. According to the author, both the data on atypical employment and the conceptualization of precarious employment from a historical perspective are alarming and create a sense of urgency for change that should be based on a new social consensus that takes seriously into account, young workers' interests and needs.

In the next chapter, *Comparing Welfare Regime Changes: Living Standards and the Unequal Life Chances of Different Birth Cohorts*, Louis Chauvel (Sciences-Po Paris) focuses on inter-and intra-cohort inequalities of living standards in a comparative perspective, comparing a corporatistic (France), a liberal (United States), a universalistic (Denmark) and a familialistic (Italy) welfare regime. Chauvel underlines the diversity of national responses to the challenges of economic slow down, stronger economic competition and globalisation and their implications on different age groups. The aim is to make a connection between national welfare regimes and the emergence of specific cohort-based economic constraint patterns in different countries, which are about to produce specific social generations. In this chapter, the emergence of "scarring effects" is highlighted; that is the irreversible and definite consequences of (short term) social fluctuations in the context of socialisation on the (long term) life chances of different birth cohorts. These "scarring effects" can affect specific birth cohorts in countries where the welfare regime provides the context for increasing polarisation between middle-aged insiders and young outsiders. Chauvel shows that the first years on the labour market are often considered to be crucial for future life chances.

While in the liberal and the universalistic regime all age groups face a similar life course, both the corporatistic and the familialistic regime fail to treat younger generations equally to the older ones. This is due to the success of the "68's Generation" to exert political pressure to create a welfare state in their interest, which is now on the retreat. So now, for the first time in a period of peace, the younger generations are no better off then their parents were, creating an atmosphere of dependency. The social value of generations changed from a relative valorisation of succeeding generations, as a positive future we have to invest in, to a valorisation of the protection of the senior citizens. The main problem, thereby, is that these developments are not protested against, because they are not well known and they are not politically recognized at all.

Hans-Peter Blossfeld (University of Bamberg) and Melinda Mills (University of Groningen) show in their chapter *How Does Globalization Affect the Life Course of Young Men and Women in Modern Societies?* that increasing uncertainty about economic and social developments is a feature of globalization in all advanced economies. However, increasing uncertainty does not impact all regions, states, organizations or individuals in the same way. There are institutional settings and social structures, historically grown and country-specific, which determine the degree to which young people are affected by rising uncertainty. In his contribution, Blossfeld and Mills develop a multi-level theoretical framework and summarize the main empirical results from the GLOBALIFE project. There is empirical evidence that youth in all countries are clearly exposed to more uncertainty in the course of globalization. However, because of strong insider-outsider markets in some countries, youth are particularly affected. In addition, uncertainty is unequal among young people, with risk accumulating in certain groups, generally those at the bottom of the qualification pyramid. Labour market uncertainty among young adults also strongly impacts family formation. Young people in more flexible positions are more likely to postpone or forgo partnership and parenthood. Youth and young adults also develop rational responses to this uncertainty, which are identified in the form of diverse behavioural strategies. The paper suggests that – in terms of social policy – it is important to help young people to reduce the level of uncertainty and to support women's employment through better pre-school and day care arrangements.

The chapter by Steffen Hillmert (University of Tübingen) looks at long-term developments in the transition from school to work. The question is whether and to what extent there has really been a de-structuring of the transition to the labour market – and linked with it of the transition to adulthood – as it has been proposed by theories of individualization. Empirical life-course data allows long-term comparisons across West German birth cohorts to be made.

The results indicate that significant changes in transition patterns can be related to the expansion of education and training since the 1950s. This is especially obvious in the case of young women. Both attaining a vocational or an academic degree and entering the labour market have become universal life events. One of the consequences is the prolongation of educational careers, which has led to later entries into employment. Hence, transitions to the labour market can no longer be equated with "youth transitions". Another consequence is increasing selectivity of educational tracks which has contributed to the deteriorating labour market position of the low qualified. Entry to (stable) employment has become more difficult, but after a period of "settling in" and increased mobility at the beginning, most people have experienced relatively stable employment careers. Differences in career patterns remain highly correlated with formal qualifications, with deficits in formal education carrying risks of exclusion. As a consequence of both social inequality in education and significant returns to education, social inequality is transferred across generations through the educational system. These "traditional inequalities" have remained strong.

School-to-work transitions are among the first events in the sequence of transition to adulthood, and are decisive for success later in life. In spite of the clear qualification-related differentiation of labour market risks, however, subjective uncertainty – deriving most prominently from the labour market – has been experienced by a large share of younger cohorts including the higher qualified. Such "new insecurities" are a likely cause of external effects like the postponement of biographical decisions in other spheres of life.

The last chapter of the first part of the book presents an exploratory survey with the members of the German Bundestag on the situation of the young generation in the labour market, carried out by Joerg Chet Tremmel (London School of Economics and Political Science) and Patrick Wegner (Foundation for the Rights of Future Generations). Their article, *German Bundestag Survey on Intergenerational Justice in the Labour Market*, first highlights changes in income and wealth distributions between 1980 and today that are disadvantageous for the young generation. The authors then introduce the theoretical groundwork for comparisons between generations on which the design of the survey was based. The survey covers general topics of generational justice in the labour market with a special focus on the "rush hour of life" and the situation of young employees at the point of career entry, as well as potential legislative measures to improve the situation of the young generation.

The second part of the chapter consists of findings of the survey. A *Generational Justice Awareness Index* is constructed on the basis of indirect comparisons between chronological-temporal generations. Moreover, the influence of outside variables like age and gender are analysed.

The authors find that the deputies' awareness of the concrete problems that the young generation faces in the labour market is generally high. Nevertheless, this does not translate into full support of decisive legislative action, for instance, introducing an age neutral dismissal law.

Part II The Rush Hour of Life

The chapter *On the Way to Life-Domains Balance: Success Factors and Obstacles* by the social psychologist Harald Lothaller serves as a starting point in the second part of the book. In a certain stage of life that we call the "rush hour of life", people face various challenges from different life domains simultaneously: they have to fulfil obligations at their workplace, at home, and elsewhere (e.g., getting a job and starting a career, establishing a family, moving towards getting their own home, but also meeting people, part taking in leisure activities, etc). As a corollary to this, they need to keep several life domains in balance. Lothaller first introduces the term "life-domains balance" and shortly explains why the more commonly used terms "work/life balance" and "work/family balance" do not meet the topic adequately. Subsequently, keeping life domains in balance is defined as the absence of negative effects ("conflicts") between life domain on the one hand, but also the presence of positive effects ("facilitation") between domains on the other hand.

In the second part of this chapter, different causes of both conflicts and facilitation between life domains are presented systematically. Dyadic aspects as well as gender aspects are considered additionally. The third part illustrates why the "rush hour of life" and the issue of life-domains balance are major challenges nowadays, in particular, and more people have to face them as compared to former generations.

In the next chapter *Shifting Parenthood to Advanced Reproductive Ages: Trends, Causes and Consequences*, Tomáš Sobotka from the Vienna Institute of Demography argues that the decision on the right timing for having children has become increasingly difficult for men and women who try to balance their education, career, and leisure activities with their partnership and family plans. The chapter outlines a remarkable shift towards later parenthood across all advanced societies and discussed determinants and consequences of this trend.

Medical literature shows that late childbearing is associated with increased risks of infertility, miscarriage, pregnancy complications, stillbirths, preterm deliveries and foetus malformations. Many of these findings have been repeatedly confirmed for mother's age, but more evidence is being gathered on the negative effects of parental age. However, social and behavioural development of children later in life does not seem to be affected by the late timing of parenthood. To the contrary, families of "late parents" often show higher stability and better family functioning. In addition, there are strong economic and career advantages for parents, especially higher-educated mothers, from postponing childbearing. Also burden-sharing within the family might be better organised if couples postpone childbearing towards the point when their parents retire and thus become available for caring about their grandchildren. Thus, the individual social and economic advantages of late parenthood may outweigh the biological advantage of early parenthood, as older parents are more experienced and knowledgeable, have more secure economic position, face lower risk of divorce, and can more easily afford childcare.

Although many people believe that medically assisted reproduction may provide a solution to infertility problems associated with postponing family formation for too long, the evidence shows that assisted reproduction is particularly ineffective at higher maternal ages and it has a very limited role in helping prospective older parents to realise their reproductive plans.

In conclusion, the author outlines possible policy actions that may support childbearing decisions at both younger and older reproductive ages. Such policies should recognise wide heterogeneity in needs and lifestyle preferences of individuals, and should not explicitly aim to encourage early parenthood.

Ute Klammer (University of Duisburg-Essen, Germany) in her article *The "Rush Hour" of Life: Insecurities and Strains in Early Life Phases as a Challenge for a Life Course-Oriented, Sustainable Social Policy* discusses the "rush hour of life" in terms of the stresses and strains in early life phases caused by uncertainties in employment, and raises this as a challenge for producing a life-course oriented, sustainable social policy. She aims to connect the question of life courses of men and women to the debate about a readjustment of social politics in view of demographic change.

In the first section, empirical data on the structure and change of life courses of both men and women are provided on an international scale. The difference in ways of handling the "rush hour of life" by different countries are shown and a comparison is made between Germany, Sweden and the Netherlands. Through this empirical data, Klammer demonstrates that the "rush hour of life" for women does not have to be resolved by a withdrawal from the labour market, as is often the case in Germany. Also discussed in this section is that unlike in past decades, women are no longer at a general disadvantage just because of their sex. In fact the vast majority of labour market flexibility risks, i.e. fixed-time contracts, temp work, unemployment etc., are taken by the young generation, the newcomers to the labour market, irrespective of their gender. The resulting insecurity, particularly in light of the increasing number of involuntary job changes, appears to be having a significant influence on young people's decision of whether or not to have children. In addition to this, periods of unemployment and temporary positions are resulting in a decrease in the accumulation of labour years during the life courses of men which will significantly affect the already delicate pensions of the young generation.

In the second section, approaches for a sustainable, life course orientated social policy are discussed. Klammer claims that what is needed are schemes that allow working time adjustments according to one's changing needs over the life course, as well as social and political support of transitions in and out of the labour market. The urgency of such a policy is required in order to alleviate the "rush hour of life". This and a general obligation to pay into the social security systems can help to make it possible for everyone to obtain pension entitlements, at least as high as the socio-cultural minimum.

Klammer concludes by stating that if social policy was geared in this direction, then it would raise awareness of the risks of such discontinuous employment and help to avoid old age poverty. Above all this would mean that young people would be encouraged to trust and rely upon the social system.

Part III On the Path to Gerontocracy?

Part III starts with an article by Martin Kohli (European University Institute, Florence). He discusses in *Age Groups and Generations: Lines of Conflict and Potentials for Integration* the extent of generational conflict in today's society and whether or not such a conflict will lead to a gerontocracy. The social question of the twenty-first century is no longer how to integrate the industrial workers (as it was at the end of the nineteenth century), but how to maintain a balanced generational contract protecting the elderly and investing in the young, while being financially sustainable and just. Differential treatment of age groups according to needs is morally acceptable, providing that each generation can expect the same at each life stage. However, this is usually not the case, which creates potential lines of conflict between the generations. As a result of demographic and economic changes, some generations are more fortunate and better-off than others all through their life course. Why, in light of this potential for conflict, are age-group or generational conflicts not more pronounced? One explanation lies in the difficulty of identifying with a particular generation when there are so many internal differentiations with regard to class, religion, ethnicity and gender. This makes any attempt to establish a feeling of "being in the same boat" almost impossible. In addition, the mediating function of political parties, unions and families explains why such conflicts do not dominate society. Elderly people are not only interested in their own well-being but also in that of their descendents, which manifests itself in the financial and social support they give to the following generations. In terms of political decision making, there is no evidence for a trend towards gerontocracy.

The next chapter *Who Wants What from the Welfare State? Socio-structural Cleavages in Distributional Politics: Evidence from Swiss Referendum Votes* comes to quite different conclusions. The authors Giuliano Bonoli (Swiss Graduate School for Public Administration, IDHEAP) and Silja Häusermann (European University Institute in Florence) investigate socio-structural cleavages in relation to social policies in Switzerland. Their article examines the extent to which vertical stratification or class, age and gender explain variations in individual social policy preferences. The goal is to investigate the pattern of multiple intersecting conflict lines, and to examine the relative weight and specific impact of each of these conflict lines. The analysis is based on survey data (VOX surveys) on reported voting behaviour in 22 direct democratic referenda concerned with distributional social policy issues between 1981 and 2004. These reforms were selected because they generally have clear distributional consequences for voters. In other words, it is relatively easy for voters to understand if they are likely to be winners or losers of these reforms.

The two main findings are the following: (1) age, i.e. a generational divide over resource allocation, seems to be the most relevant line of conflict in most distributional issues. Older generations not only massively endorse improvements in the benefits they receive, but they also tend to reject social policy proposals aimed at improving the situation of the actively employed and of young families. (2) Vertical stratification (income and education) and gender are less important in explaining individual voting decisions. The findings also suggest that material interests based on socio-structural characteristics account for only part of the variation in social policy preferences, and that value cleavages are also important.

In the next chapter, Achim Goerres (University of Cologne) analyzes demographic and survey data and reviews major findings on age-related differences in political participation in order to assess how demographic and participatory developments play out for the current young generation in Europe and what these findings mean for European democracies.

In his chapter *Being Less Active and Outnumbered?* that the political participation process in Europe is currently skewed in favour of middle-aged people who dominate in terms of their pressure potential (measured through their participation levels and demographic size) over other age groups. Young people have the lowest pressure potential due to their low participation rates and their small demographic weight. Since age groups differ in their political preferences, young people may be less able to convey information about their different preferences to, and to exert pressure on, political elites than other age groups. This finding does not imply that there is an antagonism between young and old, but the influence that young people can exert through democratic participation is more limited. In general, politicians interested in equality should not be concerned about the growing importance of older people, but the diminishing significance of the young compared to both middle-aged and older people.

Again, another aspect of the issue of gerontocracy is highlighted in the last chapter of the book: *The Emergence of Pensioners' Parties in Contemporary Europe,* Seán Hanley (University College London) examines the origins, demands and prospects of the many small pensioners and retirees' parties, which have emerged at the margins of Europe's political systems over the past two decades. Such "grey interest" parties appear at first examination to be a purely fringe phenomenon of little consequence, as they lack the potential to attract *mass* electoral support or realign political competition along age- or generational lines. Age-based political identities have historically been weak in Europe, and many older voters can be assumed to have strong established party loyalties and pre-existing political identities shaped by class, ethnicity or geography rather than generational factors.

However, Hanley argues, "grey interest" parties are sufficiently widespread and persistent to merit closer examination. As with other new minor parties, even when electorally unsuccessful, grey-interest parties may be significant as a marker for the emergence of new issues or an indication that (wider) groups of voters may be (re) defining and (re)negotiating socio-political identities or seeking vehicles for protest. Moreover, in a small number of European states "grey interest" parties have already enjoyed sufficient electoral success to gain – or come close to gaining – parliamentary representation and in some instances have exercised real political leverage. In Slovenia, Serbia and Israel pensioners' parties even entered government as junior coalition partners.

This chapter maps the emergence of pensioners' parties in both established West European democracies and in the newer post-communist democracies of Central and Eastern Europe (CEE). It first discusses their origins and demands – both of which are typically rooted in the defence of older people's welfare rights – before reflecting on the reasons for their emergence and, in certain cases, relative success. Consistent with the wider political science literature on new parties, it argues that the emergence of grey interest parties can be explained through a mixture of the "demand" for such parties generated by changes in the demographic structure, and the welfare and the opportunities afforded to them by the stability (or instability) of existing parties and the generosity of electoral systems.

However, there are important variations in patterns detectable in established Western democratic states and the newer democracies of Central and Eastern Europe (CEE). While pensioners' parties in CEE are more akin to interest groups that take to the political arena and are generally aligned to the traditional left, self-styled retirees' parties in more established Western democracies often mix interest politics with a raucous populist, anti-establishment message. The chapter concludes with a tentative assessment of the growth prospects of grey interest parties. These, it argues, will be limited by competition from bigger parties and the difficulty of translating interest and single issue demands into a coherent set of ideological principles.

Part I
The Financial Situation of the Young Generation in a Generational Comparison

Chapter 1
The Persistent Pandemic of Precariousness: Young People at Work

Lefteris Kretsos

1.1 Introduction

The emergence of a new underclass composed of young people usually described in the press as the "Precarious Generation" *or the* "Generation of 1,000 euros"[1] (and earning even less in certain cases) is, currently, one of the most widely discussed issues in the international discourse about the future of work. The obvious reasons for such a development are related to the dramatic expansion of jobs, which are precarious in nature in recent decades, as well as to the multiple and decisive ways that such a development affects the social and political inclusion of the young people,[2] as well as other vulnerable groups of the workforce, such as immigrants, women and other vulnerable groups. The contemporary context in Europe appears to be marked by an increase in economic inequalities and growing disparities in social participation and citizenship rights. In other words, current socio-economic forces have made work more *insecure*, *unpredictable* and *risky*.

However, speaking about precarious jobs today, the analysis should cover more working groups and has to reflect more, and different, working stories than that of low-paid workers or workers in atypical contracts and bad working conditions. The notion of precarious employment has become widespread and the term itself is

---

L. Kretsos
Faculty of Business, Environment and Society, Coventry University, Coventry, UK
e-mail: lefteris.kretsos@coventry.ac.uk

[1]The term, inspired by social movement activists, independent writers and radical political bloggers is currently used to describe the labour market situation of the young workers generations (18–30 years old), who have to make their own living and to organise their life under the restricted stream of low-paid and contingent jobs. Similar or associated terms used in the modern literature to describe the emergence of the new underclass include the following: contracto a vassoura, mill-euristas, Generation P (acronym from the Precarious), the contrat première embauche (CPE) generation, and Generation Kangourou.

[2]Age is a useful, but not sufficient indication to characterise the transition to adulthood. The focus of this paper is on the people age 16–30 years.

J.C. Tremmel (ed.), *A Young Generation Under Pressure?*,
DOI 10.1007/978-3-642-03483-1_1, © Springer-Verlag Berlin Heidelberg 2010

controversial. In essence, we have to talk about a combination of work precariousness elements that can be found probably in every job and working environment. However, some jobs have more elements of precariousness than others and certain social and age groups are more inclined to be found in more precarious jobs. In order to detect these elements, we have either to look on the daily biopolitics[3] of precarious workers or to restrict the analysis on the statistics of atypical and insecure forms of employment.

Based on the data from Eurostat and OECD, this paper focuses on the investigation of the position of young people in the labour market of the "old member-states" of the European Union (EU-15). The departure point of analysis is that precarious employment is a structural characteristic of the labour markets across EU-15. The analysis starts by examining the development of economic theory about precarious employment from the early stages of capitalism to date. The analysis moves next to the discussion and the presentation of the data regarding young people at work. As it will be shown there is a definite generation effect, in the sense that the young workforce was *not* exposed 30 years ago to the same extent as today to atypical employment.

1.2 The Historical Dynamics of Precarious Employment

The debate on the consequences of precarious jobs to society in general and to individuals is not something new. Such an interest is inherent to the history of capitalism, as capitalism was always characterized by inequalities in the way work was regulated and income was distributed among the workforce (Garraty 1978; Schumpeter 1954; Thompson 1981). In economic theory, the issue of precarious/contingent jobs was, for a long time, synonymous with the problem of unemployment.[4]

For most of the history of capitalism, economic theory considered seasonal and contingent workers as punks, wastrels and people in general who had low moral values and were characterised by an unproductive work ethos (Garraty 1978). Unemployment and seasonal/contingent work was an anomaly of the economy and an obstacle to economic growth that could be reduced by forcing people at

---

[3]According to this philosophical approach of precariousness, such elements are distributed across the whole time and space of life and they form an existential condition that spreads beyond the boundaries of work (Neilson and Rossiter 2005). For example, Tsianos and Papadopoulos (2006) consider precarity (the state of precariousness) as a mean to exploit the continuum of everyday life and not simply the workforce. Precarity is a form of exploitation, which operates on the level of time and forms an embodied experience.

[4]For example, Marshall described unemployment as *inconstancy* of employment. In general, the definitions of unemployment used before Keynes' theory on employment (1936) usually implied a type of work or an employment pattern characterised by inconstancy, irregularity, variability and discontinuity. For further information, see the analysis of Winch (1972) and Dedousopoulos (2000).

work (e.g. work camps) and/or by implementing policies that reduced wages (J. S. Mill) or even control the growth of the population (Ricardo, Malthus). It was also an anomaly, the overcoming of which demanded the creation of a well-disciplined workforce to the factory production system norms. According to Marshall (1920), though, the more the factory system norms were established the more the available jobs would become predictable, stable, regular and typical.

It was not until 1909 that Beveridge provided a new insight on the issue by considering the problem of unemployment and seasonal employment as a problem of industry and not a problem attributed solely to the morality and the work ethos of the unemployed and temporary workers. Unemployment and contingent work was regarded by Beveridge as an economic problem strongly related to the fluctuations of the economic cycle and not mainly to the individual characteristics of the unemployed. The creation of stable jobs was thought to eliminate contingent ones and this process was thought only to be achieved by enhancing labour mobility, strengthening occupational training and other labour market institutions and welfare policies. However, it l took more than four decades since the original conceptions of Beveridge (and to some extent those of Marshall) for work to become more standardised, typical and regulated.

Even in the 1930s, economic theory could not really disengage the discussion about precarious jobs from the problem of unemployment. According to Hicks (1932), there is a duality of the labour market in the sense that certain groups of the workforce are characterised by subnormal productivity and lower, than the average population, skills. These groups are either unemployed or temporary workers in seasonal jobs. Temporary workers are attracted by seasonal/contingent jobs because they are lazy and unable to find a better job. As such, precarious workers are like a group of socially unfit people.

As Mitropoulos (2005, p. 92) has argued: "Precarity has been the standard experience of work in capitalism the experience of regular, full-time long-term employment which characterized the most visible aspects of fordism is an exception in capitalist history that presupposed vast amounts of unpaid domestic labour by women and hyper-exploited labour in the colonies".

During the first post-war decades (a period well-known as the "golden era of capitalism"), in most central and northern European countries, the gradual establishment of the welfare state resulted in the institutionalisation of the standard employment relationship (SEP). The concept of SEP was always commonly used to describe stable and full-time employment relationships or open-ended work contracts for full-time job and stable working hours (Michon 2009). The concept of SEP was also strongly associated with the philosophy that underlined the Declaration of Human Rights by the United Nations in 1945.

According to the content of respective Articles of the Declaration (Articles 22, 23, 24): "*Everyone, as a member of society, has the right to social security and is entitled to realization, through national effort and international co-operation and in accordance with the organization and resources of each State, of the economic, social and cultural rights indispensable for his dignity and the free development of his personality*". "*Everyone has the right to work, to free choice of employment, to just and favourable conditions of work and to protection against unemployment*". "*Everyone, without any discrimination, has the right to equal pay for equal work*". "*Everyone who works has the right to just and favourable remuneration ensuring for himself and his family an existence worthy of human dignity, and supplemented, if necessary, by other means of social protection*". "*Everyone has the right to form and to join trade unions for the protection of his interests*". "*Everyone has the right to rest and leisure, including reasonable limitation of working hours and periodic holidays with pay*".

Observing the modern landscape of employment and the trends in industrial relations across Europe, it can be easily understood that those rights established more than six decades ago should *not* be taken for granted in nowadays for a significant and growing part of the workforce. The supposed periphery (workers in atypical contracts) is growing in comparison to the core segments of employment (holders of decent jobs in terms of pay, security and working conditions). In essence, the distinction between the primary and secondary labour markets is progressively *disappearing* and secondary labour market conditions spreading across the board.

A burgeoning literature has developed to explain how and why job insecurity has spread throughout the 1990s, affecting a widening spectrum of workers including skilled professional workers. Examining the case of the US labour market, Sweet and Meiksins (2008) have noted that the spread of job insecurity has occurred because of: the decline of older, more secure types of work; the changing strategies for organizing work; and the changing composition of the labour force. All these dynamics have contributed to the deconstruction of the employment relationship in a way that results in an unbalanced distribution towards and among the workers of the insecurity and risks typically attached to the labour market (Frade and Darmon 2005).

A recent policy document by the European Trade Union Confederation (ETUC 2007) provides a clear picture on the trends of precarious and contingent work in Europe. More specifically, across the EU-25 member states:

- Some 30 million workers (or 14.5% of the workforce) were employed on a fixed-term contract in 2005. This means an increase of 5 million contingent workers since 2000.
- 37 million workers are now working part-time in contrast to 32 million in 2005.
- There has been a significant fall in the share of workers having received training from their employers (from 30.6% in 2000 to 27.3% in 2005).
- 33% of workers indicate that their duties are below their skills and that they could perform more demanding tasks.

In any case, the respective figures show that the unique heritage of the European Social Model and the target of full decent employment established under the Human Rights Declaration of United Nations after the Second World War are under threat. In reality, industrial relations have become more and more individualised and commodified, losing their collective character and nature (Hyman 2007). Employers discover day by day more flexible working practices and initiate various experiments in the way work is organised and regulated at the workplace. This results in the gradual extension of atypical contracts against the normal ones.

In more political terms, other writers and academics suggest that the spread of work insecurity is the result of neoliberal economic policies to restore corporate low profit rates after the crisis of the 1970s (Callinicos 2003; Dumenil and Levy 2005; Shaikh 1999; Brenner 1998). According to Moseley (1999), several strategies were used for the wage reduction process, including: "direct cuts of wages (and benefits), the shift toward 'contingent' jobs (such as part-time jobs, temporary jobs, etc.), 'two-tier' wage systems (in which new employees are hired at much lower starting wages compared to existing employees)". During the same period, the gap between earnings of high- and low-paid employees rose dramatically.

For example, in the Mediterranean member-states of the EU, the ratio of minimum wage relative to median wages of full-time workers showed an impressive fall from 62% in 1975 to 40% in 2006.[5] Furthermore, according to Eurostat, the rate of part-time employment jobs in the EU15 economy has increased from approximately 12% in early 1980s to more than 18% in 2008 and the rate of temporary employment has increased from 8 to 15%, in the same period.

It is also important to note here the involuntary character of these growing contingent forms of employment. The distinction between full-time and part-time employments is not taken into account in the calculation of unemployment rates, but the reality is that low-registered levels of unemployment are hiding an excess supply of labour of those workers with part-time jobs. The majority of them would prefer a full-time job. Moseley (1999) and Bluestone and Rose (1997) argue that this excess labour supply is a reason for the downward pressure on wages and the "real-wage freeze impact" that are both observed in the last three decades.

1.3 A Definition of Precariousness and Young People's Exposure to Precarious Jobs

In all European countries, young people appear to have a higher inclination than the rest of the population to such types of contingent employment (Biletta and Eisner 2007). There are, though, national variations in the extent of contingent employment across Europe. Nevertheless, in all countries, young people face more difficulties than older workers in getting an entry into the labour market and have much more difficulties in finding stable and well-paid employment despite their higher level of educational attainment. The available statistics from the Labour Force Survey indicate that education definitely matters in finding a job, as unemployment is always higher for the unskilled workers in all cases, but conversely it is also evident that high achievements in education do *not* necessarily guarantee a promising career.

[5]See http://stats.oecd.org/WBOS/index.aspx.

The fact is that the majority of entrant employees face low wages results in an increasing pressure on the younger generation to make its own living. Young workers and new entrants in the labour market are two of the most heavily affected victims of this income inequality and wage-squeezing process. Young workers are more exposed to low pay in all European countries and there is an increased likelihood of young people being poor (Buchel 2002; Gallie et al. 1998; Lagarenne and Legendre 2000).

In essence, the restructuring of employment relations and the decrease in real wages have created a deep generational gap in the allocation of income and the allocation of secure jobs in the economy, raising serious issues and concerns for implementing intergenerational justice policies. As the OECD (1997) relevant study findings suggest, there is an age-specific effect with regard to self-perceived job insecurity, as job insecurity declines with increasing age.

Nevertheless, numerous national variations are observed on the way insecure employment develops. For example, in Greece and Italy, work insecurity is widespread, especially among young workers, despite the fact that at the same time both countries are characterized by one of the longest average tenures.[6] In general, different paradigms of precarious employment are hard to be compared as the characteristics that determine such employment vary among age groups or/and sectors of economic activity, making difficult a specific definition, which takes into account all different aspects of precarious employment.

An attempt to overcome the problem of comparing the actual degree of precarious employment among different labour markets was made by Rodgers (1989) who identified four dimensions to establish if a job should be called precarious or not. The first refers to the degree of certainty of continuing working, either because of short-time horizon or because of the existence of high risk of losing the job (the *temporal* dimension). The *organisational* dimension, in turn, involves the notion of control over work (control over working conditions, hours, wage and working intensity). The *absence* of trade unions is one parameter, which definitely enforces the managerial right and enhances the employers' control over the labour process. The *social* dimension addresses issues like the employee protection by trade unions, labour laws, collective agreements and the level of social protection (such as health coverage, unemployment insurance). Finally, the *economic* dimension looks at issues of salary and pay raises and the level of income. Even a stable and long-term job could be precarious if the wage is *not* sufficient and the worker is *vulnerable* to social exclusion or poverty.

As Rodgers (1989, p. 3) emphasizes "it is some combination of these factors, which identifies precarious jobs, and the boundaries around the concept are inevitably to some extent arbitrary". In a similar vein, Auer and Cazes (2003) have

[6]The Euro-Barometer (http://ec.europa.eu/public_opinion/standard_en.htm) and the European Working Conditions Surveys (http://www.eurofound.europa.eu/ewco/surveys) have come to similar conclusions regarding the work insecurity of young people for several years.

suggested that stable jobs either do not offer equal security or that they are not necessarily good jobs. Regardless of the type of employment contract (permanent, temporary), aspects of low income and bad working conditions (such as health and safety, working on tight deadlines, limited job autonomy) are also quite crucial in the definition of work insecurity. In the next part of the article, we make an effort to describe the problematic employment situation of many young people in EU-15 using available statistical evidence from OECD, Eurostat and other related surveys. The main point made is that work precariousness for young people represents a structural characteristic of labour market.

1.4 How Precarious is the Employment of Young People in Europe?

1.4.1 Labour Force, Employment and Unemployment

Table 1.1 provides an overview of the current (year 2007) state and the long-term trends regarding the shares of population, labour force, employment and unemployment by age group for the period between 1987 and 2007.

One conclusion evident here is that although the young population in EU15 and the investigated countries has decreased around 20% (with the exception of Denmark, Finland, Greece, Sweden and to a lesser extent Ireland) during the period 1980–2007, the participation rate of young people in employment has decreased even more (−30 and −25%, respectively). Another important point is that, although the unemployment rate is very high (40% and more unemployed persons are 15–29 years old in the vast majority of the EU-15 countries), the share of youth unemployment is reduced among the period under investigation.

These facts cannot be seen alone and indicate that labour market segmentation is definitely not a reflection of the population ageing effect, but a result of the expansion of unsecured forms employment. Young people in Europe extend the time devoted to the formal education system, and this comes partly as a consequence of either limited, available, good job opportunities in the labour market or broader expectations of a rising income in the future after more years in education, based on the pure notions of human capital theory (Becker 1967).

In that sense, the formal education system gradually begins to act as a buffer to the problematic conditions that prevail in the labour markets in Europe. It is more than safe to argue that if the unemployment rate and the number of insecure jobs were lower, then fewer young people would decide to stay in education for such long intervals of time. As is shown next, forms of employment, which are, by nature, flexible and contingent, have shown a dramatic rise over the years despite their involuntary character. Conversely, those countries with the highest youth unemployment rates have, at the same time, the highest rates of young people that remain longer in the education system.

Table 1.1 Demographic characteristics of young people (15–29 years old)

	Population		Labour force		Employment		Unemployment	
	Share in 2007 (%)	% change (1980–2007)	Share in 2007 (%)	% change (1980–2007)	Share in 2007 (%)	% change (1980–2007)	Share in 2007 (%)	% change (1980–2007)
EU15	27.31	−22.49	22.83	−29.81	21.64	−24.54	38.58	−36.33
Austria[a]	27.37	–	24.98	–	24.24	–	41.20	–
Belgium[b]	28.09	−21.93	21.94	−35.53	20.46	−19.93	39.95	−28.08
Denmark[b]	29.34	−14.05	24.75	−21.37	24.19	−17.30	39.66	−28.08
Finland	28.15	−13.20	23.78	−19.37	39.66	−28.08	41.30	−20.69
France	29.48	−20.07	22.68	−27.80	21.16	−29.07	40.35	−27.71
Germany	26.73	−23.05	21.57	−33.82	21.04	−34.85	27.25	−35.22
Greece	27.30	−11.84	21.06	−17.45	19.02	−16.14	27.30	−11.84
Ireland	34.81	−16.71	31.42	−26.12	30.74	−25.33	45.56	−15.95
Italy	24.96	−27.60	18.23	−40.65	16.60	−38.45	43.44	−43.16
Luxemburg[b]	27.04	−22.63	19.23	−48.95	18.58	−49.62	35.11	−42.74
Netherland	26.81	−30.42	26.74	−27.66	19.41	−62.48	19.53	−75.44
Portugal	28.38	−22.38	21.47	−42.18	20.13	−41.48	37.04	−50.76
Spain	27.33	−21.39	25.12	−29.18	23.79	−24.72	39.81	−39.89
Sweden	27.17	−10.61	22.18	−21.68	20.39	−26.28	49.95	−15.67
UK[b]	27.54	−18.86	25.39	−25.92	23.98	−25.08	50.99	−0.44

Source: OECD, Labour market Database

[a]Data for Austria are only available since 1995

[b]For Belgium, Denmark, Luxemburg and UK, % change refers to 1983–2007

1.4.2 Part-time Employment

In Table 1.2, we present the part-time rate by age group and the percentage change of part-time employment for the time span 1987–2007.

From the above evidence, we observe that part-time employment increased in all European investigated countries (except Sweden). Young people (especially those between 15 and 24 years old) have usually higher rates than the total rate in the economy in all countries. In many countries, part-time employment showed dramatic changes among young people (especially those between 15–24 and

Table 1.2 Part-time employment for selected age groups

		Total	15–19	20–24	25–29	30–34
EU15	Share in 2007(%)	18.14	42.79	19.97	13.38	14.16
	% change (1987–2007)	39.25	149.07	137.49	38.60	14.91
Austria[a]	Share in 2007(%)	17.15	9.57	15.55	14.73	17.95
	% change (1987–2007)	–	–	–	–	–
Belgium	Share in 2007(%)	18.29	42.25	13.68	14.20	14.06
	% change (1987–2007)	46.34	276.04	12.82	12.81	3.18
Denmark	Share in 2007(%)	17.74	73.86	36.23	16.17	8.97
	% change (1987–2007)	32.52	189.80	37.33	−37.12	−10.70
Finland[b]	Share in 2007 (%)	11.71	52.00	23.76	10.89	6.46
	% change (1987–2007)	51.13	–	–	–	–
France	Share in 2007(%)	13.43	18.95	19.07	10.99	10.88
	% change (1987–2007)	7.03	24.05	31.14	11.50	2.29
Germany	Share in 2007(%)	22.19	21.82	17.94	17.91	19.54
	% change (1987–2007)	102.30	1385.53	392.17	114.57	59.19
Greece	Share in 2007 (%)	7.82	15.79	10.31	7.32	6.73
	% change (1987–2007)	19.87	110.72	42.80	−2.67	−7.52
Ireland	Share in 2007 (%)	20.25	50.69	17.37	11.58	15.04
	% change (1987–2007)	125.03	268.44	186.41	74.47	69.77
Italy	Share in 2007(%)	15.14	18.52	15.48	13.81	13.63
	% change (1987–2007)	78.69	209.54	149.82	100.88	64.30
Luxemburg	Share in 2007(%)	13.12	6.56	3.57	3.50	11.28
	% change (1987–2007)	62.57	−11.36	−12.33	−46.30	27.07
Netherland	Share in 2007(%)	36.07	85.53	44.63	20.12	26.35
	% change (1987–2007)	36.84	50.43	149.55	16.50	8.80
Portugal	Share in 2007 (%)	9.95	9.56	8.27	5.23	4.40
	% change (1987–2007)	35.15	148.11	47.81	−18.37	−33.15
Spain	Share in 2007(%)	10.90	28.61	18.18	9.91	9.42
	% change (1987–2007)	116.42	208.38	208.80	78.69	148.21
Sweden[c]	Share in 2007(%)	14.36	54.84	26.21	12.75	8.79
	% change (1987–2007)	−14.80	–	–	–	–
UK	Share in 2007(%)	23.27	58.99	20.45	14.12	17.96
	% change (1987–2007)	11.79	129.05	130.79	3.62	−13.36

Source: OECD, Labour market Database
[a]Data for Austria are only available since 1995
[b]Part-time employment is available for Finland since 1989 and part-time employment by age group since 2004
[c]Part-time employment is available for Sweden since 1987 and part-time employment by age group since 2002

20–24 years old). It should be noted though that there are significant differences on the regulation of part-time contracts across Europe.

For example, in the Netherlands, where almost half of the workforce is employed on a part-time basis, many part-time jobs are characterised by decent salaries and good working conditions (Schmid et al. 1997). At the same time, the popularity of such forms of employment in all the Mediterranean countries is quite opposite to what is observed in the Netherlands. The lack of attractiveness of part-time employment in southern Europe is strongly related to the low wage levels and to the lower rates of female employment (O'Reilly and Fagan 1998).

In essence, a major issue of part-time employment in these countries is the question of who can afford living with a part-time income, given the rising cost of living. In that context, part-timers in Mediterranean countries are considered as secondary employees in comparison with the breadwinners of the family income. The income of part-timers is complementary to the family income and that itself is not enough to support family formation decisions or to eliminate poverty trap problems.

As Table 1.3 indicates, Mediterranean countries are characterized by higher than the average EU15 levels of involuntary part-time employment. In Greece, where the involuntary rates are extremely high, there is also no important difference between different age groups. Quite the opposite is the case in the Netherlands, Germany and the UK where the share of part-time is higher among the EU-15 countries. Especially in the Netherlands, the percentage of involuntary part-time employment is extremely low for all the age groups comparatively speaking.

1.4.3 *Temporary Employment*

The same conclusions made for part-time employment above can be applied to temporary employment too. Temporary employment, in all countries, is strongly

Table 1.3 Percentage of involuntary part-time employment by age group (2007)

	Total	15–24	15–39
EU15	21.0	23.6	23.9
Austria	11.7	19.4	12.6
Belgium	14.6	36.6	21.0
Denmark	21.8	24.9	21.7
Finland	23.9	17.0	21.4
France	33.2	57.6	39.8
Germany	12.8	7.2	11.5
Greece	42.8	44.7	51.5
Ireland	–	–	–
Italy	38.5	51.4	44.1
Luxemburg	5.2		9.3
Netherland	5.0	5.8	5.7
Portugal	27.2	44.2	52.1
Spain	32.1	31.0	33.3
Sweden	24.6	39.9	33.5
UK	10.1	15.6	12.9

Source: Eurostat, on-line database

Table 1.4 Temporary employment for selected age groups

		Total	15–24	15–39
EU15	Share in 2007(%)	14.80	42.80	22.00
	% change (1987–2007)	28.70	32.51	37.50
Austria	Share in 2007(%)	9.00	34.90	14.60
	% change (1987–2007)	50.00	86.63	75.90
Belgium	Share in 2007 (%)	8.30	29.50	12.50
	% change (1987–2007)	48.21	69.54	64.47
Denmark	Share in 2007 (%)	14.70	56.60	25.60
	% change (1987–2007)	26.72	53.80	43.02
Finland	Share in 2007 (%)	15.00	39.60	23.30
	% change (1987-2007)	−9.09	−20.32	−6.43
France	Share in 2007 (%)	14.20	51.40	21.40
	% change (1987–2007)	100.00	71.33	107.77
Germany	Share in 2007 (%)	8.40	23.50	13.10
	% change (1987–2007)	−24.32	−23.95	−16.03
Greece	Share in 2007 (%)	11.50	29.20	15.30
	% change (1987–2007)	−30.72	−3.63	−13.56
Ireland	Share in 2007 (%)	8.50	21.90	10.60
	% change (1987–2007)	−1.16	31.93	3.92
Italy	Share in 2007 (%)	13.30	43.30	19.50
	% change (1987–2007)	146.30	266.95	204.69
Luxemburg	Share in 2007 (%)	6.20	39.30	10.00
	% change (1987–2007)	77.14	285.29	112.77
Netherland	Share in 2007 (%)	18.20	45.20	26.60
	% change (1987–2007)	93.62	112.21	119.83
Portugal	Share in 2007 (%)	22.80	54.20	31.40
	% change (1987–2007)	36.53	44.92	41.44
Spain	Share in 2007 (%)	29.30	59.40	37.70
	% change (1987–2007)	87.82	64.09	81.25
Sweden	Share in 2007 (%)	16.10	53.60	25.60
	% change (1987–2007)	21.97	32.02	26.73
UK	Share in 2007 (%)	5.40	12.00	6.90
	% change (1987–2007)	−14.29	6.19	−11.54

Source: Eurostat, on-line database

focused on young workers (15–24 years old), while its percentage is lower among older employees. Furthermore, in the vast majority of the cases, young people's share has increased much more in comparison with the respective share for the total of the economy (Table 1.4).

Temporary contracts are widespread in Spain, Portugal and the Netherlands. In certain cases, like Italy, they also show an extremely high (more than double for the 15–24 age group) increase during the last 20 years. The picture is different, though, in other countries like the UK, Luxemburg, Germany and Ireland, where the rates of temporary employment are much lower than the EU-15 average. However, again, in all countries, young people have a much greater inclination to this form of atypical employment. Only in Finland, Germany and to some extent in the UK we observe a decrease in the share of temporary employment between 1987 and 2007. Moreover, involuntary temporary employment among young workers is usually lower than the

Table 1.5 Percentage of involuntary temporary employment by age group (2007)

	Total	15–24	15–39
EU15	57.4	33.6	52.3
Austria	18.1	4.1	13.6
Belgium	79.8	64.3	77.2
Denmark	26.7	9	18.6
Finland	64.2	40.5	57.2
France	54.8	39.1	51.8
Germany	38.5	22.5	32
Greece	82.5	62.9	79.1
Ireland	–	–	–
Italy	64.8	32.6	57.5
Luxemburg	36.5	25.7	32.5
Netherland	37.6	31.2	36.6
Portugal	81.3	72.8	80.2
Spain	84.5	71.8	82.3
Sweden	55.9	42.9	53.1
UK	43.2	34.7	45.1

Source: Eurostat, on-line database

national average level except in a few cases. The strong desire of young people for permanent employment is more than evident in southern Europe and to Belgium (Table 1.5).

1.4.4 Earnings[7]

Earnings represent one of the most decisive factors for the social situation of an individual (European Commission 2005). As it was suggested earlier, the *level* of income has a tremendous impact on the security people feel with their job. In certain cases, even stable jobs are considered as precarious if they are associated with low income that puts a great pressure on workers to cover their own and their family needs. Looking at the relevant data from the SES, we examine first the differences between the average earnings for all employees to those of young workers (15–29 years old).

The Figure 1.1 shows the mean earnings of people age up to 30 years and the total of employees across a number of EU-15 countries (plus Norway). A quite straightforward message sent by the figure is that young people (with minor exemptions) are *less* remunerated in relation to other age groups. Such a finding

[7]Data about earning by age groups come from Structure of Earnings Survey (SES) ,which was carried out in 2002 and 2006 in all EU countries. Data are available in PPS (Purchasing Power Parities), a unit which equalizes the purchasing power of different countries for a given basket of goods. Using a PPP basis is arguably more useful when comparing differences in living standards on the whole between nations (European Commission 2006).

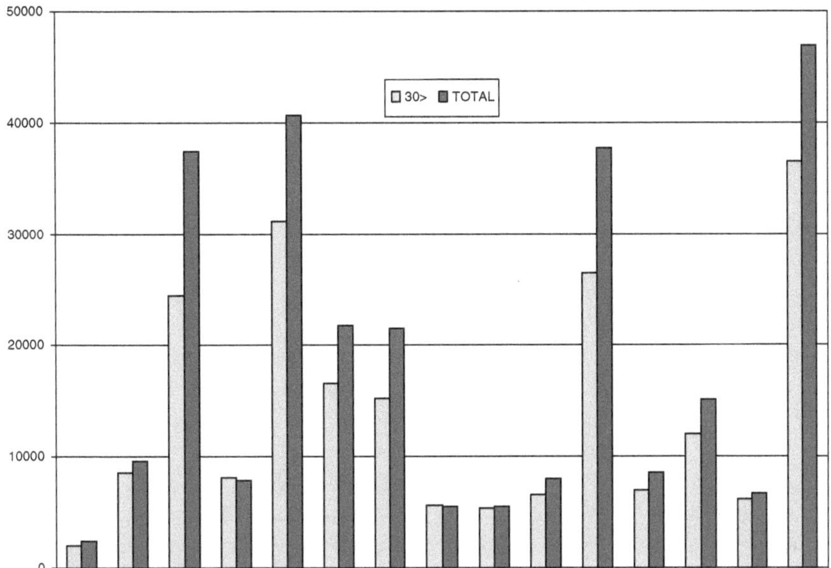

	BG	CZ	DE	EE	IE	ES	CY	LV	LT	HU	NL	PL	SI	SK	NO
30>	2002	8543	24490	8196	31144	16586	15221	5670	5333	6602	26535	6985	12038	6150	36437
TOTAL	2429	9582	37385	7940	40635	21755	21513	5510	5478	7964	37695	8562	15160	6689	46888

Fig. 1.1 Mean annual earnings, 2006
Source: Eurostat, on-line database

is *not* surprising in the sense that young workers (especially those age between 15 and 24 years) are not as experienced as their older colleagues. However, the crucial point here is that in certain cases the differences are significantly large.

Young workers experience lower levels of wages and higher levels of unemployment despite the fact that they are more qualified than older workers. In essence, their lack of working experience is penalized by high levels of unemployment and lower wages. Sometimes, this penalization is driven by certain policies that aim to increase the participation rate on higher education. Such policies set different minimum wage rates for young workers and those just entering the workforce. In Belgium, for example, those aged 16–20 are paid 70% of the minimum wage beginning at age 17. The rate increases by 6 percentage points each year until they are 21 at which time they qualify for the standard "adult" rated minimum wage.

In certain cases, the regulations that may have an adverse effect on the wages of young workers may come from various collective agreements signed by employers and the trade unions or unilateral initiatives by employers to implement an organisational restructuring exercise. For example, in Finland, the minimum wages were temporarily cut for young workers and for the long-term unemployed in the years 1995–1996. This policy was agreed to by the national level employers' associations and the trade unions. Böckerman et al. (2007) have shown that employers hardly used this opportunity to recruit young workers below the minimum wages that prevailed before the experiment. It should be noted that such two-tier wages/two-tier workforce reforms took place at times of sharply rising unemployment across Europe, and have hence found favour among the politically powerful groups in the labour market institutions.

There are serious concerns to consider young people as a group without political power in the current context.[8] These concerns justify to some extent the findings of the First EU Youth Report (2009), according to which only 4% of young people declared having participated in activities of political parties or trade unions in the past and less than 40% of young people age between 16 and 29 have trust in (or are neutral towards) politicians and political parties.

Returning to the evidence on wages, a significant question arises: Has tertiary education stopped acting as a "green light" for the employers in providing higher salaries? This hypothesis fits well with the southern EU member-states. In those countries, the number of students in tertiary education and the graduates has dramatically increased over the last decades. However, increased access to education on its own may not always allow for increased access to the world of employment. As it can be easily realized from Figure 1.2, monthly earnings vary between 50 and 86% of the EU15 average. At the same time, the respective figures for the monthly earnings of young employees are much lower and vary between 39 and 66% for young employees. This finding shows that young workers in

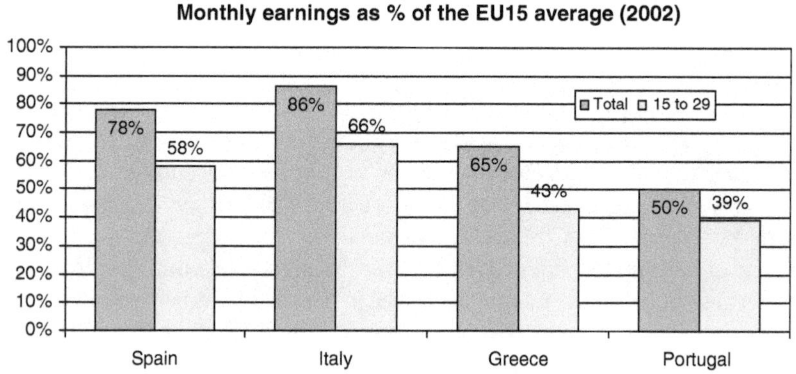

Fig. 1.2 Monthly earnings as percentage of EU15 average in Southern EU member-states, 2002
Source: OECD, on-line Labour market Database

[8]Young people cannot be considered as a powerful political group that can influence to a great or to a certain extent the decisions about labour market reforms. According to relevant publications by the European Commission (The White Paper "A New Impetus for European Youth", COM 2001/ "Renewed Social Agenda-Opportunities, Access and Solidarity in twenty-first Century Europe", COM 2008) it is argued that there is an urgent need to ensure that those for whom policies are designed are part of the policymaking process as subjects rather than objects of the planning process.

southern Europe not only receive lower wages than their EU15 counterparts, but they also have dramatic differences with the rest of the population of their country. The importance of low wages among young people becomes all the more crucial if we consider the limited state support and the rising cost of living (Karamessini 2008).

1.4.5 Undeclared Work and False Self-employment

Undeclared work and false self-employment are two forms of flexible employment contracts, which appear to be quite prevalent among young people (Commission 2007). A major problem with these forms of employment is that they are not usually taken into account in the official survey estimates of precarious employment. According to Renoy et al. (2004), around 10–28 million persons are engaged in undeclared work across the EU27 area. The size of undeclared work as percentage of GDP varies across countries. Southern European countries have a strong inclination to undeclared work with the respective figures at 16–17% for Italy, 15–20% and increasing for Spain, and over 20% with upward trends in Greece (EIRO 2005). The majority of undeclared workers are unemployed, seasonal workers, immigrants and all those who cannot choose or negotiate their employment status.

A recent report by the Commission (2007) argues that regarding the socio-demographic characteristics of undeclared workers there it is clear that undeclared work is mostly done by younger people. *As it is stated on the report (Commission 2007, p. 26):* "while amongst the youngest age (15–24 years old) almost every tenth respondent performed undeclared work during the reference period, the share is only 4% for those aged 40–54 years and declines to 2% among aged 55 years or more "as much as two-thirds of the 'undeclared workers' consist of people younger than 40 years".

Another form of precarious employment, usually seen in southern Europe and Belgium, is false self-employment or dependent self-employment. The term is used to describe cases of independent contractors that work under the same rules and conditions as typical wage workers. As a result, the pseudo-independent contractors take all the risks and costs of self-employment (e.g. Health and safety responsibility, social security costs, lack of labour law protection, etc.), and do not have access to the presumed benefits of wage workers (such as extra earnings, unfair dismissal protection rules and trade union protection).

False self-employment is usually characterized as a "grey zone" between dependent and independent employments, describing the foggy environment of work as far as it concerns certain regulations, such as social security and dismissal rules. There is no common data source on the number of false self-employed. This category of employment appears to be heterogeneous, with regard to gender, geographic areas, and occupation. It encompasses white collar groups (professionals, engineers, lawyers, etc.) as well as workers with more controlled tasks and blue collars (especially skilled workers in occupations of the construction and annexed services) (Duell 2004). For that reason, the actual size of false self-employed is rather difficult to measure at national level.

A comparative study by Pedersini (2002) highlights that such type of contingent work can be found across a range of activities, which are traditionally part of outsourcing (such as homeworking in the clothing industry) to occupations which are connected to the more recent experiences of reorganisation and contracting-out (such as maintenance work); and from activities which typically have a high rate of freelance employment (for instance, work on newspapers and magazines), to new and emerging occupations (such as ICT workers, courier workers). Young people have usually a high share in such types of activities, even if other studies suggest quite the opposite (Böheim and Muehlberger 2006).

For some countries, this type of employment is quite significant and widespread. For example, in Italy, the level of false self-employment approached around two million persons in 2000 (Frey, et al. 2002) and it is also high in Greece (Duell 2004). According to a recent study, almost 10% of employees in private sector and 8% in public sector, are false self-employed in Greece. Furthermore, the respective figure of false self-employment for the age groups between16 to 34 years old is as high as16% (GSEE 2008).

A relevant study by IRES (2005) in Italy indicated that these contracts are not so "flexible" or "independent" for the employee side. More specifically, the study focused on 640 young independent workers between 2004 and 2005. According to the results: 76% work for a single firm, 77% on the enterprise's premises, 80% had to comply with a working time schedule fixed by the employer and 74% had to be at work every day. Furthermore, 37% declare they do different work with respect to what is written in the contract and 46% of the sample had a monthly wage lower than 1,000 euros.

1.5 Discussion

From the available statistical evidence and the subsequent analysis, it is clear that young workers in Europe cannot be considered as temporarily "outsiders" of the labour market. The analysis showed that one of the main features of the European economies is the existence of a wide atypical branch where a growing part of the workforce is involved. This workforce, mainly composed of young workers, is integrated into the labour market with atypical contracts or undeclared work arrangements for more than three decades now.

In such contracts and work arrangements, employment relations are characterized by extreme informality that puts at risk even basic rights established on the national labour law framework and the results of the collective bargaining process. The difficulty of measuring in an accurate way the extension of such informal or atypical forms of employment usually leads to their dissimulation from official statistics. Official statistics use only numerical tools to define precarious employment, ignoring that in some cases that process possibly omits other important factors, thus ignoring a much more complex work reality. Nevertheless, even the official statistics leave no space for complacency regarding the difficult position of young workers in the labour market in Europe.

Probably, the most important finding we detected involving part-time and temporary employment was not their actual rates, but rather the high rates of involuntary participation in that type of employment relations. Major improvements are also needed in the field of wage formation. The introduction of two-tier wage structures and the lower average wages of young workers is another characteristic of the labour markets in EU-15 countries that promotes work insecurity among young people. Precarious employment seems to be a risk for all young people, regardless of their education level, as the comparison between the wages of manual and non-manual workers showed. In essence, many young people in Europe are trapped in low paid, contingent jobs located at the periphery of the labour market with limited and difficult prospects for upward social mobility. This situation makes urgent the need for the adoption of more effective employment policies in order to reduce intergenerational injustice and to promote a decent work agenda for the future generations of workers.

The current European debate on flexicurity which aims to bring about a compromise of the social actors between a liberal and a social democratic approach of activation and governance has not ended up in the formation of policies that can really make a difference on the daily struggle of young people in the labour market. Young Europeans must navigate a labour market that is composed of highly decentralised workplaces. The absence of protection and security young workers find themselves is enhanced by the relaxation of the labour law framework. The scary evidence about young people at work signals that the awareness of the problem is not enough and therefore, creates a sense of urgency for change that should be based on a new social consensus that takes into account young workers' interests.

Acknowledgements The author would like to thank Dr. Mary Brown (Robert Gordon University), Maria Markaki (National Technical University of Athens) Dr. Ilias Livanos (University of Warwick) and Maria Koumenta (LSE) for their contribution in the collection of the data and their comments about the analysis followed.

References

Auer P, Cazes S (eds) (2003) Employment stability in the age of flexibility. International Labour Office (ILO), Geneva

Becker G (1967) Human capital and the personal distribution of income: an analytical approach. Columbia University Press, New York

Beveridge WH (1909) Unemployment: a problem of industry. Longmans, Green and Co., London

Biletta I, Eisner M (2007) Youth and work. European Foundation for the Improvement of Living and Working Conditions, Dublin

Bluestone B, Rose St (1997) The growth in work time and the implications for macro policy. Levy Economics Institute Working Paper 204

Böckerman P, Laaksonen S, Vainiomaki J (2007) Who bears the burden of wage cuts? Evidence from Finland during the 1990s. Int J Manpow 28(2):100–121
Böheim R, Muehlberger U (2006) Dependent forms of self-employment in the UK: identifying workers on the border between employment and self-employment, IZA Discussion Papers, No. 1963, http://www.iza.org/
Brenner R (1998) The economics of global turbulence. New Left Rev 229:1–264
Buchel F (2002) Successful apprenticeship-to-work transitions. On the long-term change in significance of the german school-leaving certificate. Int J Manpow 23(5):394–410
Callinicos A (2003) Feature review: the boom and the bubble: the US in the World Economy, Robert Brenner (Verso, 2002). New Polit Econ 8(3):419–425
Dedouspopoulos A (2000) *Θεωρίες της Ανεργίας*, τόμος, vol Á. Αθ ήνα, Τυπωθήτω-Δαρδανός
Duell M (2004) Defining and assessing precarious employment in Europe: a review of main studies and surveys. Discussion paper in economix, research and consulting, Munich
Dumenil, Levy (2005) Costs and benefits of neoliberalism in Eipstein, G. A. "*Financialization and the world economy*", Edward Elgar, pp 17–45
EIRO (2005) 'Industrial relations and undeclared work', Dublin: EIRO online available: http://www.eurofound.europa.eu/pubdocs/2005/135/en/1/ef05135en.pdf
ETUC (2007) Quality of jobs at risk. ETUC, Brussels
European Commission (2005) Precarious employment in Europe: a comparative study of labour market related risks in flexible economies. European Communities, Brussels
European Commission (2006) Eurostat-OECD methodological manual on purchasing power parities. European Communities, Paris
European Commission (2007) Undeclared work in the European Union. European Communities, Brussels
Frade C, Darmon I (2005) New models of business organization and precarious employment: towards the recommodification of labour? J Eur Soc Policy 15(2):107–121
Frey L, Croce G, Pappadà G (2002) Precarious employment in Italy – a literature review, precarious employment in five countries, country report Italy. European Commission, Brussels
Gallie D, White M, Cheng Y, Tomlinson M (1998) Restructuring the employment relationship. Oxford University Press, Oxford
Garraty JA (1978) Unemployment in history: economy thought and public policy. Harper, New York
GSEE (2008) Labour and trade unions: quantitative research results. VPRC, Athens
Hicks JR (1932) The theory of wages. Macmillan, London reprinted in 1963
Hyman R (2007) How can trade unions act strategically? Paper presented for the industrial relations in Europe Conference 2007. Centre of Industrial Relations & Negotiations (CIRN), Athens, July
Karamessini M (2008) Continuity and change in the southern European social Model. Int Labour Rev 147(1):43–70
Lagarenne C, Legendre N (2000) Les Travailleurs pauvres en France: facteurs individuals et familliaux. Econ Stat 335:2000 INSEE
Marshall A (1920) Principles of economics: an introductory volume (1st edition 1890), 8th edn. Macmillan, London reprinted in 1972
Mitropoulos A (2005) Precari-us? In mute – culture and politics after the net. 1(29Spring):88–96
Moseley F (1999) United States economy at the turn of the century: entering a new era of prosperity? Cap Class 67:25–46
Neilson B, Rossiter N (2005) From precarity to precariousness and back again: labour, life and unstable networks. Fibreculture, issue 5: Precarious Labour. http://journal.fibreculture.org/issue5/index.html
OECD (1997) Is job insecurity on the increase in OECD countries? OECD employment outlook. OECD, Paris, pp 129–160
O'Reilly J, Fagan C (eds) (1998) Part-time prospects: International comparisons of part-time work in Europe, North America and the Pacific Rim. Routledge, London

Pedersini R (2002) Economically dependent workers, employment law and industrial relations, EIRO online, http://www.eiro.eurofound.eu.int/index.html, pp 1–22
Renoy P, Ivarsson St, van der Wusten-Gritsai O, Meijer Em (2004) Undeclared work in an enlarged union, an analysis of undeclared work: an in-depth study of specific items. European Commission, Brussels
Rodgers G (1989) Precarious employment in Western Europe: the state of the debate. In: Rodgers G, Rodgers J (eds) Precarious jobs in labour market regulation: the growth of atypical employment in Western Europe. International Institute for Labour Studies, Geneva
Schmid G et al (1997) The Dutch *employment* miracle? A comparison of employment systems in the Netherlands and Germany. WZB Discussion Paper FS I 97-202, Berlin
Schumpeter J (1954) History of economic analysis. Oxford University Press, Oxford
Shaikh A (1999) Explaining the global economic crisis. Hist Materialism 5(1):103–144(42)
Sweet S, Meiksins P (2008) The changing contours of work. Pine Forge Press, London
Thompson EP (1981) The making of the English working class. Pelican, Harmondsworth
Tsianos V,Papadopoulos D (2006) Precarity: a savage journey to the heart of embodied capitalism, http://precariousunderstanding.blogsome.com/2006/08/12/precarity-a-savage-journey-to-the-heart-of-embodied-capitalism/
Winch D (1972) Economics and policy: a historical study. Fontana, London

Chapter 2
Comparing Welfare Regime Changes: Living Standards and the Unequal Life Chances of Different Birth Cohorts*

Louis Chauvel

2.1 Consequences of the Welfare States' Reforms for the Different Generations

This article focuses on generational sustainability in welfare states and aims to analyse the long-term consequences that the reforms[1] carried out by these states have on the different cohorts. It is shown that in the context of conjuncture fluctuation, from the "economic miracle" (1945–1975) to the slowdown in economic growth (1975 until today),[2] a gap appeared between those who were exposed to a high rate of youth unemployment and its resulting consequences and those who were not, i.e. generations born before 1955 (the early baby boomers) and the generations born after 1955. This gap between generations would often be denied by the politicians in the public debate. These points of view imply that these generational dynamics could have major consequences for the stability of our welfare states. Furthermore, what we have observed in France in the emergence of strong inter-cohort inequalities at the expense of young adults is not seen in America. In America, the same stressors (economic slowdown and increasing competition) have resulted in a less visible inter-cohort, but a more obvious intra-cohort inequality.

L. Chauvel
Institut d'Études Politiques de Paris (Sciences-Po Paris), Observatory for Social Change, 27, rue Saint-Guillaume, 75337 Paris Cedex 07, France
e-mail: louis.chauvel@sciences-po.fr

*Part of this article appeared also in: Jones, Ian Rees 2009: Consumption and Intergenerational Change, Transaction Publishers. Piscataway, New Jersey

[1]Compare, e.g. Esping-Andersen et al. 2002.

[2]France and the US both experienced a period of post-war affluence: the American "Golden Age of Capitalism" (Maddison 1982) and the French "Trente Glorieuses" (Fourastié 1979), which contrast with the subsequent period of economic slowdown and "diminished expectations" (Krugman 1992). See, notably: Chauvel 1998 (second ed., 2002).

J.C. Tremmel (ed.), *A Young Generation Under Pressure?*,
DOI 10.1007/978-3-642-03483-1_2, © Springer-Verlag Berlin Heidelberg 2010

Reflections, here, are based on the Esping-Andersen (1990) trilogy of welfare regimes, completed by the post-Ferrera (1996) controversy. The argument is that, in the intrinsic logics of different welfare regimes, the probable set of socioeconomic responses to contemporary common challenges or stresses (economic slowdown, social distortions in the face of globalisation, obsolescence of unqualified or industrially-qualified labour, etc.) could be significantly different. As a clue to these differences, strong cohort-specific "scarring effects" are noticed in France and in Italy. Such "scarring effects" are unclear in Nordic countries and almost non-existent in the Anglo-Saxon or liberal welfare regimes.

This article will add to a theory on the intra-and inter-cohort (Mayer 2005) inequalities in an international context, and provide states with the possibility to avoid such inequalities. In the welfare states , the cohorts of young adults assist an intergenerational decline of their position, accumulating the difference between generations, the risk of a long-term destabilisation of the middle-class remains.

2.2 Different Responses of Welfare Regimes to Economic Stresses

To analyse more precisely the probable responses of different welfare regimes to the challenges of postindustrial societies, consider the standard typology of Welfare regimes (Esping-Andersen 1999); we could focus on four types of regimes, respectively corporatist (or conservative), liberal, universalist (or social democrat), and familialistic:

- Since it is based on the recognition of long-term and institutionalised social rights of members of protected social groups, the probable response of the *corporatist regime* (including France) to economic slowdown, international competition, and economic shortcomings of the Welfare regime as a redistributive agency, as a ruler of the labour force, and as an employer will be a more expensive protection of insiders, i.e. a stable workforce with higher seniority and high rates of trade-union membership. Such a response would be at the expense of young adults leaving education, women and immigrants, who have less opportunities to defend their interests. Youth unemployment results primarily from the scarcity of decent jobs in the labour market. Such scarcity is due to a (combination?) of competition with insiders and a stronger internal competition of the young for obtaining less available positions. An internal competition of this nature generates a decline in relative or absolute wages, and specific renegotiations and retrenchments of social rights of the new social generations. If seniors are victims of early retirement, they benefit from better protections of incomes and opportunities to access comfortable pension schemes and/or acceptable conditions of pre-retirement (generally better than the usual unemployment schemes of younger adults). The social generations of seniors are more equal because they are the homogeneous cohorts of the "wage earner society" of the Golden Period of 1960s–1980s. This period that brought better pension schemes for all has resulted in an increase in senior's relative income. Conversely, the new cohorts of adults face a stronger polarisation between winners and losers. (Brzinsky-Fay 2007; Bell et al. 2007). Another aspect we do not face here is the declining value of education. Working in tandem with a lack of improvement in labour market entry, a probable collective answer to the difficulties of the young is a massive increase in the post-secondary education of young cohorts. (Van De Velde 2008). However, a trend of strong educational inflation in the form of declines in the nominal value of grades, particularly for the less selective ones, can be observed.

- The *liberal regime* (including the US) is characterised by another probable answer to the same challenges: because of the centrality of market in this regime, the response to economic shortage is Welfare State retrenchments, limitation of redistributions to worse-off populations, stronger market competition, denunciation of former social rights considered as rent-economy devices, and distortions for market equilibrium. The logic, therefore, is to strengthen competition between juniors and seniors (who have less intangible rights) in order to renegotiate better positions for seniors, which were previously obtained in the context of affluence. The consequence is smoother inter-cohort inequality (the new cohorts benefit relative to the seniors). However, strengthening competition means stronger intra-cohort inequalities.
- The *universalistic regime* (including Denmark) is defined by a collective scope for long-term stability, progress, and development for all with a strong sense of collective responsibility. The quality of integration of newer cohorts is then considered as a priority, since a failure in the early socialisation of young adults is clearly seen as a massive problem for future development of society. Strong rates of youth unemployment and economic devalorisation of young adults could go with long-term risks of anxiety, sentiments of self-devaluation of the young, increasing suicide rates, or a decline in the fertility index. More generally, a better control of social risks over the complete life course is a central dimension of the Nordic Welfare State model.
- The *familialistic regime* (including Italy) shares many aspects of the corporatist one, but families here are a legitimate institution in the process of redistribution of resources, both culturally and for the regulatory activities of the state. More precisely, in this regime, some sectors of the economy are strongly protected (mainly the core sectors of the public economy and of large companies such as banks, insurance, etc.) and most of the labour regulations are based on seniority rights. In most middle- and small-sized companies, the regulation is based notably on family interconnections, where both localism and long-term fidelity of workers are fundamental institutions. In the context of post-affluent societies, and of scarcity of jobs, housing, and other resources, parents of young adults are supposed to offer help and protection, and most families act in conformity with these social pressures. The consequence is a trend of increasing dependence of young adults up until the age of 35 (or even over) in a context of declining levels

of wages and standards of living for the cohorts of new entrants into the labour market. Consequently, seniors exert political pressure to obtain a better pension in order to support their own children. This *dependency* feature generates stronger constraints for young families, increases the social pressures on women to choose between work and children, and is accompanied by a strong decline in the fertility rates. This decline in fertility rates creates a paradoxical context of "familialism without families", and becomes a major problem in the long-term sustainability of the pensions and welfare regime (shorter and less affluent careers of juniors, generational collapse of one-child families, etc.). Conversely, the decline of incomes for young families is offset by the reduction of family size. In this regime, the national homogeneity may be weaker compared to other regimes since the inter-provincial imbalances, i.e. strong unemployment rates in some localities could go with a lack of appropriate workforce in others, are structural traits of a labour market where localism and strong ties are important aspects of social regulations. This implies less geographic mobility.

While the welfare regime logics and transformations are central issues, other factors also could influence these results. These include:

- Economic acceleration: even in the short-term, a better economic situation could diminish pressure for welfare retrenchments
- Quality of the transition from school to work: close relations between the educational system and the labour market, organised internships, strong network of alumni, etc. limit the risk of "outsiderisation" of young adults
- Shape of demography: a boom in fertility rates may have an "overcrowding" effect on the labour market in 20–25 years or more. (Easterlin 1961; Easterlin et al. 1993).

The combinations of these factors are much more complex than expected. Due to the diversity of potential configurations, we should expect that the welfare regime explanation outlined here is only a part of the real history of each nation. While the welfare regime offers strong constraints, historically ascribed configurations (demography, level of development, and opportunities for growth, etc.) and achievements of social policies (educational booms, structural reforms on the labour market, etc.) could also be important explanatory factors.

2.3 The Multidimensional "Fracture Générationnelle" in France

In France, the economic slowdown has provoked a dramatic multidimensional "fracture générationnelle" since the late 1970s. This portrait is grim, but it is founded on a strong empirical base, with alternative sets of micro-data offering convergent results. Three principal topics will be highlighted here: first, the economic marginalisation of new entrants into the labour market and its direct effects on social structure; second, the long-term consequences of this deprivation in terms of socialisation and life chances; and finally, the consequences for the political participation of these cohorts and their support for the contemporary welfare regime.

2.4 The Economic Decline of Youth

The first aspect of the dynamics of social generation in France is the change in the cohort distribution of economic means. A large redistribution of earnings and incomes occurred between the 1970s and today. In 1977, the earnings gap between age groups 30–35 and 50–55 was 15%; the gap is now about 40%. During the "economic miracle," the young wage earners generally began in the labour market with the same level of income as their own parents at the end of a complete career. For the last 20 years, what is observed is , a stagnation in the wages of the young while wages for older people have grown by 20% or more. In 1997, the workers received the highest incomes when middle-aged. Today, they receive it only shortly before retiring (cf. Fig. 2.1).

There is also a new trend between the age groups, whose consequences in social sciences up to now are barely studied. The changing of the relative positions of the age groups is now double(?). During their youth, the members of the older generation (those who are around 55 years old) were in a better position in comparison to their parents. The same applies nowadays, if we compare today's older generation

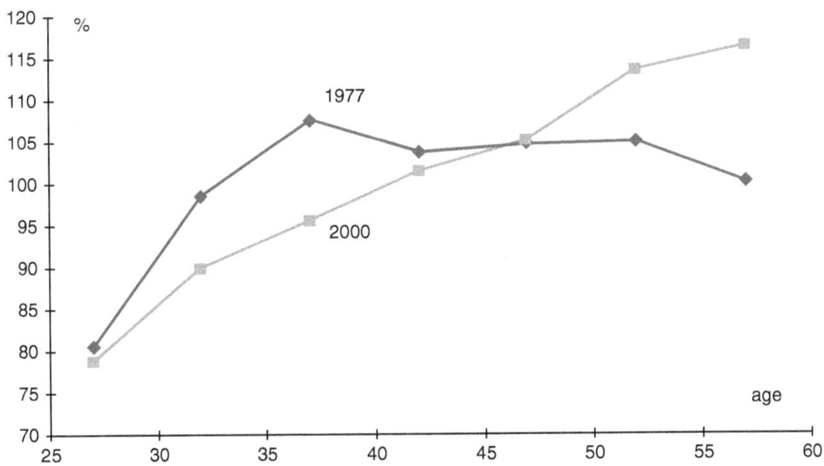

Fig. 2.1 Salaries of the age groups, in 1977 and 2000 (100 = average age group in France)[3]

[3]Enquêtes Emploi 2000 et Formation-qualification-professionnelle 1977, INSEE; archives LASMAS – Quételet.

with the young. The gap between generations is a result of a doubling in privileges as well as disadvantages.

2.5 The Unemployment Risk of the Different Cohorts

How could we explain this increasing gap? In fact, this is a consequence of a changing collective compromise, which occurred during the mid-1970s and early 1980s. This transition in the social value of generations is brought about from a relative valorisation of newer generations, as a positive feature we had to invest in, to the protection of the adults' and seniors' stability, even at the expense of the young. This is the main factor in the redistribution of well-being concerned unemployment. High unemployment rates were socially acceptable for young workers, provided that adult employees with dependent children could avoid these difficulties. In 1974, the unemployment rate of those who left school 24 months before or less was about 4%; by 1985, those who left school just then had an unemployment rate of 35%, which remained the case through till 1996. In 2002, thanks to a wave of economic recovery occurred then, it was close to 18%. The unemployment rates of youngsters who just left school are strongly reflective of the economic situation, whereas for the middle-aged and seniors the rates remain more stable. Thus, an economic slowdown has serious consequences for younger adults, and recovery firstly benefits new entrants in the labour market. Evidently, the perverse consequence of that collective compromise for the protection of adults at the expense of newcomers is due to a *lack of socialisation* of the new sacrificed generations. Due to some kind of "scarring effect", even if they are now adults with dependent children of their own, their unemployment rates remain much higher, and their earnings abnormally low when compared to other age groups.

2.6 Scarring Effect

The assessment of the long-term impact of these early difficulties is central to the interpretation; if young, deprived generations do not catch up, a somewhat long-term *hysteresis* effect appears, which can be called a "scar" or "scarring effect". This can be deemed an appropriate title as the handicap seems definitive. The age-period-cohort analysis shows that cohorts who experienced a difficult entry into the labour market, because of economic recession, continue to suffer from a relative delay in upward mobility compared to those who entered in a better economic situation.

The hypothesis presented here for France is that cohort-specific socialisation contexts imply long-term opportunities and life chances for individuals and their cohorts; when the difficulties disappear, the cohorts who faced these problems continue to suffer from long-term consequences of past handicaps.

In more concrete terms, the cohorts born during the 1940s, who benefited from the economic acceleration of the late 1960s, were relatively *privileged* compared to the previous cohorts when young and are relatively *advantaged* when compared to the newer ones due to the lack of progress for the young from 1975 to the present day.

2.7 The Devaluation of Education

An important point that cannot be developed at length here is the consequences of educational expansion. If the level of education has increased in the cohorts born in 1950–1975, that positive trend was accompanied by a strong social devalorisation of grades (Chauvel 2000). More specifically, the first cohorts of the baby boom have benefited from an expansion of education at a time when the rewards of education remained stable. Even if there were twice as many *Baccalauréat* recipients in the 1948 cohort as in the 1935, thelikelihood of their access to higher social or economic positions did not shrink. On the other hand, the generations that followed had to deal with a strong trend of devaluation in terms of the economic and social returns to education. The first consequence is a rush to the most valued and selective grades (in the "*Grandes écoles*" of the elite such as *Ecole Polytechnique*, *Ecole Nationale d'Administation*, *Sciences – Po Paris*, etc.) whose value remains stable, but whose population becomes more and more specific and may be discriminatory in terms of social origins. The second consequence is a strong devalorisation of less prestigious universities, which are less exclusive but have much smaller per capita endowments in comparison to the *Grandes écoles*. In the same way, the best secondary schools become more selective with major consequences in terms of urban segregation. In the French case, the school system was traditionally the central institution of the republic and at the heart of its idea of progress, providing the strongest support for French-style social democracy and meritocracy. The collapse of the value of grades implies a destabilisation of this myth and a pessimistic outlook on progress – developments that can be expected to have political consequences.

2.8 The 1968 Generation as Profiteers

Now that we are nearing the end of this long-term slowdown, which began 25 years ago, we can compare two social and genealogical generations.[4] For the first time in a period of peace, the youth of the new generation are no better off than their parents

---

[4]During the twentieth century, an average age gap of about 30 years separated parents and their children.

at the same age. In fact, the "1968 generation", born in 1948, are the children of those born in 1918 who were young adults in World War II and worked in difficult conditions at the beginning of the "Economic miracle". The condition of the baby boomers was incomparably better than their parents. However, the following genealogical generation, born around 1978 – that is now between 25 and 30 years old – faces diminished opportunities of growth, not only because of an economic slump, but also because of their relatively poor outcomes in comparison to those of their own parents who did very well.[5] We now observe rising rates of downward social mobility connected to the proliferation of middle-class children who cannot find social positions comparable to their parents.

Consequently, France offers an ideal typical example of a failure of a corporatist regime as it sacrifices the interests of large fractions of its population and is unable to organise its own transmission to newer generations. As a result, it is unable to distribute its benefits to young adults. This case is very interesting, since, in France, we have a country that presents specific traits. France is defined by a homogeneous culture, notably by a political culture of refusal of market rules. It is homogeneously governed by a centralised system of governance about to produce for long periods the same erroneous diagnoses and decisions on the totality of the territory. The country is based on a culture of stop-and-go policies of alternate periods of excessive and scarce investments, which are about to create backlashes and counter-backlashes. France is also a country where the first years on the labour market are strategic for future life-chances of individuals.

2.9 Is France an Exception? An International Comparison of Cohorts

A solution to test this idea of a possible French exceptionalism is to compare the dynamics of incomes on the life course in contrasted nations. Four countries will be considered here: France, Italy, Denmark, and the US. This choice gives an example of four typical welfare regimes. The four countries are characterised by similar levels of development and their trends are roughly parallel, despite the American economy doing somewhat better during the 1990s (Fig. 2.2).

[5]These parents are about to help their children in different ways with the intensification of "*solidarités familiales*" (transfers and transmissions between generations including financial, in kind, cultural, and material) that Attias-Donfut (2000) describes, but at the collective level, the first and the most efficient *solidarity* would consist of a redistribution of social positions.

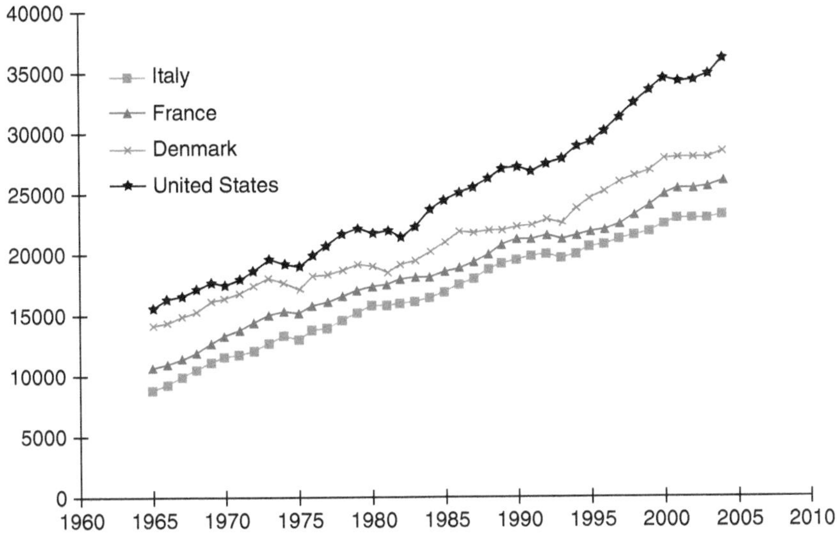

Fig. 2.2 Annual per capita GDP of four countries (in PPP $ purchasing power parity dollars)[6]

The four selected countries pertain to samples of micro-data available in the *Luxembourg Income Study Project*,[7] but other typical countries could have been selected with consistent results. Since in this chapter the major concern is about consumption, the focus will be on household level standards of living and not on personal earnings. The LIS project data offer the possibility to compute adjusted disposable income (total net income after taxes and transfers, adjusted by household size, where the equivalence scale is the square-root of the number of residents of the household) in order to compare the living standards of age groups at four different periods, respectively around 1985, 1990, 1995, and 2000.

The main results of the comparison of the relative adjusted disposable income (RADI, Fig. 2.3) are:

- In 2000, the shapes of the age distribution of the average RADI are similar with an ascending slope to age 55 and a declining standard of living after (decline of earnings or retirement).

[6]Penn World Tables 6.2 (Heston et al., 2006). Note of the editorial staff: PPP $ = average connection availability of purchasing power in Dollar.

[7]Source: Microdata of the LIS – Project (www.lisproject.org), evaluation of the Authors. : Relative Adjusted Disposable Income (RADI); RADI = 1 is related to the average of the 30–64 years old of the relative periods; Period 1, 2, 3 and 4 are related to the LIS – Data of 1985, 1990, 1995 and 2000. In the figure, the 30-year-old are part of the group 30–34 year old. Working population: according to household RADI.

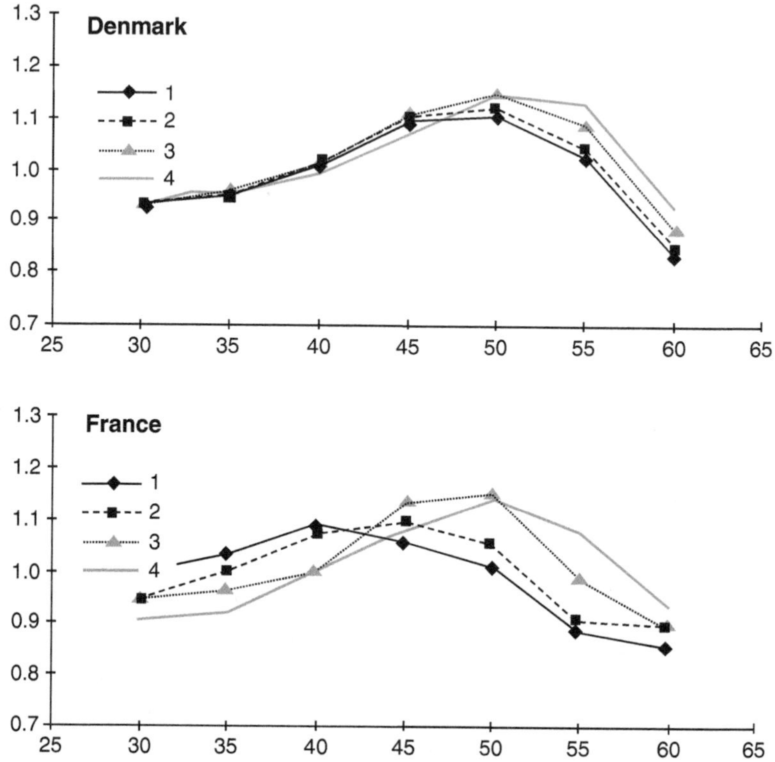

Fig. 2.3 Relative adjusted disposable income (RADI) by age group for three periods
Source: Chauvel (2007)

- From 1985 to 2000, except in the US, we note a general increase of the income of seniors, more modest in Denmark and very significant in France.
- France and Italy are characterised by a strong relative decline of the age group 35–39; the French dynamics pertain to a very clear cohort wave (there is a progressive shift of age at maximum income from age 40 to 50).
- In Italy, the decline of RADI at age 30 is less significant, but note that at age 30, most Italians are not head of their own household, and most of them continue to nominally benefit from the affluence of their own seniors.

We shall look at the situation in France a bit more precisely (cf. Fig. 2.4): those at age 33 had the highest relative loss of incomes. Those who were 33 years old about 30 years ago were lucky. The ones born after 1965 had the first "scars" that could not be recovered. On the other hand, we know for sure that those who are 60 today have known – of course on an average – a relatively perfect labour market situation and have had fair incomes.

The main point is that France and Italy show profound redistributions of living standards to the profit of seniors and at the expense of younger and mid-aged adults

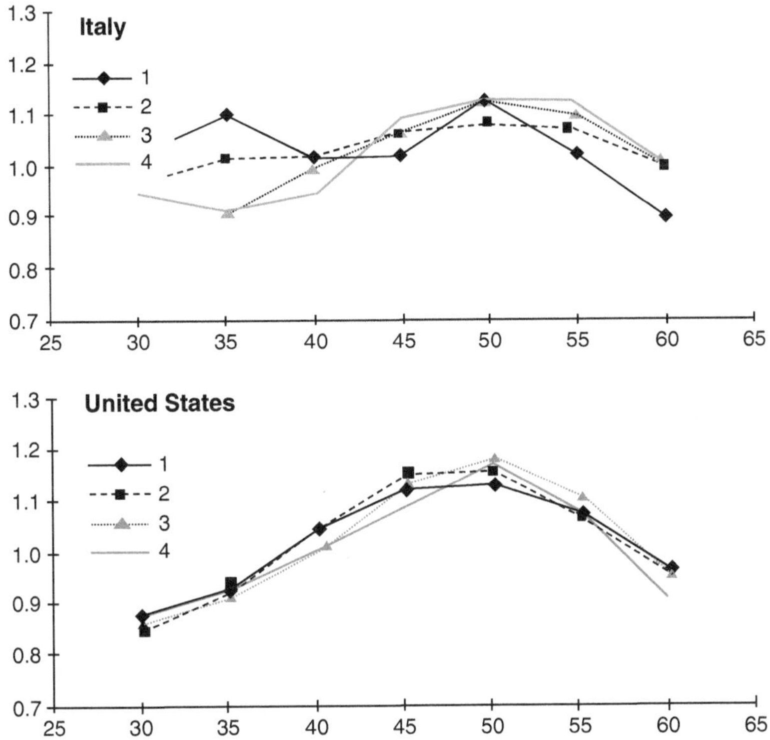

Fig 2.3 (continued)

whereas Denmark and the US face no massive transformations. When both the Nordic and Liberal welfare regimes are about to smoothen inter-cohort inequalities, the corporatist and the familialistic regimes generate visible imbalances between age groups.

2.10 Welfare Regime Ruptures and Consumption

The main conclusion is that the answers of the different welfare regimes to the economic slowdown of the post 1970s period differ substantially. The Danish model of welfare faced the challenge with a universalistic objective of stabilisation and protection of all age groups equally; the young adults are not the specific victims of any kind of retrenchments in the model. At the opposite part of the inequality spectrum, the US did not diverge from their principle of competitive market, and both the young and old face a similar life course.

Conversely, the French and the Italians have decided to answer to the new challenges with a stronger protection for the more affluent positions of seniors resulting in more difficulties for their younger cohorts. This decision created a

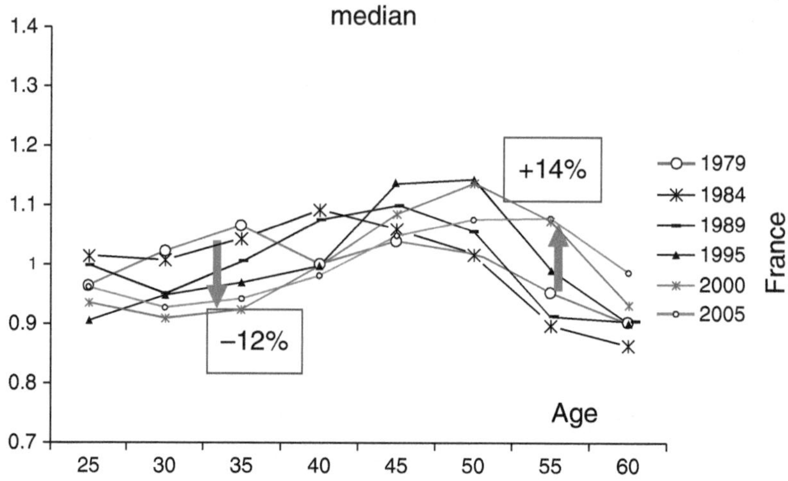

Fig. 2.4 Relative adjusted disposable income (RADI) from 1979 to 2005 by age group
Source: www.lisproject.org

paradoxical situation where social democracy seems to improve in the older cohorts while the young are destabilised. The French diagnosis of double victimisation of younger generations (victims of both fake liberalism, which give freedom only to those who have the economic means, and fake socialism, which has forgotten the young) is relevant in Italy also.

2.11 Conclusion

The central point of the conclusion relates to the long-term sustainability of welfare regimes. To be stable in the long-term, a social system must arrange its own reproduction from one generation to the next. In France and Italy, today's seniors benefit from a large welfare state, but the vast social rights they were able to accumulate were the consequence of their relatively advantaged careers; we assert that the new generations, when they become seniors themselves, will not be able to benefit from the same rights, and the large size of the present welfare state will mechanically erode with cohort replacement – since the reproduction of the welfare regime is not ascertained.

The key question is: will younger generations in France or Italy continue to sustain a system where their social condition is devalued compared to the older generations with no clear prospects of improvement? For the moment, these intergenerational inequalities are accepted, since they are generally unknown, their social visibility is low and their political recognition zero. These examples of the corporatist and familialistic impasse show that if solidarity is wanted, there is no other way than in a universalistic model (similar to the Nordic one) that supports equally the young, the middle-aged, and the elders in a long-term perspective of socialisation. In terms of consumption, these results give a better understanding of differences in the national life course perspective of standards of living.

In France, compared to the US, the young generation faces real difficulties, and at the opposite, the nowadays seniors benefit from a specific economic boom and from economic homogenisation (more equality). In France, seniors appear attractive targets for marketing products while the young are often framed in terms of social problems. The Italian situation is similar, but the demographic collapse of young generations of adults (less numerous with less children) and their increasing degree of familialistic dependence reduces the degree of immediate visibility of the social problem, but this problem will evidently appear raising the question of who will care for elders. At the opposite end, Denmark seems to be a stable model of development of a universalistic solidaristic regime of collective improvement. The social problems that appear elsewhere (deepening gaps between the rich and the poor, accumulation of social problems for the newer generations, destabilisation of the young educated middle class, etc.) seem to be relativised and smoothed, and the general atmosphere is more propitious to a socially homogeneous and the development of a "wage earner middle class" in a knowledge-based society. While recognising there are limitations to the welfare regime model approach, this analysis suggests the *universalistic* welfare regime is sustainable and maintains its own capacity for long-term development.

References

Attias-Donfut C (2000) Rapports de générations: transferts intrafamiliaux et dynamique macrosociale. Rev Fr Sociol 41(4):643–684

Bell L, Burtless G, Smeeding T, Gornick J (2007) Failure to launch: cross – National trends in the transition to economic Independence. Lis Working Paper, Nr. 456

Brzinsky-Fay C (2007) Lost in transition? Labour market entry sequences of school leavers in Europe. Eur Sociol Rev 23(4):409–422

Chauvel L (1998) Le destin des générations. Structure sociale et cohortes en France au xxe siècle. Presses Universitaires de France, Paris

Chauvel L (2000) Valorisation et dévalorisation sociale des titres. Une comparaison France – Etats – Unis. In: van Zanten A (ed) L'état de l'école. La Découverte, Paris, pp 341–352

Chauvel L (2006) Social generations, life chances and welfare regime sustainability. In: Pepper DC, Peter AH, Bruno P (eds) Changing France. The politics that markets make. Macmillan, Basingstoke, pp 341–352

Chauvel L (2007) Generazioni sociali, prospettive di vita e sostenibilità del welfare. La Riv Polit Soc 4(3):43–72

Easterlin RA (1961) The American baby boom in historical perspective. Am Econ Rev 51(5): 869–911

Easterlin RA, Schaeffer CM, Maucunovich DJ (1993) Will the baby boomers be less well off than their parents? Income, wealth, and family circumstances over the life cycle in the United States. Popul Dev Rev 19(3):497–522

Esping-Andersen G (1990) The tree worlds of welfare capitalism. Cambridge University Press, Cambridge

Esping-Andersen G (1999) Social foundations of postindustrial economies. Oxford University Press, Oxford

Esping-Andersen G, Gallie D, Hemerijck A, Myles J (2002) Why we need a new welfare state. Oxford University Press, Oxford

Ferrera M (1996) The 'Southern model' of welfare in social Europe. J Eur Soc Policy 1(6):17–37

Fourastié J (1979) Les Trente Glorieuses ou la révolution invisible. Fayard, Paris

Heston A, Summers R, Aten B (2006) Penn World Table Version 6.2. The University of Pennsylvania: Center for International Comparisons of Production, Income and prices

Maddison A (1982) Phases of capitalist development. Oxford university press, Oxford

Mannheim K (1928) Le problème des générations. Nathan, Paris

Mayer KU (2005) Life courses and life chances in a comparative perspective. In: Svallfors S (ed) Analyzing inequality. Life chances and social mobility in comparative perspective. Palo Alto, CA, Stanford University Press, pp 17–55

van de Velde C (2008) Devenir adulte. Sociologie comparée de la jeunesse en Europe. Presses Universitaires de France, Paris

Chapter 3
How Does Globalization Affect the Life Courses of Young Men and Women in Modern Societies?

Hans-Peter Blossfeld and Melinda Mills

3.1 Introduction

Young people in industrialized nations have experienced significant changes in the transition to adulthood in past decades. Globalization, via (1) the internationalization and importance of markets, (2) intensified competition, (3) accelerated spread of networks and knowledge through new technologies, and (4) the increasing dependence on random shocks, has transformed the transition to adulthood. The purpose of this paper is to inquire to which extent these changes have influenced young people's ability to establish themselves as independent adults when making the transition from school to work, to form partnerships, and to become parents. Has globalization produced a fundamental shift in youth behavior as they cope with increasing uncertainty about the future? How do different domestic institutions filter these transformations?

Our paper develops a multi-level conceptual framework of how globalization impacts the transition to adulthood and summarizes the main results from the first phase of the international research project GLOBALIFE (Life Courses in the Globalization Process) (see Blossfeld et al. 2005). This study includes 14 country-specific studies from: Canada (Mills 2005), the United States (King 2005), Great Britain (Francesconi and Golsch 2005), Germany (Kurz et al. 2005), the Netherlands (Liefbroer 2005), France (Kieffer et al. 2005), Norway (Nilsen 2002), Sweden (Bygren et al. 2005), Italy (Bernardi and Nazio 2005), Spain (Simo

H.-P. Blossfeld (✉)
Lehrstuhl für Soziologie 1, Otto-Friedrich-Universität Bamberg, Postfach 1549, 96045 Bamberg, Germany
e-mail: soziologie1@sowi.uni-bamberg.de

M. Mills
Department of Sociology/ICS, University of Groningen, Grote Rozenstraat 31, 9712 TG Groningen, The Netherlands
e-mail: m.c.mills@rug.nl

J.C. Tremmel (ed.), *A Young Generation Under Pressure?*,
DOI 10.1007/978-3-642-03483-1_3, © Springer-Verlag Berlin Heidelberg 2010

Noguera et al. 2005), Mexico (Parrado 2005), Ireland (Layte et al. 2005), Estonia (Katus et al. 2005), and Hungary (Robert and Bukodi 2005).

For our purposes, we have defined the transition to adulthood as *a stepwise process in which young people adopt specific roles and participate in certain activities*. We particularly focus on the age-graded character of labor market entry, the transition to first partnership (cohabitation or marriage), and the entry into parenthood. The study of the impact of globalization during this critical and turbulent phase of the early life course is important because at this phase youth are generally unprotected by seniority or experience and are typically outsiders in the labor market. For this reason, they are expected to experience the recent shifts towards globalization more directly.

3.2 Globalization and Increasing Uncertainty

Globalization is an inherently complex concept. Yet, in recent years, it has become a central point of reference for media, politicians, academics, and policy-makers to understand social change. Our concept of globalization can be summarized under four interrelated structural shifts, which are affecting life courses in modern societies during the last two decades. These shifts, and the mechanisms that link globalization to the transition to adulthood, are summarized in Fig. 3.1.

First, globalization refers to the *internationalization of markets and subsequent decline of national borders*. It is connected with changes in laws, institutions, or practices which make various transactions (in terms of commodities, labor, services and capital) easier or less expensive across national borders. An important consequence is that political agreements have generally liberalized financial markets (Fligstein 1998). Some have argued that this decline of national borders undermines the authority or even heralds the fall of the nation-state (Ohmae 1990; Beck 1997/2000). Our position is that the nation state, and, in particular, institutions that shape the lives of youth, do not lose their significance, but rather generate country-specific problems that call for country-specific solutions and transformations (see also Sassen 1996). Internationalization of markets also means the *integration of previously* "isolated" *nations into the world economy*.

Second, globalization relates to the *intensification of competition*, i.e., strengthens the notion that capital and labor are increasingly mobile and forces firms and national economies to continuously adjust. Within nation states, this is reflected in the increased importance of governments to make their national economies internationally competitive. These policy measures include the improvement of the functioning of markets through the removal or relaxation of government regulation of economic activities (deregulation). It also suggests a shift towards relying on the price mechanism to coordinate economic activities (liberalization), and a transfer to private ownership and control of assets or enterprises that were previously under public ownership (privatization). This neo-liberal shift demands efficiency, productivity and profitability, and often means a push to adjust prices, products,

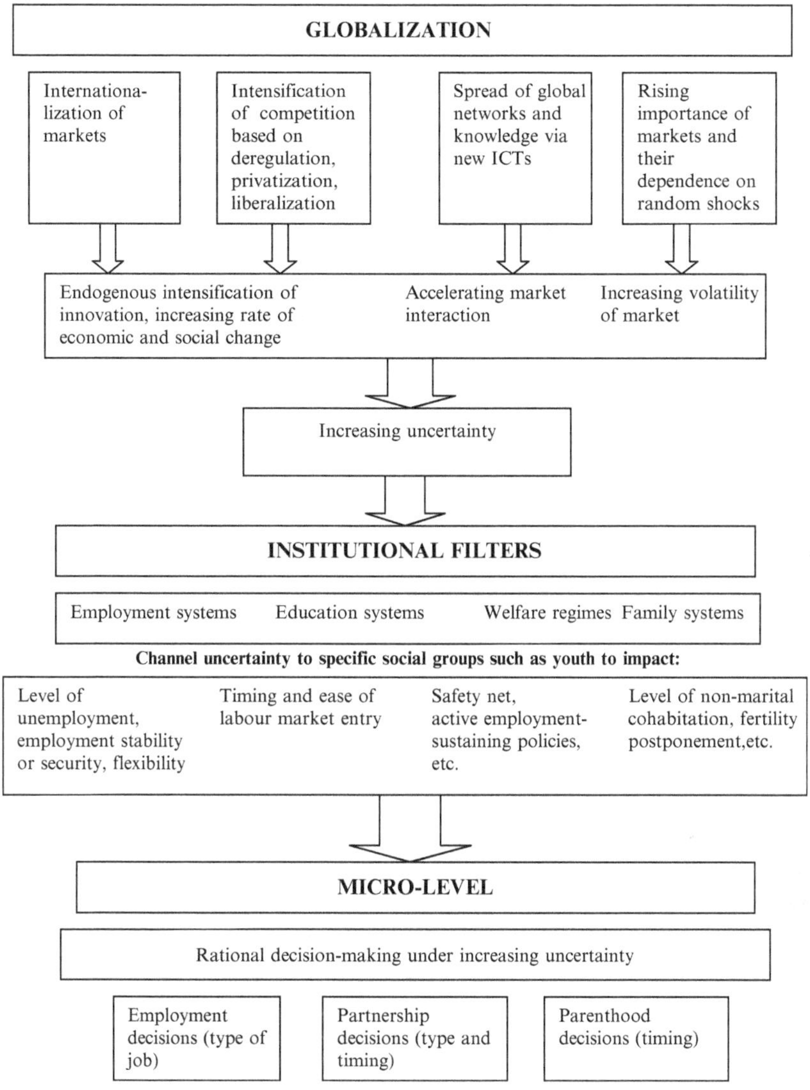

Fig. 3.1 Globalization and increasing uncertainty in the transition to adulthood

technologies and human resources more rapidly and extensively (Regini 2000; Montanari 2001).

A third feature of globalization is the *spread of global networks of people and firms linked by ICTs* (information communication technologies) such as microcomputers and the Internet. These ICTs, together with modern mass media, transmit messages and images instantaneously from the largest city to the smallest village on every continent and allow a faster diffusion of information and knowledge over long distances. They increasingly allow people to share information, in order to connect and create an instant common worldwide standard of comparison. Modern ICTs influence communications between individuals, organizations and communities by effectively rendering physical space and distance irrelevant. Thus, although the introduction of technology is not unique in itself, recent ICTs have fundamentally altered the scope (widening reach of networks of social activity and power), intensity (regularized connections), velocity (speeding up of interactions and processes), and impact (local impacts global) of transformations (Held et al. 1999).

Finally, globalization is inherently related to the *rise in the importance and the growing volatility of markets*. Globalization not only speeds up the process of exchange and communication across national borders, but due to the intensification of global competition, also increases the relevance of markets in the coordination of decisions in all modern societies. These developments inherently strengthen the worldwide interdependence of decision-making. As a consequence of these structural developments, market prices and their changes increasingly convey information about the global demand for various goods, services and assets, and the worldwide relative costs of producing and offering them. In a globalizing market, individual suppliers and consumers are increasingly exposed to a rising number of traders on each side of the market and become "price-takers," able to buy and sell any quantity at a price which they, in essence, cannot influence. Thus, prices produced by globalizingmarkets increasingly set the standards to which individuals, firms and nation states then try to comply.

However, globalization does not only mean that actors are increasingly in the hands of anonymous global markets. What is equally important is that the changes within these markets are becoming more dynamic and less predictable. First, the globalization of markets endogenously intensifies competition between firms, forcing them to be innovative, to use new technological developments or to invent new products. This, in turn, increases the instability of markets (Streeck 1987). Second, modern ICTs and deregulation and liberalization measures allow individuals, firms and governments to react faster to observed market changes and simultaneously accelerate market transactions (Castells 1996). This, in turn, makes long-term developments of globalizing markets inherently harder to predict. Third, global prices tend to become exogenously more liable to fluctuations because worldwide supply, demand, or both are becoming increasingly susceptible to random shocks caused somewhere on the globe (e.g., major scientific discoveries, technical inventions, new consumer fashions, major political upsets such as wars and revolutions, economic upsets, etc.).

The accelerated market dynamics and the rising dependence of prices on random events happening somewhere on the globe produce a higher frequency of surprises and lead to market prices which are different, to an important extent, from what people reasonably could have expected given the restricted information available to them. In other words, the increasing dynamics and volatility of outcomes of globalizing markets makes it more difficult for individuals, firms and governments to predict the future and to make choices between different alternatives and strategies. *Increasing uncertainty* about economic and social developments is therefore a definitive feature of globalization in advanced economies.

3.3 Globalization and Institutional Filters

It is not essentially increasing uncertainty as such that is important if we analyze the consequences of globalization; rather, it is how rising uncertainty is "institutionally filtered" and channeled towards specific social groups in various countries. Increasing uncertainty does not impact all regions, states, organizations or individuals in the same way. There are institutional settings and social structures, historically grown and country-specific, which determine the degree to which people are affected by rising uncertainty (Diprete et al. 1997). These institutions have a certain inertial tendency to persist (Nelson 1995; Esping-Andersen 1993) and act as a sort of intervening variable between global macro forces and the responses at the micro level (Hurrell and Woods 1995; Regini 2000) (see Fig. 3.1). Thus, we do not expect that increasing uncertainty leads to a rapid convergence of life courses in all modern societies, as claimed, for example, by neo-institutionalists (see, e.g., Meyer et al. 1992) or the proponents of the modernization hypothesis (see, e.g., Treiman 1970; Treiman and Yip 1989). Rather, we claim that there are path-dependent developments within countries (Mayer 2001; Mills et al. 2008a). The institutions having the greatest impact on the life courses of youth are employment relations, educational systems, national welfare state regimes, and the family.

3.3.1 Employment Relations Systems

Given the specific phase of the life course, we expect that *in all countries* the global increase of uncertainty is experienced more directly by *youth entering the labor market*. Youth are unprotected by seniority and experience and do not yet have strong ties to work organizations and, in general, all youth entering the labor market are more exposed to global uncertainty. In contrast, we assume that global forces should have less impact on people who are already established in their job career or have already gained several years of labor force experience.

However, countries also differ significantly with respect to the nature of employment relations between employers and workers and make it therefore more or less easy for youth to establish themselves in the labor market. These country-specific differences surface in elements such as types of work councils, collective bargaining systems, strength of unions versus employer organizations, labor legislation or administrative regulations. They produce distinct national variations of occupational structures and industries, patterns of labor–capital negotiations, strike frequencies and collective agreements on wages, job security, labor conditions, and work hours (Soskice 1993; Streeck 1992). How these systems diverge has been characterized as "coordinated" and "uncoordinated" market economies (Soskice 1998), "individualist" or "collective" regimes (Diprete et al. 1997), or "open" and "closed" employment relations (Sorensen 1983).

Based on these systems, we propose an *employment relationship hypothesis* regarding the early labor market experiences of youth in various countries.

We expect that the main consequences of the open employment relationship for young people will be: (1) comparatively low economic security (e.g., wages, benefits) for most jobs; (2) an environment that fosters precarious employment and labor market flexibility to the extent that it becomes more widespread among various social groups; (3) importance of individual human capital resources; (4) relatively easy entry into the labor market; (5) unemployment of a shorter duration; and (6) a relatively high rate of job mobility (i.e., hire-and-fire principle). The central impact of a closed employment relationship is expected to be that: (1) precarious employment forms (e.g., fixed-term contracts, part-time work) are highly concentrated among specific groups seeking access to the labor market (youth, women, unemployed); (2) individual human capital resources are less important; (3) entry in the labor force is problematic, particularly under conditions of high general unemployment; (4) unemployment is usually of a longer duration; and (5) the rate of job mobility is relatively low. Within these systems, most of the already employed workers, the so-called "insiders," which in most cases are mid-career men, will be relatively shielded against the growing uncertainty and flexibility demands of the world market. Globalization in these countries tends to create a new kind of underclass of the socially excluded, while the employed have high levels of job security with relatively high wages, reminiscent of dual and segmented labor market theories (Piore 1970; Fine 1998).

In addition, we propose a *labor market flexibility hypothesis*, which contends that firms implement different types of flexibility depending on the rigidity of the employment relation system. Not only the level or type of flexibility will differ, but also the meaning and function attributed to it. Our anticipation is that in rigid closed labor markets, functional flexibility for labor market insiders is often the primary option for employers (see Mills and Blossfeld 2005). However, for outsiders such as youth, one way to implement flexibility will be a combination of numerical/temporal flexibility in the form of fixed-term or temporary contracts. Furthermore, externalization – related to the growing number of self-employed youth not bound to a contract of employment – may also serve an increasingly important purpose (see Bernardi and Nazio 2005). Although, in more deregulated open labor markets that are built on the premises of flexibility, market economic relations, and a non-interventionist state (Mayer 2001), we expect flexibility to pervade in many forms. As new labor market entrants, youth are party to numerical flexibility and are often the last hired and first fired, a pattern likely accentuated during periods of economic recession.

3.3.2 Educational Systems

In the globalized, knowledge-based society, education and labor force experience become the most important types of human capital. Since youth are generally lacking in the latter, they have to focus on the former, which is evident in educational expansion across most the industrialized world (see Klijzing 2005).

We therefore propose a *human capital hypothesis* that gauges the significance of characteristics required in all knowledge-based economies. Educational attainment and occupational standing measure human capital, which may increase with labor force experience and age. The expectation is that those lacking human capital, such as youth with lower education, weak occupational standing or lacking experience, will feel the impact of globalization more immensely in *all* modern societies. In other words, they are at a higher risk to enter a more precarious, flexible and uncertain employment situation (e.g., fixed-term contract, part-time, irregular hours). Conversely, those with higher education or the "knowledge workers" will conceivably have more favorable experiences.

However, we expect that white-collar workers are not entirely immune to changes such as the use of temporary short-term contracts. Thus, there may be a change also for those in higher occupations or higher education. Yet, the main difference is that for them, unstable or inadequate work may serve as a bridge whereas for lower skilled wage-workers, it may become a trap (see Bernardi and Nazio 2005; Layte et al. 2005). Therefore, a second general expectation is that *globalization accentuates or even cultivates inequality* by offering better opportunities to the better educated youth and constraining the chances of the less educated.

A related point is the *degree of educational expansion* in each country. When we examine the cohort-specific attendance rates across various levels of education for the 14 countries in this study, there has been a prolonged extension of school participation over time (see Klijzing 2005). A longer stay in school works as a proxy for the degree to which the transition to economic independence has been postponed across birth cohorts in different countries. This belated timing in reaching economic independence is particularly important for our study of partnership formation and the transition to parenthood. There is a link between educational expansion and increasing youth unemployment, or an *alternative role hypothesis*. This identifies a tendency among young adults to opt – if this is structurally possible in a given educational system – for the role as a student instead of becoming unemployed in the process of transition from youth to adulthood. The educational system then serves as a reservoir for otherwise unemployed youth, which is increasingly strong in southern European countries like Italy and Spain. There is also likely a relation to the national support systems for young adults who prefer to stay in education. Some countries such as Germany, the Netherlands, Norway and Sweden have a more generous system of education grants or loans, which is limited (e.g., Canada, Great Britain, France, post-1990s Estonia, Ireland), highly insufficient (e.g., United States) or virtually non-existent in others such as Italy, Spain, Hungary, and Mexico.

3.3.3 Welfare Regimes

The impact of increasing uncertainty on social inequality among young people is strongly affected by the welfare state. Modern countries have created different welfare regimes implying diverse national ideologies about social solidarity (Flora and Alber 1981) as well as gender and social equality (Esping-andersen 1999; Orloff 1996). The five welfare regime categorizations are: liberal, social-democratic, conservative, family-oriented and post-socialistic. Differences between welfare regimes manifest themselves in the priority of:(1) active employment-sustaining labor market policies (i.e., the commitment to full employment); (2) welfare-sustaining employment exit policies (i.e., support for those who are outside of the labor market such as youth, unemployed, ill, poor, family care workers, pensioners); (3) the scope and generosity of family allowances and services (i.e., maternity/paternity leave, childcare) (Gauthier 1996); and (4) the share of the public sector in the labor force. Together, these differences form a *welfare regime hypothesis*. The expectations of the impact of each regime on the lives of youth are formulated following the description of each regime.

To varying degrees, the United States, the United Kingdom, and Canada are viewed as *liberal* welfare regimes characterized by passive labor market policies, moderate support for the underprivileged, and relatively small public sector employment. The comparatively high employment performance in these regimes is related to the reduction of rigidities such as union power, restrictive labor legislation, and general flexibility of the labor market. Due to these factors, our expectation is that although there will be an overall higher employment level for youth, it will be at the expense of greater inequality and poverty. This is the result of an environment of passive employment policies, a marginal safety net, such as limited or highly conditional unemployment benefits, and mixed (i.e., generous child allowance and limited parental leave in Ireland) or means-tested family benefits (Canada, United States), and more exposure to the competitive private sector.

Norway and Sweden are in contrast characteristic of the *social-democratic* welfare regime model. Active labor market and taxation policies in these countries are aimed at full employment, gender equality at the workplace as well as at home, and a "fair" income distribution with a high degree of wage compression. Achieving full employment is mostly attempted by a combination of Keynesian demand policies and mobility-stimulating measures such as retraining, mobility grants, and temporary jobs.

The large participation of (married) women in full-time employment in these welfare regimes rests on two factors. First, the rapid expansion of job opportunities in the service and public sector, engendered in particular by the demands of social services (kindergartens, schools, hospitals, daycare centers and homes for the elderly). Second, the highly progressive individual income tax that makes a second household income necessary for most families if they want to enjoy the products of a technologically advanced service society (Blossfeld and Drobnic 2001). In this welfare regime, the government tries to achieve full employment through an expanding public service sector with relatively low wages for public employees and a high rate of female employment, in particular. Our expectation is that youth making the transition to adulthood in this context can fall back on a relatively generous safety net, which combined with other factors such as gender equality and full employment, better enables them to combine work with family formation (i.e., forming partnership, becoming a parent).

Germany and the Netherlands are often cited as examples of *conservative* welfare regimes. Social policies in these countries are not so much designed to promote employment opportunities, job mobility, and full employment by Keynesian demand policy measures but rather to ensure that those workers who leave employment because of job loss, disability, or in some cases as part of an early retirement program, are protected against serious declines in living standards. Of course, this is costly and leads to tax increases, particularly during periods of high unemployment. This type of welfare regime is therefore strongly transfer-oriented, with de-commodifying effects for those who are economically inactive. It is also committed to the traditional division of labor in the family that makes wives economically dependent on their husbands, often referred to as the "male-breadwinner model." In particular, it supports wives and mothers who give priority to family activities (taking care of children and the elderly) and seek to work part-time. Correspondingly, welfare state provisions (e.g., daycare) are far less developed than in the social democratic model and female economic activity rates are considerably lower and mostly restricted to part-time jobs (Blossfeld and Hakim 1997). Our main prediction is that increased economic uncertainty combined with the lack of public support will impact the decision to enter parenthood for certain groups of youth, who, due to an inability to combine education or labor force participation with family careers, will increasingly postpone or even forgo parenthood (Blossfeld and Drobnic 2001). France is hard to classify since it reflects features of *various* welfare regimes. We place it next to the conservative regimes, but expect that it will exhibit sharp contrasts due to pro-natalistic policies, combined with measures that promote female employment and the combination of work and family careers (see Blossfeld 1995).

Southern European countries like Italy and Spain, and to some extent Mexico and Ireland, also share common features. They have developed a welfare regime model that is best characterized as *family-oriented* (Jurado Guerrero 1995). In terms of labor market policy, support for the less privileged, and the importance of public sector employment, this welfare regime is very similar to the liberal one. Unlike the latter, however, it is characterized by a strong ideological and indeed practical involvement of family and kinship networks in protecting its members against economic and social risks. Due to the meager or non-existent safety net (e.g., family support, unemployment benefits), the state shifts the responsibility for the support of the unemployed and other vulnerable "outsider" groups to families and kinship networks. This model is based on the deeply rooted cultural view that family and kinship represent an important institution of reciprocal help and that family members should thus support each other. Jurado Guerrero (1995) has argued that the long stay of youth in the parental home in southern Europe is "closely associated with the high labor market risks and the lukewarm protection that the state provides against them."

In reality, this family support is, however, mostly provided by women, with two important consequences: (1) their labor force participation (including part-time work) is, by international standards, extremely low (Blossfeld and Hakim 1997); and, (2) especially if young women want to make a career, there is a particularly severe conflict between family tasks and (mostly full-time) job requirements. This leads to exorbitantly low fertility levels in Spain or Italy, for example (see Mills et al. 2008b). Thus, a paradoxical result in the family-oriented Mediterranean welfare regime appears to be that the extended family is rapidly disappearing.

Finally, we add the *post-socialistic* welfare regime to include countries in the former socialist eastern Europe, which in this study includes Estonia and Hungary. However, we do note that the former socialist countries in eastern Europe have taken‘ increasingly diverse paths. Hungary is perhaps closer to the social democratic regime, characterized by both egalitarianism and de-familialization. There is relatively more generous support for the family, with the dual-earner family model favored by fiscal arrangements, but with a highly conditional to limited degree of support for unemployed youth (Robert and Bukodi 2005). Estonia has limited and next to non-existent unemployment and family benefits for youth (Katus et al. 2005). Considering the rapid transformations after 1990 and throughout the last two decades, the trajectory of these welfare regimes is still evolving.

3.4 Micro-Level Response to Increasing Uncertainty

Many decisions in the early life course have long-term implications. People have to opt for educational and professional tracks, enter job careers or make long-term binding family and fertility decisions. However, higher levels of uncertainty for youth generate insecurity and potential conflict and make it increasingly difficult to make such choices. Young people respond and adapt to the complex structural shifts brought about by globalization. A central hypothesis of this study is that the uncertainty generated by globalization at the social-structural level reduces or delays the propensity of youth to enter long-term binding commitments such as partnerships and parenthood (see Fig. 3.1). Our attention thus turns to changes in rational decision-making under conditions of increasing uncertainty and descriptions of the schema developed to measure uncertainty at the individual level.

3.4.1 Uncertainty in the Transition to Adulthood

Since a main premise of this study was to either find evidence or dispute the impact of globalization on the early life course, we required an empirical research design that offered tangible findings. We therefore devised a measurement design that captures our theoretical suppositions and is thus able to empirically gauge the impact of uncertainty that arises from globalization factors on individual transitions in the early life course. The schema consists of three types of uncertainty: economic, temporal, and employment relation.

First, *economic uncertainty* is defined as the caliber of economic precariousness of an individual's employment and educational enrollment circumstances (Bernardi 2000). We anticipate that labor market positions with high degrees of economic uncertainty will inhibit youth when making long-term binding commitments such as partnerships, and particularly marriage, or parenthood that require a secure economic basis (Oppenheimer 1988; Oppenheimer et al. 1997). Youth require a necessary minimum or what Rindfuss and Vandenheuvel (1990) refer to as the "affordability clause" to enter into a binding relationship or have a child. As Oppenheimer (1988), we expect that youth will avoid commitment such as marriage and parenthood, but still desire the rewards of having a relationship (i.e., consensual union).

In this study, economic uncertainty is measured in four central ways. First, an activity status indicator of education and employment measures it. A second dimension is occupational class, using Erikson and Goldthorpe's (1992) class schema. Our expectation is that, compared to the higher-level service or routine white-collar classes, the lower classes such as unskilled manual workers are more likely to be in economically precarious situations. In other words, skilled occupations (and as we will argue shortly, stable employment) can reduce uncertainties (Oppenheimer et al. 1997). Whether individuals receive extra benefits with their jobs (e.g., pension) is a third measure of economic uncertainty used in some of the country studies. A final measure included in several of the country studies (e.g., France, Hungary) is earnings. Thus, the comparative yardstick to measure uncertainty is against the relative "certainty" of youth holding comparatively more certain or secure statuses such as not being enrolled in education, being employed, and if so, in a higher occupational class, or receiving benefits or higher earnings.

Second, according to Breen (1997, p. 477): "Temporal uncertainty reduces the attractiveness of long-term commitment and increases that of contingent asymmetric commitment." In other words, due to *temporal uncertainty*, youth are less able to make long-term binding commitments which may translate into, for example, opting for cohabitation instead of marriage or forgoing partnership and parenthood until they feel they have obtained adequate certainty for their future life path (see also Kurz et al. 2005). Temporal uncertainty which is measured via the presence of a temporary contract, also has a highly contingent and asymmetric basis of commitment. A temporary contract is based on a relationship where one party of the agreement (employer) retains the option to withdraw from the relationship at any time, while the other party (youth) can only comply to what the first party requests.

Temporal uncertainty and the concept of "long-term commitment" is reminiscent of Elster's (1979) notion of "self-binding." In order to reduce choice complexity of long-term courses of action under uncertainty, individuals tend to constrain or bind their own future actions (i.e., commit themselves to a specific action in the future). Self-binding is an effective technique to make one's promises to significant others (e.g., partners, actors in industrial relations) more credible. This technique makes communication about what one is going to do under still unknown future conditions more reliable. According to Elster (1979), this credibility enhances the *trust* that actors will have in each other and enables them to interact and cooperate more effectively than without such self-binding commitments. Self-binding, however, is also paradoxical, particularly in a life phase in which the transition to adulthood takes place. On the one hand, it is a prerequisite for creating certainty for young people as well as credibility and trust in one's dealings with others. On the other hand, it diminishes the ability to react in a flexible manner during later stages of the life course, which clashes with the rapidly changing demands of a globalizing society.

We expect that the effects of uncertainty will, however, differ for men and women, particularly those from conservative welfare regimes. A *gender hypothesis* supposes that in countries where the male-breadwinner model is predominant, it will be more important for males to establish themselves in a more secure job as opposed to females (Oppenheimer et al. 1997). For this reason, we predict a stronger effect of uncertainty on men than women, which will be particularly evident in the male-breadwinner countries of the conservative and family-oriented welfare regimes.

3.5 Data and Methods

Our intention to search for empirical evidence to either confirm or disconfirm the impact of globalization on the lives of youth led to the use of individual-based event history data and longitudinal analytical methods and techniques (Blossfeld and Rohwer 2002). The majority of data used in this study came from retrospective or longitudinal panel surveys collected in the 1990s. This included the German Socio-Economic Panel (1984–1998), data pooled from seven retrospective life history surveys and the Panel Study of Social Integration (1987, 1989, 1991, 1995) for the Netherlands, and for France, the Young People and Careers survey (1997). The Swedish analysis draws on the Swedish Level of Living Survey (1991), with Norway using KIRUT (10% sample of public register data, 1989–1996) and the Database of Generations (1950–1990). The Hungarian study employs the Way of Life and Time Use Survey (1999–2000) and the General Youth Survey (2000). Both Estonia and Spain used the Fertility and Family Survey from 1994 and 1995, respectively. The British Household Panel Survey (1991–1999) was used for the United Kingdom, the Survey of Labor and Income Dynamics (1993–1998) for Canada, the National Survey of Family Growth (1995, women only) for the United States and the National Retrospective Demographic Survey (1989, women only) for Mexico. The analysis of Italy was based on the Italian Longitudinal Household Survey (1997) with the Irish study using both the Irish School Leavers Survey (1987–1993, 1992–1998) and the Follow-up of the School Leavers Survey (1992, 1998).

3.6 Results

This section provides a short summary of the key empirical findings from the 14 countries included in this study in addition to confronting our expectations and theoretical assumptions outlined previously.

3.6.1 The Emergence of Uncertainty

The first central finding is that in a globalizing world, *youth are increasingly vulnerable to more uncertainty when making the transition into employment across all countries*. This materializes in more precarious and lower quality employment such as fixed-term contracts, part-time or irregular work hours, or lower occupational standing (see Table 3.1). This, in turn, bestows the youngest labor market entrants with a more uncertain future. Youth, who have less labor market experience and who are not yet shielded by internal labor markets, are more greatly

Table 3.1 Summary of main results: Rising uncertainty in the labor market and impact on partnership and parenthood behavior

Welfare regime and country	Rising uncertainty in early life course				
	Uncertain labor market position for younger cohorts	Impact of employment uncertainty on hazard of:			
		Partnerships		Parenthood	
		Men	Women	Men	Women
Conservative					
Germany	↑	↓	↑	↓	↑
Netherlands	↑	↓	↑	↓	↑
[France]	↑	↓	↑/↔	↓	↑/↓
Social-democratic					
Sweden	↑	↓/↔	↓/↔	↓	↓
Norway	↑	↓	↓	↓	↓
Post-socialistic					
Hungary	↑	↓	↓	↓	↑
Estonia[a]	↑	↓/↔	↓/↔	↓/↔	↓/↔
Liberal					
Britain	↑	↔(c) ↓(m)	↓(c) ↔(m)	↔	↑
Canada	↑	↓	↓	↓	↓
United States (f)	↑	-	↓	-	↓
Family-oriented					
Mexico (f)	↑	-	↔	-	↔
Italy	↑	↓	↑	↓	↑
Spain	↑	↓	↑	↓	↑
Ireland	↓	-	↔	-	↔

Notes: ↑ = increase in hazard, ↔ = no significantly observed effect, ↓ = decrease in hazard, - = not examined, (f) = only women examined, (m) = marriage, (c) = consensual union
[a]Analysis was not divided by gender

exposed to the forces of globalization, which makes them the "losers" of globalization. This is in contrast to some groups, such as mid-career men, who generally surface as "winners" in the globalization process. As insiders, mid-career men are to a large extent shielded by labor force experience, internal labor markets and existing power structures. The forces of globalization are therefore shifted to outsiders such as youth.

The 14 studies provide evidence for youth's increased exposure to globalization in diverse ways. Young Spanish and Italian workers experienced fixed-term contracts and high unemployment, with British and Hungarian youth increasingly more likely to start their employment career in non-standard temporary jobs or as self-employed workers. As Table 3.1 demonstrates, out of the 14 countries, there was only one exception. Ireland experienced an unprecedented economic boom in the 1990s that actually reduced uncertainty for youth. The increased certainty generated by the Irish "economic miracle" and its relation to the globalization process, will be discussed in more detail shortly in relation to institutional filters.

We found strong support for our expectation that *human capital* would be an important asset to protect youth against uncertainty, particularly in the more liberal welfare regimes (see also Diprete et al. 1997). Empirical findings for Britain, for instance, show that education and labor market experience protected youth from falling into unemployment (see Francesconi and Golsch 2005; King 2005).

3.6.2 Consequences of Uncertainty for Family Formation

An uncertain *educational and labor market activity status* also had clear consequences for family formation. The lowest rate of entry into fatherhood in Spain was for men in the most uncertain position of all – the unemployed (Simo Noguera et al. 2005). As Table 3.1 illustrates, there were mixed findings of the impact of uncertainty for Sweden. Unemployment (after labor market entry) in Sweden had no effect on union formation and parenthood, which supports our hypothesis that welfare regimes with generous benefits can cushion economic uncertainty for youth (Bygren et al. 2005).

The amount of security youth possessed in their *employment relationship* and degree of *temporal uncertainty* also had real consequences for family formation. The impact of having a fixed-term contract was expected to result in higher temporal and employment relation uncertainty, which had a particularly strong effect for men (see for e.g., Bernardi and Nazio 2005; Kieffer et al. 2005; Robert and Bukodi 2005). As Table 3.1 illustrates, several patterns of the impact of uncertainty on family formation emerged within the 14 countries. First, there are clear gender-specific effects, discussed in detail shortly. Second, there was a marginal impact of labor market uncertainty on family formation in Mexico and Ireland, albeit for very different reasons. In these family-oriented regimes, partnership and fertility remained as bastions of security. Due to the relatively better economic situation brought about by globalization, young Irish youth actually opted to form partnerships and have children more so than before (Layte et al. 2005). As a rational reply to uncertainty in the Mexican context, women often worked in order to diversify the source of income and spread uncertainty over a larger base in order to support the family (Parrado 2005).

Another strategy reflects the *shift from more permanent marital unions to non-marital cohabitation.* In many of the countries, such as Sweden, Norway, the Netherlands, Britain, United States, Canada, and more recently in Hungary and Estonia, there has been a large shift among adults born in and after the 1960s to choose unmarried cohabitation as opposed to marriage. This supports our expectations that when there is growing uncertainty about behavioral outcomes and the implications of long-term commitments, a rational reaction for youth is to choose a relationship that has less of a binding obligation. There appeared to be two general groups who have a higher propensity to cohabit across the countries for very different reasons. One was youth with high amounts of human capital and good labor market prospects, who likely saw it as a flexible and non-binding commitment that did not clash with their careers. The other group was disadvantaged youth who used it as a strategy and rational reaction to uncertainty as a flexible and non-binding way to combine resources in the face of uncertain future labor market success (see Katus et al. 2005; King 2005; Robert and Bukodi 2005).

The final striking finding was the *development of gender-specific strategies in male breadwinner societies.* The first gender-specific finding is that men in uncertain positions opted to postpone family formation (see Table 3.1). A precarious employment status or lack of human capital for men had a negative impact on entry into partnership and especially parenthood, a finding that was exaggerated in the male-breadwinner nations (see Bernardi and Nazio 2005; Kieffer et al. 2005; Liefbroer 2005; Simo Noguera et al. 2005). When we examine the findings for women, we can identify two categories: family versus career-oriented. Particularly in male-breadwinner societies and conservative and family-oriented welfare regimes, certain types of women tended to enter into a marriage and have children faster (Friedman et al. 1994). Here, family formation and taking the domestic role of housewife and/or mother appears to be a particular strategy for young women with less human capital in order to reduce uncertainty. Several studies found that women who were employed part-time (e.g., Spain, Germany, the Netherlands, Britain), at a very low starting pay (e.g., France, Hungary), or were inactive or unemployed (e.g., Spain, Italy, the Netherlands, France, Britain) were *more* likely to enter a union (often marriage) or have a child.

There are perhaps three underlying reasons for the presence of the family-oriented group of women. First, worse types of jobs have very few prospects for career advancement. This prompts women to opt for motherhood to reduce their own insecurity or as a way of giving meaning and structure to their lives. Second, these women may have already been less attached to the labor force and already found domestic life more appealing. Third, following the uncertainty reduction theory of Friedman et al. (1994), being married and having children could serve as a strategy to reduce uncertainty, particularly among those who have limited or blocked alternatives to reduce uncertainty in another way. According to this theory, a stable and successful career is an important source of certainty for some, and thus lowers their likelihood to form a family. Those with marginal career prospects opt for certainty in the family realm, a strategy that may be particularly relevant for women from male-breadwinner societies.

The second group of women adopted a very different tactic and sought to obtain more individual human capital and invest in a career, which depending on the institutional context either enabled or constrained them to form a family. Women with higher education were either less likely or experienced later entry into partnerships and parenthood in countries where interdependent careers were institutionally impeded (e.g., Germany, the Netherlands, Spain). This provides support for Becker's (1981) theory of increased economic autonomy, but only in countries where the interdependence between family and work careers is incompatible. This division in the gender-specific impact of uncertainty did not hold in liberal and social democratic regimes where the dual-earner model prevails (see Table 3.1 and Mills 2005, Bygren et al. 2005). In Sweden, economic self-sufficiency has long been recognized as an important factor to increase union formation for both men and women (Bracher and Santow 1998). The high level of security afforded by the Swedish welfare state allows youth, particularly mothers, to combine work and fertility, resulting in both strong labor market attachment coupled with high fertility rates.

It is not the accumulation of human capital that is important for many women, but rather the incompatibility of employment or educational and domestic roles. In many countries entry into marriage and labor market participation does not appear to present a conflict anymore for many young women (Blossfeld 1995). This is likely due to the fact that the domestic division of labor does not change after entry into marriage, but rather after the birth of the first child. Furthermore, highly educated women do not seem to have, in general, a lower rate of *overall* entry into motherhood. Rather, as Blossfeld and Huinink (1991) argue, they simply postpone it. In Sweden and Norway, for example, men and women with the highest levels of education also had the lowest propensity to enter a first union, yet showed comparatively high first-birth rates after entry.

References

Beck U (1997/2000) What is globalization? Polity Press, Cambridge

Becker GS (1981) A treatise on the family. Harvard University Press, Cambridge

Bernardi F (2000) Employment flexibility, class and risk at entry into the labor market; Patterns of early careers in Italy, GLOBALIFE Working Paper No. 7. University of Bielefeld, Germany

Bernardi F, Nazio T (2005) Globalization and the transition to adulthood in Italy. In: Blossfeld H-P, Klizjing E, Mills M, Kurz K (eds) Globalization, uncertainty and youth in society. Routledge, London, pp 349–374

Blossfeld H-P (ed) (1995) The new role of women: family formation in modern societies. Westview Press, Boulder

Blossfeld H-P, Drobnic S (eds) (2001) Careers of couples in contemporary societies. From male breadwinner to dual-earner families. Oxford University Press, Oxford

Blossfeld H-P, Hakim C (eds) (1997) Between equalization and marginalization. Women working part-time in Europe and the United States of America. Oxford University Press, Oxford
Blossfeld H-P, Huinink J (1991) Human capital investments or norms of role transitions? How women's schooling and career affect the process of family formation. Am J Sociol 97:143–168
Blossfeld H-P, Rohwer G (2002) Techniques of event history modeling new approaches to causal analysis, 2nd edn. Erlbaum, Hillsdale, NJ
Blossfeld H-P, Klizjing E, Mills M, Kurz K (eds) (2005) Globalization, uncertainty and youth in society. Routledge, London
Bracher M, Santow G (1998) Economic independence and union formation in Sweden. Popul Stud 52:275–294
Breen R (1997) Risk, recommodification and stratification. Sociology 31(3):473–498
Bygren M, Duvander A-Z, Hultin M (2005) Elements of uncertainty in life courses: transitions to adulthood in Sweden. In: Blossfeld HP, Klizjing E, Mills M, Kurz K (eds) Globalization, uncertainty and youth in society. Routledge, London, pp 135–158
Castells M (1996) The rise of the network society. the information age: Economy, society and culture, vol I. Blackwell, Oxford
Diprete T et al (1997) Collectivist versus individualist mobility regimes? Structural change and job mobility in four countries. Am J Sociol 103(2):318–358
Elster J (1979) Ulysses and the sirens. Cambridge University Press, Cambridge, MA
Erikson R, Goldthorpe JH (1992) The constant flux: a study of class mobility in industrial societies. Clarendon Press, Oxford
Esping-Andersen G (1993) Post-industrial class structures: an analytical framework. In: Esping-Andersen E (ed) Changing classes. London, Sage, pp 7–31
Esping-Andersen G (1999) Social foundations of postindustrial economies. Oxford University Press, Oxford
Fine B (1998) From dual to segmented labour markets, Labour Market Theory
Fligstein N (1998) Is globalization the cause of the crises of welfare states? European university institute working paper SPS No. 98/5, San Domenico, Italy
Flora P, Alber J (1981) The development of welfare states in Western Europe. In: Flora P, Heidenheimer AJ (eds) The development of welfare states in Europe and America. Transaction Books, New Brunswick, NJ, pp 37–80
Francesconi M, Golsch K (2005) The process of globalization and transitions to adulthood in Britain. In: Blossfeld H-P, Klizjing E, Mills M, Kurz K (eds) Globalization, uncertainty and youth in society. London, Routledge, pp 249–278
Friedman D, Hechter D, Kanazawa S (1994) A theory of the value of children. Demography 31(3): 375–401
Gauthier AH (1996) A comparative analysis of family policies in industrialized countries. Clarendon Press, Oxford
Held D, Mcgrew A, Goldblatt D, Perraton J (1999) Global transformations. Politics, economics and culture. Polity Press, Oxford
Hurrell A, Woods N (1995) Globalization and inequality. Millennium J Int Stud 24(3):447–470
Jurado Guerrero T (1995) Legitimation durch Sozialpolitik? Die spanische Beschäftigungskrise und die Theorie des Wohlfahrtstaates. Kölner Z Soz Sozialpsychol 47:727–752
Katus K, Puur A, Sakkeus L (2005) Transition to adulthood in Estonia: evidence from the FFS. In: Blossfeld H-P, Klizjing E, Mills M, Kurz K (eds) globalization, uncertainty and youth in society. London, Routledge, pp 215–247
Kieffer A, Marry C, Meron M, Solaz A (2005) Family formation in an uncertain labor market: the case of France. In: Blossfeld HP, Klizjing E, Mills M, Kurz K (eds) Globalization, uncertainty and youth in society. London, Routledge, pp 105–134
King RB (2005) Globalization and the transition to adulthood in an individualistic regime: the case of American women. In: Blossfeld HP, Klizjing E, Mills M, Kurz K (eds) Globalization, uncertainty and youth in society. London, Routledge, pp 305–336

Klijzing E (2005) Globalization and the early life course: a description of selected economic and demographic trends. In: Blossfeld HP, Klizjing E, Mills M, Kurz K (eds) Globalization, uncertainty and youth in society. Routledge, London, pp 25–50
Kurz K, Steinhage N, Golsch K (2005) Case study Germany: global competition, uncertainty and the transition to adulthood. In: Blossfeld H-P, Klizjing E, Mills M, Kurz K (eds) Globalization, uncertainty and youth in society. Routledge, London, pp 51–82
Layte R, O'connell PJ, Fahey T, Mccoy S (2005) Ireland and economic globalization: the experiences of a small open economy. In: Blossfeld HP, Klizjing E, Mills M, Kurz K (eds) Globalization, uncertainty and youth in society. Routledge, London, pp 403–422
Liefbroer A (2005) Transition from Youth to Adulthood in the Netherlands. In: Blossfeld HP, Klizjing E, Mills M, Kurz K (eds) Globalization, uncertainty and youth in society. Routledge, London, pp 83–104
Mayer K-U (2001) The paradox of global social change and national path dependencies: life course patterns in advanced societies. In: Woodward A, Kohli M (eds) Inclusions and exclusions in European societies. New York, Routledge, pp 89–110
Meyer JW, FO Ramirez, Soysal Y (1992) World expansion of mass education, 1970–1980. Sociol Educ 65:128–149
Mills M (2005) The impact of globalization on the transition to adulthood in Canada: Irregular work schedules in a 24-hour economy. In: Blossfeld H-P, Klizjing E, Mills M, Kurz K (eds) Globalization, uncertainty and youth in society. Routledge, London, pp 277–304
Mills M, Blossfeld H-P (2005) Globalization, uncertainty and the early life course. A theoretical framework. In: Blossfeld H-P, Klizjing E, Mills M, Kurz K (eds) Globalization, uncertainty and youth in society. Routledge, London, pp 1–24
Mills M, Blossfeld H-P, Buchholz S, Hofacker D, Bernardi F, Hofmeister H (2008a) Converging divergences? An international comparison of the impact of globalization on industrial relations and employment careers. Int Sociol 23(4):563–597
Mills M, Mencarini L, Tanturri ML, Begall K (2008b) Asymmetric gender role-sets and fertility intentions. A comparative analysis of Italy and the Netherlands. Demogr Res 18(1):1–26
Montanari I (2001) Modernization, globalization and the welfare state: a comparative analysis of old and new convergence of social insurance since 1930. Br J Sociol 52(3):469–494
Nelson RR (1995) Recent evolutionary theorizing about economic change. J Econ Lit 33:48–90
OA Nilsen (2002) Transitions to adulthood in Norway. In: Blossfeld H-P, Klizjing E, Mills M, Kurz K (eds) Globalization, uncertainty and youth in society. London, Routledge, p 159176
Ohmae K (1990) The borderless World. Harper Business, New York
Oppenheimer VK (1988) A theory of marriage timing. Am J Sociol 94:563–591
Oppenheimer VK, Kalmijn M, Lim N (1997) Men's career development and marriage timing during a period of rising inequality. Demography 3:311–330
Orloff A (1996) Gender and the welfare state. Annu Rev Sociol 22:51–78
Parrado EA (2005) Globalization and the transition to adulthood in Mexico. In: Blossfeld H-P, Klizjing E, Mills M, Kurz K (eds) Globalization uncertainty and youth in society. Routledge, London, pp 327–348
Piore MJ (1970) The dual labor market: theory and implications. In: Beer S, Barringer RE, Beer S, Barringer RE (eds) The state and the poor. Winthrop, New York, pp 359–361
Regini M (2000) Between deregulation and social pacts: the responses of European economies to globalization. Polit Soc 28(1):5–33
Rindfuss R, Vandenheuvel A (1990) Cohabitation: a precursor to marriage or an alternative to being single? Popul Dev Rev 16(4):703–726
Robert P, Bukodi E (2005) The effects of the globalization process on the transition to adulthood in Hungary. In: Blossfeld H-P, Klizjing E, Mills M, Kurz K (eds) Globalization, uncertainty and youth in society. London, Routledge, pp 177–214
Sassen S (1996) Losing control? sovereignty in an age of globalization. New York, Columbia University Press

Simo Noguera C, Castro Martin T, Soro Bonmati A (2005) The effects of the globalization process on the transition to adulthood: the Spanish case. In: Blossfeld H-P, Klizjing E, Mills M, Kurz K (eds) Globalization, uncertainty and youth in society. Routledge, London, pp 375–402
Sorensen AB (1983) The structure of allocation to open and closed positions in social structure. Z Soziol 12:203–224
Soskice D (1993) The institutional infrastructure for International competitiveness: a comparative analysis of the UK and Germany. In: Atkinson AB, Brunetta R (eds) The economics of the new Europe. MacMillan, London
Soskice D (1998) Divergent production regimes: coordinated and uncoordinated market economies in the 1980s and 1990s. In: Kitschelt H-P, Marks G, Stephens J (eds) Continuity and change in contemporary capitalism. Cambridge University Press, Cambridge, p 101134
Streeck A (1987) The uncertainties of management in the management of uncertainties: employees, labor relations and industrial adjustment in the 1980s. Work Employ Soc 1:281–308
Streeck W (1992) Social institutions and economic performance. Studies in industrial relations in advanced capitalist economies. Sage, London
Treiman DJ (1970) Industrialization and social stratification. In: Laumann EO (ed) Social stratification: research and theory for the 1970s. Indianapolis, IN, Bobbs Merrill, pp 373–394
Treiman DJ, Yip K-B (1989) Educational and occupational attainment in 21 countries. In: Kohn ML (ed) Cross-national research in sociology. Sage, Thousand Oaks, CA, pp 373–394

Chapter 4
Traditional Inequalities and New Insecurities: Long-Term Trends in the Transition to the Labor Market in Germany

Steffen Hillmert

4.1 Introduction

Successful transitions from school to work are decisive for success later in life. The situation of young people at this stage is therefore an issue not only for scientific research, but also for public discussion. A high level of institutionalized coordination has traditionally been a core element of the German institutional system, not least with regard to education, training and employment (Hillmert 2002), and this has been associated with comparatively smooth transition patterns (Shavit and Müller 1998; Müller and Gangl 2003; Scherer 2005; Brzinsky-Fay 2007). Discussion in recent years has, however, increasingly focused on the problems occurring at these transitions (Hillmert 2008). When assessing this situation, it is not only important to know how many people finally make successful transitions, but also how *extended* and *complex* transitions are. Against this background, this paper asks whether and to what extent there has really been a de-structuring of the transition to the labor market in Germany – and linked with it of the transition to adulthood – as it has been proposed by theories of individualization (most prominently, Beck 1992). Possible indicators of such a de-structuring would be a de-standardization of transition patterns, a decreasing social differentiation and a declining significance of school-to-work transitions for other domains of life.

The paper combines a life-course perspective on transitions with an investigation of long-term historical trends of transition patterns. Long-term comparisons provide a frame of reference for any evaluation of the present situation. They allow distinguishing secular trends and relatively steady structural changes from temporary fluctuations. They also make the best of a systematic drawback of life-course analyses: Life courses develop over a longer period of time, so it often takes considerable time to see the individual consequences of particular events which

S. Hillmert
Department of Sociology, University of Tübingen, Wilhelmstr. 36, 72074 Tübingen, Germany
e-mail: steffen.hillmert@uni-tuebingen.de

J.C. Tremmel (ed.), *A Young Generation Under Pressure?*,
DOI 10.1007/978-3-642-03483-1_4, © Springer-Verlag Berlin Heidelberg 2010

represent the situation not of today, but of some point in the past. Yet, long-term trends may be a justification for projections into the near future of the cohorts who presently pass this point in their life. To allow for meaningful long-term comparisons within a particular economic system, the analyses of this paper concentrate on West Germany; the conditions in East Germany have been very different for most of the time and would require a separate study.

4.2 Macro-Levels Conditions of School-to-Work Transitions in Germany

Our discussion of transition systems (cf. Hillmert 2002; Raffe 2008) follows a model that distinguishes analytically between two kinds of macro-level conditions that shape transition patterns and influence their changes and long-term trends: institutions and market conditions.

4.2.1 Institutional Configurations

Transition processes are guided by social rules, and formal institutions are an important part of them. Some of these rules may directly reference incidence and timing of events as informal or legal norms (e.g., minimum ages), but their number is limited, and according to theories of modernization, and in particular individualization theory, they lose part of their relevance over time. Transition events are, however, also influenced by a whole number of other rules, notably those associated with a wide range of state institutions and their regulations (cf. Mayer and Müller 1986; Mayer 1997). Institutions may have consequences far beyond the functions that they are primarily designed for. For example, formal requirements of qualification may set *de facto* age limits; compulsory military service may lead to delayed entries to training and employment for men; demands on social positions may imply particular patterns of time use and forms of household organization; etc. It is these "latent" consequences which form probably the major part of national *life-course regimes* shaping individual life courses.

Education and training system: The main characteristics of the German educational system include a stratified tripartite secondary school system, relatively standardized tertiary education and a standardized vocational training system in which combined school and workplace training (*Duales System*) is prominent, but where there are also forms of full-time school-based training (*Berufsfachschulen* and other vocational schools). There appears to have been considerable continuity in the German educational system over the second half of the twentieth century. Qualification paths have been clear and well established, which has allowed for individual planning with a high level of information and a long time horizon.

While there are institutional differences among the various federal states, secondary school education essentially follows selective tracks, although in some states there have been major attempts of introducing comprehensive schools. In higher education, the "Bologna process" – i.e., the idea of harmonizing university degrees throughout Europe – has recently led to a shift from the conventional *Diplom/Magister* system to a system of *Bachelor/Master* courses. This shift is beginning to have an impact on career patterns, but it is too recent to affect the cohorts whose transition patterns are analyzed in this paper.

Vocational training, in its popular form of the dual system, has remained the standard experience of most young people, with an increasing number of school leavers with upper secondary education being included. The need for vocational training is commonly acknowledged and initial vocational training forms the basis for further skill acquisition. The German "training culture" has led to a normative standard, giving high preference to vocational training instead of a fast transition to the labor market at any cost. The German employment system organizes human capital in the form of vocations (*Berufe*), which allow individuals to perform a broad range of related, complex tasks and incorporate the concept of a long-term career with prospects on the basis of initial vocational training. Vocational training has been regulated by legislation (especially the Vocational Training Act (*Berufsbildungsgesetz*) of 1969). Both employers and the State have a long tradition of taking responsibility for a high level of transferable skills. Responsibility for training and certification is shared among different institutions; instructors are required to meet the standards, and formal qualifications are, therefore, widely recognized by employers.

This indicates that the education and training system is embedded in broader institutional settings, which have a direct influence also on the *labor market*. To characterize a specific institutional system, use can be made of ideal types of capitalism forms as they have been proposed by comparative political economy (Hall and Soskice 2001). Political economies differ with respect to internal coherence, for example, between the financial sector, firm co-operation, and production strategies. Germany may draw near to the model of a "flexibly coordinated market economy". This is generally characterized by corporatist decision-making and long-term trust relationships. The qualification system and industrial relations also have a strong influence on work organization. Germany can be regarded as a model for a combination of a widespread skilled occupational labor market, but also (higher level) internal and lower-level labor markets (Carroll and Mayer 1986). Relatively rigid vocational tracks may, on the other hand, be an obstacle in meeting the increasing needs of retraining and, although the German training system is widely observed as an integral part of a "high skill" production regime, it has recently come under increasing pressure to be more flexible. The employers' willingness to provide vocational training has obviously decreased. This is due, partly, to competition resulting from an expansion of higher education where academic training only partially follows clear occupational boundaries.

Deregulation and flexibilization of the labor market have, in general, been a heavily debated issue in German politics for years. The most important step to deregulate employment contracts came with the Employment Promotion Act (*Beschäftigungsförderungsgesetz*) introduced in 1985, which was followed up by various amendments. It made it easier for employers to use fixed-term contracts, thus allowing the circumvention of dismissal protection. Within companies, one can observe processes of rationalization and re-organization, e.g. decentralization and outsourcing strategies, shifts of production sites to foreign countries as well as a rising number of mergers and acquisitions since the 1980s. There has also been a growing relevance of temporary work agencies. These activities have occurred against the background of an increasing international competition and a change in management strategies, substantially orientating to global financial markets.

Besides a broad qualification system and a qualification-based labor market, there are additional features of the German institutional model which are directly relevant for transitions; many of these features can be associated with a specific *welfare regime*. According to the popular typology introduced by Esping-Andersen (1990, 1999), Germany belongs to the "conservative" welfare regime type. One element is a significant gender-specific division of labor. This arrangement is supported by a number of institutional features. Public childcare for children has been rather limited; schools have, in most cases, offered no supervision in the afternoon; parental leave legislation provides an attractive option of an employment interruption; tax regulations give strong incentives for an unequal distribution of working hours within the household. All these features foster a "male- breadwinner model". Thus, not surprisingly, women with young children are likely to be housewives or to work on a part-time basis. This makes it easier for employers to realize flexible work arrangements by increasingly offering part-time and fixed-term positions while keeping a large "core" of the workforce with secure, full-time employment relationships and stable employment careers.

As a result of the institutional arrangements in Germany, the links between qualification and employment can be expected to be relatively *close* (Allmendinger 1989; Kerckhoff 2003), providing advantages for the majority of those who hold such formal certificates and carrying risks for the minority of those who do not. Another aspect concerns *cohort relations*. Depending on the institutional situation in a society, structural changes can affect cohorts differently, giving preferences to either intra-cohort mobility or changes across cohorts (Ryder 1965). Welfare arrangements and labor-market regulations in Germany are likely to have a specific consequence in this regard (cf. DiPrete et al. 1997): Historical changes will not so much affect the mid-career phase but mainly events in the early life course such as labor market entry and family formation and events in the later life course like retirement. This may lead to observable differences across cohorts particularly with regard to the transitions at labor market entry (Buchholz 2008). Finally, patterns of transitions from school to work are influenced by the fact that Germany has had military service (or alternate service) most of the observation period. For the life courses of young men, this has often led to a further extension of the phase of transition to the labor market.

4.2.2 Market Conditions

Important as institutions are, they are not sufficient to fully explain patterns of transitions and their developments. Individual life situations are also a *function* of available resources, opportunities and constraints which receive their significance from situations of competition. This illuminates the importance of specific market conditions, i.e. factors of supply and demand on the training and labor markets. These conditions change over time, so that single cohorts may be confronted with very specific situations leading to discontinuities in the transition from school to work. Historical trends of the supply side of the German labor market during the last decades can be summarized under the following headings: demographic changes and cohort fluctuations; educational expansion and qualificational upgrading; and increasing female labor market participation.

After World War II, there has been significant variation in the size of birth cohorts, and as a result of that, in the size of the cohorts that left the educational system. Together with demand side (business-cycle) effects, this may have led to considerable differences in the labor market situation of particular cohorts beyond long-term trends (for a study on such demographic effects cf. Easterlin 1980). The birth cohort 1964 was the largest cohort ever born in the Federal Republic of Germany, so it might have been confronted with a particularly difficult situation at labor market entry.

However, the main trend affecting the supply side of the labor market has been *educational expansion* since the 1950s. It started with higher rates of participation in the intermediate and upper tracks of the general school system, but then it affected higher education as well. What is sometimes overlooked is the massive expansion also in the vocational training system. Another important aspect is *gender equalization*. Since the 1980s, girls have overtaken boys with regard to success in the general school system. The close of the traditional gender gap in education has manifested itself also in the steadily growing participation of women in vocational training. Both aspects, qualificational upgrading and gender equalization, can be determined from an inter-cohort comparison of educational attainment as it is displayed in Fig. 4.1.

Regarding the overall trend, educational expansion was successful: One can see that the proportion of people attaining no vocational training has decreased quite dramatically across cohorts, especially in the case of women. However, the remaining minority of the low-qualified people increasingly faces the risk of stigmatization. Another consequence is growing selectivity of particular (lower-level) educational tracks (Solga 2005).

A sufficient level of general education is a major precondition for successful transitions to vocational training and employment. This directly raises the issue of social inequalities in education. Such inequalities were already one of the major topics of the public debate on education in the 1960s. Since then, some dimensions of inequality in education have been greatly reduced, including gender, region or religion. It is just over the recent years that the major educational inequalities relating to

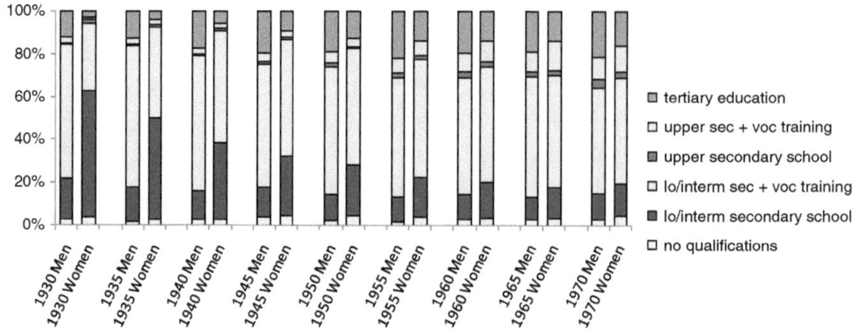

Fig. 4.1 Level of educational attainment (percentages), by birth cohort and gender. German terms: Lower/intermediate secondary school = Haupt- or Realschulabschluss; Upper secondary school = Fachhochschulreife or Abitur.
Data: Microcensus 2004 (West Germany), own calculations

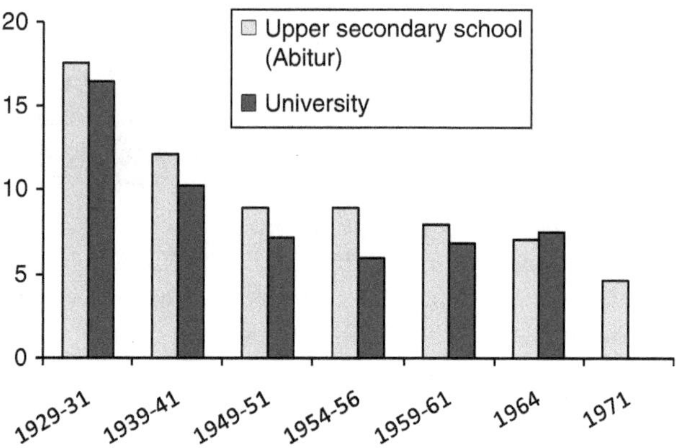

Fig. 4.2 Relative chances (odds ratios) of attaining upper secondary school/University degree, by birth cohort. Reported are relative chances of attaining Upper secondary level (or university level) vs. not attaining it for cohort members from higher educational background vs. those from lower educational background (odds ratios). Educational background is measured by the parents' education (Upper secondary education vs. below). In the 1971 birth cohort, at least the process of attaining a university degree was not yet finished at the time of the interview.
Data: West German Life History Study, own calculations

the migration background of students have received attention in both the scientific and the public discourse. Most persistent have been educational inequalities with respect to social origin. In absolute terms, educational expansion did increase the attainment rates in all social classes, but relative differences have remained significant. While sociological research has for a long time reported the close association between educational attainment and social background, large-scale comparative studies like PISA have recently brought this phenomenon to public attention again. There is evidence that origin-related inequalities in education decreased considerably during the major phase of educational expansion until the 1970s, but then leveled off (Schimpl-Neimanns 2000). A similar trend can be seen in Fig. 4.2.

The demand side of the labor market has also followed both long-term structural change and short-term fluctuations (business cycles). Structural change in the system of available jobs has been associated with fundamental shifts in the economy, like the downsizing of the agricultural sector and a trend towards services. Compared to other Western countries, these shifts happened relatively late (and the latter to a minor extent), but they were significantly driven by technological developments and rising productivity. The level of formal qualification has become increasingly important for recruitment. Most of the new arising jobs require specific skills as well as high educational attainment, while job losses mainly occur in unskilled segments. Breen (1997) argues that given global economic competition, employers will continue to shift the rising market uncertainties to their employees, most prominently to those with low bargaining power.

After a problematic phase in the immediate postwar period, the German labor market was almost balanced for around 15 years. Since the 1970s, the overall situation in the German labor market has become increasingly difficult. Along with cyclical fluctuations, unemployment has followed a clear upward trend. However, there has been a clear and growing differentiation by level of qualification (Fig. 4.3). Returns to education as measured by indicators like income and job status have on the whole been relatively stable, especially with regard to higher-level qualifications, though there are also specific developments in particular sectors (Müller 1998; OECD 2005; Becker and Hadjar 2006). Not least as a consequence of educational expansion, women have increasingly taken part in the labor market. Given their more unstable employment careers, they may have

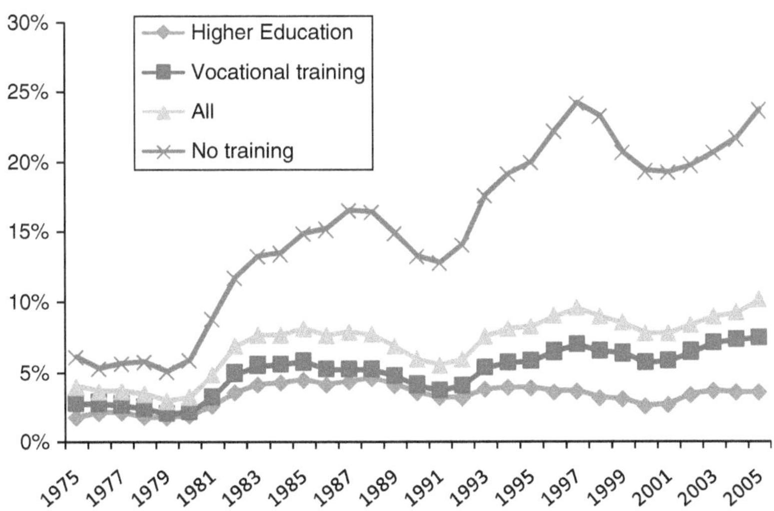

Fig. 4.3 Qualification-specific rates of unemployment (percentages), 1975–2005. West Germany (figures for 2005 without Berlin)
Source: Reinberg/Hummel 2007, p. 30

particularly been subject to the increasing demands of firms for an even more flexible work force.

As a consequence of these varying market conditions, a long-term trend towards prolonged transitions from school to work can be expected. However, our considerations also suggest that members of particular cohorts may have faced specific conditions for transitions even against the long-term trend. This applies to both large cohorts and cohorts whose members have entered the labor market in times of economic downturns.

4.3 Life-Course Data

The following analyses take a closer look at the consequences of these long-term aggregate changes for individual transitions from school to work. Central is the question of a possible de-structuring of labor market entry as it is indicated by the life-course aspects of timing, activities and work content as well as social differentiation of transition patterns (Hillmert 2002). Indicators of a de-structuring on the individual level would be that transitions become less universal and specific sequences less typical; events become temporally de-standardized, i.e. less time-specific; the impact of social differentiation diminishes; and there is less significance of the school-to-work transition with regard to other dimensions of the transition to adulthood.

Our empirical analyses draw upon various data sources, including aggregate data from official statistics. Such data either represent distributions of persons or they concentrate on selected transitions at a given point in time. With such cross-sectional data, however, it is not possible to study transition periods and patterns as they develop over time as well as their inter-individual differences.

A data source which provides detailed individual-level life-course data is the *German Life History Study* (Brückner and Mayer 1998; Hillmert et al. 2004). This project consists of a series of retrospective cohort studies, which were conducted at the Max Planck Institute for Human Development, Berlin, since the mid-1980s.

Table 4.1 The (West) German Life History Study: birth cohorts and corresponding historical periods

Birth cohort	Data collection period	*n* (Men)	*n* (Women)	Transition to labor market during historical period	Important historical events/ trends
1929–1931	1981–1983	347	361	1940/1950s	Immediate post-war period
1939–1941	1981–1983	375	355	1950/1960s	Two German states
1949–1951	1981–1983	364	369	1960/1970s	"Economic miracle"
1954–1956	1989	522	485	1970s	Educational expansion
1959–1961	1989	512	489	1970/1980s	Oil crisis
1964	1998–1999	716	700	1980s	Mass unemployment
1971	1998–1999	716	619	1980/1990s	German unification and beyond

The longitudinal data used for this paper (see Table 4.1) contain monthly life-course information for selected West German cohorts born between 1929 and 1971. There is a necessary relationship between cohorts and historical periods; taking into account the typical ages of transition to the labor market, this means that the period between the mid-1940s and the late 1990s is covered. For an illustration of historical timing, the last column lists important historical events which are likely to have an impact on transitions, but since transitions extend considerably over time and cannot be associated with specific ages, connections with specific cohorts can only be approximate. For each cohort study, separate samples were drawn, but data have been harmonized allowing for comparisons between cohorts.

4.4 Transition Patterns

An obvious consequence of educational expansion since the 1950s has been that more people have spent longer times in education and training and, as a consequence, have entered the labor market at a higher age than in older cohorts. One indicator is the rising median age for the attainment of a first vocational or academic degree (if any); median age reached a level of 21 years in the 1971 birth cohort (Hillmert and Jacob 2003). Again, the change across cohorts has been much more significant in the case of women of whom only a minority had attained vocational qualifications in the older cohorts. Another important aspect, which contributes to relatively high ages at labor market entry, is the phenomenon of multiple episodes of training (Jacob 2004): In the younger cohorts, about one-third of the cohort members have completed two or more different episodes of training when they reach the mid 1930s; in many cases, this has meant that they have further upgraded their level of qualification.

Overall educational expansion should, however, not hide the fact that particular groups have found it increasingly difficult to gain access even to basic forms of vocational training. Today, the majority of school leavers without school qualifications – but also of those with lower secondary school degrees (*Hauptschüler*) – do, in fact, not enter a regular form of vocational training in the form of an apprenticeship (*Lehre* in the dual system) or full-time school-based training (e.g., at a *Berufsfachschule*). Rather, they move into training measures which may allow making up for deficits in general qualifications or basic vocational skills, but which do not offer regular vocational qualifications on the apprenticeship level. Such measures may consist of a *Berufsvorbereitungsjahr*, special training programs, etc. This so-called "transition system" (Konsortium Bildungsberichterstattung 2006) or auxiliary system has grown considerably in its volume, nowadays accounting for a significant share of more than one-third of yearly entries into the vocational education and training system. Transitions into this system are highly determined by the level of attained school qualifications (cf. Fig. 4.4). It should also be noted that the volume of these measures reduces considerably the level of youth

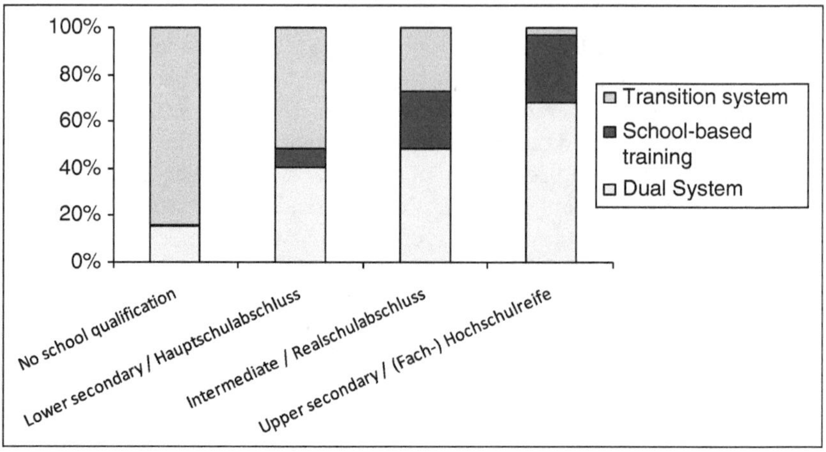

Fig. 4.4 Destination of transitions after leaving general school (percentages), by level of school qualifications, 2004
Source: Konsortium Bildungsberichterstattung 2006, p. 83

unemployment as it is reported in official statistics, so that the extent of youth unemployment is underestimated.

Major long-term developments in the transition behavior can be inferred from descriptive summaries such as the ones presented in Fig. 4.5. As a selection from a broader range of cohorts, these charts represent the monthly distribution of employment states between the ages of 14 and 30 – that is, for the ages where the major transitions between school and work take place – for members of the cohorts born around 1930 and the 1964 birth cohort. They use the categories "education and training", "employment", "unemployment", and "not in the labor force". In most cases, the latter means military service for men and family care or maternity leave for women. "Education and training" as an employment status is divided into two categories: "Still in education" and "return to education", which means that there has been a discontinuity in the educational career – at least a short gap – due, for example, to military service. An implication of this classification is that "leaving education for the first time" is a non-repeatable event which can be mapped; technically speaking, the line between the two educational states can be interpreted as a "survivor function" for leaving the educational system for the first time.

As can be seen from Fig. 4.5, members of the younger birth cohorts had much longer periods in the educational and training system than the men and women of the 1930 cohort. A small proportion of the 1964 birth cohort is in education and training at age 30 – when based on the high qualified only, this is even a significant proportion. Moreover, military service has been relevant during the transition period for many German men (indicated by the status "not in the labor force"). This has led to both a large number returning to education and also to relatively late entries into the labor market. For the older cohorts, gender differences with respect to employment status during these ages were quite obvious, with men remaining in

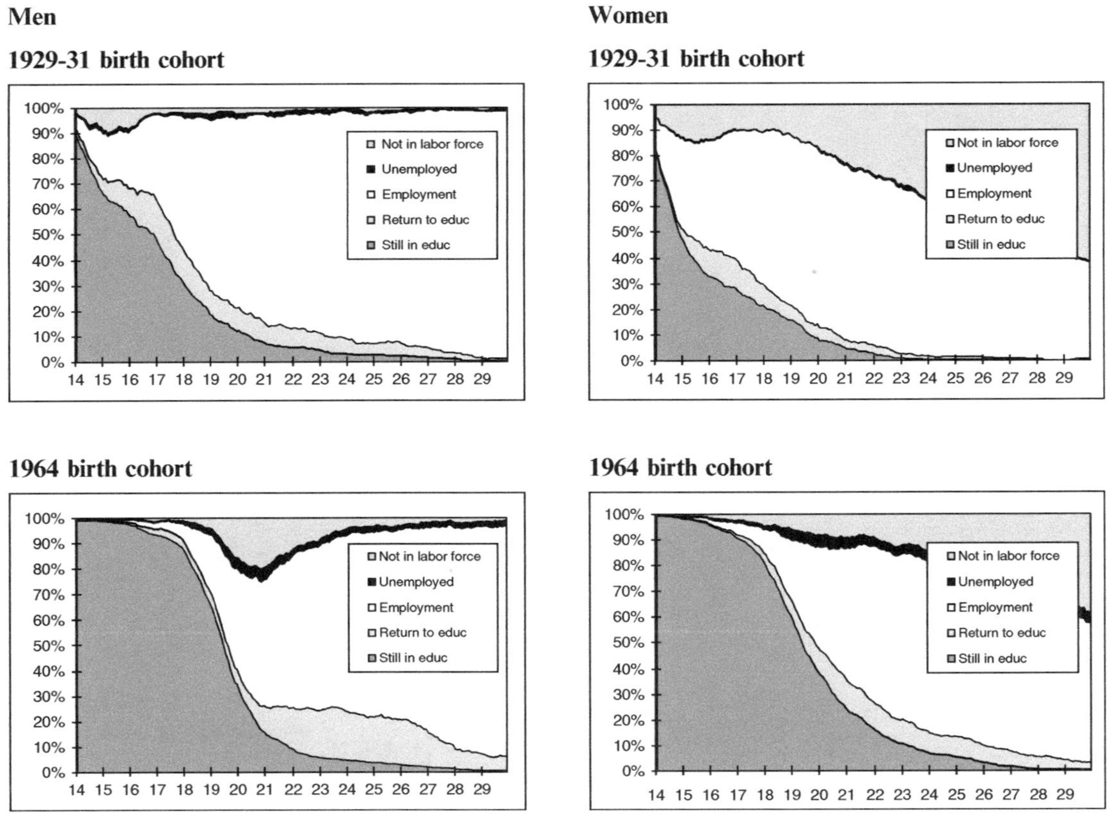

Fig. 4.5 Labor market status, by age, gender and birth cohort
Data: West German Life History Study, own calculations

education for a longer period of time and the majority of women leaving the labor force before the age of 30. Since the 1930 cohort, the educational behavior of men and women has converged, and there has been an increase in upper secondary and tertiary education across cohorts. The well-developed vocational training system in Germany has increasingly succeeded in including women. There was also a significant growth in women's labor force participation in the cohort of 1950 and the following cohorts, so that the transition patterns of men and women look more similar now. However, even in the 1964 birth cohort, gender differences in both occupations and labor market participation have been significant with many young women leaving the labor force at least temporarily before the age of 30.

After a problematic situation in the immediate postwar period (whose extent is probably still underestimated in this retrospective data), there was a booming overall labor market with little unemployment which allowed making fast transitions to employment. Later, there was a marked increase in unemployment which affected not only the labor market in general, but also young people entering the labor market; in the transition patterns of our cohorts, this becomes obvious particularly between the cohorts born around 1950 and 1960, respectively.

An alternative way of analyzing transition patterns – which can also be followed using our longitudinal data – is looking at the timing of specific transition *events*. Entry into the labor market is a decisive step in individual life courses. In order to evaluate its consequences and to compare it across cohorts, one needs to relate it to a specific point in the life course. What defines an "entry" into the labor market? On the one hand, there are well-known fluctuations between (short-term) employment, training and other activities, particularly at the very beginning of employment careers. On the other hand, one can reasonably assume that a "successful" transition to employment requires a minimum degree of stability in employment. As it appears difficult to reach a consensus on such a specific duration, one should compare different definitions of an entry into the labor market. The analyses presented in Fig. 4.6 use a relatively strong criterion for stability when distinguishing between two different definitions, the very first job (i.e., the first employment ever) and the first "stable" job (i.e., the first employment with a minimum duration of 24 months). On the basis of these definitions, they compare the median age of labor-market entry across cohorts.

One can see that from one cohort to another, entry into the labor market has happened at a later age, not least due to longer periods of education and training. However, there is also an increasing difference between the beginning of first jobs and first stable jobs. This means that an increasing number of young people have experienced an extended period of "settling in" in the employment system before reaching some degree of stability in their careers.

In addition to long-term trends, there have also been rather short-term fluctuations in the transition behavior. At least at the very beginning of employment careers, the life course situation of specific cohorts has often been influenced more by these specific circumstances than by long-term trends. One example is the transition to employment after completing an apprenticeship, i.e. the dominant form of vocational training in Germany. As Fig. 4.7 indicates, there have been

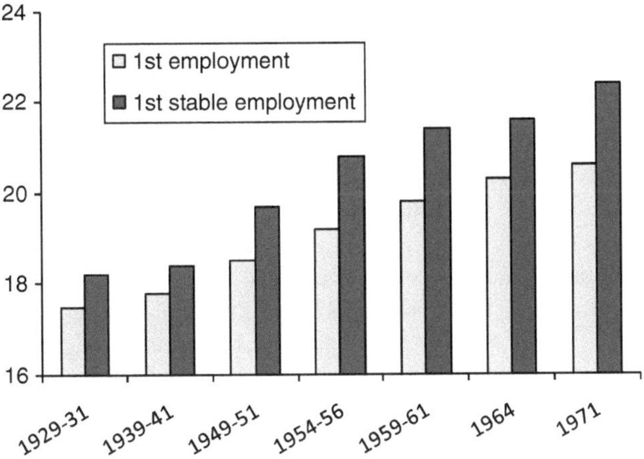

Fig. 4.6 Median age (in years) at entering (stable) employment, by birth cohort
Comments: Product-limit estimates. First "stable" employment: first employment with a minimum duration of 24 months
Data: West German Life History Study, own calculations

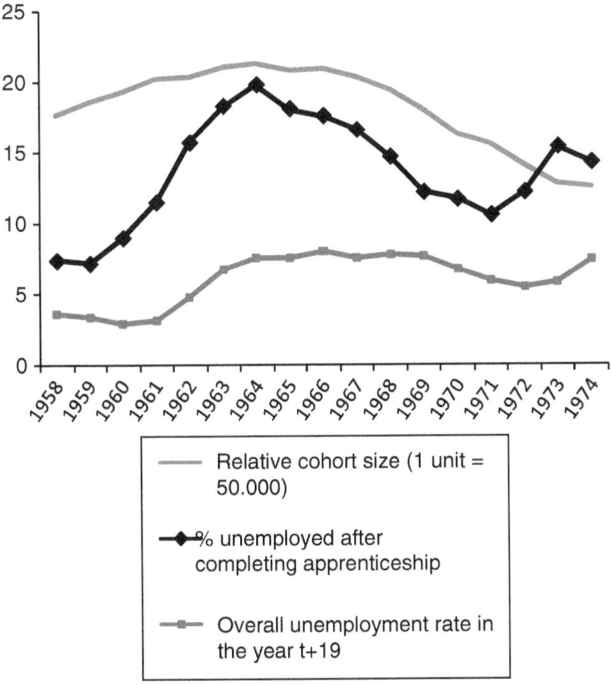

Fig. 4.7 Unemployment after vocational training (in the dual system), by birth cohort
Data: Statistisches Bundesamt, Bundesanstalt für Arbeit, various years; own calculations

considerable fluctuations among cohorts with regard to the experience of unemployment at this transition. In the 1964 birth cohort, around 20% had an episode of unemployment immediately after completing an apprenticeship. There are two cohort-specific (macro-level) determinants: cohort size and the state of the labor market at the time when the cohort members completed vocational training (on average when they were 19 years old). The information presented in this figure (and an additional analysis: see Hillmert 2004) suggests that the cohorts born around 1964 were subject to the coincidence of unfavorable historical conditions regarding both their demographic and economic situations: these baby-boom cohorts grew up under special conditions of competition about education and training opportunities, and they entered the labor market in a period of economic stagnation. The result was an exceptionally high risk of unemployment at the end of vocational training. In general, and consistent with our expectations, the cohort-related fluctuations in the unemployment risk of this group of young people seem to be more pronounced than in the labor market as a whole.

The analyses now turn to employment subsequent to labor market entry and also draw various dimensions of employment careers together. Figure 4.8 shows the stability of first employment as indicated by the dimensions: first employer, entry occupation and entry class position. The median durations are presented for these dimensions, again on the basis of both the very first job and the first stable job.

It can be seen that the stability of (very) first jobs has declined at least across the first four cohorts that have been sampled. Most interesting is a comparison of the various configurations formed by the three dimensions. The median durations of entry occupation (and social class) have been much longer than the equivalent entry

Fig. 4.8 Median durations (years) of various characteristics of first job (*left*), first stable job (*right*), by birth cohort
Comments: Product-limit estimates. Job: Median tenure with first employer; Occupation: Median tenure in entry occupation (two-digit international standard classification); Social class: Median tenure in entry social class (11 categories according to the Erikson–Goldthorpe–Portocarero classification): First "stable" job: 24 months minimum duration.
Data: West German Life History Study, own calculations

jobs; at least at labor market entry, occupations (and even more so, social class positions) have been much more stable than jobs. This means that, on average, people have stayed in their occupation (and their class position) when leaving their first employer. This pattern indicates that strong occupational labor markets do exist and that occupation-specific human capital can be transferred between different employers. The basic pattern of the three median durations has been remarkably stable over time, especially regarding the first stable job. All these descriptive results may, amongst other factors, be influenced by selective departures from the labor market. Therefore, one should also look at this information separately for men and women, since men have more stable employment careers than women. In separate analyses (that are only summarized here), however, the results become even clearer. It can be seen that, compared to the time in their first job, most German men remained in their initial occupation for a very long time.

In Germany, the phase of entry into the labor market has become more extended and the difference between transitory and stable entry jobs has increased significantly for the younger cohorts. Apart from this period of "settling in", however, the first position at labor market entry has proved to be highly significant for the quality of the further career. This means that basic structures of the labor market entry – salience of formal qualifications and occupational labor markets – have been quite stable over time. Institutional regulation and coordination has remained relatively strong, at least with regard to the labor-market "core" of skilled workers. Differences in career patterns and characteristics like income, occupational status and risk of unemployment remain highly correlated with formal qualifications, with higher-level qualifications providing relative advantages and deficits in formal education carrying risks of exclusion (for an overview, see Hillmert and Mayer 2004). Hence, there is a high degree of endogeneity in life courses, meaning that experiences and positions earlier in the life course (starting from early stages of family life and education) are significant predictors for later stages. Furthermore, as a consequence of both the significant social inequality in education and stratified returns to education, social inequality is *transferred* across generations through the educational system. Moreover, since a number of successive birth cohorts have experienced this stability, the system of qualification which supports long-term investments in occupation-specific human capital has been legitimized and established as a social standard and has allowed for the organization of collective interests along these lines.

The stability of employment patterns and qualification-related differences should, however, not hide the fact that new demands of flexibility and risks have been shifted to labor-market *entrants* in general. Most notably, the use of fixed-term contracts has spread especially among young employees under 30 years of age since the mid-1990s (cf. Fig. 4.9). This again supports the assumption that structural change and demands of flexibility are absorbed by entering (and retiring) cohorts to a higher degree than by the whole labor market. In this case, not just the low-qualified have been affected. Rather, fixed-term employment has become a characteristic also of the labor market for graduates from higher education.

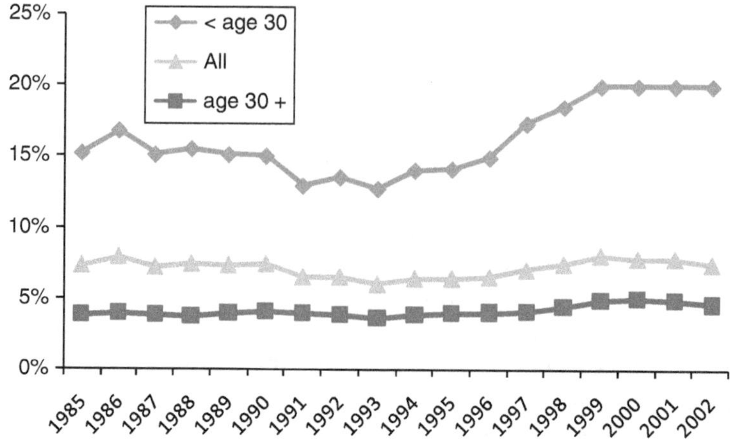

Fig. 4.9 Proportion of fixed-term contracts (percentages), by age group and year. West Germany. Data from Buchholz 2008, p. 184 (Statistisches Bundesamt and Microcensus)

The objective long-term effects of fixed-term employment on employment careers may be smaller than expected (McGinnity and Mertens 2004), but in any case, they carry a high amount of *insecurity*. The flexibilization pressures on individuals have increased also in other respects. Employees become increasingly forced to act more flexible with regard to space (e.g., commuting distances), time, income and the updating and management of skills. The aspect of insecurity may be especially important when interpreting other important transition events beyond the area of education and employment (cf. Modell et al. 1976; Hillmert 2005). Among these life events are leaving home, union formation and marriage, and becoming a parent. In a role-oriented perspective, attaining the relatively stable status of a "full adult" member of society has two major dimensions. Economic independence is reached by acquiring qualifications and entering gainful employment; emotional and social independence is primarily reached by leaving home and forming own families.

For both men and women, the median age of the event *leaving home* has shown a long-term decline, at least until the cohorts born around 1960 (cf. Fig. 4.10). Leaving home has become an individualized life event, which is *no longer* bound to marriage and family formation. The median age of *union formation* has remained rather stable across cohorts, but cohabitation has increasingly taken the place of marriage. The most striking changes concern the event of *becoming a parent*. This has been clearly postponed since the 1960s, and it has become decoupled from both household and union formation. The postponement of fertility can reasonably be interpreted as not only a consequence of the extended periods of education and training but also increasing discontinuities and insecurities that confronted the younger cohorts in the labor market (Tölke and Diewald 2003; Blossfeld et al. 2005; Brose 2008).

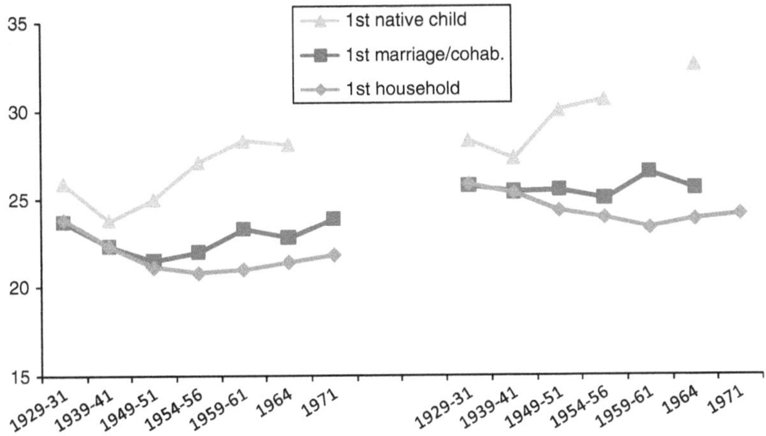

Fig. 4.10 Median ages (years) of important life events, by birth cohort, Women (*left*) – Men (*right*)
Comments: Product-limit estimates. In some of the younger cohorts less than 50% (of the women or men of the particular cohort) had experienced the specific event at the time of the interview
Data: West German Life History Study, own calculations

4.5 Summary and Conclusions

On the basis of long-term, inter-cohort comparisons, the analyses in this paper have demonstrated both significant changes and remarkable continuities regarding processes of transition to the labor market in (West) Germany. So let us finally turn back to the general question: Is there evidence for a de-structuring of school-to-work transitions and transitions to adulthood in general? There is obviously no simple answer to this question (cf. also Hillmert 2005; Mayer and Brückner 2005), but there are a number of important elements:

(1) Significant changes in the patterns of labor-market entry can be associated with the remarkable extension of education since the 1950s. This is especially obvious in the case of young women. For both genders, attaining a vocational or an academic degree and entering the labor market have become universal and, together with leaving home, the first events in the sequence of transition to adulthood. One of the consequences is the prolongation of educational careers, which has led to later entries into the labor market. This means that first transitions to the labor market can no longer be equated with "youth transitions"; they may also concern young adults at age 30 (and, in some cases, even beyond). Another consequence is increasing selectivity of educational tracks. Together with a general upgrading of educational attainment this has led to unequal starting positions at labor market entry and has constantly degraded the labor market position of the low qualified.

(2) Problems of getting entry into (stable) employment have increased, leading to extended periods of "settling in". After a period of increased mobility at the beginning of their careers, however, most people have experienced relatively stable

forms of employment. In many cases, individual mobility may be interpreted as an individual solution against the background of institutional stability. These patterns have remained relatively stable across cohorts. Major differences in career patterns remain highly correlated with formal qualifications, and deficits in formal education carry risks of exclusion. As a consequence of both social inequality in education and significant returns to education, social inequality is transferred across generations through the educational system to a high degree. These "traditional inequalities" have remained strong.

(3) In addition to such long-term trends, there have also been rather short-term fluctuations in the conditions that members of particular cohorts faced for their school-to-work transitions. At least in the short run, the situation of specific cohorts has often been influenced more by these specific circumstances than by long-term trends. The same is likely to be true for cohorts that are younger than those in our sample; hence, their specific situations always need to be evaluated in detail.

(4) In spite of a clear inter-individual differentiation of labor market risks, associated most prominently with formal qualifications, subjective insecurity – deriving most prominently from the labor market – is experienced by a large share of younger cohorts, including the high qualified. Such "new insecurities" are a likely cause of external effects like the postponement of fertility decisions.

How could at least the most dramatic inequalities and external effects be attenuated? There is certainly no definite solution, but traditional inequalities like social inequalities in the school system remain high on the agenda. However, while the renewed public interests in questions of education may be productive, there are some doubts whether demands for "more education for everyone" define a reasonable strategy. Under the present institutional circumstances, this would probably entail both new selectivities and extended phases of transitions for many young people. Necessary supplements would therefore be adequate and recognized job opportunities also for the lower-qualified as well as intensified efforts to enhance the compatibility of work and family life on all qualification levels.

References

Allmendinger J (1989) Educational systems and labor market outcomes. Eur Sociol Rev 5:231–250

Beck U (1992) Risk society: towards a new modernity, New Delhi

Becker R, Hadjar A (eds) (2006) Die Bildungsexpansion: erwartete und unerwartete Folgen, Wiesbaden

Blossfeld HP, Klijzing E, Mills M, Kurz KK (eds) (2005) Globalization, uncertainty and youth in society: The losers in a globalizing world, London

Breen R (1997) Risk, recommodification and stratification. Work Employ Soc 9:29–51

Brose N (2008) Entscheidung unter Unsicherheit: Familiengründung und -erweiterung im Erwerbsverlauf. Kölner Zeitschrift für Soziologie und Sozialpsychologie 60:27–48

Brückner E, Mayer KU (1998) Collecting life history data: experiences from the German life history study. In: Giele, Janet Z, Elder, Glen H Elder Jr (eds) Methods of life course research: Qualitative and quantitative approaches. Thousand Oaks:152–181

Brzinsky-Fay C (2007) Lost in transition? Labour market entry sequences of school leavers in Europe. Eur Soc Rev 23:409–422
Buchholz S (2008) Die Flexibilisierung des Erwerbsverlaufs: Eine Analyse von Einstiegs- und Ausstiegsprozessen in Ost- und Westdeutschland, Wiesbaden
Bundesanstalt für Arbeit (various years) Amtliche Nachrichten der Bundesanstalt für Arbeit: Arbeitsstatistik – Jahreszahlen, Nürnberg
Carroll GR, Mayer UK (1986) Job-shift patterns in the FRG: The effects of social class, industrial sector and organizational size. Am Soc Rev 51:324–341
DiPrete TA, de Graaf P, Luijkx R, Tåhlin M, Blossfeld HP Blossfeld (1997) Collectivist versus individualist mobility regimes? Structural change and job mobility in four countries. Am J Sociol 103:318–358
Easterlin RA (1980) Birth and fortune: the impact of numbers on personal welfare. Basic Books, New York
Esping-Andersen G (1990) The three worlds of welfare capitalism, Cambridge, MA
Esping-Andersen G (1999) Social foundations of postindustrial economies, Oxford
Hall PA, Soskice D (eds) (2001) Varieties of capitalism: the institutional foundations of comparative advantage, Oxford
Hillmert S (2002) Labour market integration and institutions: an Anglo-German comparison. Work Employ Soc 19:675–701
Hillmert S (2004) Berufseinstieg in Krisenzeiten: Ausbildungs- und Arbeitsmarktchancen in den 1980er und 1990er Jahren. In: Hillmert, Mayer, pp 23–38
Hillmert S (2005) From old to new structures: A long-term comparison of the transition to adulthood in West and East Germany. In: Macmillan R (ed) The structure of the life course: Standardized? Individualized? Differentiated? Adv Life Course Res, Amsterdam 9:151–173
Hillmert S (2008) When traditions change and virtues become obstacles: Skill formation in Britain and Germany. In: Mayer KU, Solga H (eds) Skill formation: Interdisciplinary and cross-national perspectives, Cambridge, pp 50–81
Hillmert S, Jacob M (2003) Bildungsprozesse zwischen Diskontinuität und Karriere: das Phänomen der Mehrfachausbildungen. Zeitschrift für Soziologie 32:325–345
Hillmert S, Künster R, Spengemann P, Mayer KU (2004) Projekt Ausbildungs- und Berufsverläufe der Geburtskohorten 1964 und 1971 in Westdeutschland. Dokumentationshandbuch, Berlin
Hillmert S, Mayer KU (eds) (2004) Geboren 1964 und 1971 – Neuere Untersuchungen zu Ausbildungs- und Berufschancen in Westdeutschland, Wiesbaden
Jacob M (2004) Mehrfachausbildung in Deutschland: Karriere, Collage, Kompensation? Wiesbaden
Kerckhoff AC (2003) From student to worker. In: Mortimer JT, Shanahan MJ (eds) Handbook of the life course, New York, pp 52–87
Konsortium Bildungsberichterstattung (ed) (2006) Bildung in Deutschland. Ein indikatorengestützter Bericht mit einer Analyse zu Bildung und Migration, Bielefeld
Mayer KU (1997) Notes on a comparative political economy of life courses. Comp Social Res 16:203–226
Mayer KU, Brückner H (2005) De-standardization of the life course: What it might mean? And if it means anything, whether it actually took place? In: Macmillan R (ed) The structure of the life course: Standardized? Individualized? Differentiated? Adv Life Course Res, Amsterdam 9:27–53
Mayer KU, Müller W (1986) The state and the structure of the life course. In: Sørensen AB, Weinert FE, Sherrod LR (eds) Human development and the life course: multidisciplinary perspectives, Hillsdale, NJ, pp 218–245
McGinnity F, Mertens A (2004) Befristete Verträge und Berufseinstieg. In: Hillmert/Mayer, pp 115–131
Modell J, Furstenberg FF, Hershberg T (1976) Social change and transitions to adulthood in historical perspective. J Family Hist 1:7–32
Müller W (1998) Erwartete und unerwartete Folgen der Bildungsexpansion. Zeitschrift für Soziologie und Sozialpsychologie, Sonderheft 38: Die Diagnosefähigkeit der Soziologie, pp 81–112

Müller W, Gangl M (eds) (2003) Transitions from education to work in Europe: the integration of youth into EU labour markets, Oxford
OECD (2005) Education at a glance – OECD indicators 2005, Paris
Raffe D (2008) The concept of transition system. J Educ Work 21:277–296
Reinberg A, Hummel M (2007) Qualifikationsspezifische Arbeitslosigkeit im Jahr 2005 und die Einführung der Hartz-IV-Reform: Empirische Befunde und methodische Probleme. IAB Forschungsbericht 9/2007, Nürnberg
Ryder NB (1965) The cohort as a concept in the study of social change. Am Sociol Rev 30:843–861
Scherer S (2005) Patterns of labor market entry – Long wait or career instability? An empirical comparison of Italy, Great Britain and West Germany. Eur Sociol Rev 21:427–440
Schimpl-Neimanns B (2000) Soziale Herkunft und Bildungsbeteiligung. Empirische Analysen zu herkunftsspezifischen Bildungsungleichheiten zwischen 1950 und 1999. Kölner Zeitschrift für Soziologie und Sozialpsychologie 52:636–669
Shavit Y, Müller W (eds) (1998) From school to work. A comparative study of educational qualifications and occupational destinations, Oxford
Solga H (2005) Ohne Abschluss in die Bildungsgesellschaft: die Erwerbschancen gering qualifizierter Personen aus soziologischer und ökonomischer Perspektive, Opladen
Statistisches Bundesamt (various years) Statistisches Jahrbuch für die Bundesrepublik Deutschland, Stuttgart
Tölke A, Diewald M (2003) Insecurities in employment and occupational careers and their impact on the transition to fatherhood in Western Germany. Demogr Res 9:42–68

Chapter 5
German Bundestag Survey on Intergenerational Justice in the Labour Market

Joerg Chet Tremmel and Patrick Wegner

5.1 The Point of Departure: Of Losers and Winners of the Income and Assets Development

Nowadays, most welfare transfer payments are made to the older generation, especially to cover pensions, nursing, and health costs. As far as distributive justice is concerned, redistributions among age groups are not unjust as such, because everybody ages. People usually experience both the state of youth and of old age during their lives, whereas they obviously keep their ethnicity and gender all life long. This distinguishes matters of intergenerational justice from gender justice or ethnic justice (Daniels 1988).

Let us assume that the young generation has only half as many voters as the old generation, so they can only rarely assert their interests at elections. It would be rash to claim that this is a generational injustice. After all, in 50 years, today's youth might be the majority and dominate the youth of 2060. Or, is it unjust that the old generation is normally wealthier than the young generation? Not necessarily. This is only the case if young people do not have a chance to be in the same situation when they grow older. Therefore, a comprehensive theory of generational justice has to focus on indirect comparisons, considering full life courses (Tremmel 2009, p. 28).

As long as the distribution of financial burdens and support does not change over time and each generation can expect to be treated in the same way as the previous or next generation, the generational contract is not unfair. However, recent studies

J.C. Tremmel (✉)
The London School of Economics and Political Science, Houghton Street, London, WC2A 2AE, UK
e-mail: J.Tremmel@lse.ac.uk

P. Wegner
Foundation for the Rights of Future Generations, P.O. Box 5115, 61422 Oberursel, Germany
e-mail: patrick.wegner@srzg.de

J.C. Tremmel (ed.), *A Young Generation Under Pressure?*,
DOI 10.1007/978-3-642-03483-1_5, © Springer-Verlag Berlin Heidelberg 2010

show that today's young generation is at a disadvantage compared to their direct predecessor.

According to life-cycle analyses, the young cohorts of today cannot expect the same increases in income as their predecessors in their professional life. In 1986, the 25–40-year-olds used to earn 11.8% less than the 50–65-year-olds, whereas the difference today is 24.2% (Fig. 5.1).

The situation in France (Chauvel 2009) is even more severe than in Germany, but nevertheless young people in Germany are clearly in a worse position nowadays than young people 30 years ago. The main reasons for the shift in income curves are the higher unemployment rates, the rising number of fixed-term employment contracts, and the increase in unpaid internships of graduates over the past three decades (compared to the previous decades) (Blossfeld and Mills 2010; Klammer 2010; Chauvel 2010).

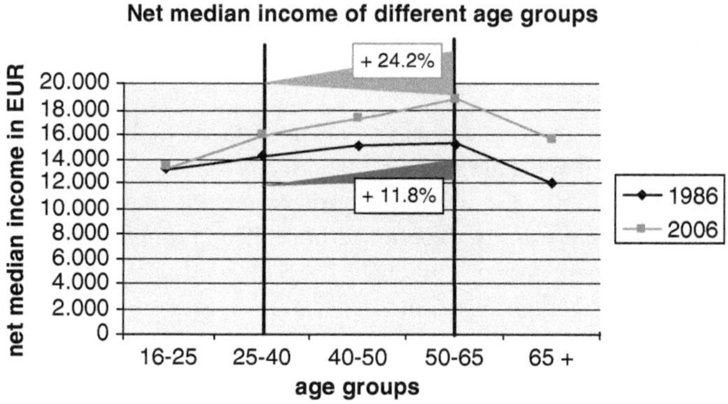

Fig. 5.1 Net median income of different age groups in Germany
Source: SOEP, persons in private households

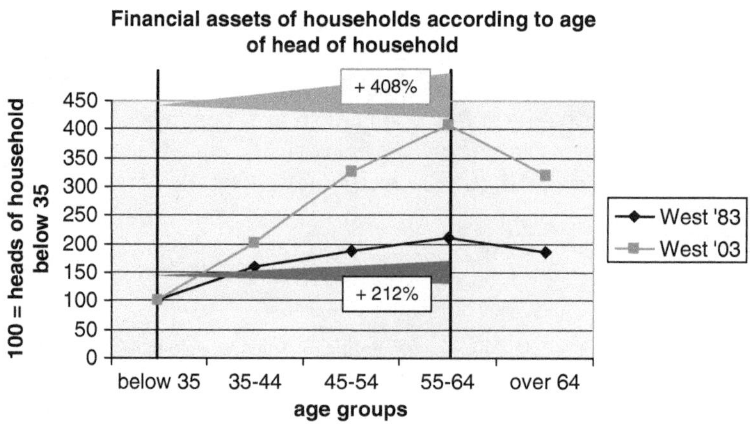

Fig. 5.2 Financial assets of households according to age of head of the household in Germany
Source: SOEP, persons in private households

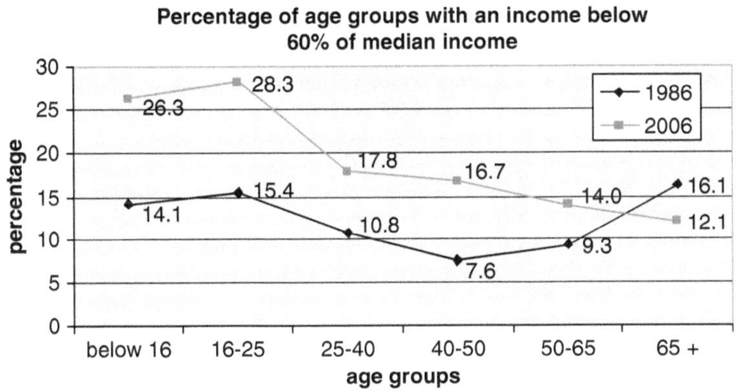

Fig. 5.3 Percentage of age group with an income below 60% of the median income in Germany
Source: SOEP, persons in private households

Compared to the distribution of income, the gap between young and old is even greater when it comes to the distribution of assets, as Fig. 5.2 illustrates. In 1983, the assets of 55–64-year-olds were roughly twice as high as those of persons below 35. In 2003, they were four times as high.

The relative poverty rates by age group also confirm the thesis that today's young people are worse off than those 20 years ago (see Fig. 5.3). About 20 years ago, 15.4% of 16–25-year-olds were poor, whereas now, 28.3% are. The graph also reveals that in 2006 in all age groups – except those above 65 – the share of the population with less than 60% of the median income increased.

In our view, a labour market is intergenerationally just if each age group (that is, young, middle and old generations) has at least the same possibilities to fulfill their needs as the predecessing group of people in the same age bracket. Young workers today are worse off compared to young workers 30 years ago considering the legal framework in the labour market, the forms of employment and their income. At the same time, older employees also find it increasingly difficult to find employment if they lose their job beyond the age of 55. Nevertheless, the disadvantages of the young generation (the so-called precarious generation) in the labour market are systemic and not comparable to the risk of old people not being (re-)employed due to their lower work productivity, protective legislature and the appeal of early retirement schemes.

As far as ecology, pensions and healthcare are concerned, generational justice is being broadly discussed, but intergenerational justice in the labour market is an underexposed issue. We believe that this is a negligence. The relevance of generational justice in the world of employment is statistically demonstrated by the rising income gaps described above. The income gap is not only widening between managers and blue-collar workers, but also between 30- and 55-year-olds. What we need is a new generational contract between young and old employees in companies. This is not being discussed at present, and the young generation is not yet making any such claims during wage negotiations and legislative procedures.

On account of this surprising fact, we have conducted an empirical survey with the deputies of the 16th German Bundestag. The questionnaire measured the members' awareness of the topics of "generational justice in the world of employment" and "rush hour of life".

In the first part, the article discusses different notions of the term "generation". This definition is necessary in order to understand the concept of comparing generations on which the article is based. In the second part, the empirical findings of the survey with the members of the German parliament (Bundestag) are presented. Finally, the article offers a discussion of the results of the survey.

5.2 Specification of Variables – Bringing Theory Back In

Unlike other empirical studies, we intend to "bring theory back in" before we lay out the design and the results of our study. It is key to be aware of the different definitions of the term *generation* and of the different possibilities to compare generations. Otherwise the result is confusion, as is the case in many other studies comparing, for instance, "the young generation" with their "parents". For example, the definition of the term "generation" by the philosopher John Rawls changes during the course of his famous study "A Theory of Justice". At first, he addresses all people living at one moment of time, therefore using the term "generation" in a wide sense.[1] But when referring to his final justification of his theory of intergenerational justice, he starts using the family-related meaning of the term "generation".[2] Somewhat more sophisticated was the distinction of Russell et al. in their empirical study on perceptions of intergenerational justice in the field of climate change. They asked their sample to distinguish between "the next generation" and the "generation of 2100" when making their assessments (Russell et al. 2003). But these are not clearcut underlying concepts of the term "generation". We doubt that the respondents could really understand the questions posed by Russell's questionnaire.

"Generational justice" consists of the two words "generation" and "justice". "Justice" is definitely the more *difficult* one to define. However, the term "generation" is also *ambiguous*. In our empirical study, we use only the chronological-temporal definition for indirect comparisons (explained below). To justify this choice, we have to first look at the different methods of comparing generations as well as the common pitfalls.

[1]For instance, Rawls (1971, p. 287): "But this calculus of advantages, which balances the losses of some against benefits to others, appears even less justified in the case of generations than among contemporaries." Or, on page 293: "We can now see that persons in different generations have duties and obligations to one another just as contemporaries do."

[2]For instance, Rawls (1971, p. 128): "For example, we may think of the parties as heads of families, and therefore as having a desire to further the welfare of their nearest descendants."

5.2.1 Family Generations

The etymological roots of the term "generation" (Latin: "generatio" = procreation, procreative capacity) refer to family relationships. Family generations are the members of a lineage (Kohli and Szydlik 2000, p. 11; Veith 2006, pp. 24–38). Therefore, they are also called "genealogical" generations. Kin relationships are not the same as cohorts and that is why the terms "children" and "parents" belong to a different context than the terms "older" and "younger" generation. After all, there are younger and older parents. Aunts and uncles can be younger than their nieces and nephews (Laslett and Fishkin 1992, p. 9).

Apart from the family-related meaning, the term "generation" has other meanings that cannot be explained by its etymological roots.

5.2.2 Societal Generations

The term "societal generation" refers to a group of people whose beliefs, attitudes or problems are homogenous.[3] In many cases, the members of the group have undergone similar political, economic, or cultural experiences[4] within a certain period of time (for instance, the "Flower-Power Generation", "Generation X", the "Generation of 89", the "Net Generation", the "Generation Internship", and the "Generation of 9/11").[5]

Only if there is a perception of peer personality, are neighbouring age groups regarded as a single generation (Bude 2000, p. 187). Such a collective generational identity can even exist among people of different origin, religion, or ethnicity. Paradoxically, such people feel close without even knowing each other. "Generations" in this sense that existed before World War II are also referred to as "historical generations". The term also plays an important role in the field of arts (e.g., the "Romanticists"), and literature ("Generation of 1898", or "Lost Generation"). In this context, age is not a decisive factor in a "societal generation". Normally, the age difference between its members is rarely more than 10 years. And yet, in arts and literature, 20-year-olds can belong to the same generation as 50-year-olds.

---

[3]Synonyms are "social generations", "sociological generations", or "historic generations".

[4]Societal generations are sometimes divided into "political", "cultural", and "economic" generations (cf. Kohli and Szydlik 2000, pp. 8–10). See also Kohli (2006).

[5]Although some societal generations might have had an international impact, each country has still predominantly its own denominations for their generations. For the US, see Strauss and Howe (1991, 1993). For Germany, see Jureit and Wildt (2005).

5.2.3 Chronological Generations

Last, but not least, there are two chronological meanings of the term "generation".[6] They are common in English, German, and other languages:

Chronological-temporal. Firstly, "generation" can refer to an age group, i.e. the young, middle-aged, or old people in a society. In this sense, several generations always live at the same time. People below 30 are usually considered "the young generation", whereas those between 30 and 60 represent "the middle-aged generation". Seniors aged 60 and above are referred to as "the old generation".[7] Authors using this definition include Easterlin (1980, p. 7), de-Shalit (1995, p. 138) and Thomson (1992, p. 207).

Chronological-intertemporal. Secondly, the term "generation" can refer to everyone alive today. Used in that sense, there is only one generation at a time (Birnbacher 1988, p. 23). This definition is of special importance if non-overlapping generations with all the concomitant problems like no possibility for direct communication, no direct reciprocity, etc. are discussed.

The result of this analysis of the term "generation" is that only one of the three meanings of the term should be used in a study on intergenerational justice in the labour market: the chronological one. "Societal generations" as entities that are formed through shared values and experiences can be ruled out from the start. Unlike chronological or family generations, they cannot be clearly distinguished from each other. For example, speaking of the "Flower-Power Generation," it is not clear whether the term refers only to those who were between 20 and 30 in the year 1968 or if it includes those who were 18 or 35, too. Does the term only refer to the students of the year 1968, or does it include those who read the newspapers, occasionally took part in a demonstration, and were below 30 in the year 1968 (Landweer 1996, p. 89)?

Family generations are clearly distinguishable from each other. Does that mean that this meaning of the term "generation" can be used in a study on intergenerational justice in the labour market? Theoretically yes, but only at the cost of conceptual clarity. Assume, a researcher ponders the following formulation of a specific question when he designs his questionnaire. The two options are:

(a) Today, young people between 20 and 45 years of age have equal prospects in the labour market as the previous generation had at this age 30 years ago.
(b) Today, young people between 20 and 45 years of age have equal prospects in the labour market as their parents had.

The first statement uses only the temporal-chronological meaning of the term "generation" whereas the second statement mixes a temporal-chronological meaning with a family-related meaning ("parents"). The parents of the young people of

[6] Synonyms are "demographic generation", "genetic generation".

[7] Further differentiations are often made, e.g., "young senior citizens" or "old senior citizens". To simplify matters, only three generations (young, middle-aged, old) shall be referred to hereinafter.

today might now be between 35 and 100 years old. The boundaries of this group are blurred. But generational justice theories require comparisons between clearly defined generations. Birth years are suitable criteria; attitudes and family lineages are not. Both the chronological-temporal as well as the chronological-intertemporal definitions allow for these comparisons. For this study on the current situation of the young generation in the world of employment, chronological-temporal comparisons are most suitable and will be used throughout the rest of the article.

5.2.4 Direct and Indirect Comparisons of Chronological Generations

Obviously, the concept of generational justice involves drawing comparisons between generations. However, this is often done improperly in the scientific (and all the more so in the public) debate. Basically, we must distinguish between direct and indirect comparisons (see Fig. 5.4).

In the Lexis diagram, the vertical axis shows the age, and the horizontal axis shows the flow of time. The diagonal line that starts above the birth year of a certain cohort represents its life course. The cohort born in 1960 is symbolised by

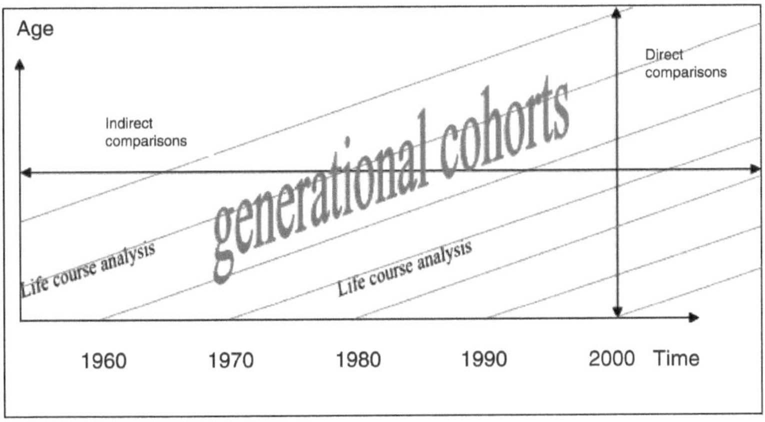

Fig. 5.4 Comparisons between generations in the Lexis-diagram
Source: *Lexis-diagram*[8]

[8]The German demographer Wilhelm Lexis developed the diagram named after him in 1875.

the diagonal line that starts in that year; it is 10 years old in 1970, 20 years old in 1980, etc.

Comparisons can either be drawn between generations at a certain point in time or between certain age groups. This fundamental difference shall be illustrated by a two-generation model. The two hatched grey generations are compared respectively (see Figs. 5.5 and 5.6a, b).

The *direct* comparison (here: vertical) is between today's "young" and "old", for example comparing the percentage of members of the old (60+ years old) and young (0–30 years old) generation who live on social security at a certain point in time (e.g., in the year 2010).

In terms of *indirect* comparisons, Fig. 5.6b might be used to show how the share of young persons on social security in 2010 compares with that in 1980 – when today's older generation was young. Figure 5.6a shows this for today's and tomorrow's old generation.

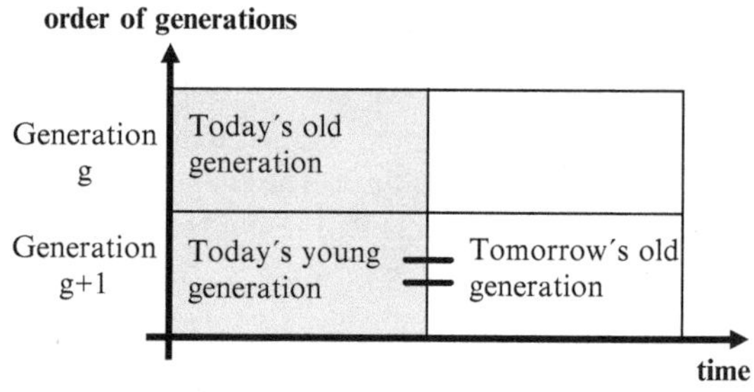

Fig. 5.5 Direct comparisons between generations. The indirect comparison (here: diagonal) compares the old with the old (see Fig. 5.6a) or the young with the young (see Fig. 5.6b)

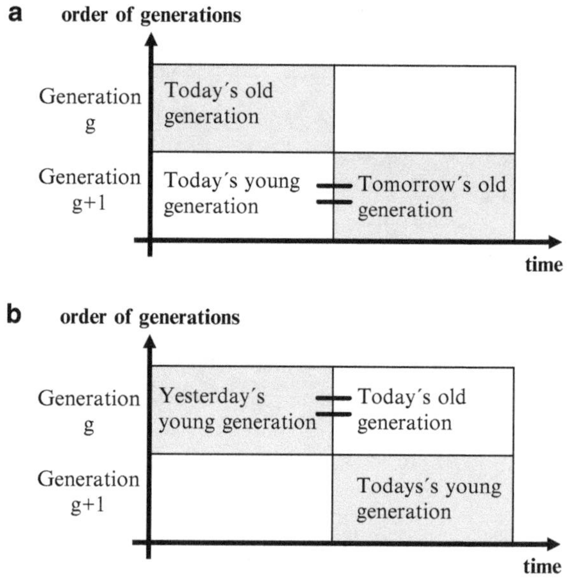

Fig. 5.6 (**a**) Indirect comparisons between generations (old/old). (**b**) Indirect comparisons between generations (young/young)

Direct comparisons would produce statements like: "Older employees in the public service receive higher salaries, profit from a significantly higher level of dismissals protection, have more vacations and work fewer hours per week than their younger colleagues even though they are doing the same work."

Unfortunately, the scientific debate on generational politics has failed for a long time to clearly distinguish both between these four meanings of the term "generation" and between the different ways of comparing them. This, in turn, produced ambiguities in questionnaires on intergenerational justice and intergenerational relations.

5.3 Description of the Survey

5.3.1 Aims of the Survey

The survey conducted with the deputies of the 16th German Bundestag was planned and conducted as exploratory research. Its first aim was to provide an overview of the knowledge and the awareness of the deputies with regard to questions of intergenerational justice in the labour market. Its second aim was to assess their willingness to support legislative initiatives in this thematic context. A number of widely discussed suggestions for reforms, aiming at enhancing the situation of young employees and career starters in the working environment, were included in the survey in order to find out how far the deputies see them as effective and approve them. The attitude of the political class towards issues and measures plays an important role in determining how quickly the public discussion will result in new laws for generational justice.

5.3.2 The Design of the Survey

The combination of a four-point scale and a "don't know" option (that is visually divided from the rest of the options) was chosen over a five-point scale in order to avoid the tendency of always checking the middle of the scale resulting from time pressure or disinterest.

The questionnaire is divided into five parts (see annex 1). The first part serves as a general introduction to the topic and evaluates the context in which intergenerational justice is seen by the deputies. The second part is divided into a part dealing with the "rush hour of life" and another part dealing with the topic "young generation and entry to the labour market". This division makes comparisons between the two main topics possible while guaranteeing a higher consistency of each part. The fourth part deals with possible reform steps for advancing generational justice in the working environment and for straightening out the rush hour of life. The fifth part surveys personal statistics like age and gender.

5.3.3 Methodology of the Survey

The German-speaking survey was implemented as a postal written study in the first weeks of March 2009. The 612 deputies of the German Bundestag were contacted with individual cover letters signed by hand by the authors.

The letters included information on the topic, as well as a self-addressed prepaid envelope. The time predetermined for returning the envelopes was set to 2 weeks (a few questionnaires handed in later were still accepted). The letters were delivered simultaneously to the German Bundestag at the beginning of a sitting week in order to ensure that the deputies would be present when the questionnaire arrives. An e-mail reminder was sent out at the end of the first week, asking the deputies for their support and including a questionnaire that could be filled in electronically and submitted via e-mail.

5.4 Analysis

5.4.1 Response Rate

The response rate of the survey was relatively low at 11%. In the scope of written surveys with an elite group, the rate is still acceptable and a sample of 67 questionnaires allows for adequate and reliable results of the analysis of the survey, considering the small size of the population.

Since some deputies gave us notice that they would not participate in the survey, we could draw some conclusions about the reasons.

One of the main reasons for a rejection was the workload of the deputies. With several questionnaires coming in daily, many deputies have a general no-participation policy regarding surveys. According to some answers we got, there seems to be a high number of surveys that students of political science try to conduct with deputies in the scope of their final thesis. This seems to lead to a general unwillingness of the deputies to take part in surveys if they are not especially interested or the survey sticks out among the others. We suppose that our survey had a relatively high response rate in comparison to other studies conducted with deputies due to it being carried out by a scientific foundation with an official letterhead and the fact that a donation was made for each participating deputy.

5.4.2 Sample Composition

Since the demographic details of the German Bundestag are known, we were in the fortunate position of being able to check how far the sample mirrored the population the survey was aimed at.

The sample featured a mean age of 49 years, which is nearly consistent with the mean age of 50 years for the Bundestag in its 16th period. Nevertheless, there are differences between the sample and the population. The age pattern is presented below in Figs. 5.7a, b.

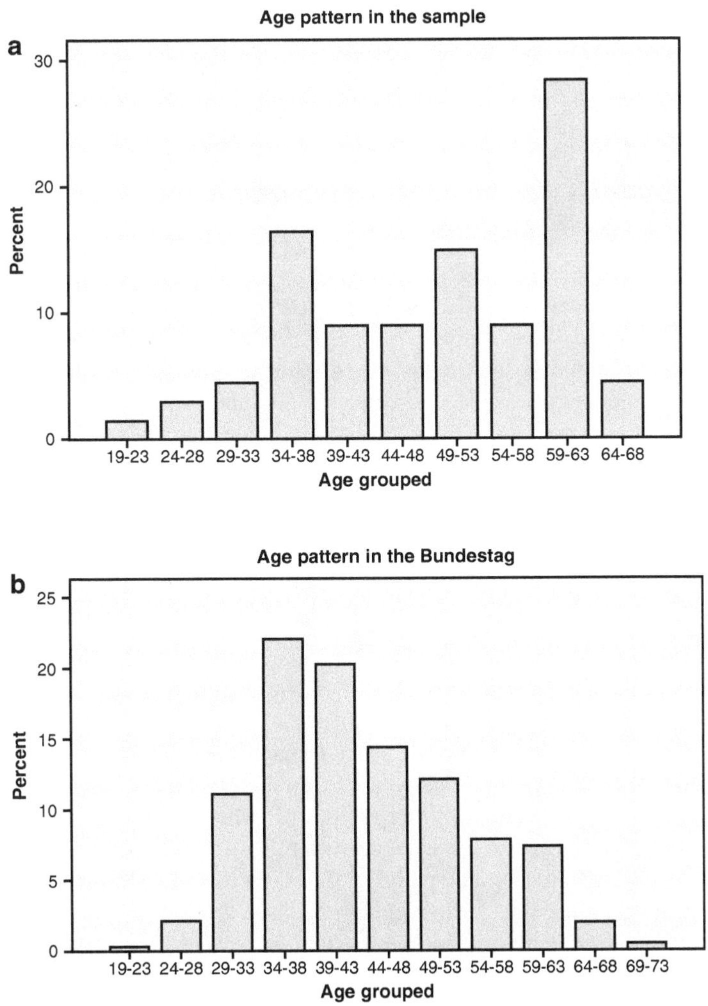

Fig. 5.7 (**a**) and (**b**): Age patterns of the sample and the population of the survey
Source: Own calculations, webpage of the German Bundestag

The group of oldest deputies is significantly overrepresented in the sample while deputies between 29 and 48 years of age are underrepresented. The participation of the youngest deputies – those less than 30 years old – equates closely with the actual proportions in the Bundestag. A reason for the comparatively low participation of the middle generations could be that they are less affected by questions of generational justice at first glance, since the concept tends to evoke comparisons between old and young generations in public opinion. This could also be the reason for the high participation rate of older deputies.

Considering gender statistics, there was an overrepresentation of female deputies in the sample with the 16th Bundestag having a 32% proportion of women while the sample has a 40% proportion. As shown later, this overrepresentation could have some influence on the results of the survey. A reason for this female overrepresentation could be that the rush hour of life concept mentioned in the cover letter is linked to topics traditionally labelled as "female" like the compatibility of family and career.

5.4.3 General Assessment of the Importance of Generational Justice

The first part was meant to offer a general overview of how the deputies assess generational justice. How important is generational justice for politics from the point of view of deputies in comparison to other concepts of justice like international, social and gender justice? Unsurprisingly, social justice was rated as the most important concept with a mean of 3.6 on a scale from 1 (no importance) to 4 (high importance). Since social justice is dominating political debates in important policy areas like labour politics, this result could be anticipated. What we did not anticipate was that generational justice would end up in a very close third place (3.0) with almost identical results to gender justice (3.1). This is also surprising taking into account the overrepresentation of female deputies, which could have led to an up valuation of gender justice. International justice comes in fourth with a mean importance of 2.5, which reflects that this concept has comparatively little importance in the scope of domestic politics which still focuses on nation states. The results are presented below in Figs. 5.8a, b.

As a second step, the deputies were asked to rate different policy fields according to their importance for generational justice (scale 1–4). Financial politics came in first, followed by education and pension politics, which tied in second place (see Fig. 5.9). The lead position of financial politics reflects the results of another survey (Tremmel et al. 2009, p. 10) that analysed the contexts in which the term "generational justice" was used in parliamentary debates. In our study, environmental politics came in fourth place tying with youth and family politics. This result is surprising if we consider that climate change has potentially the most devastating implications on the lives of future generations.

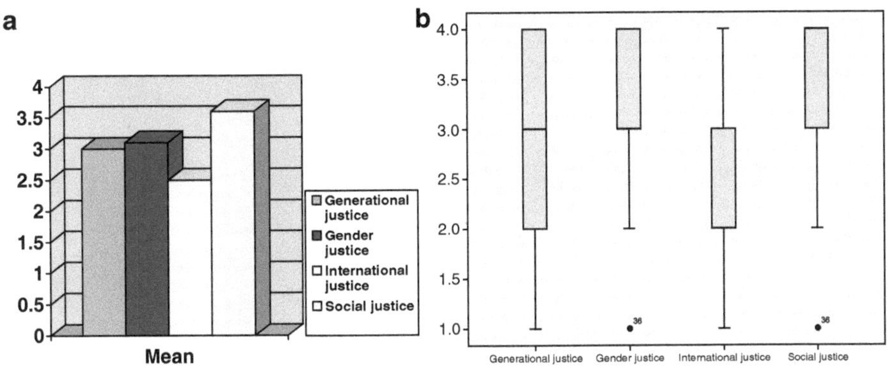

Fig. 5.8 (**a**) and (**b**): Mean and boxplot results of item 1: "In your opinion, which role have the following types of justice played so far in the political discourse?"

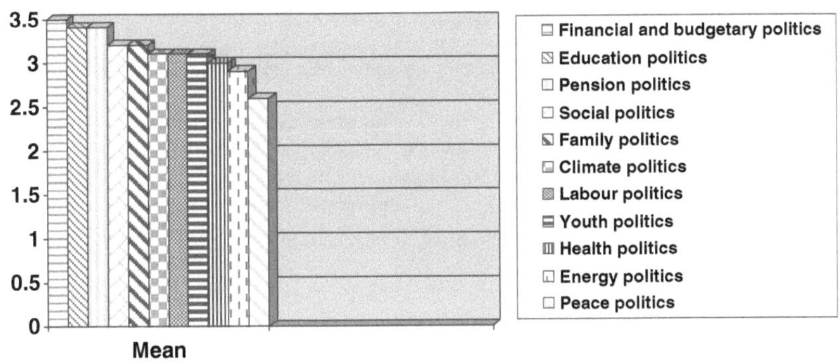

Fig. 5.9 Item: "How do you assess the importance of the following political fields within the scope of generationally just politics?"

Generally, all policy fields received a high mean ranking with the exception of peace policy coming in at 2.6. This shows that this particular policy field is not generally associated with generational justice, despite the lasting negative effects inner state wars have on the life chances of future generations in the states affected.

The last four questions of the first part present statements concerning generational justice which summarise the core problems of generational justice in our society, one example being a short time-frame in decision-making which disregards long-term consequences. These items verbatim address the concept of generational justice, thus they were placed at the beginning to avoid the possibility that their results *could be* influenced by other items detailing problems of generational justice. Overall, our society is seen as neutral concerning generational justice (2.5

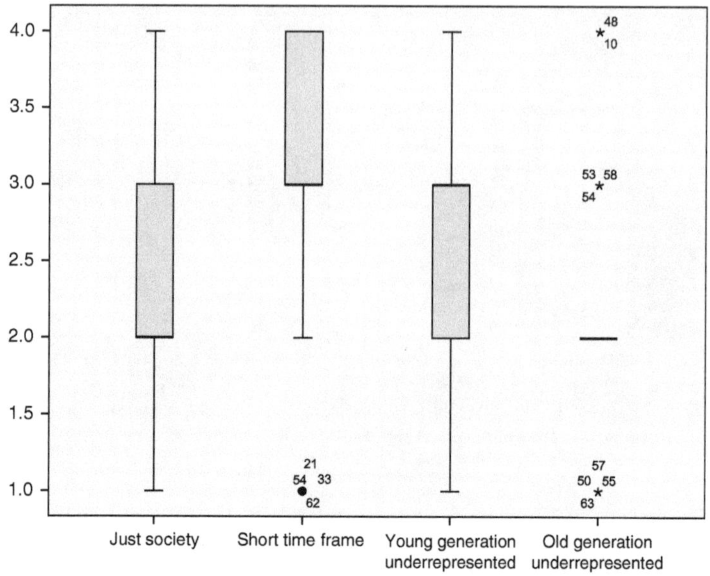

Fig. 5.10 Boxplot results for the following items. How strongly do you *agree* with the following statements? All in all we live in a generationally just society. The time horizon of politics is currently too short-term oriented to meet the requirements of generational justice. The interests of the young generation are currently not adequately represented within politics. The interests of the older generation are currently not adequately represented within politics

mean on a 1–4 scale). The problem of a short time-frame is acknowledged (3 mean) while a strong discrepancy in the representation of young and old generations is not seen. There is even a very slight correlation (0.065) of seeing both older people and younger people as underrepresented. For the boxplot results, see Fig. 5.10.

5.4.4 *The Rush Hour of Life*

The second part of the questionnaire focuses on the problems of the rush hour of life. The first question refers to the compatibility of family and working life for the young generation of today in indirect comparison with the former generation. The deputies assessed the compatibility and were asked to offer reasons for their assessment. Generally, the deputies gave the opinion that the compatibility of family and career has become more manageable nowadays with 64% saying that it is somewhat easier or easier to arrange family and careers nowadays in comparison to the situation 30 years ago. Overall, 48% of the sample offered reasons for their assessment of the situation. Better *daycare facilities* and *gender equality* were the two reasons most often given for better compatibility. The figures were 50 and

37.5%, respectively. On the other hand, higher requirements towards flexibility and an achievement-oriented society were given by 15.6% as reasons for a lower compatibility.

The following item battery consisted of questions mainly relating to the problems of the rush hour of life and the values of today's young generation regarding family life. Generally, the awareness of the deputies for the issues described in the questions was high. The items relating to problems experienced by the young generation had a mean between 2.2 and 3.5 on a 1–4 scale.[9] The item, *The respective school diplomas and university degrees offer less career prospects today than 30 years ago,* received by far the lowest approval of 2.2. All other problem items were rated with 2.6 upwards, most of them being above 3. The low approval of 2.2 for the diploma question contradicts standard views in the relevant literature.[10] *The item "The requirements on mobility and professiona flexibility have increased in the last 30 years" received the highest approval with 3.5.*

The variances of the answers were, generally, relatively low with values between 0.3 and 0.9. The large majority of the items had a variance between 0.4 and 0.7. This reflects a tendency to tick the less extreme approval or disapproval levels, being "slight disapproval" and "slight approval".

It should be mentioned that concrete problems described in the items received an average approval of 2.98.

5.4.5 Young Generation and Entry to the Labour Market

The third part of the questionnaire analysed the problems that the young generation is confronted with when trying to start a working career. The questions mainly focus on the phase between graduation and entry into the labour market. A few questions are related to job satisfaction as well as the general situation of the young generation in the labour market.

As a start, the perceived level to which insecurities in the labour market had risen for age groups and gender groups within the last 30 years was evaluated (see Fig. 5.11a, b).

The graphs show the results for each item on a scale of 1–4 as well as the boxplots. As can be seen, the deputies think the insecurities for all groups have risen within the last 30 years. Young and old employees are at the fore with high means of 3.36 and 3.28, respectively. At the same time, MPs do not see rising insecurity for male employees even though the dismissal rate in the current economic crisis affects male employees in Germany disproportionately. In May 2009, there were 224.211 additional unemployed males in comparison to May 2008, while the number of female unemployed workers shrunk by 49.410 (Bundesagentur für

[9]For the evaluation, all items were recoded in a way that high numbers indicate high awareness of generational justice issues.

[10]Cf. Chauvel (2010).

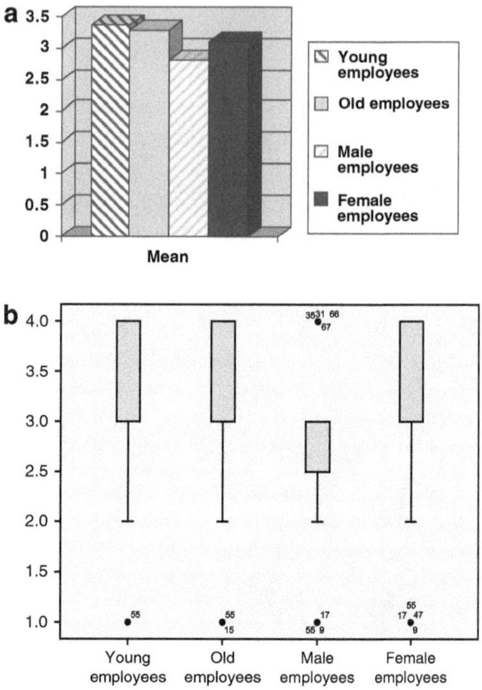

Fig. 5.11 (**a**) and (**b**): Mean and boxplot results for the following items: How much has the uncertainty of labour market conditions in Germany increased for the following groups in the last 30 years? Young employees. Old employees. Male employees. Female employees

Arbeit 2009, p. 50). The equally high numbers for young and old employees create a dilemma in the field of generational justice in the working environment, since both are affected by rising uncertainty. Current numbers show, nevertheless, that the young generation is affected disproportionately by dismissals. In Germany, the number of unemployed in the age group under 25 increased three times as much as the number in older age groups between May 2008 and May 2009 (Bundesagentur für Arbeit 2009, p. 50; Blossfeld and Mills 2010).

The deputies were asked to assess if employees can compensate financial losses in periods of early unemployment or negligible employment in the course of their careers. The findings of Chauvel clearly suggest that those periods of unemployment and negligible employment do leave their marks (cf. Chauvel 2010). On a range from 1 to 4, with four meaning a full compensation, the itemhad a mean of 2.2 with a large majority of 50% opting for "partly" compensation.

The following item battery can roughly be divided into items referring to problems the young generation faces in the labour market and items referring to statutes and laws regulating the labour market and employment. The questionnaire section on the labour market contains more items referring to laws and statutes than the rush hour of life part. There were some differences in the approval rating of items referring to legal aspects and items referring to problems. While the items referring to laws received a mean approval of 2.4, the approval of problem description items had an average mean of 2.93. Considering the tendency to opt

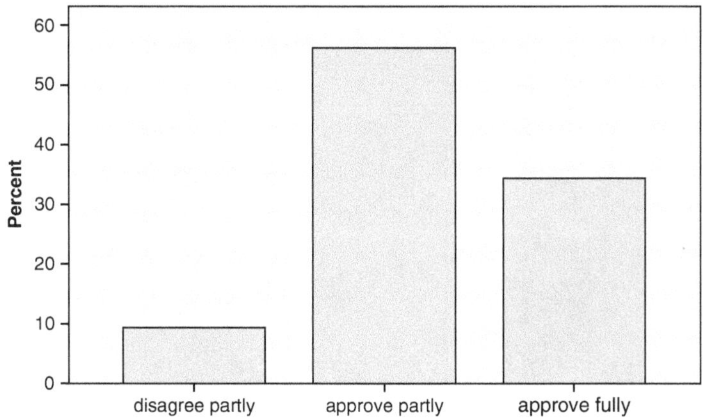

Fig. 5.12 Results of following item: In the period of family formation, the need for an adequate income is the highest since children have to be provided for and expensive purchases have to be made

for the middle of the scale (categories 2 and 3) that can be observed with the majority of the items, this difference of 0.5 *is* of relevance. The problem awareness item which received the highest approval rating was the statement: *In the period of family formation, the need for an adequate income is the highest since children have to be provided for and expensive purchases have to be made.* The item met a 54% of slight, and a 32% of full approval with no person fully disagreeing with the statement, making it one of the items with the highest approval rating in the questionnaire (Fig. 5.12).

Another item, stating that young people often have to sign part-time contracts even if they want to work full-time, also met a high mean approval of 3.1, while 44% approved slightly and 37%, fully. This means that two of the main problems of young employees (lack of financial assets and involuntary part-time employment) are met with high awareness by the deputies.

The item with the lowest mean approval of 2 was the statement: *Due to the increase of the pensionable age, positions are filled for a greater length of time, which intensifies the unemployment of the young generation.*

As Fig. 5.13 suggests, the variance in this case was higher than with most of the items, reaching 0.8. The answers considering problem awareness had a variance between 0.6 and 0.85. The item addressing the need for income of the young age group presented above was an exception with a low variance of 0.4.

Items relating to legal issues had an even higher variance between 0.6 and 1.0. The higher variances suggest that the labour market is a more controversial field than the rush hour of life, which confirms our presumptions that there would be some differences between the rush hour of life and labour market sections. However, this is not mirrored by differences in the awareness levels of problems connected with the rush hour of life or the labour market problems of

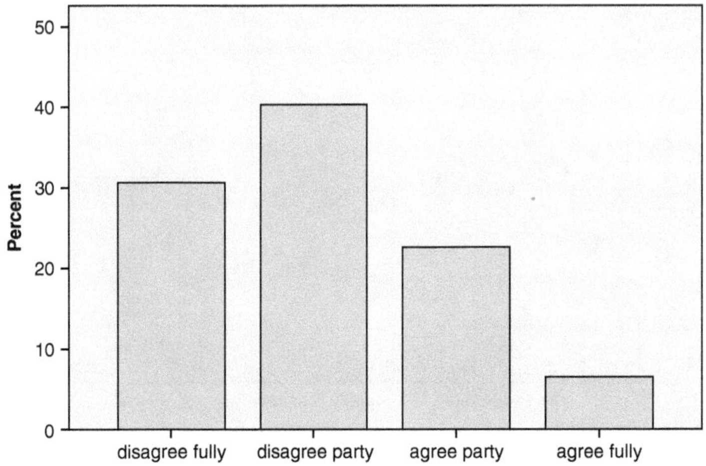

Fig. 5.13 Results of following item: Due to the increase of the pensionable age, positions are filled for a greater length of time, which intensifies the unemployment of the young generation

generational justice. The means for the items addressing problems were relatively equal with 2.93 for the labour market and 2.98 for the rush hour. As a consequence, the labour market items are more suitable for measuring awareness for generational justice problems since they are more controversial and thus provoke clearer reactions.

5.4.6 *Institutional Reforms and Measures*

The last part of the questionnaire asked the deputies to rate different legal initiatives and existing laws which were adopted either to counter problems of generational injustice in the labour market or to straighten out the rush hour of life. The first bloc asked for approval or disapproval of initiatives which aim at institutionalizing generational justice. The proposed measures and their approval levels can be found in Fig. 5.14.

As a second step, the deputies were offered *concrete* reform steps below the constitutional level. We selected a number of measures often named in scientific articles on the topic or discussed in public. The deputies were asked how far they see the measures fit to ensure that the interests of the younger generation in the labour market are taken into consideration or, respectively, to straighten out the rush hour of life. Again, the deputies were presented a scale from 1 (not at all) to 4 (completely). For the complete results, see Figs. 5.15a, b below. Percentages in the result bars not reaching a 100% were missing answers in figure a or "cannot say" answers in figure b. For the full text of the items, please refer to the questionnaire (annex 1).

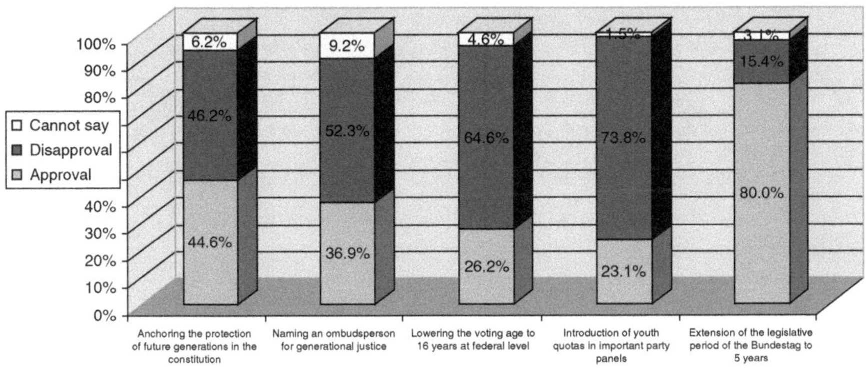

Fig. 5.14 Approval level of discussed institutional reform measures to enhance intergenerational justice in Germany

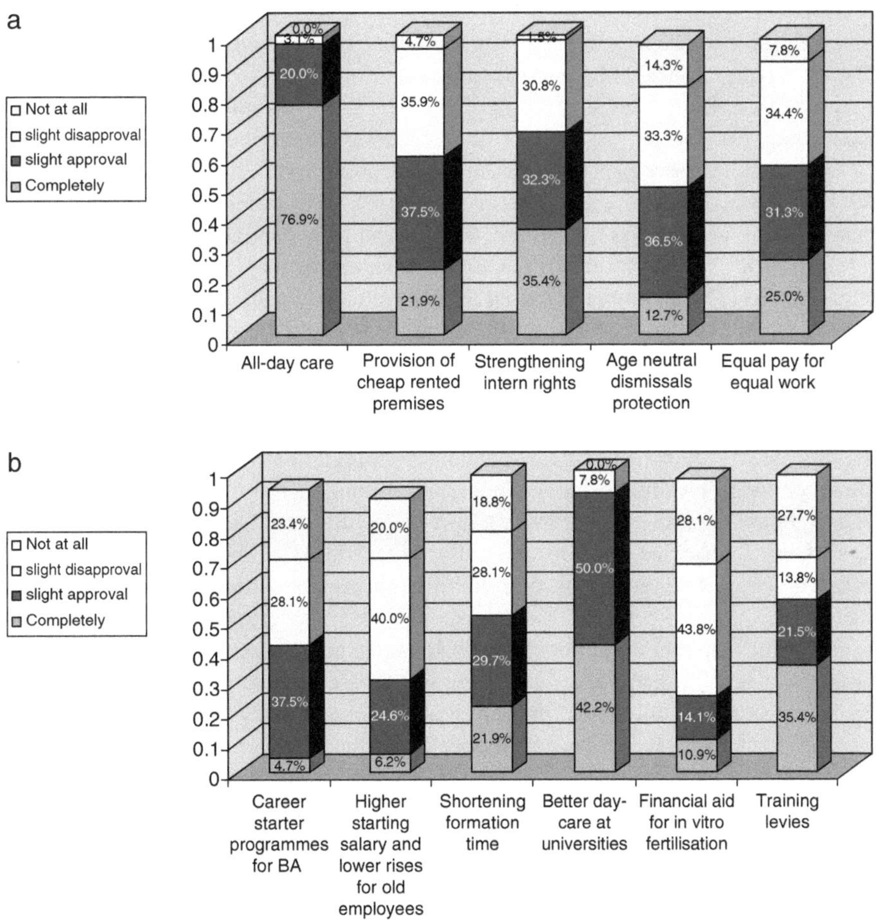

Fig. 5.15 a, b Approval levels of measures to enhance intergenerational justice in Germany

1. All in all we live in a generationally just society.
2. The time horizon of politics is currently too short-term oriented to meet the requirements of generational justice.
3. The requirements on mobility and professional flexibility have increased in the last 30 years.
4. Many employees run through periods of limited or negligible employment and unemployment respectively in the first five years of their professional career. To what degree are those employees usually able to compensate such a financial loss later in the working life?
5. Young people are increasingly being confronted with a lack of prospects on the labour market.
6. Career starters first have to complete several internships.
7. Today the young generation has equal prospects on the labour market as the previous generation had in their youth
8. Today young people are more often affected by unemployment than young people 30 years ago.
9. The pressure of competition in the labour market has not increased in the last 30 years.
10. Today young people often have to take up temporary or part-time contracts although they would prefer to take up full-time contracts.
11. The respective school diplomas and university degrees offer less career prospects today than 30 years ago.

Fig. 5.16 Items used for the GJAI

5.4.7 Indexing Awareness for Generational Justice

Measuring the awareness for generational justice is a difficult task, considering that it spans several topics and is *connected to* other problems like gender equality and social justice. In the scope of an exploratory study – usually used to survey the basic data for further research – the indexing of attributes is not common. Nevertheless, there are a number of items spread over the questionnaire used for the survey that are adequate for measuring the awareness for problems of generational justice. As described above, indirect comparisons are the most relevant from a generational justice perspective, so most items make indirect comparisons. These items were used to assemble the Generational Justice Awareness Index (GJAI) for measuring the awareness of the deputies for problems of intergenerational justice on a scale from 1 (low) to 4 (high). The items used for indexing can be found in Fig. 5.16.

While the first two items measure the awareness of generational justice directly, the other items are measuring the awareness through related problems. Thus, there are second variables falsifying the index to a certain degree. The items included are mainly items from the labour market part of the questionnaire, since they include less of third variables and are generally better suited to measure awareness for generational justice. In terms of reliability, the item battery used for indexing scored a Cronbach's α of .686, which is a bit low considering that a battery should have a value of about 0.7. One of the reasons for this comparably low value is that some items also measure other variables. Furthermore, generational justice has not yet been fully operationalised for empirical research, and hence, adequate items for measurement still have to be developed. Thus, there remain contradictions in the awareness of generational justice. For this reason, items were not weighted in the scope of indexing.

The results of the indexing can be seen in Figs. 5.17 and 5.18.

The GJAI for the sample had a mean of 2.88 with a variance of 0.188. The index is measured on a scale from 1 to 4, with 1 as the lowest and 4 as the highest score.

Fig. 5.17 Boxplot of the GJAI

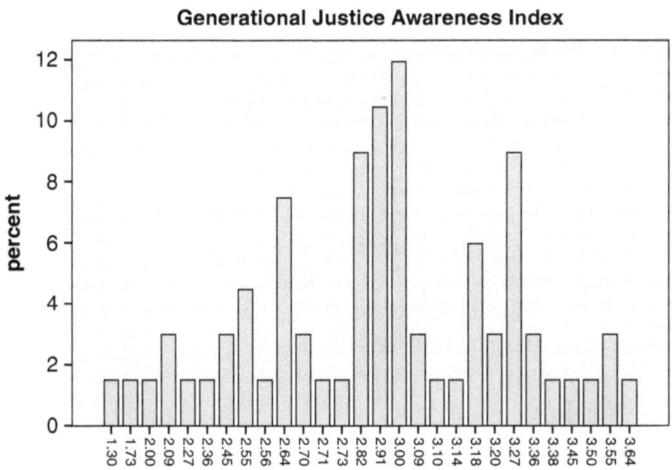

Fig. 5.18 Statistical distribution of GJAI

We can, therefore, talk of a still limited but nevertheless measurable awareness for generational justice. According to our 1–4 scale, every value above 2.5 would hint at a "real" awareness of generational justice. The median of the sample is 2.90. This is a number of some importance in this context, since the median voter is theoretically decisive in majority decisions, such as votes in parliament. The limits of the index described above should be taken into consideration though when working with these figures.

Item	Correlation * = significant on 0.05 level ** = significant on 0.01 level
1. How much has the uncertainty of labour market conditions in Germany increased for old employees in the last 30 years?	R = 0.362**
2. Many employees run through periods of limited or negligible employment and unemployment respectively in the first five years of their professional career. To what degree are those employees usually able to compensate such a financial loss later in the working life?	R = –0.276*
3. Age privileges concerning dismissal protection discriminate against young people.	R = –0.237
4. Support of training levies from companies that do not train.	R = 0.219*
5. Support for strengthening the rights of interns.	R = 0.232

Fig. 5.19 Items correlating with the age of respondents (two-tailed Spearman test)

5.4.8 Outside Variable Influences: Age and Gender

Since generational justice has a strong age connotation, a correlation between certain questions and the age of the respondent, or perhaps even a correlation between age and generational justice awareness in general, would not have been surprising (Bonoli 2010). However, the correlations of answering patterns with the age were low and irrelevant for most items. The correlations were measured with a two-tailed Spearman Test. Figure 5.19 shows the items with a significant or a comparably high correlation with the age of the respondents.

A correlation with items 1 and 3 was hardly surprising since older people are directly affected or addressed by them. On the other hand, there was support for measures to straighten out the rush hour of life in items 4 and 5 from older respondents who are not affected by the problems presented by these items. One has to keep in mind, though, that even the highest correlations listed here are still low and of limited statistical significance.

In the light of the presented findings, it is not surprising that the GJAI also did not correlate significantly with the age of the respondents. There is only an irrelevant correlation of 0.003.

As already hinted at above, gender was a more relevant factor in the survey and had some influence on a number of items. Again, the items influenced through the variable "gender" are listed below. The significance of the correlation was visualized through boxplots and measured through a one-way ANOVA test. Figure 5.20 lists the ANOVA results for the significance of the correlation. The lower the significance the higher the correlation, the direction of the correlation is indicated in parentheses.

Some of the items with a high correlation refer to topics socially labelled as "female" or directly addressing gender, which explains some of the correlations. Nevertheless, the correlations with other items hint at a higher awareness for problems of generational justice among female deputies and a higher support for certain measures to tackle those problems. There are some fairly significant

Item	Correlation
1. The interests of the young generation are currently not adequately represented within politics.	Sig.: 0.044 [negative]
2. Low birth rates are largely caused by the double burden of career and family in younger days.	Sig.: 0.016 [negative]
3. Usually companies adequately consider the familial needs of their employees.	Sig.: 0.020 [negative]
4. How much has the uncertainty of labour market conditions in Germany increased for young employees in the last 30 years?	Sig.: 0.035 [positive]
5. How much has the uncertainty of labour market conditions in Germany increased for female employees in the last 30 years?	Sig.: 0.001 [positive]
6. Many employees run through periods of limited or negligible employment and unemployment respectively in the first five years of their professional career. To what degree are those employees usually able to compensate such a financial loss later in the working life?	Sig.: 0.049 [negative]
7. Young people are increasingly being confronted with a lack of prospects on the labour market.	Sig.: 0.003 [positive]
8. Career starters first have to complete several internships.	Sig.: 0.004 [positive]
9. Today the young generation has equal prospects on the labour market as the previous generation had in their youth.	Sig.: 0.028 [negative]
10. Age privileges concerning dismissal protection discriminate against young people.	Sig.: 0.006 [negative]
11. Current legal regulations do not adequately protect school and university graduates from the exploitation by pseudo-internships.	Sig.: 0.015 [positive]
12. Approval of provision of low priced rented premises for young couples.	Sig.: 0.026 [positive]
13. Approval of strengthening the rights of interns.	Sig.: 0.004 [positive]
14. Approval of shortening school education, years of study and periods of training.	Sig.: 0.007 [negative]
15. Approval of training levies from companies that do not train.	Sig.: 0.016 [positive]

Fig. 5.20 Items correlating with the gender of respondents (ANOVA Test)

correlations for some topics concerning the rights of interns and the problematic situation of young employees in the labour market (items 5, 6, and 11 in Fig. 5.20). Furthermore, 5 of 13 items included in the generational justice index are correlated with gender (items 1, 4, 5, 6, and 7 in Fig. 5.20). Consequently, there is some correlation between the GJAI and gender as shown in Fig. 5.21.

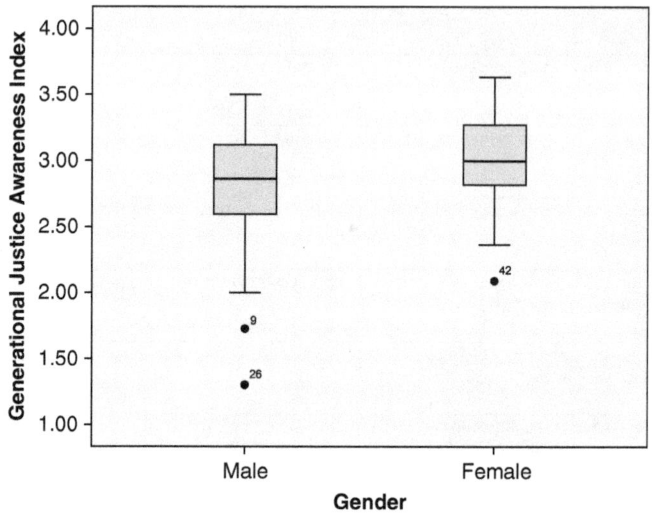

Fig. 5.21 Boxplot of the correlation of gender and the GJAI

The correlation has a significance of 0.032, which ANOVA considers sufficient (significance below 0.05 needed). The mean of the male sample lies at 2.79 while the mean for the female sample lies at 3.02 and has a lower variance.

5.5 Conclusions and Outlook

We were surprised that the level of awareness of generational justice in the world of employment is rather *strong* among members of the German Bundestag. According to official publications of the German government, age discrimination is solely understood as discrimination against older employees, *not* against younger ones. But when concrete problems of the young generations were mentioned, the approval rates of the deputies were quite high. Unfortunately, this does not always seem to lead to a readiness for legislative actions to change the grievances. On a general level, legislation to counter these problems is supported, especially in areas where there is a consensus in the society, for example, enhancing daycare and strengthening intern rights. But for other important issues like introducing age-neutral regulations of the dismissal protection, or raising the salaries for young employees while capping the salaries for older employees, there was no clear support. Furthermore, only seven deputies (about 10% of the sample) came forward with their own suggestions concerning reforms for the sake of generational justice. As soon as the issues became more controversial, the readiness to pay *lip-service* to generational justice seems to be higher than the readiness to take decisive legislative action.

References

Birnbacher D (1988) Verantwortung für zukünftige Generationen. Reclam, Stuttgart

Blossfeld H-P, Mills M (2010) How does globalization affect the life courses of young men and women in modern societies? In: FRFG (ed) A young generation under pressure? Springer, Heidelberg (in press)

Bonoli G (2010) Comparing welfare regime changes: living standards and the unequal life chances of different birth cohorts. In: FRFG (ed) A Young Generation Under Pressure? Springer, Heidelberg (in press)

Bude H (2000) Qualitative Generationsforschung. In: Flick U, von Kardorff E, Steinke I (eds) Qualitative Forschung. Rowohlt, Ein Handbuch, Hamburg, pp 187–194

Bundesagentur für Arbeit (2009) Monatsbericht Mai 2009. Bundesagentur für Arbeit, Nürnberg

Chauvel L (2010) Comparing welfare regime changes: Living standards and the unequal life chances of different birth cohorts. In: FRFG (ed) A young generation under pressure? Springer, Heidelberg (in press)

Daniels N (1988) Am I my parents keeper? An essay on justice between the young and the old. Oxford University Press, Oxford

De-Shalit A (1995) Why posterity matters. Environmental policies and future generations. Routledge, London/New York

Easterlin RA (1980) Birth and fortune. The impact of numbers on personal fortune. Basic Books, New York

Jureit U, Wildt M (2005) Generationen. In: Jureit U, Wildt M (eds) Generationen. Zur Relevanz eines wissenschaftlichen Grundbegriffs. Hamburger Edition, Hamburg, pp 7–26

Klammer U (2010) The 'rush hour' of life: insecurities and strains in early life phases as a challenge for a life course-oriented, sustainable social policy. In: FRFG (ed.) A young generation under pressure? Springer: Heidelberg (in press)

Kohli M, Szydlik M (2000) 'Einleitung'. In: Kohli M, Szydlik M (eds) Generationen in Familie und Gesellschaft. Leske und Budrich, Opladen, pp 7–18

Kohli M (2006) Aging and justice. In: Binstock HR, George LK (eds) Handbook of aging and the social sciences. Elsevier, New York, pp 457–478

Landweer H (1996) Generationenkonflikte und Sachdifferenzen. Das Beispiel Frauenbewegung. Transit 19:87–100

Laslett P, Fishkin JS (1992) Introduction. Processional justice. In: Laslett P, Fishkin JS (eds) Justice between age groups and generations. Yale University Press, New Haven/London, pp 1–23

Rawls J (1971) A theory of justice. Belknap Press of Harvard University Press, Cambridge, MA (German edition: Rawls J (1979) Eine Theorie der Gerechtigkeit, Frankfurt am Main: Suhrkamp)

Russell Y, Kals E, Montada L (2003) Generationengerechtigkeit im allgemeinen Bewusstsein? Eine umweltpsychologische Untersuchung. In: Stiftung für die Rechte zukünftiger Generationen (eds) Oekom, Handbuch Generationengerechtigkeit, München, pp 153–173

SOEP/DIW (2008) Socio-economic panel/Deutsches Institut für Wirtschaftsforschung, special analysis for the IWG BONN, Berlin

Strauss W, Howe N (1991) Generations. The history of America's future. Quill, New York

Strauss W, Howe N (1993) 13th generation. Abort, retry, ignore, fail? Vintage Books, New York

Thomson D (1992) Generations, justice, and the future of collective action. In: Laslett P, Fishkin JS (eds) Justice between age groups and generations. Yale University Press, New Haven/London, pp 206–236

Tremmel JC (2009) A theory of intergenerational justice. Earthscan, London

Tremmel J, Pöllmann K, Rohe M (2009) Die Etablierung des Begriffs,Generationengerechtigkeit' im politischen und gesellschaftlichen Sprachgebrauch, FRFG Study 1/2009, http://www.generationengerechtigkeit.de/images/stories/Publikationen/artikel_studien/studie_1_2009_begriff_gg.pdf

Veith W (2006) Intergenerationelle Gerechtigkeit. Ein Beitrag zur sozialethischen Theoriebildung. Kohlhammer, Stuttgart

Annex 1: Questionnaire of the German Bundestag Survey on Intergenerational Justice in the Labour Market

Foundation for the Rights of Future Generations

SURVEY: GENERATIONAL JUSTICE IN THE WORKING ENVIRONMENT

Please fill in the questionnaire and send it back to us using the enclosed stamp addressed envelope or via fax (06171-952566) by 14th of March 2009.

1. In your opinion, which role have the following types of justice played so far in the political discourse?

	large 4	moderate 3	small 2	none 1	don´t know 0
Generational justice	☐	☐	☐	☐	☐
Gender justice	☐	☐	☐	☐	☐
International justice	☐	☐	☐	☐	☐
Social justice	☐	☐	☐	☐	☐

2. How do you assess the importance of the following political fields within the scope of generationally just politics?

	very high 4	high 3	low 2	very low 1	don´t know 0
Youth policy	☐	☐	☐	☐	☐
Fiscal and budgetary policy	☐	☐	☐	☐	☐
Labour policy	☐	☐	☐	☐	☐
Family policy	☐	☐	☐	☐	☐
Health policy	☐	☐	☐	☐	☐
Ecological policy (without energy policy)	☐	☐	☐	☐	☐
Energy policy	☐	☐	☐	☐	☐
Educational policy	☐	☐	☐	☐	☐
Pension policy	☐	☐	☐	☐	☐
Welfare policy	☐	☐	☐	☐	☐
Policy of peace	☐	☐	☐	☐	☐

3. How strongly do you agree with the following statements?	++ fully 4	+ 3	- 2	-- not at all 1	don´t know 0
All in all we live in a generationally just society.	☐	☐	☐	☐	☐
The time frame of politics is currently too short-term oriented to meet the requirements of generational justice.	☐	☐	☐	☐	☐
The interests of the young generation are currently not adequately represented within politics.	☐	☐	☐	☐	☐
The interests of the older generation are currently not adequately represented within politics.	☐	☐	☐	☐	☐

Subject area: rush-hour of life

4. How do you assess the compatibility between work and family for the current young generation in comparison with the generation that was young 30 years ago?

easier ☐ slightly easier ☐ similar ☐ slightly more difficult ☐ more difficult ☐ don´t know ☐

Why? ______________________________

5. How strongly do you agree with the following statements?	++ fully 4	+ 3	- 2	-- not at all 1	don't know 0
Low birth rates are largely caused by the double burden of career and family in younger days.	☐	☐	☐	☐	☐
The introduction of parent's money on January 1st 2007 will in the long run result in an increase of birth rates in Germany.	☐	☐	☐	☐	☐
Long training and study periods of young people reduce the time frame for forming a family.	☐	☐	☐	☐	☐
Many young people hold the opinion that children limit their freedom.	☐	☐	☐	☐	☐
The current young generation is financially dependent on their parents for a longer period than they were 30 years ago.	☐	☐	☐	☐	☐
It has a negative effect on the career prospects of younger people if they work part-time due to family commitments.	☐	☐	☐	☐	☐
It is easier for the current young generation to maintain solid relationships than for previous generations.	☐	☐	☐	☐	☐
The introduction of the Bachelor/Master system for graduate degrees will increase the birth rates in the long run.	☐	☐	☐	☐	☐
Traditional family values are honoured by the young generation in the same way as they were by the previous generation 30 years ago.	☐	☐	☐	☐	☐
The requirements on mobility and professional flexibility have increased in the last 30 years.	☐	☐	☐	☐	☐
The currently existing care programmes for children between 1 and 5 years are adequate.	☐	☐	☐	☐	☐
The respective school diplomas and university degrees offer less career prospects today than 30 years ago.	☐	☐	☐	☐	☐
The career in the life of young people today holds a higher importance than it did 30 years ago.	☐	☐	☐	☐	☐
Usually companies adequately consider the familial needs of their employees.	☐	☐	☐	☐	☐
The transition period between training or school graduation and the entrance into the first permanent position has not extended noticeably in the last 30 years.	☐	☐	☐	☐	☐

Subject area: Young generation and entry to the labour market

6. How much has the uncertainty of labour market conditions in Germany increased for the following groups in the last 30 years?

	strongly 4	noticeably 3	mildly 2	not at all 1	don't know 0
Young employees	☐	☐	☐	☐	☐
Old employees	☐	☐	☐	☐	☐
Male employees	☐	☐	☐	☐	☐
Female employees	☐	☐	☐	☐	☐

7. Many employees run through periods of limited or negligible employment and unemployment respectively in the first five years of their professional career. To what degree are those employees usually able to compensate such a financial loss later in the working life?

fully	largely	partly	not at all	don´t know
☐	☐	☐	☐	☐

8. How strongly do you agree with the following statements?	++ fully 4	+ 3	- 2	-- not at all 1	don´t know 0
Young people are increasingly being confronted with a lack of prospects on the labour market.	☐	☐	☐	☐	☐
The rule of seniority, i.e. the increase of payment with increasing age, is reasonable and therefore should be maintained.	☐	☐	☐	☐	☐
The current labour law does not provide a fair balance to the interests of young and old employees.	☐	☐	☐	☐	☐
Career starters first have to complete several internships.	☐	☐	☐	☐	☐
Today the young generation has equal prospects on the labour market as the previous generation had in their youth.	☐	☐	☐	☐	☐
A longer staff membership in the company justifies the payment of higher incomes to those employees (rule of ancienneté).	☐	☐	☐	☐	☐
In the period of family formation the need for an adequate income is the highest since children have to be provided for and expensive purchases have to be made.	☐	☐	☐	☐	☐
Today young people are more often affected by unemployment than young people 30 years ago.	☐	☐	☐	☐	☐
Age privileges concerning dismissal protection discriminate against young people.	☐	☐	☐	☐	☐
Current legal regulations do not adequately protect school and university graduates from the exploitation by pseudo-internships.	☐	☐	☐	☐	☐
The pressure of competition in the labour market has not increased in the last 30 years.	☐	☐	☐	☐	☐
Today young people often have to take up temporary or part-time contracts although they would prefer to take up full-time contracts.	☐	☐	☐	☐	☐
The trade unions today have not tackled the problems of younger employees sufficiently.	☐	☐	☐	☐	☐
Due to the increase of the pensionable age all positions are filled for a greater length of time which intensifies the unemployment of the young generation.	☐	☐	☐	☐	☐

Subject area: Institutional Reforms and Measures

9. Which institutional reforms that promote generational justice would you support?

	yes	no	don´t know
Anchoring the protection of future generations in the constitution.	☐	☐	☐
Naming an ombudsperson for generational justice.	☐	☐	☐
Lowering the voting age to 16 years at federal level.	☐	☐	☐
Introduction of youth quotas in important party panels.	☐	☐	☐
Extension of the legislative period of the Bundestag to 5 years.	☐	☐	☐

10. Please mark how strongly you regard the following measures as applicable to considering more the needs of young employees and career starters and to ease the rush hour of life.

	++ fully 4	+ 3	- 2	-- not at all 1	don´t know 0
All-day care for children below 3 years.	☐	☐	☐	☐	☐
Provision of low priced rented premises for young couples.	☐	☐	☐	☐	☐
Strengthening the rights of interns.	☐	☐	☐	☐	☐
Age-neutral regulations of the dismissal protection.	☐	☐	☐	☐	☐
Equal wages for equal work, regardless of age.	☐	☐	☐	☐	☐
Career starter programmes for BA graduates at public employers.	☐	☐	☐	☐	☐
Higher starting salaries and lower salary rises for older employees for some years.	☐	☐	☐	☐	☐
Shortening school education, years of study and periods of training.	☐	☐	☐	☐	☐
Creation of better care programmes at universities in order to promote earlier parenthood.	☐	☐	☐	☐	☐
Financial aid for in vitro fertilisation by the state in order to promote later parenthood.	☐	☐	☐	☐	☐
Training levies from companies that do not train.	☐	☐	☐	☐	☐

Other measures you consider applicable:

____

____

Desired birthday

11. Imagine you might choose the time in which you are born. You are completely free in your choice of era, but you have to spend your life in the chosen era. Your place of origin remains the same, but you do not know which will be your social class or gender.

Set your desired year of birth: _________

Why have you chosen this era? (short phrase or headwords)

____

____

Demographic Information

12. Finally we ask you for some demographic information which has to be surveyed for the analysis of this questionnaire. Of course data will be treated anonymously.

Gender: male ☐ female ☐

Year of birth:_______

We thank you for taking your time to answer our questions.

4

Part II
The Rush Hour of Life

Chapter 6
On the Way to Life-Domains Balance: Success Factors and Obstacles

Harald Lothaller

A certain phenomenon appeared in political as well as scientific discussions in the last decade – the so-called "rush hour of life" (Bittman and Wajcman 2000). It is defined as "a certain stage of life, from the mid-twenties until the late thirties of age, when persons of both sexes who just have completed their education enter the labor market as well as start a family and thereby have to deal with both job/career demands and family/private demands at the same time" (Lothaller 2008, p. 4, translated by the author). In other words, two big life domains, namely occupation and family, are launched and become important at the same time for these persons rather than one after the other. This is because the starting age for both domains rises (e.g., due to higher and thereby longer education, people living longer at their parents' home, insecurity at the labor market at the beginning of occupation), yet the age to complete said domain does not, since missed chances do not come back (cf. Bailyn 1977; Blossfeld 2008; Chauvel 2008; Klammer 2008; and Perrig-Chiello 2008). As a corollary to this, many seem to face overwhelming demands from apparently conflicting life domains.

Current surveys indicate aspects related to occupational work and career as major reasons for having less to no children at all (Market 2005; cf. Cizek and Richter 2004). Family-related difficulties can lead to more absence from the workplace or decreased productivity in the job, but positive emotions due to the family situation can have positive effects on the job performance (cf. Eby et al. 2005; Frone 2003; and Poelmans 2001). Companies themselves make policies on family friendliness and family support. Various and diverse measures to promote family friendliness at the workplace (cf. Allen 2003; Auer 2002; and Eby et al. 2005) and initiatives to award prizes to exemplary enterprises (e.g., the European work & family audit®) are organized in cities, countries or across them. However, aside of the family domain and the job domain, other life domains add further

H. Lothaller
Department of Psychology, University of Graz, Universitaetsplatz 2/III, 8010 Graz, Austria
e-mail: harald@lothaller.net

J.C. Tremmel (ed.), *A Young Generation Under Pressure?*,
DOI 10.1007/978-3-642-03483-1_6,

demands, increasing time pressure and coordination problems. Even with leisure time, the time aspect often overlaps the leisure aspect, and activities need to be scheduled accurately. Not only from Heider's balance theory (1946; 1958) do we know that people have a drive towards balance in any system and generally do not feel good in unbalanced situations. All together, we have several interdependent life domains that we should keep in balance to decrease stress and strain and to increase our well-being and further positive outcomes, respectively (cf. Eby et al. 2005; Frone 2003; and Poelmans 2001).

The aim of this article is to give an overview on life-domains balance and related factors that lead to more or less balance. The issue of life-domains balance lacks comprehensive theories and even some clear definitions. Empirical work in the field relies on evidence-based models rather than on theoretical concepts. Therefore, we start with an exploration of the terms before dealing with the possible causes of life-domains balance and end with some considerations why this issue is of increasing importance nowadays.

6.1 What is Life-Domains Balance?

A concept called "work/life balance" has been raised in the last 25–30 years and is already common in daily life. A similar term "work/family balance" denotes a more narrow focus, but is often used synonymously. Although both terms are widely used in scientific and other literature, there is neither an explicit and comprehensive definition nor an explanation as to what it means to have different life domains "in balance". Most authors seem to take its meaning as self-explanatory and "for many writers, work–family balance represents a vague notion that work and family life are somewhat integrated and harmonious" (Frone 2003, p. 145). This still holds in particular for guidebooks or political statements; however, an increasing specification can be found at least in empirical research in the last few years (cf. Rantanen 2008).

Furthermore, there are three points of criticism with regard to this term. First, "work" is used for paid work and the occupation domain, imputing that only having a job is engaging. Second, it suggests that occupational work would be something different than life or be done elsewhere than in one's life. Third, there is no differentiation between other domains apart from the occupation domain. The more narrow term "work/family balance" overcomes the second point. Nevertheless, it also leads to overlooking the fact that a lot of (unpaid) work is done besides a job. Also, the term considers only two life domains by appellation, but not others. To overcome all three points of criticism, we had better call the concept "*life-domains balance*," as occupation, family and partnership, education, leisure time, voluntary social work, etc. are all different domains in people's lives and have to be reconciled and kept in balance (Lothaller 2008).

The two components of the terms can help us to approach the concept. The first one regards the considered *life domains*. It might be a concession or just an adequate price for becoming more precise, but in most cases the more specified publications focus on "work/family balance". In other words, they distinguish between the occupation domain, where a job is done usually for financial gain or sometimes voluntarily, and the family domain, where two or more individuals occupy "interdependent roles with the purpose to accomplish shared goals" (Eby et al. 2005, p. 126). Not surprisingly, most authors do *not* explicitly explain where they draw the line with regard to the family domain in particular; hence, it might be *assumed* that often leisure time and other activities are subsumed under the family domain too. However, this imprecise approach may fit the reality better than clear delimitations, bearing in mind different interpretations of the same activities: For instance, Shaw (1988) has shown that women consider childcare as (family) work more often than men, and men take it as a leisure time activity more often than women. So, even when we read about "work and family", it might not always be that clearly restricted by the authors, and the results (or the considerations and assumptions, at least) might hold with other life domains too. Furthermore, along with an "over-emphasis on the work domain" (Eby et al. 2005, p. 185), there is hardly any empirical evidence concerning other domains than the occupation domain and the family domain with regard to balancing life domains. Over and above, some authors criticize the inclusion of other domains in the debate. They explicitly insist on focusing on the complex interaction of occupational demands and family-related demands only, since with leisure time activities, for instance, "there is no inevitability about the obligations taken on. A child cannot be ignored; a parent with Alzheimer's cannot be left alone; a dissolving marriage cannot but interfere with concentration and performance; a teenager with a drug problem demands parental attention. In contrast, playing a game of golf or two may be good for one's morale, but it is not an obligation as such" (Edgar 1999, cit. from Russell and Bowman 2000, p. 5).

The second component of the terms is "*balance*". The widely used view of balance is the absence of conflicts between the different life domains. Balance can be jeopardized due to overwhelming demands from different life domains, or in other words due to conflicting life domains. In that, prior studies raised the concept of "work/family conflict" and defined it as "a form of interrole conflict in which the role pressures from the work and family domains are mutually incompatible in some respect. That is, participation in the work (family) role is made more difficult by the virtue of participation in the family (work) role" (Greenhaus and Beutell 1985). According to more recent literature such as Byron (2005), Frone and colleagues (1992, 1997), Frone (2003), Kinnunen and Mauno (1998), Korabik et al. (2003), or Luk and Shaffer (2002), we have to clearly distinguish between two kinds of conflicts between these two life domains: on the one side, the family domain can cause obstacles for the occupation domain (i.e., family negatively interferes with job), and on the other side, there can be obstacle from the job for the family (i.e., job negatively interferes with family). Commonly used labels (e.g., "family-to-work conflicts") once again use the short term "work" for paid work in the occupation domain. Consequently, it might be better to use the terms "family-to-job conflicts" and "job-to-family conflicts", respectively. Anyway, recent research suggests that balance is more than just a lack of conflicts. Grzywacz and Marks 1999) take the "generally accepted assumption that the interface between work and family is best characterized in terms of strain" (p. 4) as one of the most significant limitations in this respect and they note that the consequence is "an almost exclusive empirical focus" (p. 4) on conflicts between life domains. But it seems reasonable to assume that there are positive effects from one domain on another too. Experiences, skills, and positive affects gained by doing family-related activities can make it easier to fulfill demands in the occupation domain and vice versa (cf. Frone 2003; and Grzywacz and Marks 1999). Being involved in several domains can provide resources and opportunities to persons. Having a partner to talk with might help to overcome strain from the job, for instance. This supportive impact is named facilitation, enhancement, or positive spillover in current literature. Taken together, life domains should be more balanced the less the demands from different domains are conflicting and the more the participation in a domain facilitates dealing with demands from other domains. Both conflicts and facilitations between the life domains are bidirectional: Each domain can cause conflicts to or be hindered from other domains as well as each can make it easier for other domains or benefit from provided resources.

6.2 Causes of Life-Domains Balance

Life-domains balance is characterized by the extent of conflicts and of facilitation between life domains. Consistently, some aspects of a person's situation can cause conflicts and decrease balance, while others enable facilitation and increase balance. Frone (2003) summarized factors leading to life-domains conflicts and postulated two general categories, namely role environment and personality. With regard to the first, he furthermore distinguished between several kinds of role-related predictors of conflicts between life domains: behavioral involvement, psychological involvement, role-related stressors and affects, and role-related resources. Frone focused on (a) conflicts and (b) the occupation domain and the family domain only when presenting this systematization. In any case, on the superior level focusing on life-domains balance, the role-related resources in particular as well as positive affects too should be supportive and causes of facilitation. Also, equivalent causes from life domains other than job and family should have equivalent effects on life-domains balance. Figure 6.1 outlines the systematization inspired by Frone, but considers facilitation in addition to conflicts between two life domains.

Figure 6.1 is illustrated by means of empirical evidence. As the majority of prior studies with regard to life-domains balance focus on the two domains occupation and family with a "virtual omission of non-work domain variables" (Eby et al. 2005, p. 185), we rely mainly on these two life domains below. Role environment variables (i.e., originated in a certain domain) are considered with reference to life-domains conflicts *first* and life-domains facilitation *second*. In other words, we first

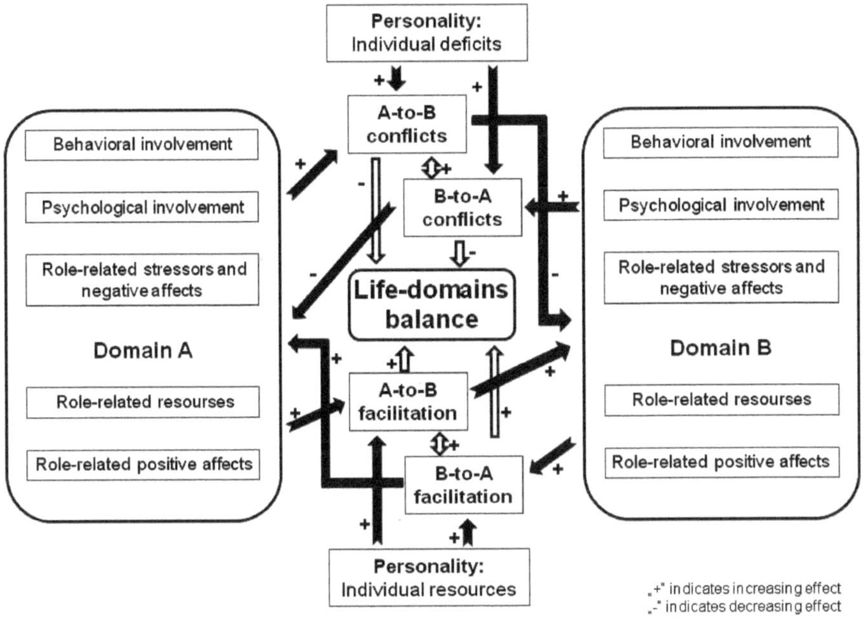

Fig. 6.1 Causes of life-domains conflicts and causes of life-domains facilitation

deal with aspects that lead to more conflicts (and their absence leads to absence of conflicts, but does not automatically lead to facilitation), while the latter lead to more life-domains facilitation (and their absence leads to no facilitation, but does not automatically lead to conflicts). Personality is discussed afterwards.

Generally speaking, demands and pressures originated in domain A as well as personal characteristics of the individual cause A-to-B conflicts. When A is the occupation domain and B is the family domain, job-to-family conflicts are caused by demands and pressures from the occupation domain or by certain individual aspects of the person. Similarly, family-to-job conflicts are caused by demands and pressures from the family domain or by certain individual aspects of the person.

Behavioral involvement represents the amount of time spent on the one or other domain. A lot of studies have shown that the more time a person spends on the occupation domain the more job-to-family conflicts she/he experiences and the more time a person spends on the family domain the more family-to-job conflicts she/he experiences (e.g., Bunk et al. 2004; Frone et al. 1997; Grzywacz et al. 2002; Luk and Shaffer 2002, 2005; Voydanoff 2004; and Wiese 2004). Other studies not separating the two kinds of conflicts have shown that more time spent on the one or the other domain increases overall life-domains conflicts (e.g., Hill et al. 2001; Milkie and Peltola, 1999; and Voydanoff, 1988). Taken together, "the more hours a person worked per week the more difficulty they had combining work and family" (Fine-Davis 2002, p. 16). Regardless of a lack of empirical evidence, we can assume that time demands of other domains' obligations lead to similar effects, e.g., spending time for voluntary social work, for maintaining friendships or for doing sports regularly. Beyond that, Guerts et al. (2003) have shown that more occupational workload leads to more job-to-family conflicts and that these conflicts furthermore lead to several negative consequences (depressive mood, health complaints, and work-related negative affects), but not the workload itself. In other words, "the direct relationship that is often found between workload and health complaints may be better understood as an indirect relationship in which WHI is a crucial intervening pathway. Workload, as such, may not cause health complaints, but rather workload exerts its negative effects on health through a process of 'spillover' of load-effects accompanied by insufficient quantitative and qualitative recovery during the non-working hours"[1] (Guerts et al. 2003, p. 552).

Psychological involvement refers to the subjective importance of a domain to a person: How much is the role linked to one's self-concept? How much does one personally identify her/himself with the respective role? How much is one engaged in a domain? Generally speaking, the higher the subjective importance of the occupation domain, the more job-to-family conflicts one experiences, and the higher the subjective importance of the family domain, the more family-to-job conflicts one experiences (e.g., Frone et al. 1992; Greenhaus and Beutell 1985; Hammer et al. 1997; Luk and Shaffer 2002, 2005; and Wiese 2004). Higher subjective importance is also linked with higher perceived demands because the importance of a domain goes along with people's role expectations, career salience or family salience for instance. To summarize it with Luk and Shaffer's words: "Consistent with most of the work–family conflict research [. . .] work role expectations had a great impact on WIF"[2] (2005, p. 502). And when a person is overwhelmed from two life domains, she/he will reduce efforts in the less important domain or will withdraw from it altogether (e.g., Korabik et al. 2003; Poelmans, 2001). Psychological involvement in hobbies or voluntary social work might act the same way too.

Role-related stressors and negative affects refer to both objective and subjective aspects. On the one side, there are requirements within a domain such as mentally demanding tasks and other characteristics of the tasks, changing situations or certain stressing events as well as within-domain conflicts or workload in general (e.g., Greenhaus and Beutell 1985; Frone 2003; and Poelmans 2001). Such stressors or "strain-based demands are linked to work-family conflict through a process of psychological spillover in which the strain associated with participating in one domain is carried over to another domain such that it creates strain in the second domain, thereby hindering role performance in that domain" (Voydanoff 2004, p. 400). The more stressors are linked with the occupation domain, the more job-to-family conflicts a person experiences, and the more stressors are linked with the family domain, the more family-to-job conflicts a person experiences

[1]Abbreviation: "WHI" for "work-home interference" (i.e., job-to-family conflict)

[2]Abbreviation: "WIF" for "work interference with family" (i.e., job-to-family conflict)

(e.g., Boyar et al. 2003; Frone et al. 1992, 1997; Hill et al. 2004a,b; Voydanoff 1988; and Wiese 2004). With respect to the occupation domain, insecurity or fear of losing one's job (Voydanoff 2004) as well as shift work (Grosswald 2003; Voydanoff 1988) are additional sources of life-domain conflicts, while the number of children is repeatedly shown as a significant predictor to increasing family-to-job conflicts (e.g., Greenhaus and Beutell 1985; Kinnunen and Mauno 1998; Luk and Shaffer 2005; and Poelmans 2001). On the other side, experiencing distress, feeling overwhelmed, taking domain-related duties as a burden, within-domain dissatisfaction or other negative affects from the occupation domain increase job-to-family conflicts as much as they increase family-to-job conflicts when they are linked with the family domain (e.g., Frone et al. 1997; Guerts et al. 2003; Poelmans 2001; and Wiese 2004). We can imagine that voluntary social work or engaging in organizations outside of job and family for instance can also bring distress or mental demands regardless of a lack of formal obligations.

While the former role-related predictors of life-domains balance increase difficulties in balancing the domains, the below-mentioned role-related resources and role-related positive affects decrease difficulties and support balance by means of facilitation. This conceptualization is in line with Voydanoff's model "that posits that within-domain work demands and resources are differentially salient for work-to-family conflict and facilitation" (2004, p. 406). Although the first group of variables predicts conflicts and the second predicts facilitation as two separate sub concepts, one might presume that on the superior level, the latter can compensate the first with regard to life-domains balance. Voydanoff additionally introduced "boundary-spanning resources" that "are expected to be negatively related to work-to-family conflict and positively associated with work-to-family facilitation" (2004, p. 401) to explain that certain resources are effecting life-domains conflicts too. This is conceptually different from the compensation presumption, but rather similar when focusing on the final consequence.

When A is the occupation domain and B is the family domain in Fig. 6.1, job-to-family facilitation is caused by supportive resources and positive affective consequences from the occupation domain or by certain individual aspects of the person. Similarly, family-to-job facilitation is caused by supportive resources and positive affective consequences from the family domain or by certain individual aspects of the person.

Concerning the occupation domain, respective resources can be work-schedule flexibility to handle family responsibilities (e.g., Greenhaus and Beutell 1985; Hammer et al. 1997; and Hill et al. 2001, 2004a, b), social support from supervisors or coworkers (e.g., Greenhaus and Beutell 1985; Frone et al. 1997; Korabik et al. 2003; Luk and Shaffer, 2002; Poelmans 2001; and Voydanoff, 2004), and supportive policies and family-friendliness of the organization (e.g., Fine-Davis 2002; Korabik et al. 2003; Luk and Shaffer 2002; Poelmans 2001; and Voydanoff 2004) for instance. When it comes to the family domain, such resources can be social supports within the family and from the partner in particular (e.g., Greenhaus and Beutell 1985; Frone et al. 1997; Luk and Shaffer 2002; and Poelmans 2001), assistance from the partner or other persons like domestic helpers in doing housework and other familial tasks (e.g., Fine-Davis 2002; Luk and Shaffer 2002), and a division of tasks between the partners that is taken for satisfactory and just (Himsel and Goldberg 2003; Milkie and Peltola 1999). In addition, some competences and skills acquired in one domain can serve as resources and be positively transferred to the other domain (e.g., Voydanoff 2004), like time management, conflict management, coping strategies, problem-solving competences or manual skills for instance. Taken together, resources from one domain ease the situation in the other domain by means of transferring positive aspects or preventing the transfer of negative aspects. The latter means that resources can help keeping one's mind free of a problem related to one domain and thereby enabling one to concentrate on tasks in the other domain, for instance. This goes beyond the fact that more resources linked with a domain decrease the conflicts resulting from this domain (cf. Frone et al. 1997; Frone 2003). Competences retrieved from leisure-time activities or a social network outside the family and social support from friends might add further benefits.

Contrary to the negative affects mentioned above, positive affects can strengthen people and cause life-domains facilitation. For instance, psychological rewards and personal enrichment, within-domain satisfaction or perceived autonomy, variety, and control in the occupation domain in particular, were indicated as relevant predictors of life-domains facilitation (e.g., Butler et al. 2005; Grzywacz and Butler 2005; Hill 2005; and Voydanoff 2004). We can imagine that the crying children might be more endurable when coming home delighted from a satisfactory and successful day on the job or that the relaxation due to a harmonious day with the family might let the big pile of files on the desk appear in a better light. Relaxation and other positive affects should follow from pursuing a hobby, meeting friends, voluntarily doing social work or further leisure time activities too.

Frone's second general category besides the role environment is personality. A differentiation should, however, be added to his systematization (see Fig. 6.1): Personality aspects often lead to more of both job-to-family conflicts as well as family-to-job conflicts, when they are individual deficits, and to more of both job-to-family facilitation as well as family-to-job facilitation, when they are individual resources. Characteristics such as mastery, self-esteem or extraversion can be considered as such individual resources. Consequently, taking oneself as being able to dealing with one's situation, having a positive and valuable image of oneself or enjoying social interaction and being talkative goes along with increasing facilitation and, consequently, a balance between life-domains. Other characteristics such as neuroticism or Type-A behavior can be taken for such individual deficits. Therefore, emotional instability with a tendency to experience negative emotional states or time urgency, impatience, and being a highly competitive stress junkie increases both kinds of life-domains conflicts (e.g., Bruck and Allen 2003; Carlson 1999; Frone 2003; Voydanoff 2004; and Wayne et al. 2004). With regard to the so-called BigFive factors in personality, Rantanen (2008) summarizes from a rare longitudinal study on antecedents and consequences of life-domains balance that "the role of Neuroticism as a risk factor, and the role of Agreeableness and Conscientiousness as resources factors for beneficial and harmful work–family interface seem most pronounced, whereas the role of Extraversion and Openness to Experience seem to be more dependable on the level of other traits they are merged with" (p. 57).

Few studies have investigated personality aspects as possible moderators, or buffers, with regard to the effects of role-environment variables or the consequences of imbalance between life-domains. Kinnunen et al. (2003) have shown that emotionally stable (i.e., low in neuroticism) "fathers were protected from negative effects of WIF on well-being at work (job exhaustion) and on general well-being (depression). In the same way, agreeable fathers were protected from negative effects of FIW on marital satisfaction"[3] (p. 1,630), for instance. Rantanen (2008) adds that both "gender and personality moderated the work-to-family conflict – psychological distress linkage simultaneously" (p. 57): There was a direct relationship and no moderation effect with men, but "women high in Neuroticism reported more psychological distress within a high work-to-family conflict experience than women low in Neuroticism who, in fact, reported low psychological distress within a high work-to-family conflict" (pp. 57–58). It seems worth noting that there were differences between women and men in occupational working hours as well as number and age of children in Rantanen's study.

Generally speaking, more individual resources should enable persons to better deal with overwhelming demands as compared to persons with less individual resources or even more individual deficits. In contrast, the latter can complicate the situation and might often make a mountain out of a molehill.

Finally, it should be mentioned that the two kinds of life-domains conflicts possibly increase each other reciprocally and both directly (e.g., Huang et al. 2004) and indirectly (e.g., Frone et al. 1997; Korabik et al. 2003). Both links are denoted in Fig. 6.1. The direct link means that job-to-family conflicts increase family-to-job conflicts or vice versa. But it also appears reasonable to assume an indirect link: We know from various studies that more conflicts from the one domain lead to worse work performance, negative work outcomes, time pressure or distress and dissatisfaction in the other domain (cf. Frone et al. 1997; Frone 2003; and Poelmans 2001). And some of these negative consequences of life-domains conflicts are shown as significant predictors of the reverse life-domains conflicts (see above). No studies have been found with regard to reciprocal effect of life-domains facilitation, yet. But there is no reason not to assume that job-to-family facilitation and family-to-job facilitation are linked with each other too, as Fig. 6.1 also denotes.

There is a wide range of possible forecasters of life-domains conflicts or life-domains facilitation considered in prior studies. But comprehensive analyzes considering them simultaneously are, nevertheless, rare. We, therefore, analyzed a data set of more than 200 Austrian dual-earner couples with young children in

---

[3]Abbreviations: "WIF" for "work interference with family" (i.e., job-to-family conflict) and "FIW" for "family interference with work" (i.e., family-to-job conflict)

consideration of conflicts between the occupation domain and the family domain.[4] First of all, we found reciprocal links between job-to-family conflicts and family-to-job conflicts. As this differentiation was not especially focused during the analyses, it is not clear whether this is a direct link or an indirect link. Nonetheless, we have seen that the job-to-family conflicts and family-to-job conflicts are interdependent and more of one goes along with more of the other. In addition, results point to the relevance of behavioral involvement and of role-related stressors and negative affects. More time spent on occupation work and higher distress at the workplace, go along with increasing job-to-family conflicts for both women and men. More time spent on family work increases family-to-job conflicts for men and higher distress at home increases family-to-job conflicts for women. In addition, the more one takes doing family work as a burden and the less sufficient one evaluates the external childcare offers, the more family-to-job conflicts increase for both women and men. The latter goes beyond pure availability of external childcare offers, which has been additionally considered in the analyzes, but refers to the fitting of such offers to the families' requirements (e.g., opening times). As a resource, sufficiency of such offers decreases family-to-job conflicts and facilitates reconciling family and occupation. It seems worth noting that the great majority of considered predictors do *not* significantly contribute to predicting life-domains conflicts in our comprehensive analyzes, such as, amongst others, the so-called BigFive personality traits.

The great majority of empirical studies and models have focused on individuals and the interaction of life-domains within a person. Partners' variables were assessed by questioning the person in focus and used as further person-related information. Fewer studies have analyzed life-domains conflicts on a dyadic level instead of the individual level. They have shown that there are so-called crossover effects with respect to life-domains conflicts between the partners of a couple (cf. Westman 2001, 2005). More life-domains conflicts of one partner can increase the life-domains conflicts of the other (e.g., Hammer et al. 1997; Westman and Etzion 2005). Hammer et al. (2003) for instance, found significant associations between both partners' job-to-family conflicts as well as between men's job-to-family conflicts and women's family-to-job conflicts for a dual-earner sample. They also conducted hierarchical regression analyzes and "in each case the ΔR^2 for spouse work–family conflict over the control variable and over one's own work–family conflict was significant ($p < .01$)" (p. 429). That means that partner's variables have effects on one's own life-domains conflicts in addition to other causes. But one identified crossover effect was contrary to their expectations, as "wives' family-to-work conflict was negatively related to their husbands' absences. Although contrary to our hypotheses, one plausible explanation is that instead of wives' family-to-work conflict predicting husbands' absences, what may

[4]Data were collected as part of the European research project Family life and professional work: Conflict and synergy ("FamWork", European Commission, Project No. SERD-2002). Further information available from www.eu-project-famwork.org. Results are presented shortly, details are available from the author on request. Outcome variables in hierarchical regression analyzes were job-to-family conflicts and family-to-job conflicts only.

actually be happening is that higher levels of family-to-work conflict for wives are the result of husbands refusing to, or not being able to, miss work to help with family demands" (Hammer et al. 2003, pp. 430–431). In addition, characteristics of the shared environment can serve as common stressors and, consequently, increase both partners' life-domains conflicts (and their family-to-job conflicts in particular as they mainly share the familial environment) simultaneously (cf. Westman 2001, 2005). Corollary, Westman and Etzion (2005) found significant associations between both partners' family-to-job conflicts with a dual-earner sample even when statistically controlling for the number of children as well as one's own job stress and family stress. Furthermore, the availability and sufficiency of external family support might serve as common resources, such as their social network, public childcare offers or financial support like the Austrian "Kinderbetreuungs-geld" (a child-related subsidy, between Euro 436 and 800 per month in 2008, depending on the overall period of receipt).

Again, we conducted respective analyzes of our data set of Austrian couples, as complete data were available from both partners of each couple. After statistically controlling for own life-domains conflicts as well as the times spent on the domain possible conflicting the other, the results do not point to crossover effects from the partners' life-domains conflicts to neither women's or men's job-to-family conflicts nor men's family-to-job conflicts. The non-identification of crossover effects to people's job-to-family conflicts simply seems reasonable as the occupation domain usually is not a shared environment of the partners. But we found a crossover effect from men's life-domains conflicts to women's family-to-job conflicts, and this holds for men's job-to-family conflicts, in particular. Increasing job-caused difficulties for the man to fulfill familial responsibilities increase the woman's difficulties in fulfilling occupational responsibilities, but not vice versa. This different finding for women and men is in line with some prior studies (e.g., Jones and Fletcher 1993; and Westman et al. 2001) and can be due to three reasons: "(a) Women experience higher levels of distress and therefore, are less resilient when facing the stress and strain of their husbands. [...] (b) Women are more empathetic to the stress of their husbands and therefore more vulnerable to crossover effects. [...] (c) Women are more vulnerable to crossover effects because of their role as providers of social support." (Westman 2005, p. 246).

Some studies examining differences between women and men indicate more job-to-family conflicts and more family-to-job conflicts with women than with men (e.g., Hammer et al. 1997; and Hill et al. 2003). For instance, Voydanoff has shown that "women [...] report higher levels of work-to-family conflict, whereas these characteristics are not related to facilitation" (2004, p. 410). Hammer et al. (2003) did not test for significance, but reanalyzing their presented means and standard deviations points to some differences between sexes with both job-to-family conflicts and family-to-job conflicts. Furthermore, it might be of interest that both sexes declared more job-to-family conflicts than family-to-work conflicts. In line with these data of Hammer and colleagues and with other studies, Kinnunen and Mauno (1998) have shown "that interference from work to family was more prevalent than interference from family to work among both sexes", but in contrast to the cited studies, "there were no gender differences in reported interference from work to family or from family to work" (pp. 167–168). It seems worthy to note that there were differences between women and men with regard to the kind of work and area of economy of this Finnish sample as "the men who participated in the study mostly worked in the factory (64% of the men) and the women either in the social and healthcare (55% of the women) or banking (27%)" (p. 164). As shown above, shift-work has been shown a cause of job-to-family conflict, the non-significance of sex differences in this study might be due to the fact that "men more often than women had non-day shift work" (p. 164).

Anyway, in his review about conflicts between the occupation domain and the family domain, Frone clearly rejects the existence, or at least the relevance, of sex differences in the extent of such conflicts as he summarizes: "Across a variety of samples [. . .], men and women report similar levels of work-to-family conflict and family-to-work conflict. Moreover, Grzywacz and Marks (2000) recently found that this lack of gender differences also extends to reports of work-to-family facilitation and family-to-work facilitation. Although some studies with large samples may report statistically significant gender differences, the absolute size of these differences is typically not large enough to be of practical importance" (Frone 2003, p. 149). He adds that even if such differences were found, they might be due to sex differences in other variables (e.g., age, family demographic characteristics) as they often disappear when controlling for the other variables.

In addition to the extent of life-domains conflicts, differences between the sexes in the relevance of certain predictors have been shown in some studies, but rather inconsistently and hardly systematically, and some other studies have rejected respective assumptions (cf. Byron 2005; and Eby et al. 2005). For instance, Bedeian et al. (1988) used a sample of fulltime-employed married persons and thereby controlled for various other influences. They did not find differences between women and in men in the extent of job-to-family conflicts. Furthermore, they did not find sex differences in their model considering occupational or role stress, parental demands, job-to-family conflicts as well as job satisfaction, marital satisfaction, and life satisfaction. From "the fact that the hypothesized model did not operate in a substantially different manner for men and women", they conclude that "future research should focus less on sex differences and more on factors mediating work–family conflict" (p. 489).

However, most studies did not examine the issue of differences between women and men (e.g., Aryee et al. 2004; Bruck and Allen 2003; Carlson 1999; Frye and Breaugh 2004, and numerous others) or only focused on either one or the other. For instance, Bayraktar and Salman (2003) focused on employed women from different occupational statuses and found "that women in better conditions (high education, profession, etc.) experienced less negative spillover" (p. 80). Brough and Kelling (2002) focused on women and found that "respondents with dependent(s) reported higher levels of inter-domain conflict, with a stronger association produced for family ⇒ work conflict" (p. 35). Also, Burke (2002) focused on women and found a significant effect of family-to-job conflicts on psychosomatic health symptoms among employed women.

With regard to the latter studies focusing on women only, it might be interesting to replicate them with men to find out whether the results hold for them too. But bearing Frone's words as well as no clear findings with regard to sex differences in mind, it might be more reasonable to set priorities on other topics in life-domains balance-related research and reviews than on sex differences. This does not mean that future research should *not* consider both sexes simultaneously, because according to Poelmans (2001), "one should by definition be suspicious of studies that do not distinguish between men and women, because they are probably ignoring the fact that the underlying mechanisms of work–family-conflicts are fundamentally different" (p. 24). In other words, we should not seek for sex differences, but we should be attentive if there are some.

6.3 And for Whom It May Concern?

We know that keeping several life domains in balance is a widespread challenge for more and more people to face (e.g., Winslow 2005). But it seems worth to mention that there is great variety in extent and complexity. The importance of domains might diverge between persons ("psychological involvement" was already discussed as a cause of life-domains conflicts above), but also more generally between situations or stages in persons' lives (e.g., Grzywacz et al. 2002; cf. Eby et al. 2005). First of all, we have to think of people who have to deal with several domains at the same time. "Every employed person is faced with the task of defining the relationship between work and family in his or her life" (Bailyn 1977, p. 1). However, traditional divisions of tasks between the partners, with one (usually male) breadwinner and one (usually female) partner caring of the family, do not raise the issue of reconciling these two domains for the persons as much as more egalitarian divisions of tasks with both partners being involved in both domains (cf. Bailyn 1977; Bailyn et al. 2001; Byron 2005; Hertz and Marshall 2001; and Waite and Nielsen 2001). In other words, taking care of several domains at the same time increases the probability of conflicts between them, much more than by focusing on either one or another life-domain. At next, families are more concerned than single persons: "If one is single, without children or dependent parents to care for, this task seems relatively easy. But even in this situation the seeming ease is somewhat deceptive. [...] The complications are generally greater, however, for working couples, where each partner must resolve this issue in a way that is congruent with the other's commitments. This joint resolution is a crucial life task for two-career families" (Bailyn 1977, p. 1). Furthermore, it seems reasonable to assume that the more important and more demanding domains are those with more time spent on. We know from various studies that occupation and family are usually the two domains with the most time spent on (e.g., Eurostat 2004; and FamWork 2005) compared to other life domains. In addition, it may be assumed that demands are higher in times of situational changes within a domain (i.e., when the priority assigned to a domain strongly increases or when a domain is newly added to a person's life situation) than when the person is somewhat experienced in dealing with a certain domain for a longer time. Beginners in a job or beginners as parents might feel more pressured as compared to colleagues or others parents, respectively. Taken together, life-domains balance might especially be a challenge for dual-earner couples with young children (cf. Hammer et al. 1997; Kinnunen and Mauno 1998; Lee and Duxbury 1998; and Roehling and Moen 2003).

Reasonably, one may assume that the members of dual-earner couples with young children are prototypes of people in the "rush hour of life" (cf. Lothaller 2008). As said above, this phenomenon and its labeling are rather new, but the underlying mechanisms are probably not that new. In the year 1977, Bailyn already described the main points of this phenomenon well and referred to life-domains balance in addition at the end: "Without some way of reducing complexity, patterns based on equal sharing may produce, particularly at certain stages of life, a serious condition of overload (cf. Rapoport and Rapoport 1976). Such a stage is likely to be reached in the late twenties or early thirties – often near the 7-year "danger" point in a marriage (Chilman 1968). Both families and work careers go through identifiable stages, which vary according to the degree of involvement they require. The difficulty at this vulnerable point in life stems from the fact that stresses in both cycles characteristically peak then: both seem to require maximum attention (Wilensky 1961; Troll 1975). Sociologically and biologically, this is the optimal time to have young children, hence family demands are maximal. It is also the time in their employee's lives when employing organizations tend to make decisions about future placement, decisions at least partially based on the degree of involvement and commitment to work demonstrated by the employee. 'I live two lives,' one male teacher in his early thirties explained; 'one is professional and one is as a family man. The two lives are neither mutually exclusive nor fully compatible. ... The main problem ... is to establish a healthy balance between the two lives in order not to sacrifice my family life now to build for a better family life in the future. The other half of the conflict is, of course, not to sacrifice my career opportunities now...' And if the wife is also working, the task of establishing a 'healthy balance' is even more complicated" (pp. 6–7). So, why do we highlight this issue nowadays if Bailyn observed similar situations more than 30 years ago? Since she was right when she argued that "all indications point to an increase in the number of dual-career couples in the future" (1977, p. 18). It might not be the phenomenon *per se* that is new, but the number of persons facing it is reasonably much higher nowadays as compared to former generations. Some data easily illustrate this proposition. First, women's participation in the labor market has increased: "Over the period 1985–1995 the male and female labor force has developed in different ways. The share of men in the labor force has been more or less constant, while the share of women has risen" (De Jong and Broekman 2003, p. 94). In this Eurostat report, the authors, furthermore, predict that "labor force participation among women aged 25–54 will continue to grow. Especially in countries currently having low female participation rates, measures will be taken in order to reconcile motherhood with paid work" (p. 16). Thereby, they clearly point to the relationship between family demands and occupation of women or, in other words, to the need for life-domains balance in this respect. Second, only small changes have been observed in the structures of households. For instance, 69.4% of all Austrian households consisted of two persons at least in 2002, compared to 74.4% in 1971 (cf. Schipfer 2003). When men's participation rate is constant and women's participation rate increases and when additionally the great majority of households consist of two or more persons, the number of dual-earner couples increases as a logical consequence. Third, more than 83% of employed mothers lived together with her partner (with only marginal differences due to the age of the children) in Austria in 2004, for instance (cf. Schipfer 2005). Fourth, several indicators point to the increased age at founding a family: The mean age of Austrian women at childbearing was 26.2 years of age in 1985 and continuously rose to 29.5 in 2004 as well as the mean age at first birth rose from 24.0 to 27.6 years (cf. Schipfer 2005). Rather, similar values were published for the European Union too, with an increase of mean age at childbearing by close on 1 year from 1991–1993 to 1997–1999 (cf. Duchene et al. 2004; and Schipfer 2005). Also, the mean age at marriage increased by about 5–28.1 years (women) and 30.3 years (men) from 1970 to 1999 in the European Union (cf. Schipfer 2003). In Austria, the median age at the first marriage has risen to 27.9 years with women and 30.6 with men in 2004 (cf. Schipfer 2005). As partnership or marriage are named as the reason for leaving the parents' home by more than half of Austrian people, it is no surprise that 76.6% of Austrian men aged 20 to 24 live with their parents and this portion goes down to 25.0% for men aged 30–34. The percentages for women are lower (60.8 and 9.6%, resp.) and this is comprehensible when bearing in mind the younger age of women at marriage (cf. Schipfer 2005; see also Perrig-Chiello 2008). Fifth, the portion of Austrian people with high education was three times higher in 2006 as compared to 1981, for instance, with a much stronger increase for women than for men (cf. Statistik Austria 2008). Taking all these data together, there is clear evidence that the "rush hour of life" and the issue of life-domains balance are major challenges nowadays in particular and more people have to face them as compared to former generations.

6.4 Conclusions

The literature review above has shown what contributes to more or less life-domains conflicts or life-domains facilitation. From a narrow view, one success factor in this respect seems to be whatever reduces conflicts between the life domains. The time spent on a domain, the psychological bond with a domain, and the felt stressors or negative affects from a domain are crucial for the extent of conflict from this domain to other domains. But over and above, success might be more than reducing conflicts but *positively influencing* and easing the situation. Resources working within a domain or from a domain for another as well as positive affects from a domain are crucial in this respect. These success factors point to a person and her/his role environment in particular. In any case, supportive measures that increase the success factors or decrease obstacles can be settled on four levels: societal level (e.g., Barkholdt 2005, proposed a lifetime account of occupational working time to flexibly deal with and thereby ease the "rush hour of life"; for reviews concerning the societal level in general, see Allen 2003; and Auer 2002), organizational level (for short reviews, see Allen 2003; Auer 2002; and Frone 2003), family or couple level (e.g., Baldock and Hadlow 2004, highlight "scheduling problems" as crucial), and individual level (e.g., Wierda-Boer et al. 2008, point to the role of adaptive strategies; for a short review, see Frone 2003). Some starting points to increase life-domains balance can be derived from the above-mentioned causes, but discussing the levels as well as reasonable measures in detail would go far beyond this article. Nevertheless, it should be mentioned that existing studies once more have a clear focus on life-domains conflicts and approaches to reducing them, but "no research has explored strategies to augment work–family facilitation" (Frone 2003, p. 156). Future psychological and sociological research on the issue of life-domains balance should focus more on this aspect in addition to life-domains conflicts to substantiate present findings, assumptions, and sometimes just speculations about possible success factors and supportive measures that can be found in literature, political discussions, and from practitioners and consultants. As can be seen in this article, there is a wide range of evidence on what contributes to more or less life-domains balance. Yet, there is still much research needed to improve some currently valid findings by differentiations into relevant details (e.g., between different kinds of occupations or of family compositions). In addition, future research about both conflicts and facilitation should include other life-domains than occupation and family too. And we strongly need more longitudinal observations of persons currently in this stage of life to know backed up by research about the long-term benefits of identified success factors and the long-term costs of identified obstacles, as well as what are the actual supportive measures to getting life-domains in balance and to easing the "rush hour of life".

This stage of life that we call the "rush hour of life" is reasonably considered as a current challenge. Anyway, it will be a future challenge too and the German Forum Demographischer Wandel des Bundespräsidenten (2006) referred to the "Generation 90" (i.e., people born between 1985 and 1995) as the next to face huge expectations from the society during their "rush hour of life". By definition, the "rush hour of life" can be mainly (but not completely, of course) described as the time in one's life to reconcile occupational demands from a new job and familial demands from a newly founded family with young children appropriately. Sometimes, one might get the impression from the literature and empirical findings, as well as from the need for discussing the issue of life-domains balance and the "rush hour of life"-phenomenon in general, that having or being a family would be a heavy burden that mainly leads to struggle, disadvantages, and abstention. For instance, Brough and Kelling (2002) conclude in their study that "dependents (children) generally decrease levels of well-being", but "the presence of a partner *per se* appeared to have little effect upon levels of inter-domain conflict" (p. 36). On the contrary, we also know that family and children can give gratifications and that the stage of life when a family is founded and maintained can be a positive one. But it might need consciousness and some active engagement. This should be somewhat easier to handle when the family is not left on its own, but when it receives external understanding and support. So, over and above, when it comes to the success factors in the role environment and the personality presented in this paper, there is a need for shifting and rethinking everywhere from the individuals' to the societal level towards more acceptance and tolerance for families with children. There is a need for structural measures (e.g., public childcare offers fitting families' requirements with regard to opening times), financial measures (e.g., child-related subsidies to overcome financial burdens from parenting instead of a full-time job), and attitude-related measures (e.g., promoting the high value of children and multichildren families for our society). This requires top-down measures to open eyes or agenda-setting like awarding prizes as well as bottom-up initiatives and everyone's own small contribution. It is not about "the others"; it is about *us*.

References

Allen S (2003) Working parents with young children: cross-national comparisons of policies and programmes in three countries. Int J Social Welf 12:261–273

Aryee S, Tan HH, Debrah YA (2004) Perceived organizational support among employed parents: The role of family-supportive work environment. Baptist University, School of Business, Hongkong

Auer M (2002) The relationship between paid work and parenthood – a comparison of structures, concepts and developments in the UK and Austria. Commun Work Fam 5(2):203–218

Bailyn L (1977) Accommodation of work to family: An analysis of couples with two careers (Working paper 905–77). MIT, Sloan School of Management, Boston

Bailyn L, Drago R, Kochan TA (2001) Integrating work and family life. A holistic approach (A report of the Sloan Work–family Policy Network). MIT, Sloan School of Management, Boston

Baldock J, Hadlow J (2004) Managing the family: Productivity, scheduling and the male veto. Social Policy Admin 38(6):706–720

Barkholdt C (2005) Ein Leben lang...Älter werdende Belegschaften und biographieorientierte Aspekte der Arbeitszeitgestaltung. Retrieved May 14, 2000, from http://www.boeckler.de/pdf/v_2005_09_05_barkholdt_text.doc

Bayraktar M, Salman M (2003) The impact of family life on work efficiency: A study of employed women from different occupational statuses in a metropolitan area in Turkey. Int J Consumer Stud 27(1):80–86

Bedeian AG, Burke BG, Moffett RG (1988) Outcomes of work–family conflict among married male and female professionals. J Manage 14(3):475–491

Bittman M, Wajcman J (2000) The rush hour: the character of leisure time and gender equity. Soc Forces 79(1):165–190

Blossfeld H-P (2008) Globalisierung, wachsende Unsicherheit und der Wandel der Arbeitsmarktsituation von Berufsanfängern in modernden Gesellschaften. Journal für Generationengerechtigkeit 8(3):21–27

Boyar SL, Maertz CP Jr, Pearson AW, Keough S (2003) Work–family conflict: A model of linkages between work and family domain variables and turnover intentions. J Manage Issues 15(2):175–190

Brough P, Kelling A (2002) Women, work & well-being: The influence of work–family and family–work conflict. NZ J Psychol 31(1):29–38

Bruck CS, Allen TD (2003) The relationship between big five personality traits, negative affectivity, type A behavior, and work–family conflict. J Vocat Behav 63:457–472

Bunk J, Reese A, Dugan A, Barnes-Farrell J (2004) Understanding work-to-family conflict among self-employed workers: Work arrangements and preferences. Summary of paper accepted for presentation at the annual conference of the American Psychological Association, Honolulu/ USA, July 2004
Burke RJ (2002) Work stress and women's health: Occupational status effects. J Bus Ethics 37:91–102
Butler AB, Gryzwacz JG, Bass BL, Linney KD (2005) Extending the demands-control model: A daily diary study of job characteristics, work–family conflict and work–family facilitation. J Occup Organ Psychol 78(2):155–169
Byron K (2005) A meta-analytic review of work–family conflict and its antecedents. J Vocat Behav 67:169–198
Carlson DS (1999) Personality and role variables as predictors of three forms of work–family conflict. J Vocat Behav 55:236–253
Chauvel L (2008) Veränderungen im Wohlfahrtsstaat: ungleiche Lebensstandards und -chancen der verschiedenen Kohorten. Journal für Generationengerechtigkeit 8(3):27–33
Chilman CS (1968) Families in development at mid-stage of the family life cycle. The Family Coordinator 172:297–310
Cizek B, Richter R (2004) Families in EU-15. Policies, challenges, and opportunities (ÖIF Materialien Heft 23). Österreichisches Institut für Familienforschung [Austrian Institute for Family Studies], Vienna
De Jong A, Broekman R (2003) National and regional trends in the labor force in the European Union 1985–2050 (Working papers and studies, Theme 3). Office for Official Publications of the European Communities, Luxembourg
Duchene J, Gabadinho A, Willems M, Wanner P (2004) Study of low fertility in the regions of the European Union: places, periods and causes (Working papers and studies, Theme 3). Office for Official Publications of the European Communities, Luxembourg
Eby LT, Casper WJ, Lockwood A, Bordeaux C, Brinley A (2005) Work and family research in IO/ OB: Content analysis and review of the literature (1980–2002). J Vocat Behav 66:124–197
Eurostat (2004) How Europeans spend their time. Everyday life of women and men (Pocket books, Theme 3). Office for Official Publications of the European, Luxembourg
FamWork (2005) Final report by the consortium of the project "Family Life and Professional work: Conflict and Synergy". Retrieved August 8, 2008, from www.eu-project-famwork.org
Fine-Davis M (2002) Fathers and mothers: Dilemmas of the work-life balance. A comparative study of 4 European countries. Retrieved November 14, 2008, from http://www.justice.ie/en/ JELR/Fathers&Mothers.pdf/Files/Fathers&Mothers.pdf
Forum Demographischer Wandel des Bundespräsidenten (2006) Familien stärken – Zukunft gewinnen. Im Blick: die "Generation '90". Retrieved November 14, 2008, from http://www. forum-demographie.de/fileadmin/user_upload/Docs/Arbeitspapier_fin.pdf
Frone MR (2003) Work–family balance. In: Quick JC, Tetrick LE (eds) Handbook of occupational health psychology. American Psychological Association, Washington, DC
Frone MR, Russell M, Cooper ML (1992) Antecedents and outcomes of work–family conflict: Testing a model of the work–family interface. J Appl Psychol 77:65–78
Frone MR, Yardley JK, Markel KS (1997) Developing and testing an integrative model of the work–family interface. J Vocat Behav 50:145–167
Frye NK, Breaugh JA (2004) Family-friendly policies, supervisor support, work–family conflict, family–work conflict, and satisfaction: A test of a conceptual model. J Bus Psychol 19(2): 197–220
Greenhaus JH, Beutell NJ (1985) Sources of conflict between work and family roles. Acad Manage Rev 10:76–88
Grosswald B (2003) Shift-work and negative work-to-family spillover. J Sociol Soc Welf 30(4): 31–58
Grzywacz JG, Butler AB (2005) The impact of job characteristics on work-to-family facilitation: Testing a theory and distinguishing a construct. J Occup Health Psychol 10(2):97–109
Grzywacz JG, Marks NF (1999) Reconceptualizing the work–family interface: An ecological perspective on the correlates of positive and negative spillover between work and family (CDE

Working Paper No. 99-03). University of Wisconsin – Madison, Center for Demography and Economy, Madison
Grzywacz JG, Marks NF (2000) Reconceptualizing the work-family interface: An ecological perspective on the correlates of positive and negative spillover between work and family. J Occup Health Psychol 5:111–126
Grzywacz JG, Almeida DM, McDonald DA (2002) Work–family spillover and daily reports of work and family stress in the adult labor force. Fam Relat 51:28–36
Guerts SAE, Kompier MAJ, Roxburgh S, Houtman ILD (2003) Does work–home interference mediate the relationship between workload and well-being? J Vocat Behav 63:532–559
Hammer LB, Allen E, Grigsby TD (1997) Work–family conflict in dual-earner couples: Within-individual and crossover effects of work and family. J Vocat Behav 50:185–203
Hammer LB, Bauer TB, Grandey AA (2003) Work–family conflict and work-related withdrawal behaviors. J Bus Psychol 17(3):419–436
Heider F (1946) Attitudes and cognitive organization. J Psychol 21:107–112
Heider F (1958) The psychology of interpersonal relation. Wiley, New York
Hertz R, Marshall NL (2001) Introduction. In: Hertz R, Marshall NL (eds) Working families: the transformation of the American Home. University of California Press, Berkeley, pp 1–20
Hill EJ (2005) Work–family facilitation and conflict, working fathers and mothers, work–family stressors and support. J Fam Issues 26(6):793–819
Hill EJ, Hawkins AJ, Ferris M, Weitzman M (2001) Finding an extra day a week: The positive influence of perceived job flexibility on work and family life balance. Fam Relat 50(1):49–58
Hill EJ, Hawkins AJ, Märtinson V, Ferris M (2003) Studying "working fathers": Comparing fathers' and mothers' work–family conflict, fit, and adaptive strategies in a global high-tech company. Fathering: J Theor Res Pract Men Fathers 1(3):239–261
Hill EJ, Märtinson V, Ferris M, Baker RZ (2004a) Beyond the mommy track: The influence of new-concept part-time work for professional women on work and family. J Fam Econ Issues 25(1):121–136
Hill EJ, Yang C, Hawkins AJ, Ferris M (2004b) A cross-cultural test of the work–family interface in 48 countries. J Marriage Fam 66(5):1300–1316
Himsel AJ, Goldberg WA (2003) Social comparisons and satisfaction with the division of housework. J Fam Issues 24(7):843–866
Huang Y-H, Hammer LB, Neal MB, Perrin NA (2004) The relationship between work-to-family conflict and family-to-work conflict: A longitudinal study. J Fam Econ Issues 25(1):79–100
Jones F, Fletcher B (1993) An empirical study of occupational stress transmission in working couples. Hum Relat 46:881–902
Kinnunen U, Mauno S (1998) Antecedents and outcomes of work–family conflict among employed women and men in Finland. Hum Relat 51(2):157–177
Kinnunen U, Vermulst A, Gerris J, Mäkikangas A (2003) Work–family conflict and its relations to well-being: the role of personality as a moderating factor. Pers Individ Dif 35:1669–1683
Klammer U (2008) Unsicherheiten und Belastungen in frühen Lebensphasen als Herausforderung für die Gestaltung einer lebenslauforientierten, nachhaltigen Sozialpolitik. Journal für Generationengerechtigkeit 8(3):8–13
Korabik K, Lero DS, Ayman R (2003) A multi-level approach to cross cultural work–family research. A micro and macro perspective. Int J Cross Cult Manage 3(3):289–303
Lee CM, Duxbury L (1998) Employed parents' support from partners, employers, and friends. J Soc Psychol 138(3):303–322
Lothaller H (2008) Die "rush hour des Lebens und" die Bedeutung der Familienarbeit und ihrer Aufteilung. Journal für Generationengerechtigkeit 8(3):4–8
Luk DM, Shaffer MA (2002) Work and family domain stressors, structure and support: Direct and indirect influences on work–family conflict (BRC Papers on Cross-Cultural Management). Baptist University, School of Business, Hongkong
Luk DM, Shaffer MA (2005) Work and family domain stressors, structure and support: Direct and indirect influences on work–family conflict. J Occup Organ Psychol 78:489–508

Market (2005) Angst vor Jobverlust steht Kinderwunsch im Wege (news Februar 05/04). Linz: market – Marktforschung. Retrieved November 2, 2008, from http://www.market.at/upload/documentbox/News_0504.pdf
Milkie MA, Peltola P (1999) Playing all the roles: Gender and the work–family balancing act. J Marriage Fam 61(2):476–490
Perrig-Chiello P (2008) Der lange Weg in die Selbstständigkeit. Journal für Generationengerechtigkeit 8(3):18–21
Poelmans S (2001) Individual and organizational issues in work–family conflict (Research paper No. 444). University of Navarra, Research Division IESE, Barcelona
Rantanen J (2008) Work–family interface and psychological well-being. A personality and longitudinal perspective (Jyväskylä Studies in Education, Psychology and Social Research). University of Jyväskylä, Jyväskyla
Rapoport R, Rapoport RN (1976) Dual-career families reexamined. London: Martin-Roberts
Roehling PV, Moen P (2003) Dual-earner couples. Retrieved November 2, 2008, from http://wfnetwork.bc.edu/encyclopedia_entry.php?id = 229&area = All
Russell G, Bowman L (2000) Work and family: Current thinking, research and practice. Commonwealth Government, Department of Family and Community Services, Canberra
Schipfer RK (2003) Familien in Zahlen. Informationen zu Familien in Österreich und der EU auf einen Blick. Vienna: Österreichisches Institut für Familienforschung [Austrian Institute for Family Studies]
Schipfer RK (2005) Familien in Zahlen. Statistische Informationen zu Familien in Österreich und der EU. Vienna: Österreichisches Institut für Familienforschung [Austrian Institute for Family Studies]
Shaw SM (1988) Gender differences in the definition and perception of household labor. Fam Relat 37:333–337
Statistik Austria (2008) Bildung in Zahlen 2006/2007: Schlüsselindikatoren und Analysen. Vienna: Statistik Austria [Statistics Austria]
Troll LE (1975) Early and middle adulthood. Monterey: Brooks/Cole
Voydanoff P (1988) Work role characteristics, family structure demands, and work/family conflict. J Marriage Fam 50(3):749–761
Voydanoff P (2004) The effects of work demands and resources on work-to-family conflict and facilitation. J Marriage Fam 66(2):398–412
Waite LJ, Nielsen M (2001) The rise of the dual-earner family, 1963–1997. In: Hertz R, Marshall NL (eds) Working families: the transformation of the American Home. University of California Press, Berkeley, pp 23–41
Wayne JH, Musisca N, Fleeson W (2004) Considering the role of personality in the work–family experience: Relationships of the big five to work–family conflict and facilitation. J Vocat Behav 64:108–130
Westman M (2001) Stress and strain crossover. Hum Relat 54(6):717–751
Westman M (2005) Cross-cultural differences in crossover research. In: Poelmans S (ed) Work and family: an international research perspective. Lawrence Erlbaum, New Jersey, pp 241–260
Westman M, Etzion D (2005) The crossover of work–family conflict from one spouse to the other. J Appl Soc Psychol 35(9):1936–1957
Westman M, Etzion D, Danon E (2001) Job insecurity and the crossover of burnout in married couples. J Organ Behav 22:467–481
Wierda-Boer H, Gerris J, Vermulst A (2008) Adaptive strategies, gender ideology, and work–family balance among Dutch dual earners. J Marriage Fam 70(4):1004–1014
Wiese BS (2004) Konflikte zwischen Beruf und Familie im Alltagserleben erwerbstätiger Paare. Zeitschrift für Sozialpsychologie 35(1):45–48
Winslow S (2005) Work–family conflict, gender, and parenthood, 1977–1997. J Fam Issues 26(6):727–755
Wilensky HL (1961) Life cycle, work situation, and participation in formal associations. In R.W. Kleemeier (Ed.) Aging and leisure. New York: Oxford

Chapter 7
Shifting Parenthood to Advanced Reproductive Ages: Trends, Causes and Consequences

Tomáš Sobotka

7.1 Introduction

In the last four decades, women and men in industrialised countries have been delaying parenthood towards ever later ages. This persistent trend, termed "postponement transition" by Kohler et al. (2002), has become characteristic for a wide range of countries with very diverse cultural, social and economic conditions. The rise of late parenthood has been enabled by the spread of modern contraception, especially the *pill*, combined with the *legalisation* of abortion; for the first time in history, young adults can enjoy a prolonged period of sexual activity without fear of unwanted pregnancy. At the same time, many social trends, including prolonged education, women's emancipation and changing family behaviour, made early parenthood increasingly unattractive. Other milestones traditionally linked with achieving adulthood, such as finishing education, leaving the parental home, and forming a couple, have been postponed towards later ages as well. However, the postponement of births receives particular attention due to the concerns about the health risks associated with it and because of the fears of persistent low birth rates that are now common in most parts of Europe and in East Asia.

The decision on the right timing of childbearing has become increasingly difficult for men and women who try to find the best way of combining their education, work career, and leisure activities with their partnership life and family plans. On the one hand, efficient contraception and the declining normative pressure for parenthood provide "freedom from children" at younger ages, when most individuals prefer to focus on non-family activities. On the other hand, the notion of biological clock and the awareness of a possible future deterioration of one's health or partnership situation provide incentives for *not* postponing parenthood until it

T. Sobotka
Vienna Institute of Demography, Austrian Academy of Sciences, Wohllebengasse 12–14, 6th floor, 1040, Vienna, Austria
e-mail: tomas.sobotka@oeaw.ac.at

J.C. Tremmel (ed.), *A Young Generation Under Pressure?*,
DOI 10.1007/978-3-642-03483-1_7, © Springer-Verlag Berlin Heidelberg 2010

gets too late for having children. This decision-making problem is further accentuated by declining compatibility of childrearing with economic aspirations, participation in education, work career, and leisure activities of young adults.

This article reviews different aspects of the shift towards later parenthood, especially focusing on the perspective of higher-educated women, who now typically become mothers in their early to mid-thirties. Although most of the issues discussed here pertain to both men and women, much of the empirical evidence explicitly focuses on women, for whom considerably more statistics and studies exist, and whose "biological clock" ticks faster. I emphasise that there is a mixture of positive as well as negative aspects of later parenthood and that the frequent negative views on childbearing postponement are exaggerated and often unwarranted.

The article is structured as follows. The shift towards later childbearing is outlined alongside an increase in childlessness and wide educational differences in fertility timing. Subsequently, I review consequences of delayed childbearing for individuals, couples, their children and society and discuss the limited role of assisted reproduction in offsetting the age-related rise in infertility. In conclusion, I outline possible policy actions that may support childbearing decisions at both younger and older reproductive ages. I argue that such policies should recognise wide heterogeneity in needs and lifestyle preferences of individuals and should not explicitly aim to encourage early parenthood. Throughout this contribution, illustrations are provided based on the research and data available for different European countries, Canada, the United States and Japan. Due to space limitations, many issues are discussed briefly and the listed references should serve for obtaining a more comprehensive picture.

7.2 The Shift Towards Later Parenthood and the Forces Contributing to It

Initiated in the early 1970s in western and northern Europe and in the most developed countries outside Europe, the trend towards later parenthood had spread to all industrialised societies by the late 1990s (Kohler et al. 2002; Sobotka 2004a). At present, women in western, northern and southern Europe as well as Japan give birth to their first child at ages 28–29 on average (Fig. 7.1). The overall mean age at childbearing for women has surpassed 30 in the majority of these countries. Fathers have also "aged" considerably and men remain on average 2–4 years older than women when having their first child (e.g., Coleman 2000; SCB 2002), in line with their later home leaving and partnership formation.

In Japan and in most parts of Europe, teenage births have become marginal, whereas the frequency of births at late reproductive ages (40+) has increased sharply since the late 1980s, bringing a reversal to the long-standing downward trend that started with the demographic transition (Prioux 2005; Sobotka et al. 2007). Among the most developed countries, the United States constitutes an important exception with an earlier first-birth pattern. This is fuelled by the

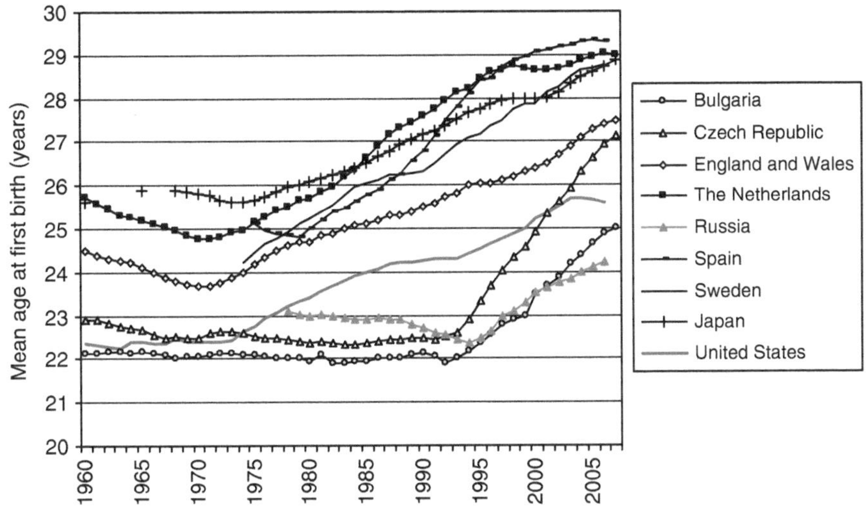

Fig. 7.1 Mean age of mother at birth of first child, selected countries of Europe, Japan and the United States (1960–2007)
Source: Computations based on Eurostat (2008 and 2009), Council of Europe (2006), Smallwood (2002), Zakharov (2008) and national statistical data

relatively high rates of teenage motherhood and an early childbearing typical of the lower-educated women (e.g., McLanahan 2004), blacks and people of Hispanic origin (for women, see Mathews and Hamilton 2002). Although many post-communist countries of Europe have experienced a pronounced shift towards later timing of parenthood after the political regime change around 1990, women in eastern and south-eastern Europe still bear their first child at younger ages (typically at ages 24–26) than their counterparts in other parts of Europe. Despite the long record of delayed childbearing in "Western" countries, there is still scope for a further shift towards later parenthood when biological limits to reproduction are considered (Goldstein 2006): most women can fulfil a typical desire for a two-child family even when they have a first child after age 30.

Many interrelated social, economic, cultural and lifestyle changes have been identified as the driving forces of delayed parenthood. Among them, the expansion of high education, especially among women, is the most important factor, contributing approximately one half to the observed rise in the age at first birth (Beets et al. 2001). Given the general perception of an incompatibility between studying and having children, later age at school-leaving directly translates into delayed parenthood (Blossfeld and Huinink 1991).

A plethora of other factors contributing to later timing of parenthood have been identified (e.g., Rindfuss et al. 1988; Gustafsson 2001; Meron and Widmer 2002; Kohler et al. 2002; Sobotka 2004a; and Billari et al. 2006). The relative decline in the economic position of young adults and the rise of temporary jobs, combined in many countries with high youth unemployment, lead to parenthood postponement (e.g., Mills and Blossfeld 2005; Adsera 2005). Traditionally, labour market prospects were most important for men, for whom achieving a relative financial security is a key precondition for their marriage and parenthood readiness (e.g., May 1982). "Women's liberation" from domesticity and economic dependence on their husbands, partly achieved through the expansion of high education, widened their life horizons and made long-term labour participation an expected and essential part of their biographies (Goldin 2006). Consequently, the possibilities for combining career and parenthood became paramount for women's childbearing decisions. Paradoxically and unlike for men, improvements of women's labour market prospects may stimulate further postponement of first birth (e.g., de Cooman et al. 1987), especially when they have high education. Furthermore, women with longer employment may achieve more secure work position and suffer lower "motherhood penalty" (i.e. income or career prospects lost due to motherhood) when having children later in life (Joshi 2002; Miller 2008; see also Sect. 7.5).

The spread of the contraceptive pill constitutes major technical innovation preventing unwanted pregnancies among younger women and it has become instrumental for most couples planning (and postponing) marriage and parenthood (Santow and Bracher 2001; Goldin and Katz 2002). Also, norms and values related to partnership and family life have changed rapidly and led to the spread of cohabitation and less stable forms of partnerships, acceptance of non-marital sex and a decline of the normative pressure for childbearing (e.g., Lesthaeghe 1995). Parenthood gradually ceases to be the main and universal goal in the lives of men and women, and is no longer considered a precondition for achieving happiness and self-fulfilment (e.g., van de Kaa 2004; Sobotka 2008). In addition, more childless people become uncertain whether they want to have children (e.g., Sobotka and Testa 2008). Consequently, the option of having children starts competing with other activities available for self-realisation, including leisure and consumer activities, which become legitimate reasons to delay or forego childbearing (Presser 2001). Nomaguchi (2006) found that Japanese married women who spent more time pursuing leisure activities became mothers 2 years later than other women. Similarly, persons with "modern" family orientation (i.e. with more individualistic, more tolerant and less family-centred attitudes) were found to prefer later timing of childbearing (Erfani and Beaujot 2006). The motivation for parenthood has changed profoundly: Having children has become a carefully planned decision of the couple, who considers various potential positive and negative effects of parenthood on their relationship, lifestyle, and economic wellbeing (see Liefbroer 2005). In this context, partnership instability and the disagreement between partners may further delay couples' childbearing.

7.3 Highly Educated Lead the Shift to Late Parenthood

Different factors driving the trends to delayed parenthood, highlighted in Sect. 7.2, are most pertinent for the group of highly educated women, for whom the competition between parenthood and other life choices is most intense (therefore, this

Table 7.1 Mean age at first birth among women by the highest achieved level of education, Czech Republic (1991 and 2001) and Norway (1980, 1990 and 1998)

Czech Republic	Year		Difference	
Highest achieved education	1991	2001	1991–2001	
Primary	20.8	21.6	0.8	
Lower secondary	21.4	24.9	3.5	
Higher secondary	23.6	28.0	4.4	
Tertiary	25.9	29.8	3.9	
Norway		Year		Difference
Highest achieved education	1980	1990	1998	1980–1998
Primary and lower secondary	23.3	23.9	24.0	0.7
Upper secondary	24.0	25.3	26.4	2.4
University, first stage	26.5	28.1	29.5	3.0
University, second stage	28.5	30.0	31.6	3.1

Source: Lappegård and Rønsen (2005) for Norway, Sobotka et al. (2008a) for the Czech Republic

section focuses mostly on women). As a result, women with university education not only postpone motherhood due to their long study period, but after completing studies they wait longer than other women before having a child. Consequently, a growing social status differentiation in the timing of parenthood has taken place among both men and women (Ravanera and Rajulton 2004). Women with tertiary education have frequently shifted birth of their first child after the age of 30, whereas women with low qualification usually give birth to their first child at an early age, often as teenagers (Beets et al. 2001; McLanahan 2004). This rising heterogeneity in first-birth timing is illustrated in Table 7.1 on an example of the Czech Republic and Norway. In both countries, the shrinking group of the lowest-educated women has hardly shown any signs of birth postponement, while the highly educated women displayed the most pronounced shift in their age at motherhood. These differences reflect, in part, different lifestyle preferences and views about ideal timing of childbearing. A recent survey in Austria has shown that the opinions about the best age for a woman to become mother are patterned by education, with low-educated women suggesting a mean age of 25 and women with tertiary education suggesting a mean of 28.5 years (own computations based on the Generation and Gender Programme survey 2008).

The rise of social status heterogeneity in first-birth timing has been most pronounced in the countries with "liberal" welfare regime (Esping-Andersen 1999) that are characterised by larger social disparities – England and Wales, Ireland and, outside Europe, in the United States (Sobotka 2004a: Table 3.5). McLanahan (2004) argues that the divergence in partnership, family, and work trajectories of low-educated and highly educated persons is linked to an increasingly disadvantaged economic position of the former group. Lochhead (2005: Fig. 7.3) provides a support to this argument, showing that income differences in Canada by mother's age at first birth have become pronounced between 1971 and 1996. Alternatively, highly educated persons may be more efficient life planners and contraceptive users, better able to delay their parenthood plans and subsequently to realise them (Neiss et al. 2002).

The contrasts in family trajectories by social status lend a nuanced perspective to the notion of the "rush hour" of life. In the 1970s and the 1980s, the "rush hour" in industrialised countries was still concentrated at young adult ages, with a very high density of major life events (leaving parental home, school graduation, marriage, first birth, and acquiring employment) occurring between ages 20 and 30 (Rindfuss 1991). At present, such a concentration of major events at young adult years remains typical for the low-educated segments of population (and some immigrant groups), who often experience complex and non-standard partnership, employment and family trajectories. For the group of higher-educated men and women, the "rush hour" has increasingly moved into their thirties.

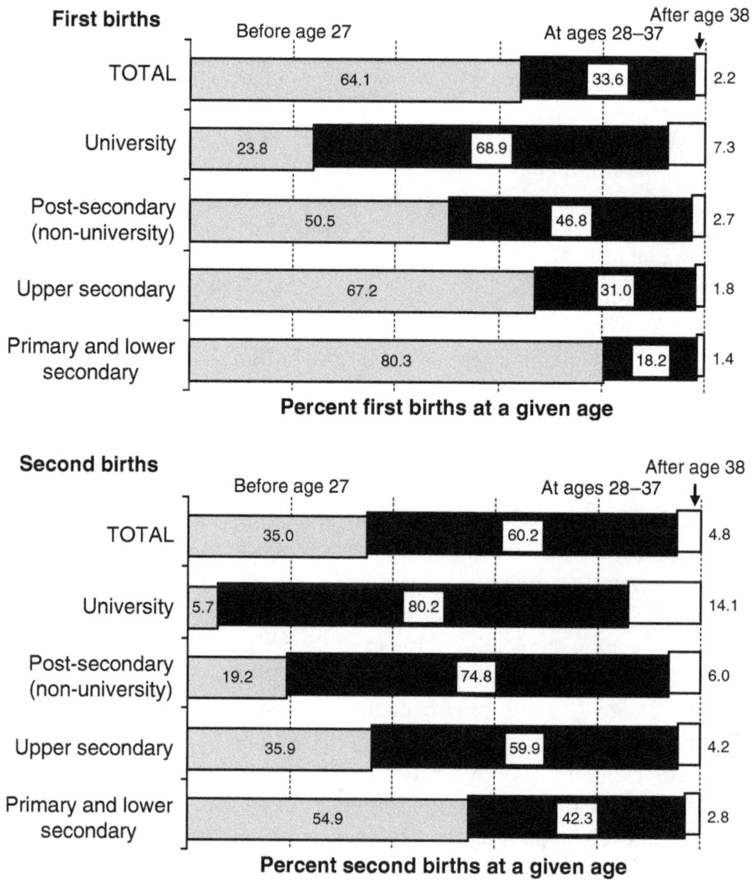

Fig. 7.2 Distribution of first and second births among women born in 1960 by age and highest education attainment, Denmark (native women only, in percent)
Source: Own computations based on the birth registry data provided by the Statistics Denmark.
Notes: Highest educational attainment is measured as of January 1, 2004. Data include only mothers and children born in Denmark. Births are observed only until age 43 (through January 1, 2004) and a very small portion of births (below 0.2%) occurring at very high reproductive ages is not included

This can be illustrated by the differences in the age distribution of first births by the highest-achieved education of mothers. Figure 7.2, looking at native Danish women born in 1960, shows that only the group of university-educated women most frequently gave birth to their first child in the age bracket of 28–37, taken somewhat arbitrarily for a delineation of the "rush hour" phase. In contrast, relatively few women with primary and lower-secondary education (one-fifth) had their first child after age 28. Arguably, the phase of *childrearing* rather than the time of entering parenthood is more important for the definition of the "rush hour". Consequently, the timing of the second birth can reveal more about the time associated with most demanding family obligations. This view increases the relevance of the "rush hour" at ages 28–37 for all educational groups: Four-fifths of the university-educated women gave birth to their second child at that stage (and 14% after age 37) and only in the lowest-educated category the majority of second births took place before age 28. In addition, younger cohorts have further shifted childbearing towards later ages.

7.4 Childlessness and Family Size Among the Highly Educated

The most obvious consequence of delayed parenthood is a rapid rise of childlessness at ages below 35 (e.g., Kneale and Joshi 2008) and a rising risk for many couples that due to biological and health constraints they will *not* be able to achieve their intended family size. The rise of childlessness has been most pronounced among the highly educated women. In the Netherlands, nine out of ten women with high level of education born in 1965–1974 remained childless by age 28, a sharp increase from about one-half in the 1940–1949 cohorts (de Graaf 2008: 20, Fig. 12). Most of these women will eventually have a child, as higher-educated usually display high rates of having second and third child in their mid- to late thirties and the early forties (e.g., Rendall and Smallwood 2003), but many will also remain permanently childless (see below).

Due to instability of childbearing plans over time and the lack of large-scale surveys tracing women's and men's plans and behaviours across their life course it is difficult to estimate how many people are not able to realise their childbearing aspirations due to postponing childbearing for too long. Different models show that this effect is not marginal: Toulemon's (2004: Table 7.1) simulation suggests that if French women born in 1950 would postpone the birth of their first child by 4 years, from 24 to 28 years on average, their childlessness would increase by almost 4% in absolute terms, from 9.7 to 13.3%. Comparable estimates were derived by a simulation of Leridon and Slama (2008: Table IV), who found that postponing a mean age of first pregnancy attempt by 6 years, from 25 to 31 years, would increase childlessness rate by 6% points. In most countries, highly educated women have the highest permanent childlessness (Nordic countries constitute an exception, see Andersson et al. 2009), but involuntary childlessness caused by "waiting for too long" to have a child usually does *not* appear to be the main reason. Childlessness by choice, partly driven by lower family orientation and the broader availability of alternative options for self-realisation, is often more prominent. However, a distinction between "voluntary" and "involuntary" childlessness remains fuzzy and ambiguous, as some reasons for childlessness (such as the perceived lack of a suitable partner or an inability to combine work career and childrearing) can be, depending on the perspective used, categorised as both voluntary and involuntary. Having these limitations in mind, de Graaf's (2008: 20, Fig. 12) analysis of Dutch women aged 35–44 expecting to remain childless sheds some light on this issue. More than one-half (55%) of these women declared being "voluntarily" childless, whereas only 5% declared they are (involuntarily) infertile after illness, accident or operation and for 7% it would be irresponsible to plan having a child due to their sickness or handicap. These latter two groups comprise many women, who had postponed motherhood until the time they became ill or infertile. Furthermore, 9% declared they have "always" been infertile.

Differently from women, childlessness among men is especially high among lower-educated (e.g., Toulemon and Lapierre-Adamcyk 2000; Coleman 2000; and SCB 2002). This apparent paradox can be explained not only by a higher risk of infertility with age for women and a high "price" paid for parenthood by the highly educated women, but also by the fact that for men, lower social status often means an exclusion from the partnership market (Toulemon and Lapierre-Adamcyk 2000).

Childlessness is only partly linked to the level of education and the timing of its completion: Hoem et al. (2006) show vast differences in childlessness by field of education among women in Sweden. This finding is corroborated by the data for Germany, which has the highest childlessness in Europe and also pronounced differences by education. Final childlessness among West German women with tertiary education is estimated at 30% for those born in 1965 – roughly double the childlessness among women with higher secondary degree from *Realschulen* (Schmitt and Wagner 2006, see Table 7.2). However, there are vast differences between women with tertiary education: those who graduated from the University of Applied Science (*Fachhoschule*, usually more practically oriented) have way lower childlessness (20%) than the women with a diploma from the university (34.5%, see Table 7.2). Migrant women that had studied abroad as well as East German women with tertiary education have particularly low childlessness.

Table 7.2 Estimated childlessness in Germany among women born in 1965 by their highest achieved level of education

	Percent childless
Lower secondary education (*Hauptschule*)	15.5
Secondary education (*Realschule*)	13.4
Tertiary education:	
West Germany: University of Applied Science (*Fachhochschule*)	20.0
West Germany: University (*Universität & Technische Hochschule*)	34.5
East Germany	7.1
Tertiary education abroad (immigrants)	9.1

Source: Schmitt and Wagner (2006): 314, computations based on German Socio-Economic Panel Study

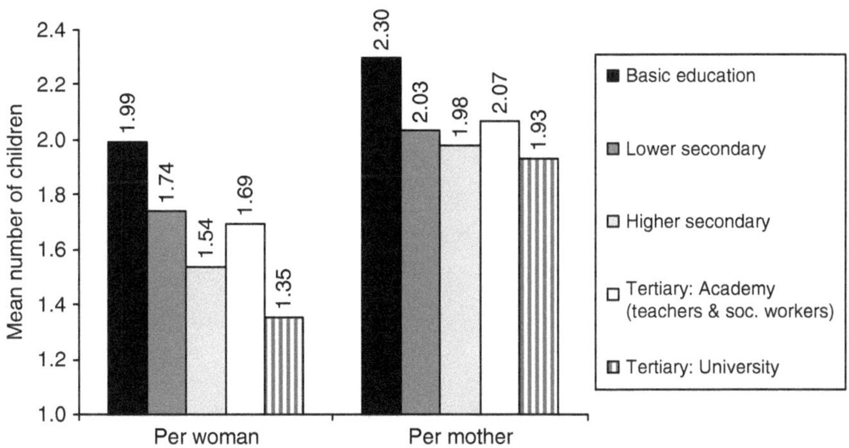

Fig. 7.3 Mean number of children per woman and per mother in Austria, women born in 1955–1960
Source: Own computations based on the 2001 Census data (Statistics Austria 2005)

These data, together with the higher frequency of voluntary childlessness in Western Germany (and also in the neighbouring Austria, see Sobotka and Testa 2008), suggest that voluntary childlessness together with institutional obstacles to the combination of work and family life are more important determinants of childlessness than the excessive postponement of motherhood. It is not by coincidence that many countries with insufficient institutional support to work and family combination and with policies favouring a prolonged work interruption among mothers have particularly high childlessness among the most educated women.

Among women who became mothers, educational differences in family size are usually small; therefore, high share of permanently childless frequently explains why highly educated women have, on average, lower number of children. Data for Austrian women born in 1955–1960 nicely illustrate this (Fig. 7.3). University-educated mothers have more than 1.9 children on average, very close to mothers with a lower degree, except those with basic education only. Due to their high childlessness, however, when all women with university education are considered, they have way lower number of children (1.35 on average) than other education categories, which range from 1.54 (women with higher secondary schooling) to 1.99 (women with basic education only).

7.5 Consequences of the Shift to a Late Childbearing Pattern for Individuals and Couples

Section 7.4 has indicated that the main reasons for high childlessness and smaller number of children among the highly educated women are not linked to their late childbearing pattern. However, evidence at hand indicates that by postponing

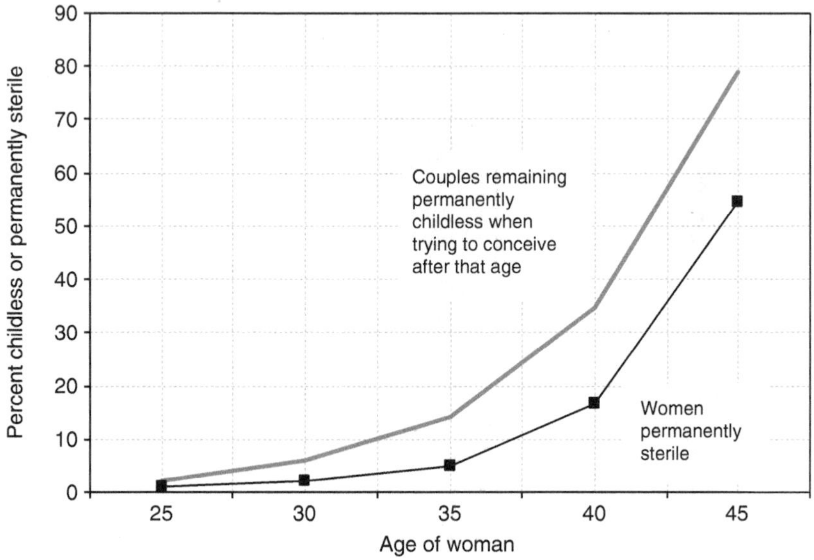

Fig. 7.4 Estimated percentage of women who are permanently sterile and of couples remaining childless at age 50 when trying to conceive after a given age
Source: Adopted from Leridon (2008: Tables 7.1 and 7.2)

childbearing until their thirties, highly educated women *risk* more than other groups being unable to reach their reproductive goals. Infertility starts rising markedly after age 35 and then accelerates after age 40. Leridon's (2008) recent estimates of permanent childlessness illustrate this well (see Fig. 7.4): at age 40, 17% of women are estimated to be permanently sterile (unable to conceive) and 35% of women would not eventually be able to have a child when starting their pregnancy attempts at that age; at age 45, permanent childlessness reaches 78%. Men's reproductive capacity declines slower with age (Kühnert and Nieschlag 2004); men are, nevertheless, often "responsible" for couple's inability to conceive. At age 55–59 men's fecundity declines by a half when compared with age 30–34 (de la Rochebrochard 2001).

For women, ages 36–42 may be thought of as a critical window for their last pregnancy attempts, when their biological clock ticks particularly fast. Data on childbearing intentions of Austrian women that are close to this critical window show that many of them still desire to have a child in the future. According to the 2001 Microcensus survey, around 8% of all women and some 18% of the tertiary educated women aged 36–40 wished to have a child (Sobotka 2009). By that age, tertiary-educated women had given birth to 1.47 children on an average and still desired to have additional 0.36 children. More recently, an Austrian GGP survey conducted in 2008 showed yet higher fraction of respondents aged 35 and older who planned to have a child. Including somewhat uncertain answers ("probably yes"), 17% of women aged 35–39 and 6% aged 40–45 intended to have a child within the next 3 years; the corresponding figures for men were as high as 28% at age 35–39 and 17% at ages 40–45 (Fig. 7.5).

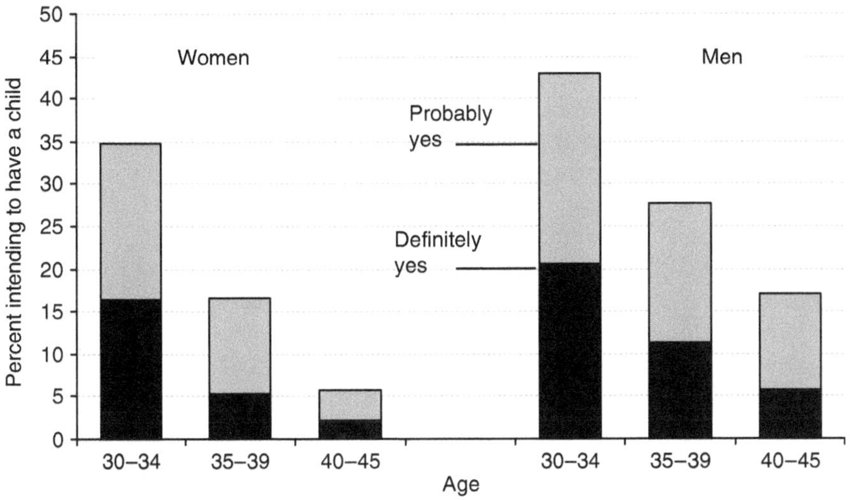

Fig. 7.5 Percent women and men who intend to have a child within the next 3 years, by age, Austria 2008
Source: Own computations from the 2008 Generation and Gender Programme survey in Austria (unweighted data)

Many of the women planning to have a child during the critical window of rapidly rising infertility will be unable to conceive or to carry pregnancy to term. This is likely to lead to a sustained rise in the demand for assisted reproduction, which remains, however, quite ineffective for women above age 40 (see Sect. 7.8 below). Psychological consequences of permanent sterility are most serious for women who are childless (Gilbert et al. 1999). As a huge body of medical literature shows, late pregnancies are associated with a rapidly increasing risk of miscarriage, higher risk of pregnancy complications and negative health outcomes for the mother, and also with an elevated risk of stillbirths, premature births and foetus malformations, such as Down Syndrome (ESHRE 2005; Heffner 2004). Some of these negative outcomes can be reduced or prevented by an extensive use of prenatal screening and selective abortion. However, motherhood at age above 35 has not been consistently found to pose long-term health risks for the mothers: while Alonzo (2002) suggests that delaying childbearing may increase the risk of cardiovascular disease, diabetes and hypertension, Spence (2008) finds no evidence of late motherhood leading to deteriorating physical health later in life (however, she detected an association with more frequent depression). Mirowsky (2005) concluded that women having first child in their early thirties subsequently display better health conditions than the younger first-time mothers. In addition, late childbearing (after age 35 or 40) has been associated with longevity among both men and women, although the effects for women are stronger (e.g., Doblhammer 2000; Yi and Vaupel 2004); this association may be influenced by selection as more healthy women are able to become mothers at higher ages.

Men's age may also negatively influence reproductive outcomes. After age 40, fathers face an increased risk of genetic abnormalities in their children (de la Rochebrochard et al. 2003; Kühnert and Nieschlag 2004). Sperm quality among healthy men deteriorates continuously from their twenties, without any evidence of an age threshold (Eskenazi et al. 2003). De la Rochebrochard and Thonneau (2002) found that women pregnant with men above age 40 have substantially higher likelihood of miscarriage and the combined effects of woman's and man's higher age produced particularly high risk. However, a large study recently conducted by Chen et al. (2008) did not find any link between parental age over 40 and adverse birth outcomes (such as low birth weight, neonatal mortality, etc.).

While medical literature frequently warns about the risks of late childbearing, late parenthood has a number of generally *positive* effects and consequences. Most children born to "older" couples are strongly desired and born into a stable family environment. Men becoming fathers after age 30 become more involved with their children and express more positive feeling about fatherhood than younger fathers (Cooney et al. 1993). Garrison et al. (2007) found that couples having their first child after age 35 were more satisfied with their marital life, experienced less parenting stress, and reported better family functioning. Few older mothers are living without a partner at the time of birth. In England and Wales, for instance, the likelihood that a woman would give birth as a single mother (without father being registered) or with a father living at a different address declines rapidly with age until about age 30, especially among young adult women. More than one-half of all teenage mothers are lone mothers or do not live with the father of their child at the time the child is born and this share steadily declines to 28% at age 20–24 and to 7% for mothers aged 30 and above (Fig. 7.6, left panel). Conversely, the proportion of women married at the time of birth increases fast until about age 30. Partnerships

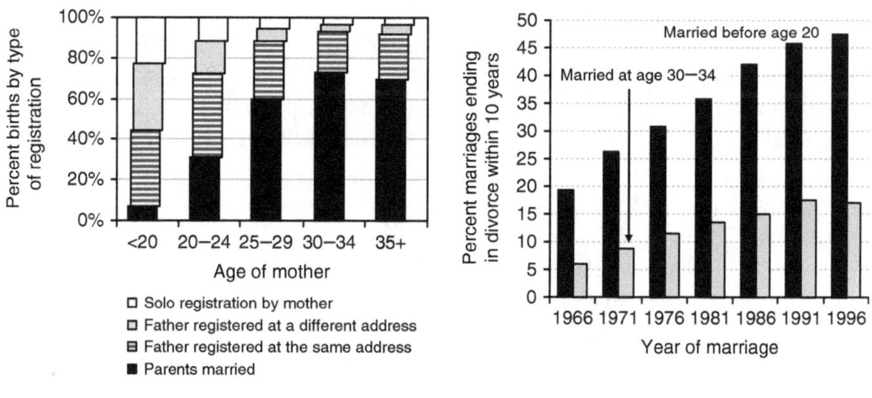

Fig. 7.6 *Left panel*: Distribution of births by age of mother and whether father was registered and resided with the mother, England and Wales 2006. *Right panel*: Cumulative percentages of first marriages ending in divorce within 10 years by age of woman at marriage and by year of marriage, England and Wales
Sources: Left panel: ONS 2007, Tables 3.6, 3.8, and 3.10. *Right panel*: Wilson and Smallwood 2008: 31, Table 7.1

and marriages are considerably more stable among couples in their late twenties and thirties than among the younger couples, reducing the risk that children will experience family disruption that has become common in the majority of developed countries (e.g., Heuveline et al. 2003). To illustrate this, consider the vast differences in the likelihood of divorce within 10 years after the marriage. In England and Wales, almost one-half (48%) of those marrying first as teenagers in 1996 divorced within 10 years, whereas only 17% of the women first-marrying at age 30–34 got divorced in a 10-year period (Wilson and Smallwood 2008, see right panel of Fig. 7.6). Cohabiting unions have even higher dissolution rates than marriages.

Late parenthood is also associated with economic and career advantages that go beyond the simple effect of longer time to accumulate material resources (savings, housing, cars, consumer goods) before having a child, which is a common motive for birth postponement (e.g., Kravdal 1994). *Economic literature* usually finds that postponing childbearing is favourable from a perspective of rational, "utility-maximising" couples (e.g., Gustafsson 2001); Happel et al. (1984: 305) suggest that such couples should delay childbearing to biological limits, when man's earnings become relatively high. Joshi (2002) analysed life-time earning profile of different categories of women in the United Kingdom and concluded that birth postponement could reduce income loss associated with motherhood, particularly among women with university degree. Similar results were obtained for Canada by Drolet (2002) and for the United States by Miller (2008), who found a *significant increase* in women's earnings associated with each year of birth postponement (women having first birth until age 33 were studied); especially college-educated women benefited from delaying births. Taniguchi (1999) concluded that women becoming mothers after age 27 suffer *lower* wage penalty due to cumulated skills and work experience.

7.6 Consequences of Late Parenthood for Children and Intergenerational Links

Later parenthood affects children, their interaction with parents and wider family relations. The impact varies for children at different life stages, which often makes different studies incomparable. However, while much research has been conducted on the possible negative influences on children of early parenthood, studies on children of older parents remain less frequent.

Studying Canadian children aged up to 5 years, Bushnik and Garner (2008) did *not* find an association of late motherhood with behavioural, cognitive or physical outcomes of children after controlling for socio-economic status of mothers and birth-related risk factors. Among many factors investigated, negative link between first motherhood after age 35 and child's development has been detected only with respect to motor and social development below age 3 and lower behavioural scores at ages 4–5. Pollock (1996) reported that at age 10, first-born children to mothers older than 30 scored significantly *higher* in various intellectual tests than first-born children of younger mothers and did not show any distinctive health outcomes. Fergusson and Woodward (1999) investigated educational and psychological outcomes at age 18 of children born to mothers over age 30 and reported that late maternal age was related to more positive outcomes for adolescent children, such as better educational achievement, lower crime rate, lower drug abuse, and fewer mental health problems. They suggested that this finding can be most of all explained by better parenting practices and family functioning, including higher family stability, in the families of older mothers (see also above). Interestingly, the effect of father's age on child health and cognitive outcomes may be more pronounced due to higher risk with age of mutations in sperm cells (Kühnert and Nieschlag 2004). A recent study by Saha et al. (2009) reported that parental age has a negative effect on a range of measures of neurocognitive performance (such as concentration, memory, learning, understanding, and reading, but also motor skills) until the age of 7 years, while, remarkably, higher maternal age had an opposite affect and was linked to a superior performance of children on all the six tested measures. Late paternal age has also been linked to long-term health outcomes such as higher risk of schizophrenia, autism, dyslexia, and Alzheimer disease (see references in Saha et al. 2009).

Late parenthood may also affect intergeneration relations. As the generation length (i.e. time span between generations) increases, parents and grandparents are more likely to have difficulties communicating with their children and grandchildren and share common values, ideas and interests. Older parents are less likely to survive until the time their children reach adulthood, marry or will have their own children; they also have higher likelihood of suffering health problems at a time when they are still caring about their teenage children. The risk of not surviving to see their own grandchildren is much higher for men, who have, at any age, *higher* mortality than women and are, on average, by about 3 years older when having children. For instance, given the current mortality levels, a woman having the first child at age 35 faces a 2% risk of not surviving until her child reaches adulthood and a 9% risk of not seeing her grandchildren, provided that her child will also become parent at age 35 (these estimates are based on contemporary mortality levels in Spain, see Table 7.3). These risks are roughly *double* the risks faced by a woman who has the first child at age 25. For men, the risks are much higher: 6% fathers having a child at age 38 (allowing for later average age at fatherhood) would not survive until their child reaches adulthood and 27% would not live to see their grandchildren, provided that their child becomes parent at age 35. However, at the same time, mortality has been declining continually in most of the developed world and the overall chances of not surviving to see own children becoming adults or having grandchildren have declined over time as life expectancy has usually increased faster than the mean age at parenthood. Moreover, given higher partnership stability among older couples (Sect. 7.5 above), their children are more likely to grow up with both of their biological parents, which gives them a great advantage in terms of emotional and material support and successful socialisation. Finally, later parenthood may lead to a better availability of childcare help by grandparents: at a time when most women remain in employment until their late fifties or early

Table 7.3 Estimated probabilities of dying before own child reaches adulthood and before having grandchildren; a comparison of early and late childbearing patterns (estimates based on mortality data for Spain in 2006)

	Women (%)		Men (%)	
	Birth at age 25	Birth at age 35	Birth at age 28	Birth at age 38
Not surviving until the child's 18th birthday	0.9	2.1	2.5	6.0
Not surviving to see own grandchildren				
– When their child becomes parent at age 25	1.8	3.9	5.2	12.0
– When their child becomes parent at age 35	4.2	9.2	12.8	27.1

Source: Own computations based on Spanish life tables in the human mortality database (http://www.mortality.org, accessed 3 May 2009)

sixties, more of them will retire and become available to help with childcare when their daughters or sons become parents at age 30 and above.

7.7 Societal-Level Consequences of Delayed Childbearing

On an aggregate level, a shift to a later timing of childbearing depresses birth rates and may generate distinct baby busts, bringing a temporary decline in the number of births, even if the number of children that women have over their life course does not change. One can also think of this effect in terms of an expansion of an interval between generations during which fewer births fall into each calendar year. In the past decade, demographers have extensively debated the importance of this so-called *tempo effect* for fertility measurement and for explaining extreme low fertility rates that were recorded in many countries of Europe (note that the term "fertility rates" is used here, following demographic conventions, to denote childbearing rates among women of reproductive age). By the year 2002, the most common indicator of period fertility, the total fertility rate (TFR), fell below the "lowest-low" level of 1.3 (Kohler et al. 2002) in 16 out of 39 European countries with more than 100 thousand inhabitants, representing 56% of Europe's population (Frejka and Sobotka 2008). This is way below the fertility rate of 2.08, needed to keep the population stable in the absence of migration. Since then, the TFR has increased in all parts of Europe, but this was largely a consequence of slowing down in the increase of the mean age at childbearing (i.e. declining tempo effect) rather than a real rise in fertility rates (Sobotka and Lutz 2009; Goldstein et al. 2009). This is generally a welcome trend; however, it creates a minor baby boom that may put a strain on childcare and school institutions, downscaled during the prolonged baby bust period.

While it is clear that a number of European countries have very low fertility levels irrespective of the negative impact of the tempo effect, without shifting age at

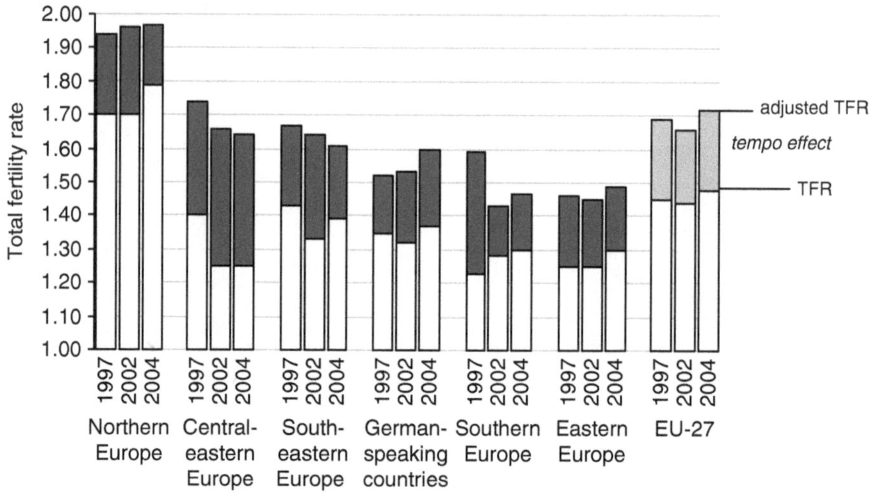

Fig. 7.7 Total fertility rate, observed (TFR) and in the absence of changing age at motherhood (adjusted TFR), major European regions 1997–2004
Source: VID 2008. *Notes*: Years shown in the graph refer the following periods: 1997 to 1995–2000, 2002 to 2001–2003, 2004 to 2003–2005. Adjusted TFR computed with the method by Bongaarts and Feeney (1998). See more details at http://www.oeaw.ac.at/vid/datasheet/box2.shtml

childbearing fertility rates would be considerably higher in most parts of Europe (e.g. Bongaarts 2002; Kohler et al. 2002; and Sobotka 2004b). Estimates produced by the Vienna Institute of Demography (VID 2008) show that in the absence of the ongoing increase in age at childbearing the TFR for the European Union in 2003–2005 would reach 1.72 instead of the observed value of 1.48. This effect was most pronounced in Central and Eastern Europe, where the observed TFR was as low as 1.25, whereas the estimated TFR in the absence of the tempo effect was substantially higher, 1.64 (Fig. 7.7, tempo effect was estimated using an adjustment proposed by Bongaarts and Feeney in 1998).

Besides the temporary effect of motherhood postponement on the number of births and fertility rates, delayed childbearing also leads to permanently lower fertility rates due to rising infertility at higher ages, which prevents some women from achieving their desired number of children (see also Sect. 7.5 above). The magnitude of this effect is difficult to estimate. Kohler et al. (2002) estimated that 1 year of delay of the mean age at first birth reduced the completed fertility of women in different European countries by 1.6–5.1% (for other estimates, comparable in magnitude, see Leridon and Slama 2008; Billari and Borgoni 2005). Noticeably, this effect was smaller for younger cohorts that experienced motherhood later in life. This is not a small effect, but a comparative analysis suggests that delayed childbearing has, so far, played a minor role in the observed shift to low fertility levels and that other factors are responsible for very low fertility experienced especially in southern Europe, eastern Europe, and German-speaking countries (e.g. Billari and Kohler 2004; Frejka and Sobotka 2008). Some of the countries that have reached the highest ages at first motherhood, including France, Norway, and Sweden, also record relatively stable fertility rates, which remain the highest in Europe.

The shift of childbearing to higher reproductive ages indicates that there will be a sustained increase in the demand for infertility treatment (see below) and, possibly, also for more reliable tests of ovarian reserve that can identify women with reduced reproductive lifespan (Broekmans et al. 2007). Later childbearing also implies rising need of specialised counselling to pregnant women, more extensive monitoring of pregnancy complications and, potentially, a threat of worsening of some aggregate health-related indicators of births (e.g. stillbirth rate, low birth weight rate, and pre-term delivery rate).

7.8 Is Assisted Reproduction a Solution to Infertility Due to Postponement?

Medical treatment of infertility might be perceived as a potential solution for women who have postponed childbearing until the age when they face infertility. The use of assisted reproduction technology (ART), which involves surgical removal of woman's oocytes ("eggs"), has been increasing rapidly in developed countries. At present, between 1 and 4% of children born in different European countries are conceived through ART (Nyboe Andersen et al. 2007). In countries where these methods are most widespread, ART has a small but rising impact on fertility rates (Sobotka et al. 2008b; Leridon and Slama 2008). Some contributions on the ongoing "reproductive revolution" envision that advances in assisted reproduction might solve the problem of women's "biological clock" in the foreseeable future by allowing them to store their oocytes at a younger age and use them later in an in vitro fertilisation once they are ready to become mothers (Nowak 2007).

These expectations might be overblown, however. With the present knowledge and technology assisted reproduction remains an ineffective method to cope with infertility caused by childbearing postponement. For each cycle initiated with the use of woman's own oocytes, success rates, as measured by the chances of achieving a live birth ("take-home-baby rate") decline steadily from about age 32. Pregnancy rates and live birth rates are particularly low for women aged 40 and older: In the United States, where ART industry is very competitive, only 23% of cycles using fresh non-donor eggs result in pregnancy at age 40 and 16% result in live birth (CDC 2007; data refer to 2005). At age 42, live birth rate declines below 10% (Fig. 7.8) and this figure might be even lower in Europe (Gleicher et al. 2006). Given that these women have little time left to try many repeated ART cycles, the overall chances of getting pregnant through assisted reproduction are rather low. Leridon's (2004) simulations estimated that after the age of 40, only a small percentage of women experiencing infertility can achieve pregnancy and live birth through ART as compared to the scenario of *no ART use*. Consequently, costs of treatment per one ART child born are very high after age 40: In Australia,

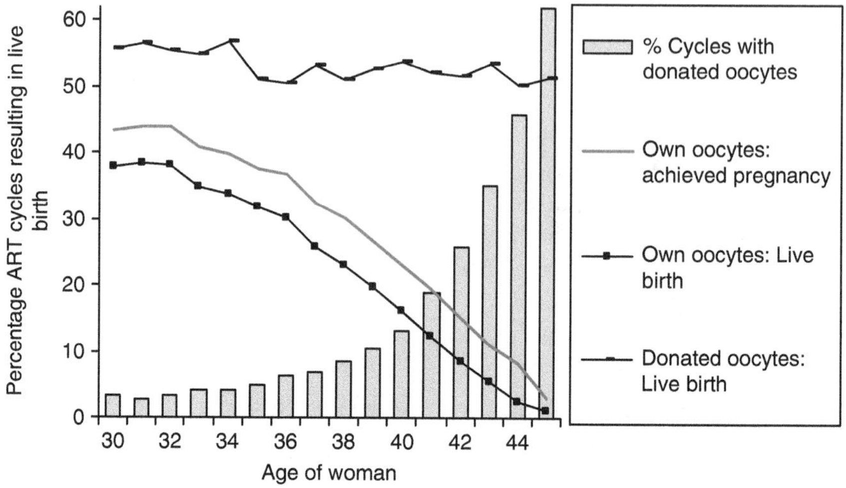

Fig. 7.8 Percentage of ART cycles resulting in pregnancy and live birth by age of woman undergoing ART, Unites States 2005
Source: CDC 2007, Figs. 14, 44, and 45

estimated costs per live birth using fresh ART cycles skyrocket to 307,559 Australian Dollars for women aged 42 or older, a tenfold increase when compared with the costs of life birth among ART users aged 30–34 (Chambers et al. 2006; ART data refer to 2002 and cost estimates pertain to 2005). This low effectiveness of treatments at advanced maternal ages results in many countries in defining age 40 as a threshold after which assisted reproduction is no longer subsidised through health insurance funds.

Many infertile women wishing to have a child after age 40 achieve high success rates of around 50% per cycle by using *donated* oocytes. Remarkably, the use of donated oocytes, commonly originating from much younger women, does not diminish chances of achieving successful pregnancy and delivery with age of woman undergoing ART (Fig. 7.8). This suggests that using cryopreservation ("egg freezing") at younger ages *may* give many women a chance to get pregnant with their own fertilised oocytes later in life. However, at present, cryopreservation of oocytes is – in contrast to the commonly used sperm and embryo cryopreservation – still in an early stage of technological development (Nowak 2007; Tucker 2008) and only a few cases of its successful use have been documented. It is unclear when will long-term cryopreservation reach high "survival" rates coupled with very low risk of chromosomal damage to the oocytes stored so that the technology can become reliable. Even if that happened literally tomorrow, its adoption would be slowed down by high costs, ethical questions raised, legal regulations, and, possibly, also by a limited acceptance of oocyte collection among women. Clearly, there are many reasons to be sceptical about the potential impact of "egg storing" on late birth rates in the next two decades.

7.9 Concluding Discussion and Policy Recommendations

7.9.1 Rationales for Having Children Later in Life

This article has highlighted a remarkable *shift* towards "late" parenthood taking place in all advanced societies and discussed numerous determinants and consequences of this trend. Medical literature generally perceives delayed childbearing negatively, emphasising high risks of infertility and high rates of negative pregnancy outcomes and foetus deformations. However, the biological rationale for early childbearing is increasingly in conflict with social and economic rationales favouring late childbearing. Late parenthood has a number of potentially benefiting effects for both parents and their children. It is also a strategy consistent with the decline in the relative importance of children and family life at younger ages and with the general extension of life span, prolonged education and delayed economic activity (Lee and Goldstein 2003). The "postponement transition" has been led by highly educated individuals, who display a rapid increase in fertility rates after age 35 and who also have the strongest economic motivation to postpone their family formation. At the same time, lower-educated women show only a modest increase in age at motherhood and social status heterogeneity in fertility timing has widened in most countries. Early parenthood, which is also frequently unplanned, has been increasingly associated with disadvantaged social and economic position, unstable family situations, and poor career prospects. In an evolutionary perspective, this social differentiation can be seen as a manifestation of age-related reproductive strategies that are linked to socialisation in early childhood. Belsky et al. (1991) suggest that individuals whose childhood experiences led them to perceive others as untrustworthy, relationships as opportunistic, and resources as scarce or unpredictable, will develop a "quantity orientation" in mating and reproductive strategies, orient themselves towards short-term pair bonds, and accelerate their reproductive efforts.

7.9.2 Policy Recommendations

Educational, social and economic policies may affect decisions on fertility timing. Lutz and Skirbekk (2005) outline two ways in which policies may support earlier timing of parenthood: (1) by reordering life course events (e.g. by having children before finishing education) and (2) by shortening different phases that lead to parenthood (e.g. by shortening the time spent in higher education), but maintaining the "usual" sequence of events. Rindfuss and Brauner-Otto (2008) have recently investigated this issue in detail and discussed how policies and regulations related to education, labour market and housing market may stimulate earlier timing of births.

Large individual heterogeneity in living arrangements, family life course and the timing of childbearing need to be taken into account by policy actions that aim to ease the work-family combination during the "rush hour" stage of life. Hakim (2003) has argued that women differ in their work-family preferences and policies *need to reflect* these differences. Arguably, "old-style" policies assuming uniform experiences, needs and preferences might be counterproductive as they may lead to different reactions among individual men and women. For instance, the policy stimulating an extended period of generous parental leave without offering an alternative option of short work interruption and easily available institutional child care may discourage career-oriented women from having children earlier in life. Similarly, policy that increases taxation of childless people and redistributes these resources to families with children might have an unintended effect of restricting income of young men and women who are planning to become parents. Policies for the twenty-first century need to reflect heterogeneous family forms and lifestyle preferences and, at a very general level, should aim to spread "more innovatively paid and unpaid duty-free time over the entire life course" (Avramov and Cliquet 2003).

Taking these general observations as a starting point and drawing on the existing research, a stylised "wish list" of policy recommendations can be formulated as follows:

- Aim to reverse trends in relative income of younger workers below age 35, which was falling in comparison with the older workers (aged 45–54) between the mid-1970s and the mid-1990s (Lutz et al. 2006). Lower income at younger ages makes resource accumulation before family formation a more difficult and longer process.
- Make labour market more flexible and open for young adults, and limit employment policies favouring older workers, thus reducing youth unemployment rates. Unemployment has been found an *important determinant* of delayed childbearing (Meron and Widmer 2002), whereas flexible labour legislation and high proportion of part-time employment have a positive effect on fertility (Adsera 2004).
- Give both men and women greater flexibility over their employment and family time. Allow broad choice in the length of weekly work time, duration of parental leave (including a system of short family leaves for parents with children below age 15) and its sharing by both partners. Similarly, allow wider choice in retirement age.
- Make institutional childcare inexpensive and well accessible and with full-day coverage, also for parents with children below age 3 and for school-aged children. Support alternative childcare arrangements, including private provision and small neighbourhood parental groups. Childcare availability might particularly affect childbearing decisions of younger women (Rindfuss et al. 2007).
- Give unmarried couples and their children equal legal recognition, rights and duties as given to the married couples.
- Enable an easy and cheap access to all types of infertility treatment to women and couples who are infertile and have a non-marginal chance of becoming

pregnant. The treatment should be provided irrespective of family status and current number of children.

- Provide detailed information about reproductive ageing, infertility and pregnancy complications at secondary schools and medical establishments. At the same time, provide detailed information about contraception in primary and secondary schools and disseminate contraception for free to non-economically active young adults.
- Support affordable and accessible housing, both rental and privately owned (see discussion in Rindfuss and Brauner-Otto 2008). Ability to establish an independent household is one of the most important preconditions for parenthood.
- Support more efficient system of higher education that does not stimulate unnecessary prolongation of studies among young adults (see also Lutz and Skirbekk 2005).

These policies should not explicitly aim at reducing age at childbearing, as there is no clear support for the notion that an earlier timing of births should be preferred when different positive and negative consequences of late parenthood are compared. To some extent, the outlined policy actions would prop up childbearing at younger ages by facilitating parenthood among younger couples who wish to become parents and face obstacles to realising this desire. At the same time, some of these policies may also encourage "recuperation" of delayed childbearing at later reproductive ages and thus lead to a continuous increase in fertility rates of women past age 30.

7.9.3 Concluding Remarks

On balance, the shift to a late childbearing pattern does *not* need to be perceived negatively, especially when most women have their first child at ages when they can achieve their desired family size, which is, in most countries and in most social groups, centred at two children. In other words, as long as a majority of women, including those with high education, have the first child before age 35, age-related decline in fecundity may not have a very strong effect on their ability to achieve their plans and on aggregate cohort fertility rates. As Stein and Susser (2000) suggest, the "social advantage" of late parenthood may *outweigh* the biological advantage of early parenthood, as older parents are more experienced and knowledgeable, have better economic situation, face lower risk of divorce, and can more easily afford childcare.

Postponing parenthood does not constitute the major reason for rising childlessness and for the observed educational differences in childlessness levels. The rising numbers of women who are childless or with only one child after age 30 and who express a desire to have a child later in life indicate that the trend of rising birth rates at advanced reproductive ages will *continue* in most countries, although with a diminishing intensity. The persistence of the current institutional and cultural framework in most developed societies, which favours non-family orientation at younger ages and postponement of stable partnership and family formation is likely to contribute to a further shift towards later parenthood. The late parenthood "revolution" is not over yet.

Acknowledgements Many thanks to Egbert te Velde for his comments on the first draft of this contribution. Helpful suggestions by three reviewers and the participants of the WannseeForum workshop on "Easing the rush hour of life – diversity of life courses in international comparison" were also highly appreciated.

References

Adsera A (2004) Changing fertility rates in developed countries. The impact of labour market institutions. J Popul Econ 17(1):1–27

Adsera A (2005) Vanishing children: From high unemployment to low fertility in developed countries. Am Econ Rev Paper Proc 95(2):189–193

Alonzo A (2002) Long-term health consequences of delayed childbirth: NHANES III. Women's Health Issues 12(1):37–45

Andersson G, Rønsen M, Knudsen LB, Lappegård T, Neyer G, Skrede K, Teschner K, Vikat A (2009) Cohort fertility patterns in the Nordic countries. Demogr Res 20(14):313–352

Avramov D, Cliquet R (2003) Economy of time and population policy. Rethinking the 20th Century life course paradigm. Zeitschrift für Bevölkerungswissenschaft 28(2–4):369–402

Beets G, Dourleijn E, Liefbroer A, Henkens K (2001) De timing van het eerste kind in Nederland en Europa. Report No. 59, NIDI, Den Haag

Belsky J, Steinberg L, Draper P (1991) Childhood experiences, interpersonal development, and reproductive strategy: An evolutionary theory of socialization. Child Dev 62:647–670

Billari FC, Borgoni R (2005) Assessing the use of sample selection models in the estimation of fertility postponement effects. Stat Method Appl 14(3):389–402

Billari FC, Kohler H-P (2004) Patterns of low and very low fertility in Europe. Popul Stud 58(2):161–176

Billari FC, Liefbroer AC, Philipov D (2006) The postponement of childbearing in Europe: Driving forces and implications. Vienna Yearb Popul Res 2006:1–17

Blossfeld H-P, Huinink J (1991) Human capital investments or norms of role transition? How women's schooling and career affect the process of family formation. Am J Sociol 97(1):143–168

Bongaarts J (2002) The end of the fertility transition in the developed world. Popul Dev Rev 28(3):419–443

Bongaarts J, Feeney G (1998) On the quantum and tempo of fertility. Popul Dev Rev 24(2):271–291

Broekmans FJ, Knauff EAH, te Velde E, Macklon NS, Fauser BC (2007) Female reproductive ageing: current knowledge and future trends. TRENDS in Endocrinol Metab 18(2): 58–65

Bushnik T, Garner R (2008) The children of older first-time mothers in Canada: Their health and development. Research Paper, Catalogue no. 89-599-M – No. 005. Statistics Canada, Ottawa

CDC (2007) Assisted reproductive technology success rates 2005. U.S. Department of Health and Human Services, Centers for Disease Control and Prevention, Atlanta. Accessed at.: http://www.cdc.gov/ART/ART2005/download.htm

Chambers G, Ho MT, Sullivan E (2006) Assisted reproductive technology treatment costs of a live birth: an age-stratified cost-outcome study of treatment in Australia. MJA 64(4): 155–158

Chen X-K, Wen SW, Krewski D, Fleming N, Yang Q, Walker MC (2008) Paternal age and adverse birth outcomes: Teenager or 40 + , who is at risk? Hum Reprod 23(6):1290–1296
Coleman DA (2000) Male fertility trends in industrial countries: Theories in search of some evidence, Chapter 1. In: Bledsoe C, Lerner S, Guyer JI (eds) Fertility and the male life-cycle in the era of fertility decline. Oxford University Press, Oxford, pp 29–60
Cooney TM, Pedersen FA, Indelicato S, Palkovitz R (1993) Timing of fatherhood: Is "on-time" optimal? J Marriage Fam 55:205–215
Council of Europe (2006) Recent demographic developments in Europe 2005. Council of Europe Publishing, Strasbourg
De Cooman E, Ermisch J, Joshi H (1987) The next birth and the labour market: A dynamic model of births in England and Wales. Popul Stud 41(2):237–268
De Graaf A (2008) Vruchtbaarheid in de twintigste eeuw [Fertility in the 20th Century]. Bevolkingstrends 1/2008:14–22
de la Rochebrochard É (2001) Sterility, fecundity: What about men? Popul Soc 371:1–4
de la Rochebrochard É, Thonneau P (2002) Paternal age and maternal age are risk factors for miscarriage: Results from a multicentre European study. Hum Reprod 17(6):1649–1656
de la Rochebrochard É, McElreavey K, Thonneau P (2003) Paternal age over 40 years. The "amber light" in the reproductive life of men? J Androl 24(4):459–465
Doblhammer G (2000) Reproductive history and mortality later in life: A comparative study of England and Wales and Austria. Popul Stud 54(2):169–176
Drolet M (2002) Wives, mothers and wages: Does timing matter? Research Paper, Catalogue No. 11F0019MIE – No. 186. Statistics Canada, Ottawa
Erfani A, Beaujot R (2006) Familial orientations and the rationales for childbearing behaviour. Can Stud Popul 33(1):46–67
ESHRE (2005) Fertility and ageing. ESHRE Capri Workshop Group. Hum Reprod Update 11(3):261–276
Eskenazi B, Wyrobek AJ, Sloter E, Kidd SA, Moore L, Young S, Moore D (2003) The association of age and semen quality in healthy men. Hum Reprod 18(2):447–454
Esping-Andersen G (1999) Social foundations of postindustrial economies. Oxford University Press, Oxford
Eurostat (2008, 2009). Population and social conditions. Online database of Eurostat accessed in May 2008 and March 2009 at http://epp.eurostat.ec.europa.eu
Fergusson DM, Woodward LJ (1999) Maternal age and educational and psychological outcomes in early adulthood. J Child Psychol Psychiat 43(3):479–489
Frejka T, Sobotka T (2008) Fertility in Europe: Diverse, delayed and below replacement. Overview Chapter 1. In: Frejka T et al (eds) Childbearing trends and policies in Europe. Demogr Res, Special Collection 7, 19(3):15–46
Garrison ME, Blalock LB, Zarski JJ, Merritt PB (2007) Delayed parenthood: An exploratory study of family functioning. Fam Relat 46(3):281–290
Gilbert WM, Nesbitt TS, Danielsen B (1999) Childbearing beyond age 40: Pregnancy outcome in 24, 032 cases. Obstet Gynecol 93(1):9–14
Gleicher N, Weghofer A, Barad D (2006) A formal comparison of the practice of assisted reproductive technologies between Europe and the USA. Hum Reprod 21(8):1945–1950
Goldin C (2006) The quiet revolution that transformed women's employment, education, and family. Am Econ Rev 96(2):1–21
Goldin C, Katz LF (2002) The power of the pill: Oral contraceptives and women's career and marriage decisions. J Pol Econ 110(4):730–770
Goldstein JR (2006) How late can first births be postponed? Some illustrative population-level calculations. Vienna Yearb Popul Res 2006:153–165
Goldstein JR, Sobotka T, Jasilioniene A (2009) The end of "lowest-low" fertility? Population and Development Review 35(4):681–718
Gustafsson S (2001) Optimal age at motherhood. Theoretical and empirical considerations on postponement of maternity in Europe. J Popul Econ 14:225–247

Hakim C (2003) Preference theory: A new approach to explaining fertility patterns. Popul Dev Rev 29(3):349–374
Happel SK, Hill JK, Low SA (1984) An economic analysis of the timing of childbirth. Popul Stud 38:299–311
Heffner L (2004) Advanced maternal age – How old is too old? N Engl J Med 351(189): 1927–1929
Heuveline P, Timberlake JM, Furstenberg FF Jr (2003) Shifting childrearing to single mothers: Results from 17 Western countries. Popul Dev Rev 29(1):47–71
Hoem JM, Neyer G, Andersson G (2006) Education and childlessness. The relationship between educational field, educational level, and childlessness among Swedish women born in 1955–1959. Demogr Res 14(15):331–380
Joshi H (2002) Production, reproduction and education: Women, children and work in a British perspective. Popul Dev Rev 28(3):445–474
Kneale D, Joshi H (2008) Postponement and childlessness: Evidence from two British cohorts. Demogr Res 19(58):1935–1968
Kohler H-P, Billari FC, Ortega JA (2002) The emergence of lowest-low fertility in Europe during the 1990s. Popul Dev Rev 28(4):641–680
Kravdal Ø (1994) The importance of economic activity, economic potential and economic resources for the timing of first births in Norway. Popul Stud 48(2):249–267
Kühnert B, Nieschlag E (2004) Reproductive functions of the ageing male. Hum Reprod Update 10(4):327–339
Lappegård T, Rønsen M (2005) The multifaceted impact of education on entry into motherhood. Eur J Popul 21(1):31–49
Lee RD, Goldstein J (2003) Rescaling the life cycle. Longevity and proportionality. In: Carey JR, Tuljapurkar S (eds) Life span. Evolutionary, ecological and demographic perspectives. Supplement to Popul Dev Rev 29:183–207
Leridon H (2004) Can assisted reproduction technology compensate for the natural decline in fertility with age? A model assessment. Hum Reprod 19(7):1549–1554
Leridon H (2008) A new estimate of permanent sterility by age: Sterility defined as the inability to conceive. Popul Stud 62(1):15–24
Leridon H, Slama R (2008) The impact of a decline in fecundity and of pregnancy postponement on final number of children and demand for assisted reproduction technology. Hum Reprod 23(6):1312–1319
Lesthaeghe R (1995) The second demographic transition in Western countries: An interpretation. In: Mason KO, Jensen A-M (eds) Gender and family change in industrialized countries. Clarendon Press, Oxford, pp 17–62
Liefbroer AC (2005) The impact of perceived costs and rewards of childbearing on entry into parenthood: evidence from a panel study. Eur J Popul 21(4):367–391
Lochhead C (2005) Growing disparities among first-time parents: 1971–1996. Health Policy Research Bulletin, 2005/10, Health Canada, pp 11–14
Lutz W, Skirbekk V (2005) Policies addressing the tempo effect in low-fertility countries. Popul Dev Rev 31(4):699–720
Lutz W, Skirbekk V, Testa MR (2006) The low fertility trap hypothesis. Forces that may lead to further postponement and fewer births in Europe. Vienna Yearb Popul Res 2006: 167–192
Mathews TJ, Hamilton BE (2002) Mean age of mother 1970–2000. National Vital Statistics Reports 51(1):1–14. National Center for Health Statistics, Hyattsville, MD
May KA (1982) Factors contributing to first-time fathers' readiness for fatherhood: An exploratory study. Fam Relat 31(3):353–361
McLanahan S (2004) Diverging destinies: How children are faring under the second demographic transition? Demography 41(4):607–627
Meron M, Widmer I (2002) Unemployment leads women to postpone the birth of their first child. Population-E 2002 57(2):301–330

Miller AR (2008) Motherhood delay and the human capital of the next generation. Available at SSRN: http://ssrn.com/abstract = 1079832
Mills M, Blossfeld H-P (2005) Globalization, uncertainty and the early life course: A theoretical framework. In: Blossfeld H-P et al. (eds) Globalization, uncertainty and youth in society. Routledge, London, pp 1–24
Mirowsky J (2005) Age at first birth, health, and mortality. J Health Social Behav 46:32–50
Neiss M, Rowe DC, Rodgers JL (2002) Does education mediate the relationship between IQ and age at first birth? A behavioural genetic analysis. J Biosocial Sci 34:259–275
Nomaguchi KM (2006) Time of one's own: Employment, leisure and delayed transition to motherhood in Japan. J Fam Issues 27(12):1668–1700
Nowak R (2007) Egg freezing: A reproductive revolution. New Scientist 21 March 2007:8–9
Nyboe Andersen A, Goossens V, Gianaroli L, Felberbaum R, de Mouzon J, Nygren KG (2007) Assisted reproductive technology in Europe, 2003. Results generated from European registers by ESHRE. Hum Reprod 22(6):1513–1525
ONS (2007) Birth statistics. Review of the Registrar General on births and patterns of family building England and Wales, 2006. Series FM1, No. 35, Office of National Statistics, London
Pollock JI (1996) Mature maternity: long term associations in first children born to older mothers in 1970 in the UK. J Epidemiol Commun Health 50:429–436
Presser HB (2001) Comment: A gender perspective for understanding low fertility in post-transitional societies. In: Bulatao RA, Casterline JB (eds) Global fertility transition, supplement to Popul Dev Rev 27, New York, Population Council, pp 177–183
Prioux F (2005) Late fertility in Europe: some comparative and historical data. Revue d'épidémiologie et de santé publique 53:2S3–2S11
Ravanera ZR, Rajulton F (2004) Social status polarization in the timing and trajectories to motherhood. Discussion Paper 04-06, Population Studies Centre, University of Western Ontario, London. Accessed at http://sociology.uwo.ca/popstudies/dp/dp04-06.pdf
Rendall MS, Smallwood S (2003) Higher qualifications, first-birth timing, and further childbearing in Englands and Wales. Popul Trends 111(Spring 2003):18–26
Rindfuss RR (1991) The young adult years: Diversity, structural change, and fertility. Demography 28(4):493–512
Rindfuss RR, Brauner-Otto SR (2008) Policies, institutions, and the transition to adulthood: Implications for fertility tempo in low fertility settings. Vienna Yearb Popul Res 2008: 57–87
Rindfuss RR, Morgan SP, Swicegood G (1988) First births in America. Changes in the timing of parenthood. University of California Press, Berkeley, California
Rindfuss RR, Guilkey D, Morgan SP, Kravdal Ø, Guzzo KB (2007) Child care availability and first birth timing in Norway. Demography 44(2):345–372
Saha S, Barnett AG, Foldi C, Burne TH, Eyles DW, Buka SL (2009) Advanced paternal age is associated with impaired neurocognitive outcomes during infancy and childhood. PLoS Med 6(3):e1000040:1–9
Santow G, Bracher M (2001) Deferment of first birth and fluctuating fertility in Sweden. Eur J Popul 17:343–363
SCB (2002) Mammor och pappor. Om kvinnors och mäns föräldraskap 2001. [Mothers and fathers. Women's and men's parenthood 2001]. Demografiska rapporter 2002:7. Statistics Sweden, Stockholm
Schmitt C, Wagner GG (2006) Kinderlosigkeit von Akademikerinnen überbewertet. DIW Wochenbericht 73(21/2006):313–315
Smallwood S (2002) New estimates of trends in births by birth order in England and Wales. Popul Trends 108:32–48
Sobotka T (2004a) Postponement of childbearing and low fertility in Europe. PhD Thesis, University of Groningen. Dutch University Press, Amsterdam
Sobotka T (2004b) Is lowest-low fertility explained by the postponement of childbearing? Popul Dev Rev 30(2):195–220

Sobotka T (2008) The diverse faces of the second demographic transition in Europe. Overview Chapter 6. In: Frejka T et al (eds) Childbearing trends and policies in Europe. Demogr Res, Special Collection 7, 19(8):171–224

Sobotka T (2009) Subreplacement fertility intentions in Austria. Eur J Popul, doi: 10.1007/s10680-009-9183-0

Sobotka T, Lutz W (2009) Misleading policy messages from the period TFR: Should we stop using it? *European Demographic Research Papers* 2009–4, Vienna: Vienna Institute of Demography

Sobotka T, Testa MR (2008) Attitudes and intentions towards childlessness in Europe. In: Höhn Ch, Avramov D, Kotowska I (eds) People, population change and policies: lessons from the population policy acceptance study, vol 1. Springer, Berlin, pp 177–211

Sobotka T, Kohler H-P, Billari FC (2007) The increase in late childbearing in Europe, Japan and the United States. Paper presented at the 2007 Annual Meeting of the Population Association of America, New York, 29–31 March 2007

Sobotka T, Šťastná A, Zeman K, Hamplová D, Kantorová V (2008a) Czech Republic: A rapid transformation of fertility and family behaviour after the collapse of state socialism. In: Frejka T et al (eds) Childbearing trends and policies in Europe. Demogr Res, Special Collection 7, 19(14):403–454

Sobotka T, Hansen MA, Jensen TK, Pedersen AT, Lutz W, Skakkebæk NE (2008b) The contribution of assisted reproduction to completed fertility: An analysis of Danish data. Popul Dev Rev 34(1):79–101

Spence NJ (2008) The long-term consequences of childbearing: Physical and psychological well-being of mothers in later life. Res Aging 30(6):722–751

Statistics Austria (2005) Volkszählung 2001. Haushalte und Familien. Statistics Austria, Vienna

Stein Z, Susser M (2000) The risks of having children later in life. BMJ 320:1681–1682

Taniguchi H (1999) The timing of childbearing and women's wages. J Marriage Fam 61(6): 1008–1019

Toulemon L (2004) La fécondité est-elle encore naturelle? Application au retard des naissances et à son influence sur la descendance finale. In: Entre nature et culture: quelle(s) démographie(s)? Louvain-la-Neuve: Academia-Bruylant: 15–42

Toulemon L, Lapierre-Adamcyk É (2000) Demographic patterns of motherhood and fatherhood in France, Chapter 12. In: Bledsoe C, Lerner S, Guyer JI (eds) Fertility and the male life-cycle in the era of fertility decline. Oxford University Press, Oxford, pp 293–330

Tucker MJ (2008) The freezing of human oocytes (eggs). Georgia reproductive specialists, Atlanta, Georgia. Available at http:/www.ivf.com/freezing.html

Van de Kaa DJ (2004) The true commonality: In reflexive societies fertility is a derivative. Popul Stud 58(1):77–80

VID (2008) European demographic data sheet 2008. Vienna Institute of Demography, IIASA, Population Reference Bureau. Accessible at http://www.oeaw.ac.at/vid/datasheet/index.html

Wilson B, Smallwood S (2008) The proportion of marriages ending in divorce. Popul Trends 131 (Spring 2008):28–36

Yi Z, Vaupel J (2004) Association of late childbearing with healthy longevity among the oldest-old in China. Popul Stud 58(1):37–53

Zakharov S (2008) Russian Federation: From the first to second demographic transition. In: Frejka T et al (eds) Childbearing trends and policies in Europe. Demogr Res, Special Collection 7, 19(24):907–972

Chapter 8
The "Rush Hour" of Life: Insecurities and Strains in Early Life Phases as a Challenge for a Life Course-Oriented, Sustainable Social Policy

Ute Klammer

8.1 From Cross-Sectional to Longitudinal Data

In order to get a wider scope, one should look not only into different income patterns and familial time arrangements at a *certain point in time*, but also at how these patterns *develop through a respective life course*. Certain working time models, such as regular or marginal part-time, must be analysed with regard to the long-term effect on the workers employed under such conditions. Are these short episodes of employment only temporarily accepted at certain points of time, e.g. at point of career entry or during times of increased need? Or, are these work forms permanently obtained – be it "voluntarily"[1] or not? In certain strata of the work force, is there a concentration of problematic working time models, such as part-time employment? Which financial consequences for the income and social transfers are there for unemployment or part-time work in the long run? Do uncertain labour perspectives lead to delays or even to the renunciation of parenthood and family – and do uncertain labour perspectives, in this respect, have a direct impact on the demographic "problem" of low fertility rates?

A longitudinal perspective enables the viewing of different distribution of time necessities in individual biographies and identifies stages of time pressure, such as the "rush hour" of life. This term coined by European time researchers describes the challenge of middle age when small children have to be cared for and time has to be invested in a professional career simultaneously. At the same time, the analysis of time distribution over the life course allows for an interpersonal comparison – not only do certain time necessities, for example for care tasks, occur for different people at different stages in their lives, they also may cumulate to large "time

U. Klammer
University of Duisburg-Essen, Universitätsstraße 2, 45117 Essen, Germany
e-mail: ute.klammer@uni-due.de

[1]The quotation marks denote that "voluntariness" depends on the predominant framework as well as cultural norms.

J.C. Tremmel (ed.), *A Young Generation Under Pressure?*,
DOI 10.1007/978-3-642-03483-1_8, © Springer-Verlag Berlin Heidelberg 2010

masses", while, in other biographies (of both sexes), they hardly occur at all. These results put forward different demands to social politics to influence the intertemporal and interpersonal distribution of time and money.

Some European countries, as well as the European Union, have recently shown an increased interest in these and similar questions. In the European Union, the life course perspective has gained importance due to the discussion about "life-long learning" and the generally increased interest in education in the context of a "social policy of investing". At the same time, the aims of the European Employment Strategy of raising income rates for women and elderly people, as well as profoundly raising the actual retirement age, poses questions for the *course* of employment records and the options to influence economic and social politics. Consequently, the European Directives for National Employment Policies have been demanding for several years that a comprehensive national strategy be developed based on the life course approach (Council of the European Union 2003: Paragraph 15). This was explicitly confirmed in 2005 by the new employment guideline No. 18, *Promote a life-cycle approach to work* (European Commission, Guidelines 2005, 2005/600/EC).

Thus, this article connects the question of (different and changing) life courses of men and women to the debate about a readjustment of social politics in view of demographic change. The first section will provide some empirical data on the structure and change of life courses of men and women both in Germany and on the international scale.[2] The following chapter discusses approaches for a sustainable, life course-oriented social policy.

8.2 Changing Income Records of Men and Women: Some Highlights

Abundant empirical data analyses from my own projects and others prove that labour market risks are unbalanced in Germany and that discontinuities in professional life are extensive (cf., for example, Klammer and Tillmann 2002). Despite a similar entry into professional life of young men and women, the labour participation and weekly work hours of women significantly decrease when children are born. Using cross-sectional data to analyse different life and family stages, one finds that young partnered women without children today work on average 38 h per week, whereas the average drops to 16 h among partnered women with small

[2]The results were partly taken from longitudinal analyses of AVID data (Old-Age Provision in Germany) and from the IAB employee sample of a research project supervised by the author, cf. Klammer and Tillmann (2002).

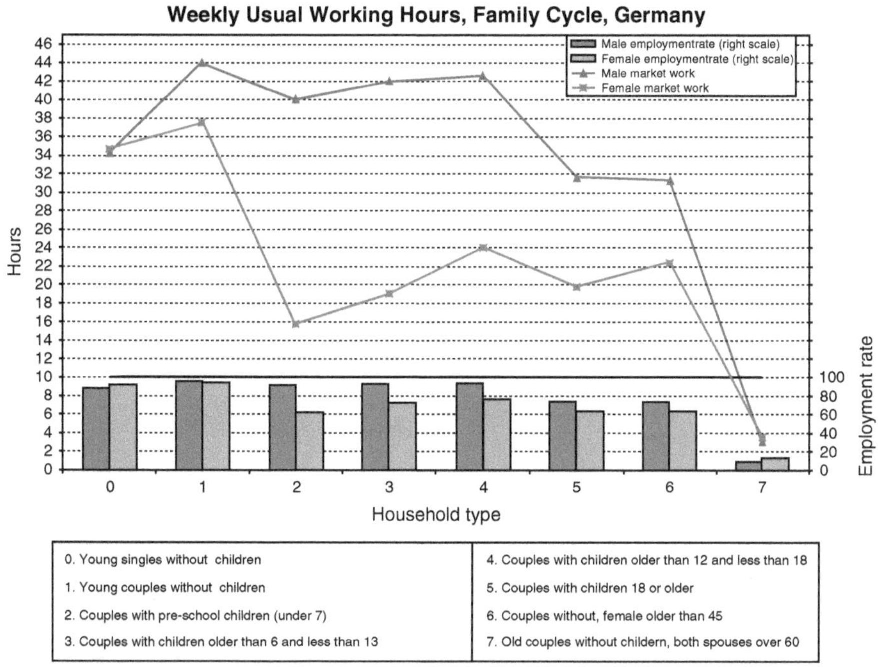

Fig. 8.1 Labour market participation rates and average weekly work hours of men and women during the family cycle: Germany. *Note*: Average weekly working hours refer to ALL members of the respective household type, including inactive persons (working time = 0 h)
Source: ECHP, data for 2000. Calculations for the author's project "Towards a new organisation of working time throughout working life", European Foundation (2006)

children (below the age of 7) in the household (see the lines in Fig. 8.1[3] above). This average reduction (referring to all members of the household type) results from both a reduction shift from full-time to part-time work as a drop in labour market participation rates (see columns in Fig. 8.1).

The *rush hour of life* is thus alleviated by women through lower labour market participation. But even after school enrolment, the weekly work hours of mothers are considerably lower than those of fathers. Actually, German mothers on average

[3]Calculations based on data of the European Community Household Panel (ECHP) for the project "Towards a new organisation of working time throughout working life". Cf. Anxo et al. (2006) and Klammer et al. (2005). The construction of the family cycle based on cross-sectional data (here: 2000) is advantageous because every household type can be shown in a specific point in time – and in the context of a specific institutional framework. However, the disadvantage is that this does not show "real" life courses with potential cohort effects having to be taken into account (which means that men and women who have small children nowadays may possibly show different labour market participation patterns later on than those who are in a later life phase today).

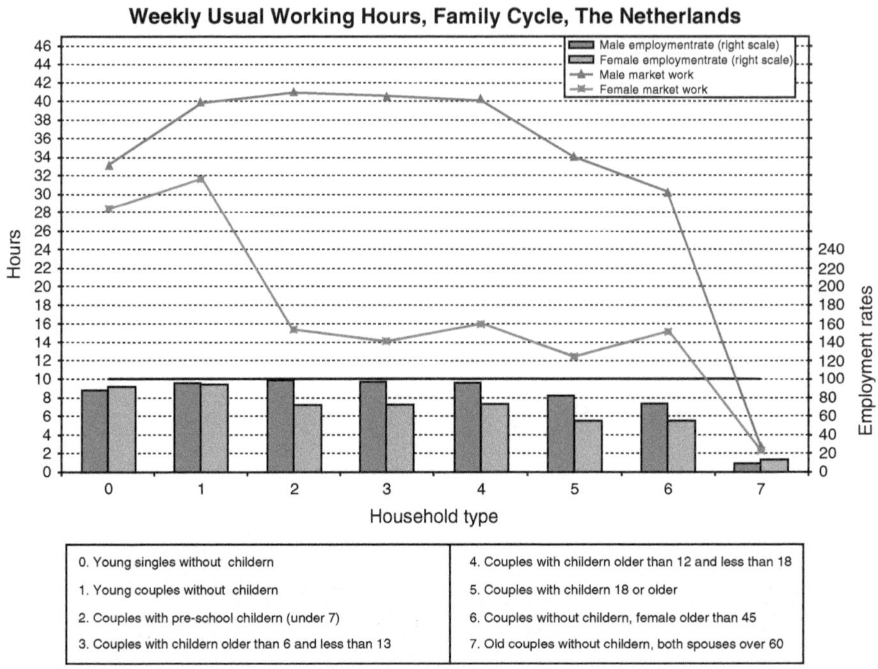

Fig. 8.2 Labour market rates and average weekly work hours of men and women during the family cycle: The Netherlands. *Note*: see Fig. 8.1 and footnote 3
Source: ECHP, data for 2000. Calculations for the author's project "Towards a new organisation of working time throughout working life", European Foundation 2006

do not reach the same level of labour participation and average weekly work hours as their male partners in any later life phase.

As the following figures of the Netherlands and Sweden illustrate, there are differences between the employment courses of men and women in every country, especially when it comes to the "rush hour" of life, when small children have to be attended to. Nevertheless, the welfare states differ significantly in terms of the level and the continuity of labour market participation and the average work hours of men and women in different life stages – during as well as after the "rush hour" of life. This suggests that there are different possibilities and strategies to deal with the special challenges of different life phases.

In the Netherlands (Fig. 8.2), the average weekly work hours of females decrease significantly when children are born, and continue at a low level as long as small children have to be attended to. However, contrary to German women, instead of withdrawing totally from the labour market, Dutch women alleviate the "rush hour" of life primarily by reducing their working hours.

Sweden differs significantly from other West European countries (Fig. 8.3). The labour market participation of Swedish women decreases only minimally after childbirth or when small children have to be attended to; on average, they only cut down by about 4 h (from 26 to 22 h). Later on, their labour participation rises

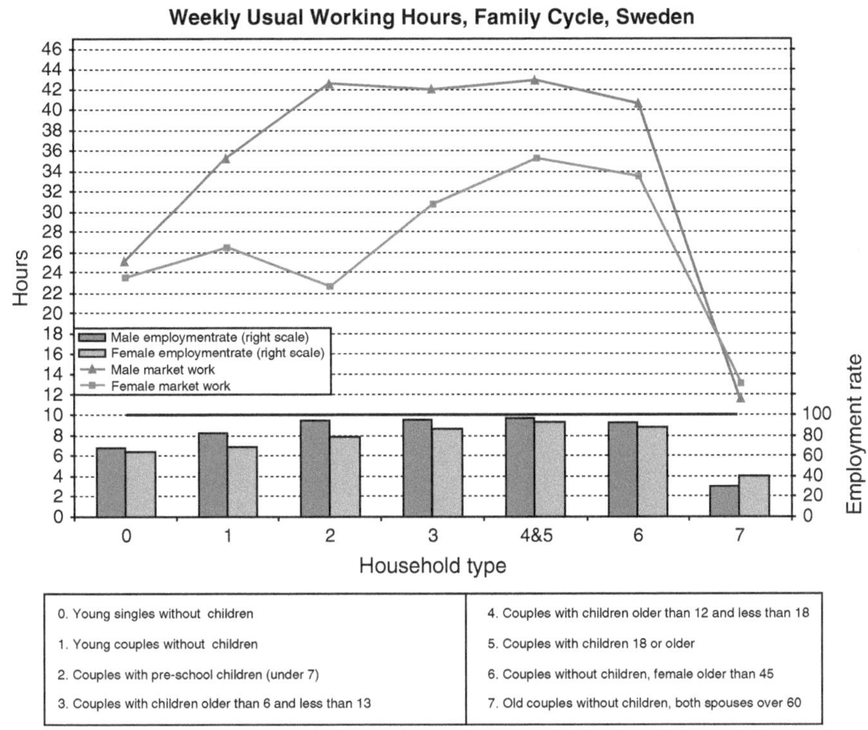

Fig. 8.3 Labour market rates and average weekly work hours of men and women during the family cycle: Sweden. *Note*: see Fig. 8.1 and footnote 3
Source: HUS, data for 1998. Calculations for the author's project "Towards a new organisation of working time throughout working life", European Foundation 2006

almost to the level of male labour participation, far more than in other countries. This suggests that, apart from different role models, institutional factors such as legal and company work time arrangements and leave options for certain life stages are of importance in the Swedish welfare state. Together with the general accessibility of public childcare, these options lead to fewer "compatibility problems" in the first stages of family life than in other countries. As demonstrated here, these "problems" do not have to be resolved by the mothers' withdrawal from the labour market.

In Germany, desire and reality differ significantly when it comes to working hours – this goes for both sexes, but especially for women. Men's desired work hours are at the norm of a full-time job, whereas their real working hours are often higher because of extra hours. Many women who work long hours would like to work less, but women with short part-time jobs wish for longer working hours (with the accompanying income). West German women regard a "long part-time job", i.e. 27 h per week, as the ideal and East German women prefer a "short full-time job", i.e. 34 h per week.

8.3 The Changes in the Labour Market Entry Phase in Germany in an Intergenerational Comparison

Regarding the life course in Germany, one can see that, among younger cohorts, about 80% of all women will have phases of part-time work of at least 1 year in their lives. This is compared to only a small number of men. Fewer women pause their careers because of childcare and this is a continuing trend. However, of the women born from 1951 to 1955, about two-thirds withdrew from employment for at least 1 year because of childcare. On the other hand, a significant number of men – depending on the birth year (1936–1955) about 16–20% – had one or more periods of self-employment, which is often accompanied by social insurance gaps (cf. Klammer and Tillmann (2002), based on AVID data).

But women are no longer at a general disadvantage just because of their sex. The majority of flexibility risks (e.g. fixed-time contracts, temp work, unemployment, etc.) are taken by the young generation, the *newcomers* on the labour market, as well as unskilled people – irrespective of their sex.

Therefore, the youngest cohorts on the labour market are seven times more likely to have a temporary position than the oldest cohorts. All cohorts born after 1945 had to face an increased risk of unemployment in the early years. Among the cohorts of 1961–1965, already 53% of all men and women had experienced unemployment at least once before the age of 30 (see Fig. 8.4).[4,5] This is dangerous as a prolonged labour market entry phase (when compared to earlier times) with (financial) uncertainties often *cuts* into the potential phase of family planning. One has every right to assume that this has a significant influence on young people's decision of whether or not to have children.

Although the average job tenure is surprisingly stable in Germany, no less than 15% of all employees have already had five employers or more – and often they were unemployed in between. Among temporary employees, the ratio is 22%, which means that temp workers have a higher risk to experience frequent job changes.

Even if two-thirds of all job changes are voluntary and the majority of all job changers claim to have improved themselves, one notices an increasing number of involuntary job changes (e.g. employer-initiated) from cohort to cohort, and ever fewer job changes actually lead to professional improvement (cf. Klammer and Tillmann 2002).

Concerning the accumulation of labour years during the life course (based on data of the AVID), one finds a significant decline for men and a moderate increase

[4] Percentage of employees who have experienced unemployment at least once before the age of 30 as related to all employees under 30, sorted by cohorts.

[5] Additional sample I of the IAB employee sample, project calculations for Klammer and Tillmann (2002).

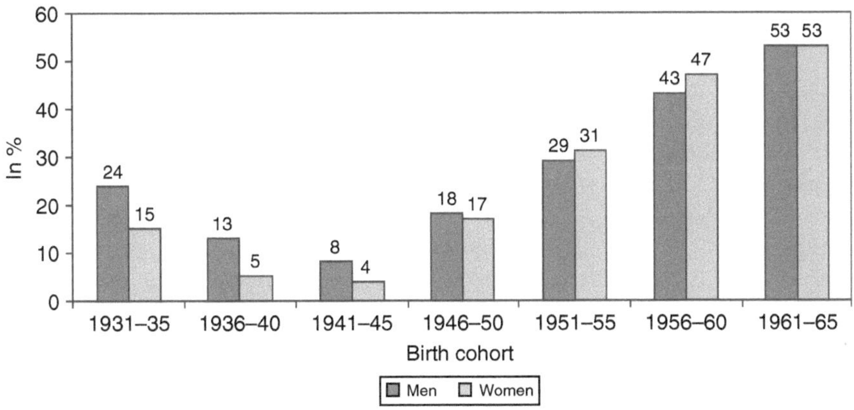

Fig. 8.4 Occurrence of unemployment the age of 30, sorted by cohorts, West Germany
Source: Klammer and Tillmann 2002

for women. Of the men born from 1936 to 1940, 42% had a "complete" (in terms of old-age pension claims) labour record, whereas in the cohorts of 1951–1955, the percentage will only be about 30%. The female ratio increases from about 8 to around 13%. Today's 50-year-old females will still have around 7 (in West Germany, 9) years less on their work records than their male contemporaries. This shows that there are still gender-related labour and income gaps, which continue to affect retirement income.

Looking at the labour courses of the cohorts from 1936 to 1955, an increasing "compression" of life income becomes apparent – mostly on the male side. The long-term trends of late career entry and early retirement have led to a concentration of labour income in the middle phase of life. That is problematic, because this period of time is the "rush hour" of life, when family duties and the general pressures of life and professionals developemnt are gathering to a peak. Furthermore, because of the concentration of life income at this stage, discontinuities – for example, unemployment – become dangerous as they have an even greater impact an our's lifetime income.

Econometric data on the effects of labour interruption show significant impact on long-term income capacity and human capital. These are often underestimated by the people concerned (Among others, Beblo and Wolf 2002). When discontinuities occur in early life phases, the loss of human capital is normally lower and the damage is limited. The assessed postponing of motherhood to a later point in life is critical in this respect. On the other hand, several surveys ascertain that those part-time jobs that are subject to social insurance contribution (not including marginal employment) are better than their reputation when it comes to long-term human capital and income losses. In addition to that, they often have a bridging function, or, as in the case of East Germany, a hinge function, between full-time employments (cf. Klammer and Tillmann 2002).

8.3.1 Policy Response I: Socio-Political Support of Transition

Changing life courses and, in particular, the problems identified during the "rush hour of life" require a reorientation of social security systems. One important task in this respect is the shift from securing status to securing (and promoting) transitions. According to the theory of transitional labour markets, (for example, Schmid and Gazier 2002) this includes: transitions from (further) education, household tasks or unemployment towards employment and vice versa, transitions into retirement, changes from full-time to part-time work, other job changes etc. An increased concentration of social state provisions on securing transitional phases has to include securing both voluntary and involuntary transitions, and not just financially stabilising life standards in case of loss of income. Examples include help for re-entering the labour market after parenting or care tasks, offers for support and financial provisions which enable people to change jobs or start their own business. Other possibilities include the development of more flexible ways to retire and further improvements in transferring company pension claims in case of employment interruption or job changes.

In most European countries, the support of transitions is strongly connected with the (re-)integration of people into the labour market, which might be called the heart of the "activating welfare state" paradigm. Compared to other European countries, the German labour law entered this path relatively late, but in the past few years it has made an impact (Klammer and Leiber 2004). In terms of activation terminology, parallels can be observed internationally. This is probably due to the European employment strategy (EES). However, there have been major differences in applying the activation paradigm, varying from paternalistic approaches to those which emphasise the autonomy of the individual (Berkel and Hornemann-Moeller 2002, p. 54). However, knowledge about long-term effects of activation is still insufficient. For the time being, it appears that the chances of re-entering the labour market primarily depends on the general situation of the economy (the ratio between labour demand and labour supply), and to a minor extent to a favourable relationship between staff in the job placement and labour agencies and those seeking employment as well as to the existence of local and target group-oriented programmes (Cebulla 2002). In Germany, each and everyone of the aforementioned points shows deficits – despite the improved aims of the Hartz laws.

German research studies on the approach of the transitional labour markets have already identified numerous elements and structures which could function as support for the change of status (for example, Rabe and Schmid 1999; Schmid and Gazier 2002). The transitional labour market approach has to be developed further in order to create criteria for "good" and "bad" transitions and the accompanying supporting measures – by taking into account specific needs of specific life stages.

What should be viewed as especially demanding tasks are the beginning and the end of professional life, which have more and more developed into entire phases of work life (Gautié 2003). As mentioned above, the entry phase into professional life often lasts for several years and is characterised by unstable jobs and short interims of unemployment; the exit phase can also be accompanied by unemployment, or by illnesses, invalidity or partial retirement. Bearing in mind this shortening and compression of professional life as an increasing trend, a future key task is to work towards once again "straightening out" professional life. Shortened school and study phases might be one way, but there also has to be a sustainable employment policy. Such a policy is a prerequisite for later retirement, as targeted in the European Union's Lisbon strategy. Introducing *real* old-age part-time models would improve the flexibility of retirement transition as these would lead to an actual reduction of working hours in the latest labour phase.[6] However, does not mean opting for a higher amount of total working hours during the life course. Instead, opting for earlier work entries and later exits the priority of "straightening out" the labour record is to better distribute the income risks over the life course and to alleviate the "rush hour(s)" of life by giving way to other time necessities during the life course, e.g. care tasks and further education.

8.3.2 Policy Response II: Financing – Individual Options for Distributing the Life Income and for Readjusting the Collective Support Systems

In many European countries, a concentration of social policy on the activation and reintegration of all people fit for employment into the labour market can be observed. However, this trend has not rendered monetary transfers for certain life phases obsolete. On the contrary – new discontinuities and time necessities over the life course raise questions about how to ease the financial needs in such life stages. A currently discussed approach[7] concentrates on giving individuals more options to dispose of their estimated life income. Up until now, the Netherlands have done this most effectively. Since the beginning of 2006, there is the so-called *levensloopregeling*, a new framework legislation which enables employees to save up part of their salary (up to 12% of the gross monthly salary and up to a total of 210% of their gross monthly salary) and also time, e.g. extra hours, privileged by taxes, in order to use this credit later on, for example to finance sabbaticals, a family break, further education phases, old-age part-time or even an early retirement (SZW 2006). In order to use this credit in earlier life phases – in the "rush hour" of life – when only small savings have been acquired, it is possible to take out a loan on the estimated future income (for example, company pension claims).

Without doubt, such approaches could improve the individual's possibilities to manage their specific time needs according to personal necessities over the life

[6]The existing German old-age part-time work model – contrary to its original purpose – is mostly used as a block model for early retirement.

[7]For example in the Netherlands, but in the European Commission as well, cf. Stuurgroep Verkenning Levensloop (2002), Naegele et al. (2003), Klammer et al. (2005), Waas (2004).

course. However, this should be viewed critically, as younger cohorts – contrary to today's pensioners – will anyway have problems in gaining a poverty-defying income and in building up decent pension claims. A premature consumption of potential income and pension claims could therefore increase the pressure on the further professional life and also pose a risk of poverty in old-age. Also problematic is the fact that these models promote the further privatisation of social risks – such as childcare and care for frail, elderly family members. If we argue that everybody can compensate for "life risks" by re-arranging their personal life income from work, we may very well assume that a collectively funded scheme for the coverage of social risks and socially important forms of unpaid work was obsolete. But as income risks and care tasks are unequally distributed among the population, such schemes are, in fact, indispensable. However, there has to be a renewed discussion about *which* life phases legitimate an interpersonal reallocation by collective systems. There are arguments for giving time options with monetary support ("integrated options") preferably to people in the "rush hour" of life who have care tasks and are short on time, instead of using them to provide an easier retirement, as is still common in Germany. One approach would be a collectively supported model of "part-time work for people with care tasks". Financial means for this could be gained from the expensive and questionable family support system of the married couples' tax splitting (Deutscher Bundestag 2002, pp. 257–260). Therefore, it makes sense to combine and adjust improved, individual options of redistributing money (and time) over the life course with specifically aligned, collectively funded financial support systems for certain life risks.

In addition to the aforementioned developments, the readjustment of support systems requires a broad access to social security systems. In Germany, contrary to those European countries that have more of a general security system, certain flexible employment forms and gaps are accompanied by gaps of social security coverage (Klammer 2000) although part of the risks are still alleviated through marriage-associated rights. As numerous surveys have shown, the most recent of which being the AVID data published in November 2007, (Rische 2007, in critical reference: Hauser 2007; Klammer 2008) young people, through cutbacks in the statutory pension insurance, are more and more confronted with the risk of old-age poverty – even if they use governmental aid for private retirement plans.

In order to build up sufficient social security claims with the aim of a population-wide coverage for certain social risks, which have yet to be defined, we recommend an extension of the statutory insurance duty. This should include a (basic) health insurance. In terms of old-age provision, there has been the German pension reform of 2001 which has introduced a means-tested minimum standard. However, this is only meant as a repair mechanism for – as compared to the norm – "failed" biographies.[8] The actual reasons for the lack of pension entitlements – namely, employment and insurance interruptions – are neither identified nor remedied. Any answer to altering the labour and life course, based upon a general insurance

[8]Consistently, this has been included in the social assistance law of the new SGB XII.

obligation over the life course, would have to decide who would bear the costs of maintaining such an insurance status in certain labour and life conditions e.g. in case of unemployment or care phases Vielle 2001; Vielle and Walthery 2003). The aim has to be to make it possible for every individual to independently obtain non-means-tested pension entitlements at least as high as the socio-cultural minimum standard. Not only would this help to avoid old-age poverty among men and women with discontinuous employment records, it would also help raise public awareness for the long-term risks and costs of such discontinuous employment records. It may also help to impede the *free rider behaviour* and raise acceptance for the collective support of those still in need. This would invoke a trust in the social security system amongst younger cohorts enabling them, in spite of increased labour market risks, to rely on the social security system.

References

Anxo D, Boulin J-Y, Cebrian I, Fagan C, Keuzenkamp S, Klammer U, Klenner C, Moreno G, Toharía L (2006) Working time options over the life course: New work patterns and company strategies. European Foundation, Office for Official Publications of the European Communities, Luxembourg

Beblo M, Wolf E (2002) Wage penalties for career interruptions. An empirical analysis for West Germany. ZEW Discussion Paper No. 02/45. Mannheim

Berkel RV, Hornemann Møller I (Eds.) (2002) Active social policies in the EU. Inclusion through participation? Policy Press, Bristol

Cebulla A (2002) Flexibilität und soziale Sicherung in Großbritannien unter besonderer Berücksichtigung des New Deal. In: Klammer U, Tillmann K (eds) Flexicurity – Soziale Sicherung und Flexibilisierung der Arbeits- und Lebensverhältnisse. Landesarbeitsministerium MASQT 1106, Düsseldorf, pp 585–636

Council of the European Union (2003) Council Decision of 22 July 2003 on guidelines for the employment policies of the Member States. Official J Eur Union. 5.8.2003, L197 13–L197 21

Deutscher Bundestag (2002) Bericht der Bundesregierung zur Berufs- und Einkommenssituation von Frauen und Männern. BT-Drs. 14/8952, Berlin

Gautié J (2003) Transitions et trajectoires sur le marché du travail en France: mutations et conséquences. Troisièmes entretiens de l'emploi. ANPE. Mars

Hauser R (2007) Anmerkungen zur Untersuchung "Alterssicherung in Deutschland", Vortrag gehalten auf der Tagung "Sozialpolitische Herausforderungen in der Alterssicherung gestalten", Berlin 22.11.2007, unpublished manuscript

Klammer U (2000) Auf dem Weg zu mehr Flexicurity in Europa. WSI-Mitteilungen 5/2000, pp 313–321

Klammer U (2008) Armut und Verteilung in Deutschland und Europa – eine kritische Bestandsaufnahme, WSI-Mitteilungen 3/2008

Klammer U, Leiber S (2004) Aktivierung und Eigenverantwortung in europäisch-vergleichender Perspektive. WSI-Mitteilungen 9/2004, pp 514–521

Klammer U, Tillmann K (2002) Flexicurity – Soziale Sicherung und Flexibilisierung der Arbeits- und Lebensverhältnisse. Landesarbeitsministerium MASQT 1106, Düsseldorf

Klammer U, Keuzenkamp S, Anxo D, Boulin J-Y, Cebrián I, Fagan C, Klenner C, Moreno G, Toharía L (2005) Working time options over the life course: Changing social security structures. European Foundation, Office for Official Publications of the European Communities, Luxembourg

Naegele G, Barkholdt C, de Vroom B, Goul Anderson J, Krämer K (2003) A new organisation of time over working life. European Foundation, Office for Official Publications of the European Communities, Luxembourg

Rabe B, Schmid G (1999) Eine Frage der Balance. Reform der Arbeitsmarktpolitik. Aus Politik und Zeitgeschichte. B 37/1999, pp 21–30

Rische H (2007) Vorstellung der Studie "Altersvorsorge in Deutschland (AVID)". 3. Aktuelles Presseseminar der Deutschen Rentenversicherung Bund. Würzburg 20–21.11.2007. http://www.deutsche-rentenversicherung.de. download 25/11/2007

Schmid G, Gazier B (Hg.) (2002) The dynamics of full employment. Social integration through transitional labour markets. Edward Elgar Publishing, Cheltenham

Stuurgroep Verkenning Levensloop (2002) Verkenning Levensloop, Den Haag

SZW (2006) Levensloopregeling: informatie voor werknemers. http://home.szw.nl/navigatie/rubriek/dsp_rubriek.cfm?rubriek_id = 1001&subrubriek_id = 1003&link_id = 77624. download 15/3/2006

Vielle P (2001) La sécurité sociale et le coût indirect des responsabilités familiales. Bruylant, Brüssel

Vielle P, Walthery P (2003) Flexibility and social protection. European Foundation for the Improvement of Living and Working Conditions, Dublin

Waas B (2004) Die 'lebensverlaufbezogene' Politik in den Niederlanden. Ein Beispiel für Deutschland? Sozialer Fortschritt 7/2004, pp 173–178

Part III
On the Path to Gerontocracy?

Chapter 9
Age Groups and Generations: Lines of Conflict and Potentials for Integration

Martin Kohli

9.1 Introduction

The "rush hour" of life may be regarded as a manifestation of cleavages between age groups or generations. Cleavages inherent in social structure create the potential for conflicts; whether and to what extent these conflicts manifest themselves openly depends on the mobilisation of the actors on both sides of the rift. However, there are also links which reach across the cleavages. In our societies marked by demographic discontinuity, we heavily depend on these links in order to maintain societal integration. They are created by a range of institutions, above all, political institutions such as parties and unions on the one hand and families on the other. The potential for generational integration is threatened, though, by the current changes in social structure and the welfare state. This chapter will treat both the cleavages and the potentials for their integration.

9.2 Old and New Inequalities

The "social question" dominating the end of the nineteenth century was the integration of the industrial workers, or in other words, the pacification of class conflict. This was achieved by giving workers some assurance of a stable life course, including the institutionalisation of retirement as a normal stage of life funded through public social security (Kohli 1987). At the beginning of the twenty-first century, class conflict seems to be defunct and its place taken over by generational conflict (Bengtson 1993; Kaufmann 2005). The new social question consists in maintaining a balanced generational contract, which should protect the

M. Kohli
European University Institute, Florence, Italy
e-mail: Martin.Kohli@EUI.eu

J.C. Tremmel (ed.), *A Young Generation Under Pressure?*,
DOI 10.1007/978-3-642-03483-1_9,

elderly and invest in the young while being financially sustainable and socially just (Albertini et al. 2007, p. 319). This is due both to the success of the welfare state, which has created age-graded claims and obligations and turned the elderly into its main clients, and to the demographic challenge of low fertility and increasing longevity (Kohli 2006, p. 456).

Are we thus moving from class conflict to generational conflict? (cf. also Hernes 1987; Mirowsky and Ross 1999; Esping-Andersen and Sarasa 2002). Such an assertion needs to be qualified in two ways (Kohli 2006, p. 456). First, it should be noted that conflict or competition between young and old over scarce resources is by no means new; it is a common theme in historical and anthropological accounts of pre-modern societies as well. But with the evolution of the modern welfare state, the form and arena of this conflict have changed. Secondly, and more importantly for our present concerns, it remains essential to assess the extent of the generational cleavage *per se* and the extent to which it masks the continued existence of the class cleavage between wealthy and poor (or owners and workers). There are, moreover, other cleavages that are usually categorized as "new" dimensions of inequality (as distinct from the "old" ones of class), such as those of gender and ethnicity (or "race"). Emphasizing the generational conflict as the new basic cleavage in society tends to downplay other inequalities, and by this, risks being ideological: It may function as a way to divert attention from the still existing problems of poverty and exclusion *within* generations, e.g., those based on class or gender (Kohli 2006, p. 467).

Age is the foremost basis for public entitlements and obligations. Public redistribution over the life course has been one of the strongest elements of what I have called the institutionalisation of the life course as a sequence of clearly delimited periods of life, each with its own profile of social roles and positions, of cultural expectations, and of legal obligations and claims (Kohli 2007). As shown by life course profiles of benefits and contributions, the elderly have become the main clients of welfare state redistribution, mostly through pensions and healthcare. In terms of legitimacy and distributional justice, redistribution among age groups is (relatively) unproblematic because we can expect everyone to live through the different stages of life. Unlike gender or ethnic groups, age groups do not have a fixed membership but a regularly changing one where all individuals progress through the life course from one stage to the next according to an institutionalised schedule (Kohli 2006, p. 458). Thus, differential treatment of age groups is morally acceptable (cf. Daniels, 1988) and may be justified by the different needs that age groups have, or by reasonable political goals (cf. Esping-Andersen et al. 2002; Esping-Andersen and Sarasa 2002; Preston 1984). The only problem here is posed by the fact that people do *not* all live equally long. This differential longevity is socially stratified, and thus constitutes a massive social inequality that is compounded by demographic aging.

Generational redistribution, on the other hand, is inherently problematic. "Generation" can be defined in terms of position in the family lineage or, at the societal level, in terms of being born in a certain time period and sharing the same historical experiences. Thus, societal generations have a fixed membership (Kohli 2006,

p. 458), and there is no legitimisation for an unequal treatment of them – indiscriminately of the question of how far into the future (or into the past) the standard of equality should be extended. The intergenerational sharing of burdens and rewards is just or fair to the extent that each generation can expect to receive the same treatment as the preceding and following ones while moving through the stages of life. Financing the elderly during one's professional life through a pay-as-you-go system is not problematic as long as one can expect to have one's own retirement funded by the next generation as well (Kohli 2006, p. 463). Unfortunately though, this is rarely the case; generational differences are the rule rather than the exception.

9.3 The Impact of Historical and Macro-Structural Changes

The reason for this phenomenon is linked to the experience of historical watersheds such as wars or system changes. These have varied massively from country to country, and have been more numerous in some countries than in others. Switzerland is an example of a rather fortunate country which has had a less-eventful recent history than others, and the US is another such example with much more continuity than most European countries. Like most social science literature, the literature on generations is still to a large extent an American literature, and therefore does not take into account what people across most of Europe have experienced in terms of historical discontinuity. The inclusion of a European perspective is therefore highly necessary.

As an illustration, here are some data on how Germans view the impact of historical events on their past lives (cf. Scherger and Kohli 2005). It is taken from the German Aging Survey of 1996, a nationally representative survey of the German population aged 40–85 and living in private households (cf. Kohli et al. 2000). The two major events in recent history for the respondents were World War II and the "turn" (*die Wende*), i.e., the demise of socialism and German reunification. Whereas West Germans attach more importance to World War II, in the East of the country the "turn" has been the key event (cf. Table 9.1). Other events or changes that are mentioned to some extent in the West, but by almost no one in the East, are the cultural and political transformation of the 1960s ("1968") and the nuclear accident and fallout of Chernobyl.

This overall result varies by age (cf. Fig. 9.1). For the 70–85-year-old West Germans, World War II remains the paramount historical event, while the Turn is almost non-existent. The impact of the Turn is higher for the younger groups while the impact of the War decreases. Among the East Germans, the role of World War II is slightly weaker than that in the West, with an identical age profile, while the role of the Turn is much stronger, with over nine-tenths of the 40–54-year-olds asserting that it has left a special imprint on their lives.

Figure 9.2 shows a Lexis diagram of how German birth cohorts of the twentieth century have moved through historical time. Following Karl Mannheim (1928), we may ask which periods in life are especially likely to leave an imprint of historical

Table 9.1 Historical watersheds in West and East Germany (in %)

	West	East
World War I	0.7	0.8
World War II	55.1	31.6
"Turn" (unification)	30.0	80.7
Chernobyl	5.6	0.3
"1968"	4.1	0.8

Answers to the question "This question concerns how people think about their past. There have been many events or changes in our country and in the world in this century. Please name one or two such events or changes that have left a special imprint on your life". Own calculations based on the German Aging Survey 1996

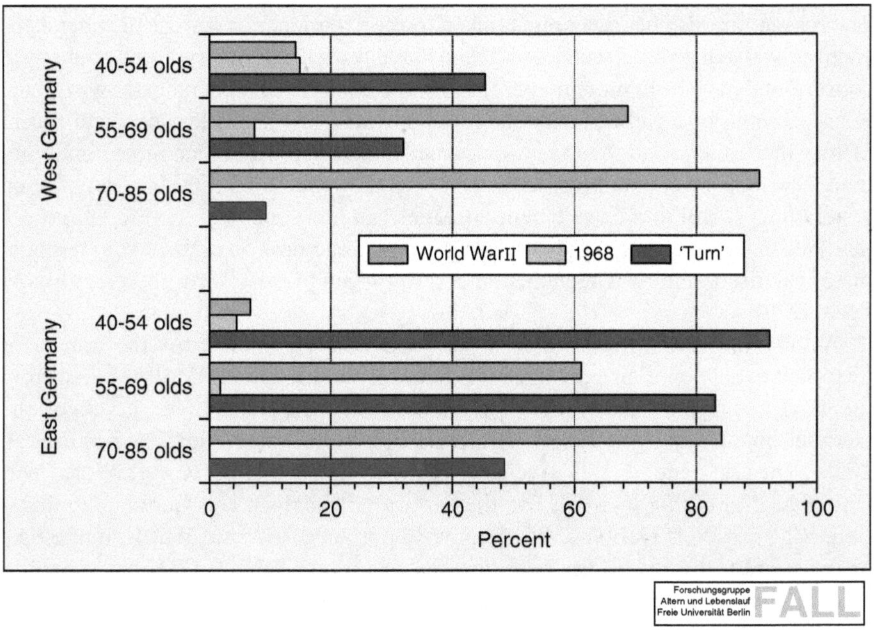

Fig. 9.1 Historical watersheds by age groups in West and East Germany. Own calculations based on the German Ageing Survey 1996

events. For Mannheim, this was the period of adolescence. In the wake of psychoanalysis, some developmental experts might favour the period of early childhood instead. Glen Elder, in his pioneering study (1974), has examined the long-term impact of the Great Depression of the early 1930s in the US on two cohorts which experienced this event at different ages, early childhood or early adolescence, during the great depression. Where due to the Depression men became

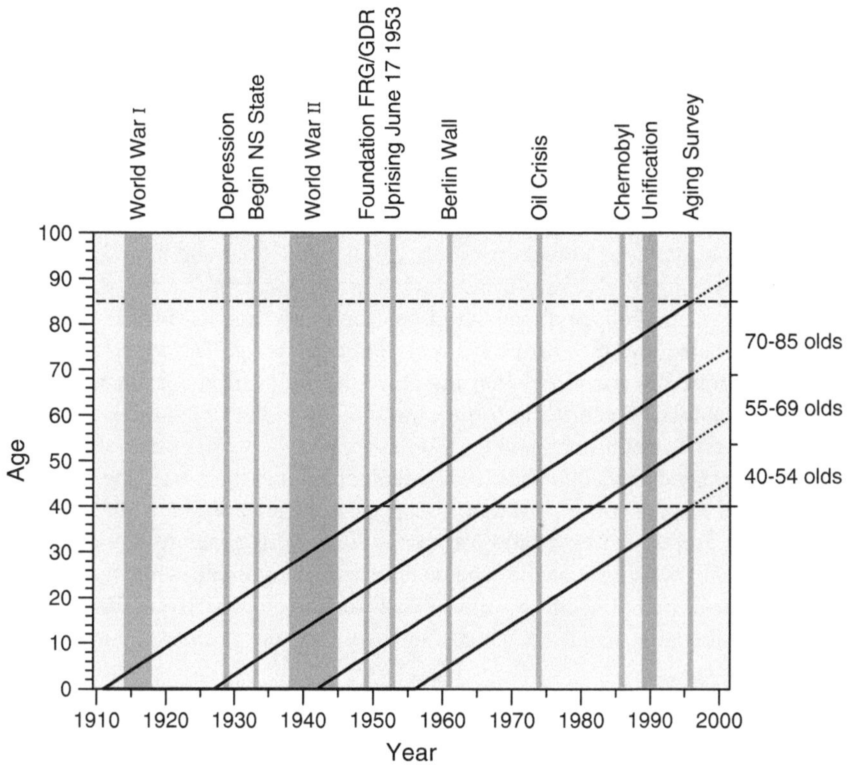

Fig. 9.2 Cohorts in historical time (From Kohli et al. 2000, p. 10)

unemployed, the (mediating) family dynamics changed and the family members were hit by economic insecurities. Elder showed that the impact of the Depression was, in the long run, more negative for those who lived through it in early childhood than in early adolescence. Another important aspect is the extent to which it is later possible to make up for this vulnerability. Depending on later conditions, there is substantial resilience: those cohorts that have been disadvantaged in earlier stages can make this up later if offered special opportunities.

Another element of generational cleavages is macro-structural changes in demography or the economy, such as the major shift from agriculture to industry and services in our societies across the past decades. This shift occurred with greatest speed in the Mediterranean countries, Scandinavia and Ireland. Finland, for example, experienced a massive contraction of agriculture during the life course of the current elderly. Its agricultural labour force decreased from 71% in 1920 to 46% in 1950 and 8% in 1990. In rough measure, this means that about three-fifths of the current Finnish retirees were born on farms – an experience which obviously is not easily forgotten.

9.4 The Economics of Demographic Discontinuity

Cultural shifts such as those of the 1960s as well as changes in institutionalised life course patterns leading to age-graded experiences, obligations and entitlements are other factors that create generational cleavages. Richard Easterlin (1980) has offered a poignant analysis of economic cleavages among generations based on the demographic discontinuity of baby boom and baby bust. His argument is that large birth cohorts face more competition in schools, labour and marriage markets and will thus remain relatively disadvantaged over their life course. As a consequence, they also produce fewer children; for these smaller birth cohorts, the opposite holds, so that they will have more children again. The argument has not been corroborated in countries other than the US, but is an important reminder of how demographic and economic fortunes may interact with each other to produce different cohorts. David Thomson (1989) has treated the welfare state as a generational conspiracy. He tried to show for New Zealand that there was one generation which played the system so well that it reaped all the advantages while both those living earlier and those living later had to pay for it. This generation first created a youth-state with housing subsidies and benefits for young families and then, over its own life course, turned it into a welfare state for the elderly (Kohli 2006, p. 466) This is a challenging assertion which, however, has not found support for other countries so far.

How do the different generations fare in terms of economic well-being? The best comparative overview over the income positions of age groups or cohorts is available in an OECD paper by Michael Förster and Marco Mira D'Ercole (2005). It contains unified data for the beginning of this century for different countries, some of which are selected for Table 9.2. The relative disposable incomes are equivalised, i.e., individual incomes are adjusted for household size. Hundred is the average for the population over all ages. The children and partly but not always the young aged 18–25 are below this average, and the elderly (with a few exceptions) even more so.

A precise differentiation between life course (age) and generational (cohort) effects would require data over time for corresponding age groups. In France, as an example, the age group from 18 to 25 has clearly lost in the decade from 1984 to 1994 and then has made up some of it again. Other countries have gone through a different evolution. In Italy, for instance, this age group has lost in both periods, and this is also the composite pattern for all 17 OECD countries for which these data are available (cf. Table 9.2).

Overall, there has been stability in the relative income of children and adolescents (those aged 1–17) in the decade from 1985 to 1995 and a slight increase in the half decade from the mid-1990s to 2000. Young adults have lost ground over both periods, which may be the result of the expansion of higher education, or in other words, the later transition into the labour force. Children have lower relative equivalent disposable incomes than the active population whereas for young adults the picture is uneven. In most countries, incomes peak in middle adulthood and then

Table 9.2 Relative incomes by age groups, ca. 2000

Country	Age						
	0–17	18–25	26–40	41–50	51–65	66–75	76+
Australia, 1999	87.6	120.4	108.6	122.0	92.0	67.0	63.5
Change, 1984–1994	−2.0	−9.5					
Change, 1994–1999	3.0	0.1	−2.1	−1.4	2.1	–0.5	−2.3
France, 2000	93.4	98.2	99.7	111.6	114.6	88.5	86.4
Change, 1984–1994	0.4	−5.0	−5.9	2.7	6.5	7.4	0.4
Change, 1994–2000	–1.5	1.6	–0.3	−3.0	5.1	−5.2	4.0
Germany (old Länder), 2001	89.1	95.8	100.2	114.3	113.1	89.4	83.5
Change, 1984–1994	–3.0	−3.1	–4.2	8.5	0.7	4.8	0.4
Change, 1994–2001	0.4	–0.1	0.0	–6.1	3.0	2.4	2.2
Hungary, 2000	92.9	109.2	105.7	109.2	107.8	80.3	82.3
Change, 1991–1995	–6.2	1.9	−2.2	2.9	3.8	6.6	1.7
Change, 1995–2000	–0.6	−1.8	3.5	−9.9	6.4	−5.0	3.8
Italy, 2000	89.1	101.8	105.6	105.3	112.8	86.2	77.2
Change, 1984–1995	−3.4	−2.2	−1.3	0.9	3.5	5.7	5.4
Change, 1995–2000	2.3	−2.8	0.6	−1.4	1.6	−1.8	−6.1
Japan, 2000	90.6	104.3	98.5	109.2	113.0	90.6	88.8
Change, 1985–1994	−1.4	−1.8	2.0	1.0	1.7	−1.9	−5.4
Change, 1994–2000	−0.5	−1.4	0.1	0.4	0.3	1.1	1.7
Sweden, 2000	98.3	91.7	99.1	111.8	125.3	88.3	68.6
Change, 1983–1995	−2.2	−10.7	−4.7	0.8	7.7	5.8	8.8
Change, 1995–2000	2.9	0.5	1.4	−2.8	2.9	−5.0	−7.5
Switzerland, 2001	85.5	109.2	101.2	109.5	114.5	91.0	78.2
Change, 1998–2001	1.5	4.4	0.6	1.4	−5.1	−3.4	−1.3
United Kingdom, 2000	88.4	106.2	108.0	121.3	108.5	77.2	71.0
Change, 1985–1995	−3.8	−2.2	1.3	−0.5	2.6	5.9	2.0
Change, 1995–2000	2.6	−5.4	1.5	−1.7	0.7	−2.7	−3.2
United States, 2000	86.7	93.6	103.5	113.9	121.4	96.8	80.6
Change, 1984–1995	2.5	−5.1	−1.8	0.7	3.1	−0.3	−2.4
Change, 1995–2000	2.6	0.0	1.2	−4.3	−2.3	−2.0	−1.5
OECD 17, 2000	91.7	99.8	103.7	112.3	113.2	86.3	77.8
Change, 1985–1995	−0.1	−5.7	−1.3	2.6	2.7	2.4	0.0
Change, 1995–2000	0.5	−1.3	1.0	−3.7	1.6	−1.0	−0.3

Changes in relative incomes by age groups, ca. 1984–2000

Note: Relative incomes are in percent of mean equivalized income of the total population. Changes are in percentage points

Source: Förster and Mira D'Ercole (2005), pp. 68–71

decrease again. The elderly fare worse than the active population, and also somewhat worse than children; the US, together with Switzerland, is again an outlier in this respect. The "old olds" (76+) have especially low incomes, considerably lower than those of the "young olds" (66–75). The incomes of the elderly grew from the mid-1980s to the mid-1990s due to the expansion of old-age security; this trend was reversed after the mid-1990s, however.

A different assessment of the economic well-being of the age groups and cohorts is given by the poverty rates, measured here as the proportion below 50% of the median equivalised income (cf. Table 9.3). Overall, the rate at the beginning of this century amounted to 10.4% in the OECD 24. In the liberal countries – Australia,

Table 9.3 Relative poverty rates by age groups, ca. 2000

Country	Age							Total
	0–17	18–25	26–40	41–50	51–65	66–75	76+	
Australia, 1999	11.6	5.6	8.0	8.6	14.0	20.6	28.8	11.2
Change, 1994–1999	0.7	−0.5	1.1	3.1	−0.3	6.7	8.3	1.9
France, 2000	7.3	7.6	5.6	5.2	6.6	9.9	11.3	7.0
Change, 1994–2000	0.2	−0.7	−0.4	−0.7	−1.2	1.5	−3.5	−0.4
Germany (old Länder), 2001	13.1	15.6	9.6	4.9	9.0	8.9	11.1	10.0
Change, 1994–2001	2.5	1.9	0.9	−1.7	1.1	0.3	−1.3	0.6
Hungary, 2000	13.1	7.1	7.5	8.2	7.2	5.5	4.8	8.1
Change, 1995–2000	2.8	0.0	0.8	2.2	2.2	−0.2	−6.2	0.8
Italy, 2000	15.7	14.0	11.0	11.7	10.7	14.6	16.4	12.9
Change, 1995–2000	−2.9	0.4	−3.1	1.2	−1.2	−0.1	0.2	−1.3
Japan, 2000	14.3	16.6	12.4	11.7	14.4	19.5	23.8	15.3
Change, 1994–2000	2.3	2.5	2.0	1.5	1.0	−1.7	−2.3	1.6
Sweden, 2000	3.6	14.4	4.9	2.8	2.4	4.6	11.5	5.3
Change, 1995–2000	1.1	2.0	1.5	0.6	0.4	2.2	6.2	1.6
Switzerland, 2001	6.8	5.5	5.9	3.7	7.6	10.4	12.7	6.7
Change, 1998–2001	−3.6	−5.3	−0.7	−3.7	0.7	0.2	−5.1	−1.9
United Kingdom, 2000	16.2	11.9	8.7	7.9	7.6	11.4	19.2	11.4
Change, 1995–2000	−1.2	1.6	−0.8	2.1	1.2	1.6	4.4	0.5
United States, 2000	21.7	19.1	13.8	11.0	13.0	20.3	29.6	17.1
Change, 1995–2000	−0.6	0.2	0.1	0.8	0.0	3.4	4.0	0.4
OECD 24, 2000	12.3	11.5	8.7	7.5	8.9	11.4	16.5	10.4
Change, 1995–2000	0.9	0.7	0.5	0.8	0.5	0.1	−0.2	0.5

Changes in relative poverty rates by age groups, ca. 1995–2000
Note: Relative poverty rates in percent, changes in percentage points. Poverty threshold set at 50% of the median disposable income of the total population
Source: Förster and Mira D'Ercole (2005), pp. 72–74

the UK and the US – both children and the elderly have much higher poverty rates than the population at working age. This is not the case in most other countries. 17% of the population of the US live in relative poverty as against 5% of the Swedish population. This clearly shows how welfare regimes make a difference.

The welfare state has succeeded in smoothing lifetime consumption chances, and thus in keeping economic cleavages between generations at bay. The stylised picture presented above shows a massive variation of relative poverty rates among nations, and especially between the two welfare regimes at opposite ends, the "liberal" (Anglo-Saxon) versus the "social-democratic" (Scandinavian) regime. Children and the elderly fare worse than the active population in the liberal regime but not in the social-democratic regime. The other two regimes – the "conservative" regime of continental western Europe and the "familistic" regime of the Mediterranean – are situated somewhere in between. As an example of the latter, Italy does not have a "residual" welfare state but a welfare state which is focused on the male breadwinners. In spite of some recent changes, pension levels for these male breadwinners are still very high.

In a longer overall perspective, poverty has remained stable or increased among children. It decreased among the elderly after the 1970s but this trend has stopped in the mid-1990s; one can already detect some effects of recent pension "reforms" – or rather retrenchments (Liebig et al. 2004). The fairly even distribution of economic resources is now threatened both by the primary distribution of income on the labour market and by its redistribution through the welfare state. Increasing labour market inequalities as well as welfare state retrenchment may deepen economic cleavages. In policy terms, it is necessary to target support for children (and their parents) but there is no reason to strip the elderly of their benefits considering how they fare compared to the total population.

There is thus no obvious possibility for generational mobilisation. On the one hand, economic cleavages are (still) modest, and on the other hand such a mobilisation would have to overcome several difficulties. One is that the temporal boundaries of generations or cohorts are inherently fuzzy – usually the result of a simple act of will. This fuzziness does not facilitate the perception of a common destiny: we may take 5-year birth cohorts or 20-year generations, and even then it is not clear where they start and where they end. A second difficulty is that generations are internally differentiated with regard to class, religion, ethnicity or gender, which makes any attempt to establish a feeling of "being in the same boat" not very convincing. In spite of these difficulties, major revolutions have been driven by youth movements. This has been the case for the French revolution just as for the Bolshevik revolution, for the Fascist revolution in Italy just as for the National-Socialist revolution in Germany. Most of the leading cadres of the National Socialist Party, for example, were in their early thirties in 1933 and in their mid-forties after the "Thousand Years". On another note, the Fascist anthem "Giovinezza, giovinezza, primavera di bellezza" celebrated youth as the "spring of beauty". The Fascists attempted to mobilise youth as the vanguard of cultural and political change, necessarily at war with the adult world (Wohl 1979). The problem of internal differentiation was countered by generational elites, which succeeded in presenting themselves as carrier groups for other strata as well.

9.5 Moving Towards Gerontocracy?

What are the chances for the "new" or upcoming economic conflicts to lead to a likewise mobilisation? As to age-specific attitudes towards social policy issues such as whether pensions should be increased, decreased, or remain the same, most people surveyed in 1996 supported pensions to remain the same or even increase, with only modest age effects (cf. Table 9.4, Hicks 2001). Pensions were thus (still) popular among all age groups. Even when it was pointed out that taxes might have to be raised in order to increase government spending on retirement benefits, large parts of all age groups still opted for such an increase. The largest support for increasing pensions among the countries selected for Table 9.4 was obtained in the UK where the public pension level was the lowest. On the other hand, a Eurobarometer survey of 2001 showed that increasing the age of retirement was very unpopular – again across all age groups (Kohl 2003; cf. also Kohli 2006, p. 473).

Table 9.4 Age-specific attitudes towards government spending on pensions

Percentage indicating that they would like to see more, or much more, government spending on retirement benefits (being asked to remember that if you say "much more", it might require a tax increase to pay for it)

	Age group				
	under 30	30–39	40–49	50–64	65+
Canada	34.8	23.4	24.6	30.5	20.5
Germany	45.5	41.6	41.6	48.4	51.7
Italy	55.8	60.4	65.8	65.8	75.6
Japan	54.6	48.0	53.9	57.9	60.9
Sweden	41.7	51.3	51.9	59.8	66.8
United Kingdom	63.3	79.2	79.7	79.8	87.1
United States	55.0	51.0	45.7	48.9	45.2

Source: Hicks (2001) based on the International Social Survey Program (ISSP) 1996

How do attitudes translate into party voting? Age differences are absent in the US and counterintuitive in Germany, if one assumes that older people should support the party most in favour of the welfare state, i.e., the Social Democrats (cf. Kohli et al. 1999). Through the pension reform of 1957, the Christian Democrats succeeded in capturing the agenda of welfare. This has translated into higher vote shares for the among the elderly than among other parts of the population. Although the Left currently profits from protest votes mainly by the elderly, age effects have favoured the, which among the 60+ in federal elections has always been above the mean for the total population.

Much more important are period effects, which either favour the Left or the Right and which have a strong impact on the young generations. First-time voters are especially sensitive to period effects and, as a cohort, tend to retain their original voting decision for the rest of their life course. In the US, which has frequent issue voting at the local and the state level, the age effects are usually somewhat stronger with regard to "young" issues such as education than with regard to "old" issues such as pensions or health. But this is mediated by community tenure. With regard to the votes on the expansion of schools, for instance, the population who has lived in the community for some time does not show any age effects. However, there are age effects in those communities where people move in retirement. Moving into a community as an old person does not create a sufficient connection to the local political agenda to foster generational integration.

The elderly have an increasing weight in public voting not only because of their increasing demographic share, but also because they have a higher participation in elections than the young (cf. Binstock 2000). A similar pattern emerges for party membership. The ageing of party members and party elites is uneven. In Germany, the Greens are basically a one-generation party which has aged with its generation. Their elites are now around 50 years old. The Post-Socialist Party has been mostly a party of retirees, but since the formation of the Left party there has been some infusion of younger members as well. All parties except the Greens are faced with a higher membership among retirees than among the active population.

But party membership does not necessarily translate into power. In the German case – unlike apparently in France (cf. Louis Chauvel's text in this issue) – there exists a paradox of representation: The elderly have a much lower representation in parliament and government than their population share, and since the 1960s the mean age of the members of the Federal Parliament has even decreased somewhat. Non-traditional participation is also low but to some extent growing, and we may assume that these new forms of old-age activism will gain in importance with the aging of the 68ers.

Some proponents of "generational equity" argue that the window of opportunity for implementing reforms of the welfare state is closing because the older population increasingly dominates the political arena by its sheer voting weight. They see a point of *no return* when the power of the elderly will be such that they will be able to block any attempt at reducing their benefits. In a model for Germany, Hans-Jürgen Sinn and Silke Uebelmesser (Sinn and Uebelmesser 2002, p. 155) took into account both demography and age-specific voting participation, and made a projection of the median age of voters and of the "indifference age" where one is affected neither positively nor negatively by a pension reform. Above this threshold, people are more likely to profit from improvements in old-age security; below it, they are more likely to have a negative pay-off with the costs outweighing the benefits. The assumption is that reform will be feasible only if the median voter favours it. The authors conclude that until 2016 a reform can be democratically enforced because a majority of the voters will still be below the indifference age. 2016 is "Germany's last chance"; after that year it will be a gerontocracy, with no possibility of cutting old-age benefits anymore because the majority will vote for them. Such a model of self-interest is of course highly flawed; it presupposes that people's votes are based only on their current individual interest position and that voting shares fully translate into specific policies – both of which are manifestly not the case (Kohli 2006, p. 466). There is among the elderly an interest in the following generations, in one's own family but also on a societal level, and thus possibly an even stronger tendency for group-oriented ("socio-tropic") voting than among the general population. A simple rational choice model which assumes that voters maximise their own perceived current interests does not provide a valid account of the act of voting.

9.6 Parties and Unions as Mediating Organizations

Why are age conflicts not more pronounced? One reason – at least in the corporatist pattern of Germany – is the mediating function of political organizations such as parties and trade unions (Kohli et al. 1999). These organizations have created special groups for the elderly, just as for other hitherto neglected categories such as women and the young. They have set up these groups as a form of internalised interest groups that mobilise these categories for the goals of the overarching organization. Another advantage of such groups is that they offer further possibilities of participation for political cadres beyond the main organizational hierarchies. Those who, e.g., leave the Federal Parliament and have to hand over their mandates to younger colleagues can then take over functions in the parties' senior groups. The idea is to appropriate the demands of these population categories by giving them a special organizational niche, and thereby hoping that they will neither mobilise outside the party nor weigh on its core business. This is even more the case with the trade unions, where the dilemma is heightened by the fact that unions' avowed purpose is directed to the working population. But unions also depend on their retired members for support and as a signal to their active members, and therefore offer them special groups for organising within the union but detached from its core business (cf. Wolf et al. 1994).

The shifting generational agenda is mirrored by the weight of these groups. In the Christian Democratic Party, for example, the past years have seen a shift from privileging the young to aiming for a balance between the generations. In the build-up for the 2009 election, the heads of the *Junge Union* and *Senioren-Union* were therefore called upon to cooperate on an agenda of generational integration. To the extent that these special groups are successful, age conflicts remain within the organizational reach of the parties and do not manifest themselves on the open political market. The exceptions are the grey parties, which have had some electoral success in some countries, especially in the Netherlands. But as with most one-issue parties, they have usually not lasted because other parties took up their issue or because they self-destructed over their own internal issue divisions. The only successful one-issue party in Germany so far has been the Greens, and they were successful by broadening their agenda.

9.7 Family Relations

Another reason for the low salience of age conflicts is family relations and inter-family transfers. Families are the prototypical institutions of age integration. An example is given by Peter Uhlenberg's (2009) analysis of data from the US General Social Survey that asked adult respondents to identify up to five other adults with whom they had discussed important matters over the past 6 months. The result was very clear: the discussion partners were either age peers or family members. No one under age 30 identified any non-kin over 70 as a personal discussion partner, and vice-versa. In other words, no members of other generations and ages were mentioned except within the family.

The importance of the family for age-integration is corroborated by data on residential patterns and support. While household co-residence of adult family generations in western Europe today has become rare, except for some Mediterranean countries, geographical proximity is high. The same applies to emotional closeness and to social and financial support. The other side of the coin is a surprisingly low prevalence of intergenerational family conflicts. In Germany, these issues were first studied through the *German Aging Survey (Alters-Survey)*

(Kohli 1999; Kohli and Künemund 2005), at the European level through the *Survey of Health, Ageing and Retirement in Europe (SHARE)* (e.g., Albertini et al. 2007). Elderly parents are net givers in terms of *inter vivos* financial transfers; their net contribution to their descendants in Germany in 1996 amounted to 9% of the yearly pension sum. Volunteering and family support activities of the elderly made up another 21% (Kohli 1999). Parental altruism, in terms of an orientation towards the special needs of their children, is strong, even though there may also be expectations of reciprocity (Kohli 2006, p. 474). Inheritance is another major and substantive concern of the elderly, as even those with modest means usually want to leave something to their children. There is a systematic difference between the generations here: parents have a stake in continuation by transferring their social, material and cultural capital to their children, while children have a stake in becoming autonomous. Both family sociology and evolutionary theory concur on this (Giarrusso et al. 1994; Low 1998). It is often argued that this is a recent development. In the family of the nineteenth century, before the full onset of industrialisation – so the argument goes – the elderly were supported by their children, and children were seen as an insurance for old age. But this is less evident than it seems at first sight. A revisionist social history of generations now claims that parents have always given more to their children than vice-versa (e.g., Ehmer 2000).

Figure 9.3 (from Kohli et al. 2007) provides information, for a range of European countries, on those aged 50 or more who have given or received financial transfers (above the threshold of 250€) or social support across family generations over the past 12 months before the interview.[1] That these elderly Europeans are net givers emerges clearly: Financial transfers have been given on a much more massive scale than received. The same applies for social support, defined here as personal care, practical household help, help with paperwork, and grand-parenting. Looking after grand-children (without the presence of the parents) is included here as social support because it helps young parents (especially mothers) to reconcile parenthood and employment. This can be critical for the mother's participation on the labour market as well as for the decision to have children in the first place.

Another aspect is co-residence of adult generations in the same household. As mentioned above, this has become rare in the Continental and Nordic countries, but is still frequent in the Mediterranean regime where much intergenerational support occurs in the form of co-residence. While it is difficult to precisely pin down the extent and direction of transfer flows within a household, there is indirect evidence

[1]See Albertini et al. (2007) for a more detailed analysis. Figures 9.3 and 9.4 are based on SHARE Wave 1 (2004), release 1. This release is preliminary and may contain errors, which will be corrected in later releases. The SHARE data collection has been primarily funded by the European Commission through the 5th Framework Programme (Project QLK6-CT-2001–00360 in the thematic programme Quality of Life). Additional funding came from the US National Institute on Aging (U01 AG09740–13 S2, P01 AG005842, P01 AG08291, P30 AG12815, Y1-AG-4553–01 and OGHA 04–064). Data collection in Austria (through the Austrian Science Fund, FWF), Belgium (through the Belgian Science Policy Office) and Switzerland (through BBW/OFES/UFES) was nationally funded. The SHARE data set is introduced in Börsch-Supan et al. (2005); methodological details are reported in Börsch-Supan and Jürges (2005).

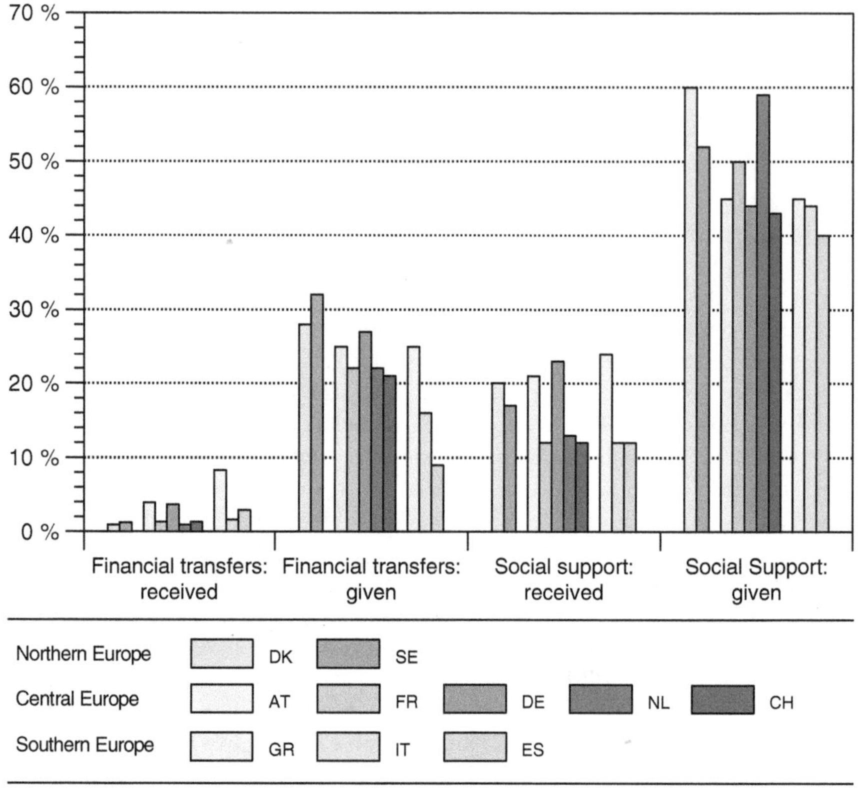

Fig. 9.3 Frequency of financial transfers and social support among adult family generations
Data source: SHARE 2004 release 1, own calculations

that here as well parents are net givers. The Mediterranean countries are characterized by very late exit of the young from their parental homes, which means that the highest rates of co-residence in the SHARE sample are found among the 50- to 60-year-old parents; but there are also very clear differences among the regimes for the over 80-year-olds. Co-residence in Scandinavia practically does not exist at that age, while in Italy it is still in the range of 30%. The Nordic regime is thus much more individualised. While the Nordic countries offer good community services for the elderly and an extended sector of old-age homes, both of these practically do not exist in Italy or in Spain where everything depends on the family. Recently, the family has started to care for its older members through the low-wage work of immigrant women – allowed to work in large numbers in spite of the rampant current anti-immigration discourse in Italy.

Figure 9.4 shows the variation among welfare regimes in the amounts of intergenerational support. This balance of giving and receiving combines financial transfers and social support; each hour of social support has been calculated with a wage rate of 7.50€. The overall picture confirms the evidence presented so far: Up

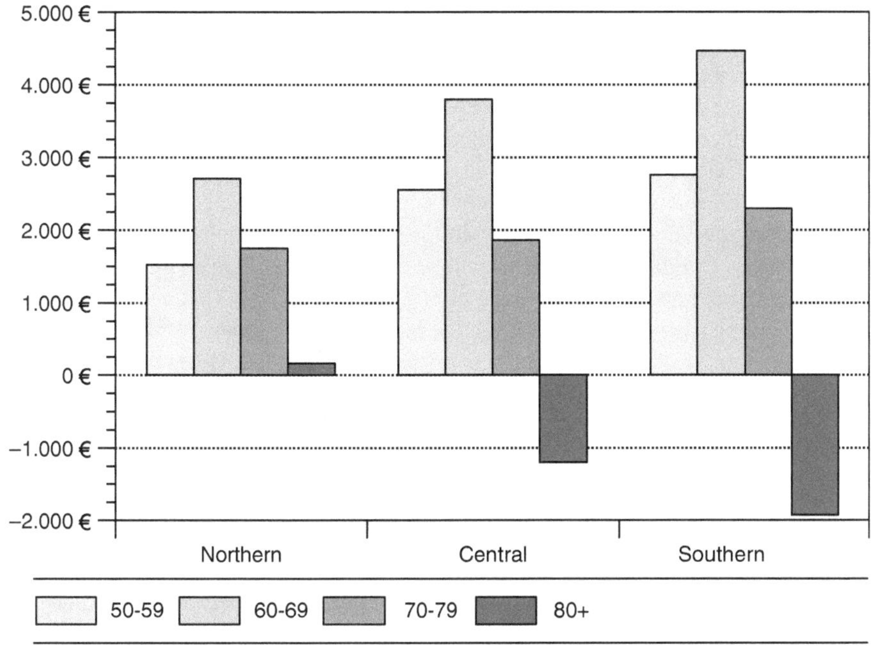

Fig. 9.4 Balance of financial transfers and social support among adult family generations by age group and regime
Data source: SHARE 2004 release 1, own calculations (cf. Kohli et al. 2009)

to age 80 people are net givers, whereas after this age they become net recipients in central and southern Europe but remain net givers in the Nordic countries.

9.8 Generation and Class: Cleavages and Integration

In Western societies, social stratification in terms of labour incomes and welfare (transfer) incomes is historically increasing. The aging of the population is likely to deepen class inequalities because important dimensions of the life course such as morbidity and mortality, functional capacity, pension income as well as social participation and embeddedness are socially stratified. Inter-individual variation is to a considerable extent socially stratified variation, and it increases with age: The class divide matters more in old age than at any other time of life. The historically increasing stratification also increases inequalities within age groups. This historical (period) effect interacts with the age effect with regard to the lifetime accumulation of benefits and deficits, vulnerability and resilience. But while class cleavages deepen, class mobilisation seems to fade away. Class mobilisation is still institutionalised in the systems of industrial relations as well as in most party systems. However, industrial relations are nowadays characterized by weakening trade union power and weakening corporatist arrangements. Stable party attachments as well as traditional left–right cleavages are weakening, too.

As to generations, current structural trends – demographic discontinuity, economic insecurity and welfare state retrenchment – lead to a high and increasing salience of generational cleavages, which offer a considerable potential for generational mobilisation. Nevertheless, the likelihood of a gerontocracy is low and support for the public generational contract is still broad among all age groups. The age-integrative effects of family solidarity are strong, and political organisations play a key mediating role. However, the increasing salience of class cleavages may change this picture. The salience of class is especially high among the elderly and also among the young, i.e., among the more vulnerable parts of the population. This interaction of class and age or generation may create new lines of mobilisation as new cohorts grow up and enter old age.

References

Albertini M, Kohli M, Vogel C (2007) Intergenerational transfers of time and money in European families: common patterns–different regimes?. J Eur Soc Pol 17(4/2007):319–334

Bengtson VL (1993) Is the "contract across generations" changing? Effects of population ageing on obligations and expectations across age groups. In: Bengtson VL, Achenbaum WA (eds) The changing contract across generations. Aldine de Gruyter, New York, pp 3–24

Binstock RH (2000) Older people and voting participation: past and future. Gerontol 40(1/2000):18–31

Börsch-Supan A, Jürges H (eds) (2005) The survey of health, ageing and retirement in Europe – methodology. MEA, Mannheim

Börsch-Supan A et al (eds) (2005) Health, ageing and retirement in Europe: first results from SHARE. MEA, Mannheim

Daniels N (1988) Am I my parents' keeper? An essay on justice between the old and the young. Oxford University Press, Oxford

Easterlin RA (1980) Birth and fortune: The impact of numbers on personal welfare. Basic Books, New York

Ehmer J (2000) Ökonomische Transfers und emotionale Bindungen in den Generationenbeziehungen des 18. und 19. Jahrhunderts. In: Kohli M, Szydlik M (eds) Generationen in Familie und Gesellschaft. Leske + Budrich, Opladen, pp 77–96

Elder GH Jr (1974) Children of the great depression: social change in life experience. University of Chicago Press, Chicago

Esping-Andersen G, Sarasa S (2002) The generational contract reconsidered. J Eur Soc Pol 12(1/2002):5–21

Esping-Andersen G et al (2002) Why we need a new welfare state. Oxford University Press, Oxford

Förster M, Mira d'Ercole M (2005) Income distribution and poverty in OECD countries in the second half of the 1990s. In: OECD social employment and migration working papers 22. OECD, Paris. http://ideas.repec.org/p/oec/elsaab/22-en.html (16.07.2008)

Giarrusso R, Bengtson VL, Stallings M (1994) The "Intergenerational Stake" hypothesis revisited: parent-child differences in perceptions of relationships 20 years later. In: Vern LB, Warner Schaie K, Burton LM (eds) Adult intergenerational relations. Springer, New York, pp 227–263

Hernes HM (1987) Welfare state and women power. Norwegian University Press, Oslo

Hicks P (2001) Public support for retirement income reform. OECD labour market and social policy occasional papers no. 55. http://ideas.repec.org/p/oec/elsaaa/55-en.html (16.07.2008)

Kaufmann F-X (2005) Gibt es einen Generationenvertrag? In: Kaufmann F-X (ed) Sozialpolitik und Sozialstaat: Soziologische Analysen, 2nd ed. Wiesbaden: VS (1st edition 2002), pp 161–182.

Kohl J (2003) Citizens' opinions on the transition from work to retirement. Paper for the ISSA 4th International Research Conference on Social Security in a Long Life Society, Antwerp

Kohli M (1987) Retirement and the moral economy: an historical interpretation of the German Case. J Aging Stud 1(2/1987):125–144

Kohli M (1999) Private and public transfers between generations: linking the family and the state. Eur Soc 1(1/1999):81–104

Kohli M (2006) Aging and justice. In: Binstock RH, George LK (eds) Handbook of aging and the social sciences, 6th edn. Academic Press, San Diego, CA (1st edn 1981), pp 456–478

Kohli M (2007) The institutionalization of the life course: looking back to look ahead. Res Hum Dev 4 (3-4/2007):253–271

Kohli M, Künemund H (eds) (2005) Die zweite Lebenshälfte. Gesellschaftliche Lage und Partizipation im Spiegel des Alters-Survey (2, erweiterte Auflage). VS Verlag für Sozialwissenschaften, Wiesbaden

Kohli M, Neckel S, Wolf J (1999) Krieg der Generationen? Die politische Macht der Älteren. In: Niederfranke A, Naegele G, Frahm E (eds) Funkkolleg Altern, Bd. 2. Westdeutscher Verlag, Opladen, pp 479–514

Kohli M, Künemund H, Motel A, Szydlik M (2000) Grunddaten zur Lebenssituation der 40–85 jährigen deutschen Bevölkerung. Ergebnisse des Alters-Survey. Weißensee, Berlin

Kohli M, Künemund H, Vogel (2009) Giving and receiving: the balance of intergenerational exchange. Poster presented at the Geront Soc Am 62nd Annual Sc Meeting, Atlanta, GA, Nov 18–22

Liebig S, Lengfeld H, Mau S (2004) Einleitung: Gesellschaftliche Verteilungsprobleme und der Beitrag der soziologischen Gerechtigkeitsforschung. In: Liebig S, Lengfeld H, Mau S (eds) Verteilungsprobleme und Gerechtigkeit in modernen Gesellschaften. Frankfurt/M: Campus, pp 7–26

Low BS (1998) The evolution of human life histories. In: Crawford C, Krebs DL (eds) Handbook of evolutionary psychology: ideas, issues, and applications. Erlbaum, Mahwah, NJ, pp 131–161

Mannheim K (1928) Das Problem der Generationen. Kölner Vierjahrshefte für Soziologie 7(2-3/1928):157–185, 309–330

Mirowsky J, Ross CE (1999) Economic hardship across the life course. Am Soc Rev 64(4/1999):548–569

Preston SH (1984) Children and the elderly: divergent paths for America's dependents. Demography 21(4/1984):435–457

Scherger S, Kohli M (2005) Eine Gesellschaft – zwei Vergangenheiten? Historische Ereignisse und kollektives Gedächtnis in Ost- und Westdeutschland. BIOS – Zeitschrift für Biographieforschung, Oral History und Lebensverlaufsanalysen 18 (1/2005):3–27

Sinn H-W, Uebelmesser S (2002) Pensions and the path to gerontocracy in Germany. Eur J Pol Econ 19(1/2003):153–158

Thomson D (1989) Selfish generations: the ageing of the welfare state. Allen & Unwin, Wellington

Uhlenberg P (2009) Children in an aging society. Journal of Gerontology: Social Sciences 64B (4/2009):489–496

Wohl R (1979) The generation of 1914. Harvard University Press, Cambridge, MA

Wolf J, Kohli M, Künemund H (eds) (1994) Alter und gewerkschaftliche Politik. Auf dem Weg zur Rentnergewerkschaft? Bund-Verlag, Köln

Chapter 10
Who Wants What from the Welfare State? Socio-structural Cleavages in Distributional Politics: Evidence from Swiss Referendum Votes

Giuliano Bonoli and Silja Häusermann

10.1 Introduction

Research on individual social policy preferences has highlighted a number of socio-structural cleavages as determinants. Studies investigating public opinion on the various redistributive schemes that make up today's welfare states have shown the relevance of class-related factors such as income or education as key explanatory variables (Ferrera 1993; Taylor-Gooby 1995, 1998; and Svallfors 1997). More recent studies, however, have suggested that other factors are also likely to play a role. Among these, the most important are age, gender, and individual values (Armingeon 2006; Deitch 2004; and Roller 2000, 2002). The scenario that emerges from the existing literature is one of multiple intersecting cleavages, but it remains unclear as to what today is the relative weight and specific impact of each of these cleavages.

In addition, studies on policy preferences with regard to distributional issues suffer from a key weakness: they rely on survey data. Individual responses to questions asked in public opinion surveys are problematic for several reasons (Gaxie 1990; Kangas 1995; Berclaz 2002). Respondents may not be familiar with the subject of the survey or may not have an opinion on the question asked. Questions tend to be rather general, whereas people hold specific opinions on particular policies. In addition, researchers have pointed out the existence of a pro-altruism bias, or a tendency to reply in a "politically correct" manner (Taylor-Gooby 1998).

Against this background, our objective is to examine the structure of social policy preferences on the basis of reported voting behaviour in direct democratic referendums on social policy reforms. Switzerland has a strong tradition of

G. Bonoli (✉) and S. Häusermann
Swiss Graduate School for Public Administration (IDHEAP), University of Lausanne, Lausanne, Switzerland
e-mail: Giuliano.Bonoli@idheap.unil.ch

J.C. Tremmel (ed.), *A Young Generation Under Pressure?*,
DOI 10.1007/978-3-642-03483-1_10, © Springer-Verlag Berlin Heidelberg 2010

referendums since 1848.[1] The paper analyses voting patterns in 22 referendums on distributional issues that took place between 1981 and 2004. These include a variety of proposals ranging from lowering the age of retirement to cutting unemployment benefits or introducing a brand-new maternity insurance scheme. Using multivariate logistic regression analysis, we assess the relative importance of the various putative cleavages.

Data on reported voting behaviour are not unproblematic, either. Turnout is socially structured: non-nationals (about 20% of the Swiss population) are barred from voting and, as in other democracies, participation is related to age and education levels. We have tested empirically for this likely bias where possible. However, these new referendum-data do have a particular value: voting behaviour reflects actual decisions, often informed by public debates. It can be seen as a rather solid indicator of what people want from the welfare state. Therefore, data on reported voting behaviour can usefully complement our knowledge in this field.

An additional caveat concerns the country where the referendums have taken place. Switzerland is rather unique among Western democracies in several respects: consensus-democratic political institutions have forged a tradition of consensual policy-making. In addition, in international comparison, the overall level of material well-being has been high throughout the twentieth century. One might think that economic affluence may weaken the salience of the economic (class) conflict in comparison with other countries, and thereby affect our results. However, social stratification on income and education is even higher in Switzerland than in most continental European countries, and party positions on economic welfare issues are as polarized as in the neighbouring countries (Bornschier 2007). Hence, the distribution of preferences in Switzerland should not be completely idiosyncratic. Nevertheless, given the particular consensus-democratic institutional framework, our findings may not necessarily apply to other democracies.

10.2 Theoretical Framework: Conflict Lines in Social Policy Making

Social policy preferences may be structured by a number of cleavages. For the sake of conceptual clarity and in response to data limitation problems, we focus our investigation on a set of hypotheses based on a simple utility-maximising reasoning. In other words, we expect social groups to support policies that bring them advantages, and to oppose those, which bring them material costs. In so doing, we do not claim that differences in values and norms are irrelevant for people's preferences. On the contrary, as will be seen below, we even interpret the inability

[1]The Swiss constitution makes provision for various types of referendums. Constitutional change can be put forward by means of a 'popular initiative', backed by 100,000 signatures. Voters can also challenge at the polls any act passed by parliament, if they are able to produce 50,000 signatures to that effect.

of utility-maximisation-based hypotheses to account for some of our findings as an indication that values matter. However, questions on personal values have been asked only in the latest post-referendum surveys, and therefore with our data we cannot deal directly with the issue of the impact of values. Hence, the focus of this article is clear: how far can we go in explaining individual social policy preferences with a simple utility-maximization assumption?

On the basis of existing scholarship, we identify three crucial cleavages supposed to shape social policy preferences: vertical stratification, age and gender.

10.2.1 Vertical Stratification as the Main Cleavage in Social Policy Making

Traditionally, redistributive social policies have widely been understood as the result of the mobilisation of economically disadvantaged groups. In most cases, these groups could be equated with the working class (Stephens 1979; Korpi 1983; and Esping-Andersen 1985). In addition, as pointed out by Peter Baldwin, other disadvantaged groups, such as farmers in the Nordic countries, have occasionally joined forces with industrial workers (Baldwin 1990). Overall, the hypothesis implied by this strand of literature is that on most distributional issues, the main cleavage line will be vertical stratification based on material resources. Quite simply, lower income groups are expected to be more supportive of redistributive measures, because they are the ones who can expect to gain most.

Subsequent research, however, has questioned the unique role of vertical stratification in structuring welfare state conflicts. With regard to the Nordic welfare states, some authors argue that welfare states are also the result of an alliance between the middle and the lower classes and of class compromise (Baldwin 1990; Swenson 2002; and Palier 2003). Finally, authors such as van Kersbergen (1995) and Manow (2002) have insisted on religious actors as drivers of reform and main allies of the working class.

This literature shows that welfare states are not simply the result of vertically structured class conflict. Nevertheless, all these authors do emphasize the role of the materially most disadvantaged groups as a consistently pro-welfare force in industrial welfare states. For the purpose of this paper, we thus include income and educational stratification as socio-structural determinants in the analysis, and we expect people in social strata that are less endowed with those resources to be more supportive of redistributive measures than people in higher strata.

10.2.2 A Generational Conflict Over Resource Allocation?

The debate on a generational conflict over the allocation of resources has made its appearance in the 1980s, first in the US. According to some commentators, the pro-elderly bias of the welfare state, coupled with population ageing, will result in increasingly large transfers from the working age to the retired population. The pro-elderly bias is probably the unintended result of welfare state design choices made several decades ago (Lynch 2006). However, in the ongoing era of welfare state restructuring, the age bias of social policy reinforces the stakes that older age groups have in the welfare state. Assuming an interest-led rational voting behaviour, older voters should be particularly inclined to preserve the high level of social entitlements achieved during the post-war years (Longman 1987; Thurow 1996).

More systematic research carried out in subsequent years has provided substantial evidence that the generational divide increasingly constitutes a cleavage over the allocation of resources. Pampel, for instance, found that the pro-aged bias in social policies depended very much on the interest representation system of different countries: in the US, issue-based representation encourages fragmentation, including along generational lines (Pampel 1994). Poterba, studying spending on education in the US over the 1960–1990 period, found that increases in the proportion of the older population are a significant determinant of reductions in per-child educational spending (Poterba 1997). Hence, empirical studies increasingly confirm the thesis of generational competition in the allocation of public sector resources.

Finally, public opinion research on social policy preferences is also of relevance. Here, the age variable seems to play an important role. In general, older respondents favour more spending on programmes like pensions and healthcare, but less on education or unemployment benefit (Armingeon 2006; Esping-Andersen 1999; and Roller 2002). The cleavage seems to be somewhat asymmetric, though: older people are less supportive of policies for the young, while the younger generations tend to be equally supportive of all policies. This can be explained with a simple interest-based hypothesis, making reference to the likelihood of being a one-day beneficiary of the relevant programme. There is little longitudinal research on these issues, but one study on Germany shows that an age cleavage in policy preferences over income guarantee programmes has emerged over the last few decades (Roller 2002).

Assuming an interest-based behaviour, we can expect age groups to favour policies that benefit them. In addition, we can also expect an age cleavage to emerge more clearly in policies for the young, such as family policy or education, than in those benefiting older voters.

10.2.3 Gender as a Cleavage Line in Distributional Issues?

The study of gender-based divisions in attitudes towards welfare states is less developed than the study of age or economic cleavages. Political scientists have paid more attention to gender as a determinant of electoral behaviour, and have identified a gender gap: in a majority of advanced democracies, women today are more likely to be left voters than men (Inglehart and Norris 2000; Iversen and Rosenbluth 2006), whereas they were more likely to be on the right during the post-war years.

Women's inclination to prefer left-wing parties is reflected in analyses of social policy preferences. Public opinion researchers have found a small but consistent gender gap in attitudes towards welfare state support in all western countries, with women being more supportive of social policies (Armingeon 2006; Deitch 2004; and Svallfors 1997). The effect is weakened if one controls for class, party and union membership, but does not disappear. But how can we account theoretically for the gender gap in both voting behaviour and social policy preferences?

First, some authors have argued that socialization resulting from women's typical biography as primary caregivers results in higher levels of compassion, which is supposed to be associated with left-wing party support (Deitch 2004). This view, however, is incompatible with the change of direction in the gender gap. When women were more likely to be primary carers (the post-war years) they tended to be more conservative. In addition, women who are full-time carers are at present less likely to be on the left than those who are involved in paid employment (Iversen and Rosenbluth 2006).

A second perspective puts more emphasis on a shift in women's material interests over the last 30 to 40 years. According to this view, women have shifted their social policy preferences in parallel with their increased propensity to engage in paid employment. Women wishing to engage in paid employment can be expected to support social policies that facilitate female labour market participation, such as gender equality or childcare policies (Inglehart and Norris 2000; Iversen and Rosenbluth 2006).

A utility-maximising hypothesis would thus expect women who are involved in paid employment to support work and family life reconciliation policies; it would expect women who have chosen homemaking to support a more traditional form of family policy. Unfortunately, our data do not allow us to distinguish between these two categories of women. We will thus simply hypothesise that women are more likely than men to support policies targeted on them.

10.3 Data and Methods

Our analysis covers 22 referendums, which took place between 1985 and 2004 in the fields of old-age pensions, labour market regulation and family policy.[2] These reforms were selected because they generally have clear distributional consequences for voters. In other words, it is relatively easy for voters to understand if they are likely to be winners or losers of these reforms.

[2]During the period considered, 209 national votes were held. The full list of referendums is available on www.admin.ch/ch/f/pore/va/index.html.

Our data come from the VOX surveys,[3] which are carried out after every referendum vote. Respondents are asked how they voted as well as a series of socio-demographic and attitudinal questions. The number of respondents varies between about 800 in earlier surveys and about 1,200 in more recent surveys.

In the empirical analysis presented below, we included only the actual participants in the votes (on average about 55–60% of respondents) for two reasons: first, we want to exploit the advantage of referendum – instead of general survey-data. Therefore, it is important that we include the preferences of those people, who have actually made a concrete choice on a particular policy. And second, reform proposals are oftentimes rather complex issues and non-voters are far less informed on them than actual voters (Di Giacomo 1993). Therefore, the analyses presented in this article include only respondents who actually voted.

However, the choice to include only participants has also a downside, since turnout is socially structured: participation is strongly related to age, income and education level. Excluding people who abstained from voting reduces variation in these variables and may thus weaken our results. Until 1999, VOX-data also included information on the opinions of non-voters. Hence, where available, we have also made the calculations for all respondents. However, we do not report the results in the article, since all the effects we find are confirmed and some even strengthened. Consequently, our choice to present results for participants only can be viewed as a conservative estimate of the effects.

For each vote we estimated logistic regression models where the individual voting decision (yes or no) is the dependent variable. Our independent variables reflect the cleavages we are interested in: gender, age and vertical stratification.

In relation to socio-economic stratification, we were confronted with data problems. The only stratification-variable, which is consistently available throughout the period, is education. The sole use of education, however, may be problematic, since education not only reflects material aspects of stratification, but is also one of the main determinants of cultural values (Kitschelt 1994), which may offset the propensity to vote according to material interests. After 1993, household income is also available, and preferable for our purposes. For this reason, in the votes prior to 1993 we use education as a measure of stratification, and in those after that date, income.[4]

The inclusion of age in the models also proved problematic, because the expected shape of the relationship between age and support for redistribution depends on the precise features of the reform at stake. Support for more generous pensions may be linearly related to age, but approval for reductions in the age of retirement can be expected to be the strongest among middle-aged people (40–65).

[3]Brunner, Matthias, Hanspeter Kriesi and François Lorétan. VoxIt: enquêtes post-votations standardisées (jeux de données informatiques). Production: SIDOS, Service Suisse d'information et d'archivage de données pour les sciences sociales, Neuchâtel. See www.sidos.ch for more information.

[4]Income is operationalised by means of the following categories of monthly household earnings in Swiss francs: <3,000, 3,001–5,000, 5,001–7,000, 7,001–9,000, >9,001.

In order to capture both linear and non-linear relationships between age and voting behaviour, we used age categories, rather than a continuous age variable.

After careful consideration, we decided not to include the political orientation of respondents as a control variable in the main models. In fact, even though a variable on self-positioning on the left–right axis is available for several votes, its inclusion could have confused the analysis for several reasons. First, self-positioning on the left–right axis may depend on someone's view on social policy, making it difficult to identify the direction of causality. Second, the left–right dimension reflects a variety of cleavages. Hence, one is unable to disentangle the exact meaning of a respondents' self-positioning. We did, nonetheless, run models with left–right self-positioning as a robustness control, and we report the result where relevant.

10.4 An Empirical Analysis of Referendum Voting on Social Policy Issues

The sample of referendums we analysed is rather heterogeneous, including votes in different policy areas. A joint analysis and discussion of all the 22 referendums is thus very difficult to interpret meaningfully. It can be, nonetheless, pointed out that of the three cleavages we are interested in, age comes out as a relevant division most frequently (in 18 out of 22 votes), followed by vertical stratification (7 out of 22) and gender (3 out of 22).

10.4.1 Pension Policy

During the period covered by this study, 10 referendums in the field of pension policy took place. All concerned the basic pension scheme, which is a universal, redistributive social insurance scheme. Five of them were about lowering the age of retirement; three were about bringing more funds to the scheme; one was about introducing gender equality; and one was about shifting the financing of the basic scheme from payroll taxes to an eco-tax.

Pension policy is an extremely promising field to compare the effects of different cleavages. In fact, we can develop clear hypotheses in relation to at least two of the cleavages. Regarding vertical stratification, lower income earners can be expected to support measures that strengthen the scheme, since they gain from its redistributive character. Higher income earners, in contrast, are likely to oppose such measures. Things are a bit more complex in relation to the age cleavage. We assume that measures that bring more finance to the pension scheme are going to be supported more strongly by older people. The relationship between age and support for reductions in the age of retirement, instead, can be expected to have an inverted U shape, meaning that the middle-aged (between 40 and 64) whose

Table 10.1 Logistic regression: Estimates for the odds of accepting pension reforms, 1988–2000

vote n°		Lowering of the age of retirement				
year		1	2	3	4	5
		1988	1995	1998	2000	2000
Sex	Man	r	r	r	r	r
	Woman	0.964	1.106	1.621**	1.234	1.286
Age	18–9	r	r	r	r	r
	40–64	0.714	0.895	1.867**	1.145	1.124
	65 and older	0.197***	0.605	0.81	0.46**	0.492**
Vertical stratification	Income		0.825	1.069	0.9	0.822*
	Low level of education (mandatory school)	r				
	Medium level of education (secondary school)	0.793				
	High level of education (tertiary school)	0.498				
(constant)		0.887	0.672	0.335***	1.031	1.484
Pseudo R2 (Nagelkerke)		0.077	0.019	0.064	0.046	0.048
N observations		632	357	540	462	465

Figures shown are the odds ratios of the chance to vote yes to the reform as compared to vote no or blank. *** = significant at the 0.001 level; ** = significant at the 0.01 level; * = significant at the 0.05 level; r = reference category

aspiration to quit the workforce is the highest should be the strongest supporters. Younger people may not find the prospect of a lower retirement age so essential, and older people (aged 65+) can be expected to oppose reductions in the age of retirement, because this essentially means more competitors for pension resources. Finally, we do not expect a gender cleavage to emerge in pension policy issues, unless the reform is specifically about gender-related aspects such as in referendum No. 9.

The first striking result is that age seems to be the main cleavage line in pension politics (see Tables 10.1 and 10.2). In eight votes out of ten, age is a significant predictor of voting behaviour. Income stratification instead, is much less likely to be a significant determinant (three out of nine votes). As expected, gender does not generally foster conflict in pension politics. Even though the basic pension is strongly vertically redistributive, it today generates mostly generational rather than stratification-based cleavages.

This finding is confirmed by looking at more specific aspects of the analyses. Of particular interest are the five votes on reductions in the age of retirement. In all cases, older people (65+) are far less likely than young and middle-aged people to support such measures, and in three out of five cases the results are statistically significant. Our expectation was that middle-aged voters are the staunchest supporters of reductions in the age of retirement. This indeed happens in the three most recent proposals (in one of them, the result is statistically significant). In the remaining two votes, middle-aged people are less likely to support reductions in the age of retirement than younger people, but are more likely to do so than older people.

Table 10.2 Logistic regression: Estimates of the odds of accepting the reforms, 1993–2001

Vote n°		More funds to basic pension			Gender equality	Ecotax
		6	7	8	9	10
Year		1993	2002	2002	1995	2001
Sex	Man	r	r	r	r	r
	Woman	0.994	1.03	1.081	0.83	1.252
Age	18–39	r	r	r	r	r
	40–64	0.989	1.591*	0.512**	0.795	0.962
	65 and older	2.436**	2.429***	0.774	1.981*	0.642
Vertical stratification	Income	1.289**	1.028	0.958	1.218*	1.207
(constant)		0.743	0.388**	1.192	0.787	0.138***
Pseudo R2 (Nagelkerke)		0.042	0.03	0.029	0.044	0.029
N observations		546	509	497	375	391

Figures shown are the odds ratios of the chance to vote yes to the reform as compared to vote no or blank. *** = significant at the 0.001 level; ** = significant at the 0.01 level; * = significant at the 0.05 level; r = reference category

Household income, as expected, is negatively related to support for a lower age of retirement. This is understandable, since high-income groups in Switzerland tend to rely on occupational and private pensions, and have less interest in a more generous basic pension scheme. The income effect, however, is considerably less strong than the age effect. It is in the expected direction in three votes, but in only one case (No. 5) do members of a higher income category support the reform significantly less than people of the next lower category.

If we now turn to measures designed to bring more funds to the basic pension, we find again a rather strong age effect. Older people (65+) are in general more likely to support increasing funds for pensions than other age groups. In two cases (No. 8 and No. 10), however, older people were less likely to support more funds. Vote No. 8 took place at the same time as vote No. 7 and was merely a less-generous alternative. Opposition to more funds in this case may simply have meant support for the more-generous alternative.[5] Vote No. 10 was about using an ecotax to (partly) replace payroll taxes as a source of finance for the basic pension. Survey data show that it was overwhelmingly perceived as an environmental measure rather than a way to bring extra finance to the pension scheme (Zürcher et al. 2002). This helps to explain the absence of an age cleavage.

Income stratification, instead, seems less relevant for the assignment of extra funds to the basic pension. Again, given the strong redistributive character of the scheme, we would expect lower income groups to favour such measures. However, income is significantly related to voting behaviour on only one occasion (vote No. 6), and in the opposite direction.

[5]Both referendums were about how to spend some 20 bn CHF resulting from the sale of part of the National bank's gold reserves. Referendum No.7 proposed assigning the whole sum to the basic pension, whereas referendum No.8 was about sharing the windfall among the basic pension, a solidarity foundation and the cantons.

The votes on increased funding are of particular interest, because they contain both left-wing and right-wing solutions to the problem of financing pensions. Vote No. 6 was about increasing VAT by one percentage point for the basic pension scheme. This governmental proposal was supported by all major parties. In the referendum, however, support for it came predominately from left-wing voters. Vote No. 7, instead, was about assigning to the basic pension some CHF 20 billion resulting from the sale of gold by the National bank, and was put forward by a right-wing party. In the referendum, it was mostly supported by right-wing voters. What is intriguing, however, is that old age (65+) remains a statistically significant predictor of voting behaviour in both cases, even when controlling for self-positioning on the left–right axis (models not shown).

Finally, in line with our expectations, this set of votes does not show any clear evidence of a strong gender cleavage in pension policy issues. Vote No. 9, which introduced gender equality, was in fact a mixed blessing for women. While introducing contribution credits for childrearing and contribution sharing between spouses, these measures were also coupled with an increase from 62 to 64 in women's age of retirement. This helps to explain the absence of a significant gender cleavage. Vote No. 3, instead, which was about bringing back women's age of retirement to 62, was undoubtedly beneficial to women, and indeed saw a stronger prevalence of 'yes' votes among female voters.

The analysis of voting behaviour in pension policy issues suggests that the main cleavage in this field of social policy is age. Measures aimed at extending coverage to younger age groups are forcefully and consistently opposed by older voters (65+). In addition, it emerges that the prevalence of interest-based voting is very strong among groups defined by age, and somewhat less so among groups defined by income level.

10.4.2 Labour Market Policy

Eight reforms of labour market policy have taken place between 1985 and 2003. They can be easily divided into two groups according to the main aim of the proposals. Three votes were popular initiatives working time reductions (such as introducing a 35 h week) (No. 11–13) and five votes were about labour market deregulation. (No. 14–18).

With regard to age, we expect retirees to oppose social policy expansion in favour of working age generations. With regard to the young and the middle-aged however, hypotheses are more difficult to formulate. On the one hand, the middle-aged can be expected to be particularly favourable to working-time reductions and labour market protection because it is harder for them to re-enter the labour market. On the other hand, the young are likely to be the staunchest supporters of such measures, because they are the ones who will have to stay longer in the labour market. It is an empirical question, which of these two age groups will be most favourable to these bills.

Table 10.3 Logistic regression: Estimates of the odds of accepting labour market reforms, 1985–2002

Vote n°		Lowering of working time		
Year		11	12	13
		1985	1988	2002
Sex	Man	r	r	r
	Woman	0.841	0.933	0.694
Age	18–39	r	r	r
	40–64	0.462**	0.741	0.861
	65 and older	0.306***	0.451**	0.307***
Vertical stratification	Income			0.994
	Low level of education (mandatory school)	r	r	
	Medium level of education (secondary school)	0.591	1.153	
	High level of education (tertiary school)	1.053	1.566	
(constant)		1.728	0.492*	0.402*
Pseudo R2 (Nagelkerke)		0.07	0.034	0.05
N observations		340	674	607

Figures shown are the odds ratios of the chance to vote yes to the reform as compared to vote no or blank. *** = significant at the 0.001 level; ** = significant at the 0.01 level; * = significant at the 0.05 level; r = reference category

Hypotheses on expected income and gender cleavages are somewhat less straightforward, notably because unemployment protection, labour law and labour time regulation are not very redistributive, and generally apply to all labour market participants in the same way. However, the lower income groups are more vulnerable and should thus support workers' protection and labour time reductions more strongly than higher income groups. Finally, women could tend to be more favourable to labour protection, since they are also more vulnerable in the labour market.

Again, the impact of age is the most consistent result with regard to working time (see Tables 10.3 and 10.4). The oldest age category, retired people (65+), was consistently and highly significantly less likely to support working time reductions than the youngest (18–39). The impact of age seems to be nearly linear, since the middle-aged also tended to reject the reduction in working time more often than the young. Part of the voting behaviour of the oldest generation can be explained by them being more conservative, but the effects remain identical when controlling for left–right self-positioning (results not shown).

Vertical stratification, by contrast, has no consistent impact in the referendums dealing with the lowering of working time. Education, generally accounts for only minor differences and in 1988, the higher-educated were even more favourable to lowering working time than those with low and intermediate education. This effect, however, is not significant and remains the same when controlling for left–right self-positioning, which might indicate that education probably captures values as much as material interest. Income has no significant effect on voting behaviour, which might be explained by the fact that working-time regulation affects all labour

Table 10.4 Logistic regression: Estimates for the odds of accepting labour market reforms, 1995–2001

vote n°		Labor market liberalization (reduction in employment protection and unemployment benefits)				
year						
		14	15	16	17	18
		1995	1996	1997	1998	2002
Sex	Man	r	r	r	r	r
	Woman	1.329	0.992	0.567**	0.694	0.943
Age	18–39	r	r	r	r	r
	40–64	1.242	1.958**	1.217	1.080	1.258
	65 and older	1.489	1.693	2.806***	1.742*	1.995**
Vertical stratification	Income		1.263*	1.180*	1.174	1.072
	Low level of education (mandatory school)	r				
	Medium level of education (secondary school)	1.675				
	High level of education (tertiary school)	2.248*				
(constant)		1.611	0.147***	0.407**	0.738	0.595
Pseudo R2	(Nagelkerke)		0.026	0.041	0.076	0.033
0.019						
N observations		509	502	521	425	473

Figures shown are the odds ratios of the chance to vote yes to the reform as compared to vote no or blank. *** = significant at the 0.001 level; ** = significant at the 0.01 level; * = significant at the 0.05 level; r = reference category

market participants in the same way. It is probably for similar reasons that gender has no significant impact on these issues either. These results suggest that the split between the active and the retired generations has become the structuring conflict line in working-time politics.

The emerging picture is similar with regard to employment protection legislation. In four out of five votes, the oldest age group was the staunchest supporter of a reduction of workers' protection or cutbacks in unemployment protection. In the 1990s and 2000s, the retired were about two to three times more likely to support liberalization than the young. The impact of age is again linear, the middle-aged being somewhat (though mostly insignificantly) more open to labour market liberalization than the youngest generation. This result is robust when we control for left–right self-positioning: in two out of four votes, the odds of the oldest generation to accept liberalization remain significantly lower than those of the young (results not shown). The only exception is the 1996 vote on labour law, when the middle-aged were even more favourable to the bill than the old. This vote was particularly controversial because it would have allowed Sunday openings for shops, a highly symbolic measure, whose tradition-breaking nature made it unacceptable to large sections of older voters.

In addition, it can be observed that the more highly educated and higher income groups were significantly more inclined to accept retrenchment and cutbacks in labour protection, even though this effect weakened after 1998. Hence, there is an effect of vertical stratification on the preferences with regard to labour market liberalization. The results are robust, but weaken considerably (i.e. become insignificant) when controlled for left–right positioning. Finally, women – whether on the right or on the left – tend to be more attached to workers' protection than men, particularly so in the 1997 labour law reform, in which men were twice as likely as women to accept labour market liberalization.

Overall, the age cleavage is again the most important socio-structural factor explaining voters' choices. The oldest age group (65+) consistently rejected working-time reductions and was clearly more favourable to reductions in workers' protection than the active generations.

10.4.3 Family Policy

The sample of votes on family policy issues is more homogeneous than previous ones, as all four votes were about the introduction of maternity insurance (Switzerland lacked a mandatory maternity insurance until 2004).

Most obviously, one might expect stronger support for maternity insurance by women compared to men. In fact, except in the event of adoption, men could not directly benefit from any of the four schemes proposed. At the same time, however, the impact of gender could be blurred by the fact that only younger women can potentially benefit from maternity insurance and thus be more inclined to support the introduction of this scheme. Controlling for age does not help here, because it does not allow us to distinguish between the voting behaviour of women within different age groups. For this reason, we also ran models using an interaction term to test the propensity of young women to support maternity insurance.

Finally, hypotheses on the impact of vertical stratification are not straightforward, either. On the one hand, one could expect a strong impact, because lower income groups are most dependent on income replacement from maternity insurance. On the other hand, employment rates and hence the likelihood of relying on maternity insurance, are higher among highly educated women. Theoretical reasoning alone does not allow us to produce a clear-cut hypothesis. Hence, the issue must be settled empirically (Table 10.5).

It is most interesting to note that gender does not consistently structure the voting behaviour on family policy. Indeed, only in one out of four models do women support maternity insurance more than men. The differences between male and female votes are insignificant in all other referendums. To some extent, this may be due to the fact that people think in terms of household income. A man, living with a woman who interrupts employment because of maternity, will be better off if a maternity scheme exists.

With regard to the link between age and gender, we hypothesised that young women would be the most favourable to maternity protection of all socio-structural

Table 10.5 Logistic regression : Estimates of the odds of accepting the introduction of maternity insurance, 1984–2004

vote n°		Maternity insurance			
year		19	20	21	22
		1984	1987	1999	2004
Sex	Man	r	r	r	r
	Woman	0.885	1.688**	0.963	0.714
Age	18–39	r	r	r	r
	40–64	0.410**	0.578***	0.411***	0.807
	65 and older	0.275***	0.876	0.357***	0.362***
Vertical stratification	Income			1.014	1.027
	Low level of education (mandatory school)	r	r		
	Medium level of education (secondary school)	0.503*	0.891		
	High level of education (tertiary school)	1.311	3.359***		
(constant)		0.789	0.491**	1.391	3.954***
Pseudo R2 (Nagelkerke)		0.112	0.095	0.053	0.06
N observations		342	617	581	531

Figures shown are the odds ratios of the chance to vote yes to the reform as compared to vote no or blank. *** = significant at the 0.001 level; ** = significant at the 0.01 level; * = significant at the 0.05 level; r = reference category

groups. We have tested this hypothesis by introducing an interaction term in the model (results not shown). Young women are indeed more likely than the rest of the population to support maternity insurance, but in none of the cases significantly so.

Age again provides more consistent results in terms of our rational utility-maximising assumptions. In all four referendums, age has a significant effect on the odds of approval for maternity insurance. Generally, the youngest generation was two to three times more likely to approve the bills than the middle-aged and the oldest generation of people (65 and older). This negative effect of age on the odds of approval holds stable when we control for left–right self-positioning and becomes insignificant only in the last referendum in 2004. Hence, the effect of age is only partly due to the more conservative profile of older persons. Even among ideologically like-minded persons, the elderly reject those policies more clearly than the young.

In the 1987 vote, however, the middle-aged were more sceptical against the bill than the oldest-age category, contrary to our expectation of a linear relation between age and approval. This can tentatively be explained by the fact that this bill was strongly supported by the government, the federal parliament and all four governmental parties. Older voters are, in general, more likely to follow the position of the government and this high level of unanimity may explain the unusual approval rate among the oldest generation.

Finally, income effects are negligible. The different income groups displayed very similar patterns of voting behaviour.

The only interest-based effect in this field is related to age. Income and gender on the other hand, seem to have no effect on policy preferences with regard to maternity insurance. As suggested in the introduction, we may see here the limits of a rational-choice model of voting decisions: social policy dealing with family models is, of course, strongly value-laden. Our data do not allow us to test value-based hypotheses, but our results suggest that these may help explain voting behaviour.

10.5 Conclusion

In this paper, we have analysed the extent to which socio-structural characteristics, such as vertical stratification, age and gender, influence voting behaviour on redistributive social policy issues. We have started with very straightforward, rationalistic hypotheses, i.e. we expected a conflict line to appear if the bill proposal in question had diverging distributional effects for different age, gender or income categories.

This hypothesis is most strikingly confirmed in relation to age. In eight out of ten votes on pension policy, in seven out of eight referendums on labour market policy and in four out of four votes on maternity insurance, age was a relevant and significant predictor of voting behaviour. The direction of the age effect is almost always consistent with a rational utility-maximising behaviour. Even after controlling for self-positioning on the left–right axis – elderly people being more conservative – age remains in most cases a significant predictor and the direction of the effect does not change. Older generations not only massively approve improvements in the benefits they receive, but they also tend to reject social policy proposals aimed at improving the situation of the actively employed and of young families. The votes on labour market policies most clearly show the turning point at the age of retirement. People of the age of 65 and more significantly reject working-time reductions and approve labour market deregulation, whereas the active generations between 18 and 64 do not differ significantly in their voting behaviour. The importance of the age cleavage in contemporary opinion formation on social policy issues is the most important and most consistent result of this article.

Vertical stratification, by contrast, has a relevant effect on social policy preferences only with regard to certain issues, most clearly so with regard to labour market liberalization, of which higher income-strata are more supportive than the less privileged.

But why is utility-maximising voting stronger in relation to age than in relation to income? One hypothesis may be that, it is more straightforward to ascertain one's position in relation to the former than to the latter. Ideas on social mobility blur the estimations of costs-and-benefits people may make regarding the effects of social policy on their income and socio-structural status. In addition, the welfare state itself has contributed to the weakening of class-consciousness. With regard to age, by contrast, the calculation is easier, especially from the viewpoint of the elderly: a retired person will never again rely on labour market regulation, unemployment benefits or family policy. Hence, cost-benefit calculations are more straightforward and rational decision-making plays out more directly in individual decisions.

Appendix

List of Referendums

22 Referendums on Distributional Conflicts 1984–2004

No.	Date	VOX No	Title (PT popular initiative)	Content	% yes
1	June 12th, 1988	352	P1 "on lowering the retirement age to 62/ 60"	Lowering of retirement age to 62 for men and 60 for women	35.1
2	Nov 28th, 1993	513	Federal bill on the stabilisation of the social insurance schemes	Increase of the VAT by 1 percentage point earmarked for pensions	62.6
3	June 25th, 1995	571	Federal law on old-age insurance AHV (revision)	Splitting of pension contributions, increase of women's retirement age to	60.7
4	June 25th, 1995	572	P1 "for an expansion of pension and disability insurance coverage"	Lowering of retirement age	27.6
5	Sept 27th, 1998	643	P1 "for the 10th revision of AHV without an increase in the retirement age"	Lowering of women's retirement age back to 60 (after vote No. 3)	41.5
6	Nov 26th, 2000	721	P1 "for a flexibilisation of the basic pension scheme"	Lowering of retirement age	39.5
7	Nov 26th, 2000	722	P1 "for a flexible retirement age at 62 for men and women"	Lowering of retirement age and ecotax for financing of pensions	46.0
8	Dec 2nd, 2001	752	P1 "for a stable pension scheme - taxing energy instead of work"	Ecotax to finance basic pensions	22.9
9	Sept 22nd, 2002	781	PI "excess gold for pension funds"	Excess gold of National Bank to be transferred to the basic pension scheme	47.6

No.	Date	VOX No	Title (PT popular initiative)	Content	% yes
10	Sept 22nd, 2002	782	Alternative proposal to the PT 781	Excess gold of National Bank to be shared between a solidarity foundation, the pension scheme and the cantons	46.4
11	Mar 10th, 1985	251	PI "for longer paid holidays"	Statutory right to 4 or 5 weeks of paid holidays (depending on age)	34.8
12	Dec 4th, 1988	362	PI "for the lowering of working time"	Introduction of the 40 h working week	34.3
13	Mar 3rd, 2002	762	PI "for a shorter working week"	Introduction of the 40 h working week	25.4
14	Sept 26th, 1993	505	Federal bill on measures in unemployment insurance	Cuts in unemployment benefits and extension of their duration	70.4
15	Dec 1st, 1996	602	Federal labour law (revision)	Limited opening of shops on Sundays, allowing women's night work, more flexible conditions for night work	33.0
16	Sept 28th, 1997	622	Federal bill on unemployment insurance financing	Cuts in unemployment benefits	49.2
17	Nov 29th, 1998	654	Federal labour law (revision)	Allowing women's night work, more flexible conditions for night work	63.5
18	Nov 24th, 2002	792	Federal law on unemployment insurance (revision)	Cuts in unemployment benefits	56.1
19	Dec 2nd, 1984	241	PI "for an effective protection of mothers"	Paid maternity leave	15.8
20	Dec 6th, 1987	342	Federal law on health insurance (revision)	Health insurance reform with paid maternity leave	28.7
21	June 13th, 1999	685	Federal law on maternity insurance (introduction)	Paid maternity leave for working mothers, birth benefits for all mothers	39.0
22	Sept 28th, 2004	854	Federal law on the income replacement scheme (revision)	Paid maternity leave for working mothers	55.5

References

Armingeon K (2006) Reconciling competing claims of the welfare state clientele. In: Armingeon K, Bonoli G (eds) The politics of post-industrial welfare states. London, Routledge, pp 100–122
Baldwin P (1990) The politics of social solidarity. Class bases of the European welfare state 1875–1975. Cambridge University Press, Cambridge
Berclaz M (2002) Les transformation de la communication politique, Geneva, University of Geneva, unpublished MA dissertation
Bornschier S (2007) The transformation of historical cleavages and the rise of right-wing populist parties in Western Europe. Ph.D. thesis, University of Zurich, Switzerland
Deitch C (2004) Gender and popular support for the welfare state: Cross-national trends in a period of restructuring, Paper prepared for the ISA RC19 annual conference, September 2–4, 2004, Paris, France
Di Giacomo F (1993) La decision des abstentionnistes. In: Hanspeter K (ed) Citoyenneté et démocratie directe. Seismo, Zurich
Esping-Andersen G (1985) Politics against markets. Princeton University Press, Princeton, NJ
Esping-Andersen G (1999) Politics without class? Postindustrial cleavages in Europe and America. In: Kitschelt H et al (eds) Continuity and change in contemporary capitalism. Cambridge University Press, Cambridge
Ferrera M (1993) EC citizens and social protection. European Commission, Brussels
Gaxie D (1990) Des points de vue sociaux. La distribution des opinions sur les questions sociales. In: Gaxie D, Collovald A, Gaïti B, Lehingue P, Poirmeur Y (eds) Le social transfiguré. PUF, Paris
Inglehart R, Norris P (2000) The developmental theory of the gender gap: women and men's voting behavior in global perspective. Int Polit Sci Rev 21(4):441–463
Iversen T, Rosenbluth F (2006) The political economy of gender: explaining cross-national variation in the gender division of labour and the gender voting gap. Am J Polit Sci 50(1):1–19
Kangas O (1995) Interest intermediation and popular will. Comments on Peter Taylor-Gooby. In: Svallfors S (ed) In the eye of the beholder. opinions on welfare and justice in comparative perspective. The Bank of Sweden Trecentenary Foundation, Umeä
Kitschelt H (1994) The transformation of European social democracy. Cambridge University Press, Cambridge
Korpi W (1983) The democratic class struggle. Routeledge and Kegan, London
Longman P (1987) Born to pay: the new politics of ageing in America. Houghton Mifflin, Boston, MA
Lynch J (2006) Age in the welfare state. Cambridge University Press, Cambridge and New York
Manow P (2002) The good, the bad and the ugly, Esping-Andersens' Wohlfahrtsstaatentypologie und die konfessionellen Grundlagen des westlichen Wohlfahrtsstaates. Kölner Z Soz Sozialpsychol 54:203–225
Palier B (2003) Gouverner la sécurité sociale. PUF, Paris
Pampel F (1994) Population ageing, class, context and age inequality in public spendin. Am J Sociol 100:153–195
Poterba J (1997) Demographic structure and the political economy of public education. J Policy Anal Manage 16:48–66
Roller E (2000) Ende des sozialstaatlichen Konsenses? Zum Aufbrechen traditioneller und zur Entstehung neuer Konfliktstrukturen in Deutschland. In: Niedermayer O, Westle B (eds) Demokratie und partizipation. Westdeutscher Verlag, Wiesbaden
Roller E (2002) Erosion des sozialstaatlichen Konsens und die Entstehung einer neuen Konfliktlinie in Deutschland? *Aus Politik und Zeitgeschichte*, 1–11
Stephens JD (1979) The transition from capitalism to socialism. Macmillian, London
Svallfors S (1997) Worlds of welfare and attitudes to redistribution: a comparison of eight western countries. Eur Sociol Rev 13(3):283–304

Swenson P (2002) Capitalists against markets. The making of labor markets and welfare states in the United States and Sweden. Oxford University Press, New York
Taylor-Gooby P (1995) Who wants the welfare state? Support for state welfare provision in European countries. In: Svallfors S (ed) In the eye of the beholder. Opinions on welfare and justice in comparative perspective. The Bank of Sweden Trecentenary Foundation, Umeä
Taylor-Gooby P (1998) Commitment to the Welfare State. In: Jowell R, Curtice J, Park A, Brook L, Thomson K, Bryson L (eds) British and European social attitutdes. How Britain differs. The 15th Report. Ashgate, Aldershot
Thurow L (1996) The future of capitalism. Nicholas Brealy, London
Van Kersbergen K (1995) Social capitalism. a study of christian democracy and the welfare state. Routledge, London
Zürcher L, Mahnig F, Milic T (2002) Analisi delle votazioni federali del 2 dicembre 2001, Bern/ Zurich, GfS/IPW, Vox No.75

Chapter 11
Being Less Active and Outnumbered?

The Political Participation and Relative Pressure Potential of Young People in Europe

Achim Goerres

> "I am afraid to say that we are currently witnessing the early signs of a pensioners' democracy. Older people are becoming more numerous, and all political parties pay extraordinary attention to them. This development could end in a situation in which older people would plunder the young."
> Roman Herzog, ex-judge at the Federal Constitutional Court (1983–1994) and ex-president of Germany (1994–1999), on the announcement of the German government in April 2008 to raise public pensions by 1.1% and to deviate thereby from the pension formula (Blome et al. 2008)

There are increasingly panicky discussions about the "war of generations," the "grey power," and "pensioner's democracy" in European countries. Advocates of such apocalyptic visions of politics in ageing democracies seem to follow a simple argument: demographic change leads to a growing number of older people. Older people are politically very active, especially in electoral politics. They share common political interests and use their political activities to pursue them. Policy-makers anticipate this development and make policies in order not to disenchant older people. As a consequence, young people are on the losing side in the politics of ageing democracies.

This chapter challenges some aspects of this simplistic argumentation and tries to give a more balanced view by looking at the whole array of political actions. It compares the patterns of political participation and preferences of young, middle-aged and older people in Europe and explores the question whether differences in participation matter. It is young people who are losing out relatively both to middle-aged and to older people due to their low participation levels and relatively small demographic share of the population. This finding does not imply that there is an antagonism between young and old, but that the influence young people can exert through democratic participation is more *limited*. In general, politicians interested in equality

---

A. Goerres
University of Cologne, Köln, Germany
e-mail: Agoerres@uni-koeln.de

J.C. Tremmel (ed.), *A Young Generation Under Pressure?*,
DOI 10.1007/978-3-642-03483-1_11,

should not be concerned about the growing importance of older people, but the diminishing significance of the young compared to both middle-aged and older people.

The analysis proceeds in six steps. Firstly, it is argued that individual political participation is becoming more heterogeneous in contemporary Europe due to the large-scale societal changes. Secondly, I demonstrate how the universe of political participation can be meaningfully structured. Thirdly, I trace the shift of age group sizes in the last 30 years to show the demographic weight of each age group, most importantly the shrinking relative size of the age group of those younger than 30. Fourthly, I present the evidence for contemporary Europe regarding differences between age groups for various types of political participation and for the pressure potential of each age group due to their mean participation levels combined with their demographic size. Fifthly, the political preferences of each age group are shown to be different on a diverse set of policy issue domains, a finding that makes differences in political pressure potential all the more noteworthy. Sixthly, the findings are juxtaposed with results from existing studies.

11.1 The Growing Heterogeneity of Individual Political Participation

Individual political participation is becoming more heterogeneous in European democracies. The reasons for this development in Europe and many other advanced industrial democracies lie in broad societal changes.

In a liberal democracy, citizens are free to participate in politics. Political participation can be defined as individual actions that are intended to affect public policy, institutional arrangements or the selection of political personnel (Verba et al. 1995; Goerres 2009b, pp. 5–6). This definition circumscribes a whole universe of political actions: voting, participation in organizations (political parties, trade unions, NGOs and others), and participation outside of organizations (contacting a public official or politician, signing a petition, taking part in demonstrations, buying or boycotting a product for political reasons and others). Most of these actions are legal and open to everybody. However, in practice, not all actions are pursued with equal probabilities, with *voting* being the most common form of political action.

Political participation typically has two kinds of impact. On the one hand, an action conveys a certain array of preferences of participants to political elites in government or in bureaucracy. On the other, the total impact by many in a certain type of political action exerts different degrees of pressure on elites to react (see Verba and Nie 1972). For instance, voting shows very little preferences of the voter as she/he can only cast one vote. However, since governments depend on election and re-election, voting exerts a lot of pressure on the elites. Petitions, as another example, show very detailed preferences of those who sign them, but exert relatively little pressure on elites in power to act.

For a few years now, scholars have detected a change in the political participation process in advanced industrial democracies. The forms of political actions that were most common in the early years of liberal democracies, e.g., in the two decades after World War II, are on the decline. These include voting, participation in political parties and participation in trade unions. This decline in popularity is not uniform across all countries. For example, membership in political parties is on the decrease in most West European party systems. It is on the rise in Spain and some of the post-communist countries like Poland (Mair and van Biezen 2001). At the same time, other forms of participation are on the increase, for example, participation in single-issue organizations, non-institutionalized forms of participation that do not require long-term commitment and that are sometimes labeled as "consumerist" (Meyer and Tarrow 1998; Norris 2002).

Inglehart (1995) attributes these changes in participatory patterns to a broad societal process of post-modernization. As an element of that process, he identifies the shift from scarcity to post-modern values. Among these latter values, individual self-expression and political participation take important places. Individuals' basic material needs tend to be satisfied in recent times, for example, hunger and lack of shelter remain a problem only for a very small minority in established democracies. Individuals are therefore striving for higher, post-material goods. Also, individuals are less accepting of bureaucratic authority because states and governments are less able to exert their powers in a growingly complex world. The declining control by the state adds to the lessened social control of religion and promotes individuation. The shift towards post-modernism is more prevalent in countries that are characterized by high levels of economic development and high life expectancy, such as in most European countries.

Dalton (2004) presents an abundance of empirical evidence on declining trust in state authorities and on the decline of party identification in established democracies. He argues that the spread of education and civic skills leads to cognitive mobilization and the increased usage of elite-challenging forms of participation. The simultaneous spread of media usage and increasing negative media coverage of politicians and governmental politics add to declining trust and the resort to other forms of participation.[1]

This change in the participation process has generational implications. Younger cohorts tend to be more inclined towards those forms of participation that are becoming more en vogue. Thus, members of younger generations tend to show a greater inclination towards elite-challenging behavior, such as taking part in a street demonstration, and consumerist political behavior, such as boycotting a product for political reasons (see Goerres 2009b, chap. 6).

There is a debate about the implications of declining turnout among young voters in many European countries, such as the United Kingdom. Some authors, like Martin Wattenberg (2008), fear that declining voting participation among younger people is a sign of an increasing detachment of those groups from the

[1]Other factors that accompany the post-modernisation process are (Norris 2002: 22–3): suburbanisation (individuals tend to be more mobile and less embedded in the same social networks for decades) and de-unionisation due to the shift to the services sector (individuals become less mobilised by trade unions).

political process and of political apathy. A similar view is shared by Robert Putnam (2000) in a broader conception of declining engagement in civic life. Other scholars, like Russell Dalton (2008), take a more optimistic view as the decline in participation in elections is also accompanied by an increase in participation through other channels. Thus, younger generations are not becoming more detached, but their "linkage" (Lawson 1988) to politics is different from that of other age groups. For example, one British study showed that the meaning of politics is changing for younger British citizens, with them losing interest in the traditional "formal" politics of elections and parties while retaining interest in other types of politics (Henn et al. 2002).

The discussion about whether these changes in the empirically measurable participation process alter the nature of democracy remains open. A greater variety of political participation among younger cohorts may be viewed as a positive development from the viewpoint of a participatory theorist (such as Pateman 1970) because multiple actions of participation increase an individual's bond to the system. In contrast, since most democratic systems are built on structures of representative democracy, power, legitimacy and public resource allocation still largely depend on formally organized structures of the state the key personnel of which is still recruited through parties and elections.

What remains neglected in this debate, is the changing demographics of numbers, i.e., alongside the change in the participation process, a demographic shift is taking place. Younger people are becoming relatively fewer; and this fact together with the changing nature of political participation overall needs to be looked up more closely, which is the objective of this essay. To that end, I will now – after a short description of what constitutes dimensions in the universe of political participation – look at demographic figures, participation rates by age groups and at what the picture looks like when we bring these two types of evidence together.

11.2 The Nature of Political Participation in Europe

If I define all individual actions as political participation that are intended to influence political outcomes (public policy, institutional arrangements or personnel), what is the underlying structure of this universe of actions? Political participation is a type of behavior that has several dimensions. Citizens of all ages who want to become involved politically have several options to choose from. These options differ in the nature and target of the political action carried out (Table 11.1).

One way to structure this universe[2] is to differentiate between actions that the individual carries out on his or her own or those that are collective, i.e., group-based

[2]There is an extensive discussion in the literature of political participation about which conceptualization is most appropriate, which I am not presenting here. Readers interested in this shall be referred to van Deth et al. (2007).

Table 11.1 Types of political participation

	Institutionalized	Non-institutionalized
Individual	Voting	Consumer participation (e.g., buying or boycotting a product for political reasons), contacting a public official or politician, wearing a badge, signing a petition
Collective	Involvement in parties, single-issue organizations, organizations of the economic sphere	demonstrating

Source: own illustration

types of actions. In terms of motivation, stand-alone actions cannot be motivated by some of the social incentives of collective actions. Collective actions provide the participants with the interactions of a group as another mobilizing and gratifying factor (e.g., making friends). Furthermore, it is advisable to differentiate between the degrees of institutionalization. Political participation by individuals can take place in an organized context or in a more spontaneous, non-institutionalized setting. In the first instance, the political action is dependent on a regular social organization that has permanent character. In the latter instance, the political action is not regulated, but has a temporary nature. Broadly speaking, this non-institutionalized behavior is on the rise in popularity whereas the other form is on the decline in many European democracies. Once the distinction between individual and collective behavior is combined with the degree of institutionalization, political actions can be sorted in this two-by-two scheme.

The European Social Survey 2002/2003, which I am going to use for the analysis, includes 25 individual political actions in 21 European countries.[3] These items include: voting, contacting a public official or politician, wearing a badge, signing a petition, taking part in a legal or illegal demonstration, boycotting or buying a product for political reasons, involvement (membership, donations, participation in activities and voluntary work) in political parties, trade unions, professional organizations, humanitarian/ human rights organizations, environmental organizations, peace organizations, animal rights organizations and consumer organizations. The last five types of organizations are often called "single-issue organizations" as their activities tend to focus on a limited set of political issues only.

In this scheme, individual, institutionalized participation is captured in voting. Collective, institutionalized participation is represented by involvement in political parties, in single-issue organizations and organizations of the economic sphere (trade unions and professional organizations). Individual, non-institutionalized

[3]Austria, Belgium, Czech Republic, Denmark, Germany, Great Britain, Greece, Finland, France, Hungary, Ireland, Italy, Luxembourg, the Netherlands, Norway, Poland, Portugal, Slovenia, Spain, Sweden, Switzerland. Some types of participation were not asked for in Hungary and Switzerland.

participation includes such things as contacting a public official, consumer participation, wearing a badge and signing a petition. The last combination of non-institutionalized, collective participation is represented by taking part in demonstrations.

Whereas this scheme is useful to guide the analysis, the boundaries between the various combinations are fluid. So, for instance, involvement in single-issue organizations often goes hand-in-hand with non-institutionalized forms of participation. Another example may be that party activists act as initiators of demonstrations, trying to reach a broader audience than their own members. In addition to fluid transitions between types of activities, all types of political participation are correlated albeit only at moderate levels, meaning that people active in one type of channel are also more likely to be active in another.

11.3 Demographics in Europe

In this section, I demonstrate that the demographic weight of older and middle-aged people has increased significantly whereas young people are a diminishing group as a percentage of the total and the adult population.

It is helpful to define older people in Europe as those who are 60 and older, with 60 being about the mean retirement age in Europe.[4] Retirement is an important social division point. Retirees have left the labor market; their expectations from the state are different with them paying less tax and being increasingly dependent on state services. Also, their social life is characterized by more free time and a focus on their own social lives. Those who are younger than 60 can be divided into two subgroups: young people (18–29) and middle-aged people (30–59). Young people are likely still to be in education or in their early professional careers. They are likely to be exposed to various pressures from the labor market and their social environment to build their careers and organize their lives. Middle-aged people are likely to be economically active, have family responsibilities in the form of children or older individuals that they care for. They are on average fully embedded in the labor market. In contrast to young people, their lives tend to be more organized already.

European countries underwent a remarkable demographic shift in the last three decades (see Table 11.2). After the population expansion following World War II, population growth stagnated from the 1960s onwards. In the 21 countries under investigation here, the total population was 405 million in 1970. In 2000, the closest data point to the survey period, it was 465 million.

As a consequence, the size of age groups changed as well. Here, the most important change was the ageing of the baby-boomer cohort, i.e., the large

[4]The rate of economically active people between ages 60 and 64 tends to be much lower than the rates for younger age groups. On average, it stands at 29.4% in the 21 European countries. The rate of economically active individuals aged 65 and older lies at an average of 5.1% (ILO 2006).

Table 11.2 Demographic change in 21 European countries by age group 1970–2000

	1970	2000	Diff. 1970–2000
Very young (0–18), mill.	125.1	99.1	−26.0
% of total population	30.9	21.3	−9.6
Young (18–29), mill.	63.5	67.3	3.7
% of total population	15.7	14.4	−1.2
% of adult population	22.7	18.3	−4.3
Middle-aged (30–59), mill.	146.8	188.1	41.3
% of total population	36.2	40.4	4.2
% of adult population	52.4	51.3	−1.1
Older (60+), mill.	69.8	111.4	41.6
% of total population	17.2	23.9	6.7
% of adult population	24.9	30.4	5.4
Total, mill.	405.2	465.9	60.6
Total adult, mill.	280.1	366.7	86.6

Note: 1970 without East Germany, United Nations Common Database (2007)

generation of people that was born in the first two decades after World War II. That generation still belonged to the very young in 1970 and was among the middle-aged in 2000.

The number of minor children between ages 0 and 18 decreased from 125 million in 1970 to 99 million in 2000. The group of young individuals (18–29) increased slightly from 64 to 67 million. The groups of middle-aged and older people increased dramatically. Middle-aged residents numbered 147 million in 1970 and 188 million in 2000. Older residents increased from 70 to 111 million. The relative proportion of the total population changed as well. The youngest age group decreased by almost 9.6%, the group of the young decreased by about 1.2%, the middle-aged increased by about 4.2% and the oldest age group increased by about 6.7% of the total population.

For a discussion of political participation, it is necessary to look at changes of the adult population (defined as 18 and older) because some of the dimensions of participation require the participant to be an adult. Here, the relative changes clearly show a decrease of the groups of the young and the middle-aged by 4.3% and 1.1%, respectively and an increase of the group of older people of 5.4%. In 2000, the adult population comprised 18.4% young people (18–29), 51.3% middle-aged individuals and 30.4% older people.

Thus, a dramatic shift can be seen in the age composition of the European population. Older people are the strongest growing age group, and the youngest and the young are the ones losing in relative numerical importance. The population changes mean for political participation that the pool of potential participants changes as well. Increasingly, the pool of citizens who can potentially become active consists of middle-aged and older people. As a consequence, the following analysis of the variation in political behavior of young, middle-aged and older people should take the demographic weight of each group into consideration.

11.4 Age Group Imbalances in Political Participation in Europe

In general, differences in participation between age groups can be due to cohort differences or differences along the life-cycle. Cohort differences are rooted in varying socialization experiences at young age that are experienced by a group of individuals born in the same period. For example, cohorts differ in the extent to which they have internalized the sense of duty to vote. Life-cycle differences are the same for all cohorts. They stem from the fact that the individual endowment with resources and motivation to engage in political behavior varies across the life-cycle. For example, the older individuals are, the more likely they are to be hampered by illness (see for a detailed discussion Goerres 2009b, p. 52).

11.4.1 Participation Rates by Age Groups in Europe

Figure 11.1 summarizes the results in eight variables by age group. Each variable captures whether an individual was active in the 12 months before the survey or not for a given kind of participation. The numbers for each age group indicate the average probability of someone in that age group to be active in that type of activity.

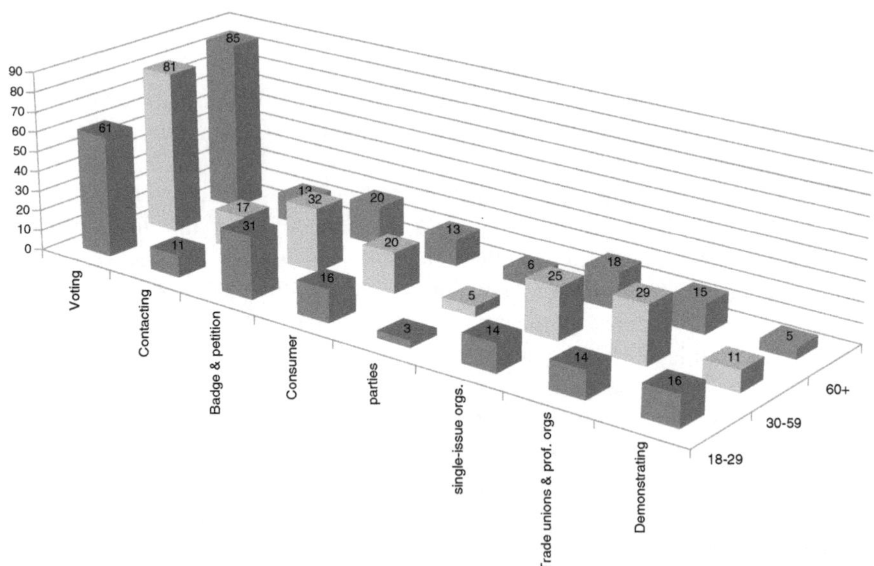

Fig. 11.1 Average participation rates on eight kinds of political participation by age groups *Source*: ESS 2002/2003. Observations weighted

At a first glance, it can be seen that voting is still by far the most common form of political participation across all age groups. Young people have a likelihood of 60% to have voted, middle-aged people 81% and older people 85%. So, older people are most active on this participation channel. The difference of 25 percentage points is also the most substantive difference across age groups as can be judged from the comparison with other types (Fig. 11.1).

Across all areas of participation, young people are the least active compared to the other two age groups – except for demonstrating where young people have a 16% chance of having taken part in a demonstration compared to 11% for middle-aged and 5% for older people. In some areas, young people hardly differ from middle-aged people, such as for having worn a badge/signed a petition or consumer activities. Thus, young people are most likely to use non-institutionalized individual and collective forms of participation, relative to the other age groups. Older people clearly dominate the traditional ways of participation through voting and party involvement; even with regard to involvement in organizations of the employment sphere (trade unions and professional organizations), which are likely to be tied to working life, they have a higher likelihood (15%) of being involved than young people (14%). Older people tend to be retirees who are economically inactive. Still, their high level of involvement in trade unions or employers' organizations seems to result from the effort of these organizations to maintain relations with retirees.

Thus, with regard to simple participation rates, young people are at a disadvantage with regard to all dimensions of political participation. This is already a remarkable finding given the strong normative importance of political activity in liberal democracies. However, since I am ultimately interested in the potential impact of participation by young people, I should also take into consideration how many individuals belong to each age group.

11.4.2 Participation by Age Groups Weighted by Demographic Size

In a democracy, numbers do matter. So, when there are more individuals in a certain age group, there exists a larger reservoir of people who can become active and can potentially exert pressure on elites (as well as reveal political preferences). This pressure potential can be approximated by multiplying the average likelihood of participation of an age group with its relative size in the adult population. This number combines the relative numerical power of an age group together with their participation patterns.

Figure 11.2 presents the participation rates by age groups weighted by their relative demographic sizes. Recall that in 2000, the adult population comprised 18.4% young people (18–29), 51.3% middle-aged (30–59) and 30.4% older people (60+). For example, if all three groups have a participation rate of 10%, younger people have a pressure potential of 1.84, middle-aged a 5.13 and older people a

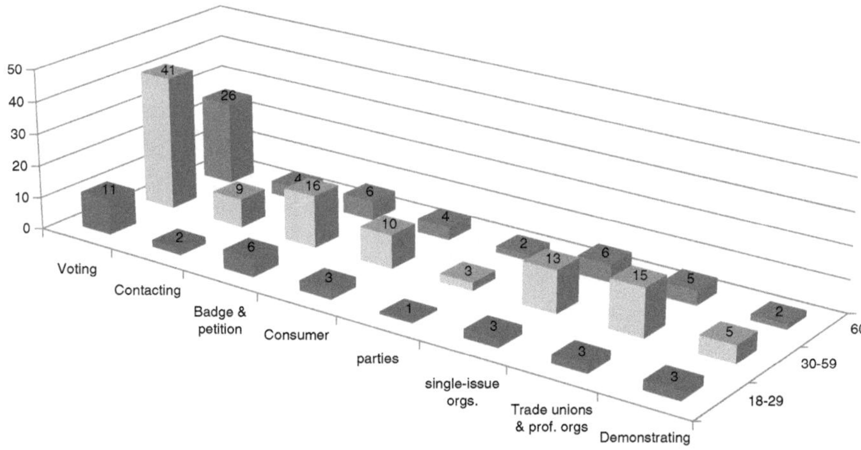

Fig. 11.2 Pressure potential by age groups in Europe in 2002
Note: Pressure potential = average likelihood to participate*relative demographic weight of age group. Values are those from Fig. 11.2 times the proportion of the respective age group of the adult population (18.3% for young, 51.3% for middle-aged, 30.4% for older individuals)

3.04. The impact of the middle-aged through that participation dimension on elites and the political system, as a whole, is potentially higher than for older or younger individuals.

The results in Fig. 11.2 are even clearer than the unweighted results before with regard to age distortion of the participation process. The columns of the middle-aged are higher than the other two columns for all dimensions. Middle-aged individuals dominate in their pressure potential over the young and older people in all channels of participation. The strong demographic weight of middle-aged citizens makes up for any lower participation rate that they might have, e.g., in voting. In addition, young people have the lowest pressure potential compared to the other two age groups in all dimensions – except for wearing a badge/signing a petition where there is a tie with the 60+ age group. Seen from this perspective, the relatively high levels of non-institutionalised participation of young people is lost with regard to pressure potential through their low and declining number in the population.

These results show that the varying participation rates that could be seen above are not so much of importance with the clear demographic differences between young, middle-aged and older individuals being considered. The picture in 2000–2002 is now clear: due to their average participation rates and their relative demographic size, young people are at a disadvantage with regard to their pressure potential, compared to middle-aged and older individuals. Older people are almost always second in the size of their impact relative to the other two groups. The clear "winner" in this comparison of pressure potential is the middle-aged group. Their overall relatively high participation rates and their large demographic size make them outperform the other two groups on all dimensions.

Coming back to the structuring principles, I can also see that the domination of the middle-aged is comparatively higher in the institutionalized dimensions of participation (voting, involvement in parties, single-issue organizations and organizations of the economic sphere). Their domination in the non-institutionalized forms, which are considered to be on the rise, is slightly smaller. Since middle-aged people dominate in their pressure potential on all types of participatory channels, their relative impact potential in conveying information about their preferences as well as their potential to exert pressure on political elites is always higher than for the other age groups.[5]

If it is accepted for the moment that the streams of political participation are *distorted* between age groups, does that mean that public policy can be distorted to one age group or the other, depending on the influence of various forms of political participation? This is what Robert Dahl (1982) called the "distortion of the public agenda" in his discussion of *Dilemmas of Pluralist Democracy*. Those groups that are more active can determine the content and scope of the public policy agenda. I therefore need to go one step further. The answer lies in the last step of the analysis, the investigation into the political preferences of older, middle-aged and young people in order to decide whether there are any systematic differences.

11.5 Age Differences in Political Preferences

If older, middle-aged and young people wanted the same in politics, differences in pressure potential would not matter. If the same kind of people (with regard to political interests) use different routes for their political expression, the aggregate outcome *cannot* be affected by these participatory differences.

Let us look at attitudes in a broad range of policy domains: the role of the state in the economy, immigrant immigration and sexual life-style policy. In the European Social Survey, respondents were given a statement and were then asked to what extent they agreed with them:

---

[5]Obviously, this result is contingent in the age separation that I suggested here: 18–29, 30–59, and 60+ . However, this categorization might be considered to be conservative as far as young people are concerned. The defining line of young people being not as settled as middle-aged people might be drawn at even earlier ages than 30. If I did so, the differences would even be starker. As to the other division line, 60 seems the most plausible social division point as it is the mean retirement age across Europe. One could argue that early retirement regimes in, for example, Italy would call for a lower division point, but the analysis is quite robust even for cut-off points between 50 and 60. Thus, we can say with confidence that currently, middle-aged people dominate in their pressure potential due to their high participation rates and demographic weight, relative to other age groups whereas young people are the least influential and older people are always in between.

- The less the government intervenes in the economy, the better it is for your [country].
- It is better for a country if almost everyone shares the same customs and traditions.
- Gay men and lesbians should be free to live their own life as they wish.

Table 11.3 reports the percentages of young, middle-aged and older people who agreed or fully agreed with the statements. I split the analysis by participation channels in order to get a sense of to what extent older people using one certain type of participation are different from younger people using the same type. The highlighted columns present the difference in percentage of people supporting the respective statement. For instance, among voters, 38% of older people compared to 24% of young people agree with the statement that *less* government intervention in the economy is *better*. So there is a difference of 14% between the young and older people.

The most important finding in this table is that the direction of difference is the same, no matter what the channel of participation, with regard to all three policy domains. Thus, young people active in politics are on average more in favor of a stronger involvement of the state in the economy, more in favor of a culturally heterogeneous society and more in favor of a liberal sexual life-style policy. Depending on the policy domain, the difference between young and older people varies, but not to a large degree (and could easily stem from sampling errors). In the area of the state and the economy, the difference is as small as 8% for those who are active in contacting, parties and demonstrations. However, it is 20% for consumer participation. In the sexual life-style policy area, there are no differences as the numbers only vary between 15 and 21. In the area of migration policy, the difference varies between 16% (demonstrators) and 22% (active in consumer participation, wearing a badge/signing a petition and voting). On all three policy domains, however, young citizens are less conservative than middle-aged or older ones.[6]

In sum, political preferences vary between age groups. In three diverse policy domains (the role of the state in the economy, migration policy and sexual life style policies), older people are always more conservative than middle-aged who are more conservative than young people. Probably, these differences are due to changing socialization effects at young adulthood (see Sect. 6), meaning that they are differences between cohorts than across the life cycle. Middle-aged individuals who have the strongest pressure potential through their participation given their demographic weight are always between younger and older individuals in their political preferences.

Therefore, the differential impact of age groups that has been unveiled in Sect. 4 matters. Age groups are different in their political preferences. Since middle-aged

[6]The literature on preference formation and age effects tends to explain these differences with a generational account. Thus, older people are not becoming more conservative. If society moves into a certain direction with its mean value position, older people tend to maintain on average an ideal point that was prevalent during their time of early political socialization (see for example Tilley 2005; Danigelis and Cutler 1991).

Table 11.3 Political attitudes of young, middle-aged and older people in three policy domains across Europe

	State and the economy				Sexual life styles				Immigrant integration			
	Young	MA	Older	Diff.	Young	MA	Older	Diff	Young	MA	Older	Diff.
Voting	24	31	38	−14	78	76	59	19	43	48	65	−22
Contacting	26	31	34	−8	80	76	59	21	39	43	57	−18
Badge and petition	24	29	37	−13	86	82	66	20	31	38	54	−22
Consumer	23	29	43	−20	86	83	68	18	28	33	50	−22
Parties	30	32	38	−8	77	76	62	15	41	44	61	−20
Single-issue orgs.	27	32	43	−16	85	83	68	16	32	35	53	−21
Trade unions and prof. orgs	23	29	37	−14	82	80	66	16	36	40	55	−19
Demonstrating	22	28	30	−8	86	84	69	17	32	34	48	−16

Source: ESS2002/3, Questions (B43, B46, D40), 21 European countries, trade union/single issue = 19 countries. Cell entries are percent who agree or strongly agree, all differences are significant at the 0.05 level. Weighted observations, MA = middle-aged

people have a *higher* pressure potential than young people and older people, their preferences can potentially have *more* of an influence.

11.6 Discussion

Let us now put the results into perspective with some findings of other researchers. In sum, this chapter reveals three empirical findings for Europe at the beginning of the third millennium: (1) young people are at a disadvantage relative to middle-aged and older people on most forms of political participation; (2) young people's potential to exert political pressure through means of mass participation and due to their number is lower than that of middle-aged and older people; and (3) young people differ in their political preferences from middle-aged and older people. Thus, their lower pressure potential *can matter* as to political outcomes.

The first finding is just another description of what has been found by many scholars, namely that the current generation of young people in Europe is less active than people of higher age in many forms of participation. Some aspects of these lower levels of especially institutionalised participation are typical of the current generation who are socialized into being less interested in formal politics, but may be still interested in "the political" (Dalton 2004; Henn et al. 2002). Future generations of young people may receive a different kind of socialization, such as through civic education at schools, and be more active again (Galston 2001). Other aspects of this lower level of participation are linked to the life course and may be more difficult to change. For example, there is strong evidence that early experience of voting is hindered by the exigencies of setting up an adult life (Plutzer 2002). Since there are both cohort and life cycle effects at work, it is difficult to judge for the near future what the political participation of young people will look like.

Secondly, the lower level of pressure potential is contingent on the lower levels of political participation of young people. If future generations of young people are *socialized* into more political activity, their pressure potential will rise again. However, the demographic trends in European democracies are very rigid; low fertility seems to be a characteristic of post-industrial societies. Policy-makers' attempts to raise it seem mostly to be in vain, although some demographers think solutions are viable (Morgan 2003). So, overall, the pressure potential of young people is likely to remain rather low due to *demographics*.

But age group differences in political pressure potential may only be a problem if there is a conflict between generations. There exists very little evidence for conflicts between cohorts in post-industrial democracies. Apart from the differences in some political preferences, which have been shown above and will be discussed further down, generational conflicts seem not to be an issue in politics. This lack of conflict may be due to the two things: (a) members of birth cohorts have links to members of other birth cohorts in their families and (b) intermediary organizations like parties and trade unions historically created and managed varying generational demands (Kohli 1999, 2008).

Some social scientists claim that the shifting demographics can close doors for fundamental reforms, such as a reform of the public pension system (Sinn and Uebelmesser 2002; see for counter-arguments Goerres 2007). Their assumption is a very simplistic notion of material self-interest and voting: older people will use their increasing pressure potential to block any political change that worsens their material status quo like the adjustment of pension levels to sustainable formulae. However, studies of actual voting patterns of older people (Bonoli and Häusermann (2009); Goerres 2008, 2009a) show that such a materialistic outlook on politics does not determine voting choices of older people. Also, there is evidence that in those European countries in which the necessity for reform, for instance due to a high old-age dependency, young people are more active compared to older people than in countries where the necessity is less urgent (Goerres 2009b).

Another concrete proposal to improve the political situation of young people as to their pressure potential is to *lower* the voting age. There are three variations to this idea: to lower the age (typical at 18 at the moment) to another threshold, such as 16, as was done in Austria in 2007 for elections at all levels, to get rid of any voting age (effectively setting it to 0) or to give parents extra votes for their minor children until these children can take on their own right (see Goerres and Tiemann 2009; Krieger 2006). These proposals once put into practice would effectively increase the numerical size of the group of "the young" as voters and thereby increase their pressure potential, although it would not affect other areas of participation where often legal age is the minimum (for example, for full party membership). However, with regard to generational conflict, such changes could be counter-productive (although no study has yet been carried out in order to empirically assess this claim). It could be that solidarity between generations would decrease if older and middle-aged people saw that those younger than 18 had access to the political process. The consideration by middle-aged and older people for the young when casting their vote or acting politically in general could vanish. If anything, these reforms should be produced due to normative considerations among which generational justice may be an important aspect (see Kohli 2006).

Finally, there is the evidence for differences in political preferences across several policy domains. The differences in political preferences between young and middle-aged or older people can be due either to life-cycle or cohort differences (Goerres 2009b, Chap. 2). The longitudinal evidence that exists seems to point towards cohort differences being the main determinant of these differences between age groups (Danigelis and Cutler 1991; Tilley 2005). Thus, the low pressure potential of young people linked to preferences different from those of middle-aged or older people because of cohort membership could only lead to less impact of these cohort specific interests, i.e., political impact could be *skewed* in favor of the interests of the current cohorts of middle-aged or older people, not their interests in the position of the life-cycle. Overall, there is little evidence for differences in political preferences linked to the life-cycle. The little there is may be due to very specific circumstances of the country and the existing political institutions. Simple material self-interest linked to the life-cycle is definitely not the main answer to these findings (Bonoli and Häusermann (2009); Busemeyer et al. (2009); Wilkoszewski 2008). Thus, for example, the policies towards same-sex marriage may not be optimal for the current generation of young people who are more progressive than the current generations of middle-aged and older people who are more conservative. But the political output is unlikely to be skewed against the interests of those who are younger than 30 (education, childcare, etc.).

11.7 Conclusions

Political participation by individuals is becoming more heterogeneous in European democracies due to large-scale societal changes. In addition, demographic changes made the group of young people shrink in the past, which will continue into the future.

This essay argues that the political participation process in Europe is currently skewed in favor of middle-aged people who dominate in pressure potential measured through their participation levels and demographic size. Older people, the fastest growing age group, come in second on almost all dimensions. Young people, who are unlikely to increase in the near future, have the lowest pressure potential due to their low participation rates and their small demographic weight. The evidence also showed that young, middle-aged and older individuals differ in their political preferences. Therefore, seen from this non-specific perspective, young people are less able to convey information about their preferences and exert less pressure on political elites relative to other age groups. It is important to point out that this chapter is about broad dynamics and the potential for pressure. Whether young people in a *particular country* and with regard to a *certain policy* exert less pressure, remains another empirical question.

Overall, the empirical evidence throws up the question as to what extent preferences for channels of political participation by groups and political preferences of these groups can influence political outcomes that are produced in a democracy. Whereas the literature tends to be pre-occupied with a mismatch of the preferences of those who participate and those who do not (Verba et al. 1978, Verba et al. 1995; Verba and Nie 1972), there is also a case to be made that among those who participate, differences in preferences could lead to diverging political results. Politicians interested in equality in participation and outcome should not be concerned about the growing importance of older people, but rather the *diminishing significance* of the young compared to both middle-aged and older people.

This chapter demonstrated that the demand for policies expressed through channels of participation varies among age groups. Therefore, it needs to be investigated how the intermediary organizations, such as political parties, trade unions and NGOs deal with these differences. In addition, there are still too few studies that look at differences in political preferences among age groups more closely. What are the policy interests that are immediately tied to young age and to what extent are they context-dependent? The evidence that is known hints at very few truly life-cycle related differences in political preferences that are also highly dependent on the institutional context. Still, if a vote is carried out on matters such as pension reforms in very specific circumstances where only one policy is at stake, these life-cycle interests may be played out.

Acknowledgment For detailed comments, I would like to thank Aaron Boesenecker, Frank Nullmeier, Armin Schäfer and Pieter Vanhuysse and two anonymous referees.

References

Blome N, Hoeren D, Koch E (2008) Roman Herzog warnt vor Rentner-Demokratie. Bild 11-04-2008

Bonoli G, Häusermann S (2009) New socio-structural conflicts in social policy issues: evidence from Swiss referendum votes. Eur Soc 11(2):211–232

Busemeyer MR, Achim G, Simon W (2009) Attitudes towards redistributive spending in an era of demographic ageing: the rival pressures from age and income in 14 OECD Countries. J Eur Soc Policy 14(2):582–610

Dahl RA (1982) Dilemmas of pluralist democracy. Autonomy vs. control. Yale University Press, New Haven, CT

Dalton RJ (2004) Democratic challenges. Democratic choices. The erosion of political support in advanced industrial democracies. Oxford University Press, Oxford

Dalton RJ (2008) The good citizen: how a younger generation is reshaping American politics. CQ Press, Washington, DC

Danigelis NL, Cutler SJ (1991) Cohort trends in attitudes about law and order: who's leading the conservative wave? Public Opin Q 55:24–49

Deth V, Jan W, Montero JR, Westholm A (eds) (2007) Citizenship and involvement in European democracies. A comparative analysis. Routledge, London

Galston WA (2001) Political knowledge, political engagement, and civc education. Annu Rev Polit Sci 4:217–234

Goerres A (2007) Can we reform the welfare state in times of 'grey' majorities? The myth of an electoral opposition between younger and older voters in Germany. Max Planck Institute for the Study of Societies Working Paper 07/05

Goerres A (2008) The grey vote Determinants of older voters' party choice in Britain and West Germany. Elect Stud 27(2):285–304

Goerres A (2009a) Das Wahlverhalten älterer Menschen. Ein Beitrag über die Unterschiede zwischen älteren und jüngeren Wählern. In: Kocka J, Kohli M, Streeck W (eds) Altern: Familie Zivilgesellschaft, Politik. Deutsche Akademie der Naturforscher Leopoldina, Halle (Saale)

Goerres A (2009b) The political participation of older people in Europe: the greying of our democracies. Palgrave Macmillan, Basingstoke

Goerres A, Tiemann G (2009) Kinder an die Macht? Die politischen Konsequenzen des stellvertretenden Elternwahlrechts. Politische Vierteljahresschr 50(1):50–74

Henn M, Weinstein M, Wring D (2002) A generation apart? Youth and political participation in Britain. Br J Polit Int Relat 4(2):167–192

ILO (2006) EAPEP Data (Version 5) 2006 [cited 28-02 2006]. Available from http://laborsta.ilo.org/

Inglehart R (1995) Changing values, economic development and political change. Int Soc Sci J 145:379–404

Kohli M (1999) Private and Public Transfers between Generations: Linking the Family and the State. Eur Soc 1:81–104

Kohli M (2006) Aging and justice. In: Binstock RH, George LK (eds) Handbook of aging and the social sciences. Academic, San Diego, CA

Kohli M (2008) Altersgruppen und Generationen – Konfliktlinien und Integrationspotenzial. J Generationengerechtigkeit 8(3):34–38

Krieger Tim (2006) Generationengerechtigkeit und das "Wahlrecht" von Geburt an - kritische Anmerkungen aus Sicht der Public-Choice-Theorie. J Generationengerechtigkeit 3:27–29

Lawson K (1988) When linkage fails. In: Lawson K, Merkl PH (eds) When parties fail Emerging alternative organizations. Princeton University Press, Princeton

Mair P, van Biezen I (2001) Party membership in twenty European democracies, 1980–2000. Party Polit 7(1):5–21

Meyer D, Tarrow S (eds) (1998) The social movement society. Contentious politics for a new century. Rowman and Littlefield, Lanham

Morgan SP (2003) Is low fertility a twenty-first-century demographic crisis? Demography 40 (4):589–603

Norris P (2002) Democratic phoenix: reinventing political activism. Cambridge University Press, Cambridge

Pateman C (1970) Participation and democratic theory. Cambridge University Press, Cambridge

Plutzer E (2002) Becoming a habitual voter: inertia, resources, and growth in young adulthood. Am Polit Sci Rev 96(1):41–56

Putnam RD (2000) Bowling alone. The collapse and revival of American community. Simon and Schuster, New York

Sinn H-W, Uebelmesser S (2002) Pensions and the path to gerontocracy in Germany. Eur J Polit Econ 19:153–158

Tilley JR (2005) Libertarian-authoritarian value change in Britain, 1974–2001. Polit Stud 53 (2):442–453

United Nations (2007) Population by sex and age groups (UN Population Division's quinquennial estimates and projections) [code 13680] 2007 [cited 31-10 2007]. Available from http://unstats.un.org/unsd/databases.htm

Verba S, Nie NH (1972) Participation in America: political democracy and social equality. Harper and Row, New York

Verba S, Nie NH, Kim Jae-on (1978) Participation and political equality. A seven-nation comparison. Cambridge University Press, Cambridge

Verba S, Schlozman KL, Brady HE (1995) Voice and equality: Civic voluntarism in American politics. Harvard University Press, Cambridge

Wattenberg MP (2008) Is voting for young people?. Pearson Education, New York

Wilkoszewski H (2008) Demographic pressure and attitudes towards public intergenerational transfers in Germany: how much room left for reforms? In: Tremmel J (ed) Demographic change and intergenerational justice: the implementation of long-term thinking in the political decision-making process. Springer, Berlin

Chapter 12
The Emergence of Pensioners' Parties in Contemporary Europe

Seán Hanley

12.1 Introduction

Party politics in contemporary Europe often exhibit marked generational biases. Older voters are both more likely to turn out to vote to support political parties at elections and also to be members of political parties (Goerres 2009). Conversely, younger voters are increasingly disinclined to participate in formal party-electoral politics leading to concern over the 'greying' of party democracy and of socio-political organizations (Henn et al. 2002; Phelps 2006; Goerres 2009; and Robertson 2009). Certain (types of) parties are disproportionately supported by older age groups. Indeed, in certain cases – as with the members of the British Conservative Party during 1990s (Whiteley et al. 1994) or the electorate of the Czech Republic's Communist Party (Hanley 2001) – older age cohorts can find themselves in the majority, significantly affecting the way such parties understand, prioritize and respond to issues of the day and often tending to narrow their political appeal over time.

However, the possibility that population ageing and the growing salience of issues relating to ageing societies might generate pressures for the emergence of *new* parties has been largely overlooked. This is in many ways unsurprising. Despite the emergence at the margins of political systems across Europe of pensioners and retirees' parties over the last two decades, such 'grey interest' parties' (Goerres 2009, p. 148), appear on first examination a fringe phenomenon of little importance (Walker 1998; Goerres 2009, pp. 72–74).[1] Nevertheless, grey interest parties arguably merit closer examination both as socio-political phenomena in

S. Hanley
Senior Lecturer in Politics at the School of Slavonic and East European Studies, University College London, London
e-mail: s.hanley@ssees.ucl.ac.uk

[1]Following Goerres (2009, p. 72), I take a 'grey interest' party to be any organization contesting (or planning to contest) elections which signals through its name and/or founding documents that it seeks mainly to represent the interests of pensioners and/or older voters.

J.C. Tremmel (ed.), *A Young Generation Under Pressure?*,
DOI 10.1007/978-3-642-03483-1_12, © Springer-Verlag Berlin Heidelberg 2010

themselves and as a potential new party family in the making in European politics. As Herzog (1987) suggests, regardless of their vote-getting potential, newly emerging minor parties can serve as a marker for emergence of new issues and an early indicator that (wider) groups of voters may be redefining and re-negotiating socio-political identities or seeking vehicles for protest. Moreover, in a number of European states grey interest parties have already enjoyed sufficient electoral success to exercise political leverage. Indeed, in a small number of cases, they have even entered government.

This chapter maps the emergence of pensioners' parties over the last two decades in both established West European democracies and the newer post-communist democracies of Central and Eastern Europe (CEE). It then examines the reasons for the emergence and, in certain cases, the relative success of pensioners' parties highlighting both the 'demand' for such parties generated by socio-economic and demographic change and the 'supply' of political opportunities for their emergence thrown up by electoral systems and configurations of established parties. It concludes with a brief assessment of the prospects of pensioners' parties and the possibility that they might establish themselves as a minor party family in European politics.

12.2 The Emergence of Pensioners' Parties

Pensioners' interest organizations in western Europe generally date from the 1940s and 1950s and in some cases the interwar period. The precise form of such organizations varied both historically and by national context, reflecting specific patterns of 'pillarization' and/or 'partification' of social life or specific strategies of mass organization. A further wave of new older people's social and political organizations emerged sporadically across from 1970s across western Europe in the context of the 'new politics of old age' generated by the twin processes of population ageing and the contraction and reconfiguration of post-war welfare states (Walker 1998; Evers and Jürgen 1999).

In West European democracies, pensioners' parties emerged as a fringe phenomenon in the late 1980s and early 1990s. Although there were reports of an 'Autonomous Party of Pensioners' contesting Italian parliamentary elections as early as 1972 (*Time*, 22 March 1972), as Table 12.1 shows, the first pensioners' party to emerge in a Western democracy for which firm evidence is available was founded in Israel in 1981 – the first in a series of generally peripheral 'grey' groupings to emerge in Israeli electoral politics before the unexpected electoral breakthrough of the GIL party in 2006 (Iecovich 2002; Derfner 2006; Susser 2007). The first grey party to emerge in western Europe proper was Italy's *Partito dei Pensionati (PP)* founded in 1987. Thereafter, pensioners' parties were formed in Germany, Scandinavia, the Benelux countries and Portugal. More recently, several pensioners' parties have also emerged seem the United Kingdom. The Scottish Senior Citizens' Unity Party (SSCUP) was founded in 2003 and had one

Table 12.1 Pensioners parties in Western Europe and Israel

Belgium	*Waardig Ouder Worden* (WOW) Founded 1994 European elections 1994 2.14% Flemish parliamentary elections 2004, 0.02%
Denmark	Active Pensioners Party (*Partiet Aktive Pensionister*) Founded 1997 Contested local elections 2005 Has not contested national elections
Finland	1. Joint Responsibility Party of Pensioners and Greens Parliamentary elections 1991, 0.1%
	2. Independent Non-Aligned Pensioners in Finland Parliamentary elections 1991, 0.19%
	3. Pensioners for the People (EKA) Parliamentary elections 1995, 0.2% Parliamentary elections 1999 0.2%
	4. Finnish Pensioners' Party (SEP – *Suomen eläkeläisten puolue*) 1987, 1.22% Parliamentary elections 1991, 0.39% Parliamentary elections 1995, 0.1% Parliamentary elections 1999, 0.2%
Germany	1. The Greys – Gray Panthers *Die Grauen – Graue Panther)* Founded 1989 (as pressure group 1975) Formally dissolved in 2008 1990 0.8%% PR lists? 1994 0.4% Single Member Districts, 0.5% PR lists 1998 0.3% Single Member Districts, 0.3% PR lists 2002 0.2% Single Member Districts, 0.2 PR lists 2005 0.0 Single Member District (6340 votes), PR list 0.4% 2004 European elections 1.2%
	2. The Greys – Party of Generations (*Die Grauen – Generationspartei*) Founded 2008
	3. Grey Panther Alliance (*Allianz Graue Panther)* Founded 2008
Holland	1. General Elderly Alliance (*Algemeen Ouderen Verbond*, AOV) Founded 1993 1994 parliamentary election, 3.6% 6 seats (of 150) Did not contest subsequent parliamentary elections Represented at sub-national (provincial) level (provincial elections in 1995–2003). Gained seats in upper chamber 1995–1998 on basis on provincial representation
	2. Union 55+ Founded 1992 1994 parliamentary election, 0.8%, 1 seat Sub-national (provincial) representation in coalition with AOV
	3. Elderly Union (*Ouderenunie*). Formed 1998 from merger of AOV and Union 55+ 1998 parliamentary election, 0.5%
	4. United Seniors Party (*Verenigde Senioren Partij* – VSP) Formed 2001 from merger of Elderly Union and Seniors Party 2002 parliamentary elections 0.4% 2003 parliamentary elections – not contested

(*continued*)

Table 12.1 (continued)

	2006 parliamentary elections 0.1% Limited sub-national representation
Italy	1. Autonomous Party of Pensioners Contested parliamentary elections 1972
	2. Pensioners' Party: *Partito Pensionati*) Founded 1987 1999 European elections 0.8%, no seats 2004 European elections, 1.1%, 1 seat 2006 parliamentary elections, 0.88% Part of centre-left Union grouping 2008 parliamentary election – candidates presented as part of People of Freedom bloc
Israel	1. Older Persons and Pensioners Party of Israel (*HaGimlain Vhakshishim BeIsrael)* Founded 1981 1981 parliamentary elections, 0.1%
	2. 'Pensioners' (*Gimlaim*) Founded 1988 1988 parliamentary elections, 0.73% 1992 parliamentary elections in coalition with Hand by Hand (*Yad beyad*) party representing ex-Soviet immigrants, 0.31%
	3. Power for Pensioners (*Koah LaGimlaim*), parliamentary elections 1999, 1.1%, no seats
	4. Pensioners of Israel to the Knesset (GIL) *Gimla'ey Yisrael LaKnesset* Founded 1996 1996 parliamentary elections, 0.57%, 2006 parliamentary elections, 5.92%, 7 seats (of 120) 2009 parliamentary elections, 0.52%
Luxembourg	1. Alternative Democratic Reform party (ADR)[a] (*Alternativ Demokratesch Reformpartei/ Parti réformiste d'alternative démocratique/Alternative Demokratische Reformpartei*) Founded 1987 1989 parliamentary elections 7.3%, 4 seats (of 60) 1994 parliamentary elections 9.0%, 5 seats 1999 parliamentary elections 11.3%, 7 seats 2004 parliamentary elections 9.9% 5 seats 2009 parliamentary elections, 8,1% 4 seats Subnational representation since 1993
	2. Party of the Third Age (*Partei vum 3. Alter, Parti du troisième age*) 1999 parliamentary elections 0.1% 2004 parliamentary elections 0.4% in one constituency Now disbanded
Norway	Pensioners Party *(Pensjonistpartiet*) Founded 1985 1985 parliamentary elections 0.3% 1989 parliamentary elections 0.3% 1993 parliamentary elections 1.0% 1997 parliamentary elections 0.6 2001 parliamentary elections 0.7% 2005 parliamentary election 0.5% Never represented at national level Some subnational representation

(*continued*)

Table 12.1 (continued)

Portugal	Party of National Solidarity (*Partido da Solidariedade Nacional* – PSN) Founded 1990 1991 Parliamentary elections 1.7%, 1 seat (of 230) 1995 Parliamentary elections 0.2% 1999 Parliamentary elections 0.2% 2002 Parliamentary elections 0.0%
Spain	Active Pensioners' Party (*Partido de los Pensionistas en Acción* – PDLPEA Founded 2007 2008 parliamentary elections 0.01%
Sweden	Swedish Senior Citizen Interest Party (*Sveriges Pensionärers Intresseparti*) Founded 1987 1991 parliamentary elections 0.04% 1994 parliamentary elections 0.04% 1998 parliamentary elections 1.0% 2003 parliamentary elections 0.71% 2006 parliamentary elections 0.52% Never represented at national level Some subnational representation
UK	
– Scotland	Scottish Senior Citizens Unity Party (SSCUP) Founded 2003 2003 Scottish parliamentary elections, 0.1% in Single Member Districts, 1.5% of regional list votes, 1 seat 2007 Scottish parliamentary elections, 1.92% of regional list vote, no seats
– England and Wales	Senior Citizens Party 2005 European elections

[a]Name since 2006. Previously 'Action Committee – 5/6 Pensions for All' (1987–1999), 'Action Committee 5/6' (1989–1992), 'Action Committee for Democracy and Pensions Justice'
Sources: http://www.parties-and-elections.de; Iecovich (2002); Israeli Knesset; http://www.knesset.gov.il/description/eng/eng_mimshal_res.htm; *The Times*, 5 May 2007; German Federal Returning Officer http://www.bundeswahlleiter.de; www.electionresources.org; Statistics Norway www.ssb.no; Swedish Election Authority www.val.se and personal communication 10 January 2008; Statistics Norway www.ssb.no

representative elected to the Scottish Parliament in elections of that year. Several more peripheral and localized groups emerged in England and Wales around the time of the 2005 general election. Overall, it appears only three countries in western Europe saw no grey interest parties form: Ireland, Iceland and France.

As Table 12.1 shows, West European pensioners' parties have so far remained a largely peripheral phenomenon. Some have almost no electoral support at national level, although most have been able to gain 1–2% of the vote in national elections on at least one occasion and many have some representation at sub-national level. A small number of 'grey' parties have exceeded this level of support, the most notable cases being Holland's General Elderly Alliance (AOV) (van Stipdonk and van Holsteyn 1995; Thornton 1995), which was represented in the Dutch parliament between 1994 and 1998, and Luxembourg's Alternative Democratic Reform

Party (ADR), which has polled close to 10% of the national vote in successive parliamentary elections and has become an established parliamentary party. In neither case, however, did these grey interest groupings enter government, nor were they considered as potential coalition partners. Israel thus offers the only instance of a pensioners' party holding government office in an established Western democracy. The Israeli pensioners' party GIL, which was represented in the Knesset between 2006 and 2009, was a junior partner in the coalition administration led by the centrist Kadima movement. Pensioners' parties have also contested European elections on several occasions. However, only one, Italy's *PP* which gained one MEP in 2004, has had any representation in the European Parliament.

Pensioners' parties have also widely emerged in post-communist Europe but, as in western Europe, have remained a largely peripheral and short-lived phenomenon. As Table 12.2 shows, 'grey' groupings formed in almost all post-communist democracies in CEE, the earliest emerging in the early-mid 1990s in the rapidly reforming Central European states. Pensioners' parties have also developed more recently in Russia, Ukraine and South East European states such as Croatia, Serbia and Bulgaria, where the region's newest grey party, the Social Solidarity Movement, was founded in July 2007 after months of protest demonstrations by older people in Sofia against the Bulgarian government's failure to uprate pensions (Novinite 2007). In post-communist Europe, despite the existence of numerous electoral lists for the 'underprivileged' or 'social justice', pensioners' parties seem to be absent in Albania, Latvia, Lithuania and Moldova.

As in western Europe, the success of eastern and central Europe's grey interest parties has been limited and few have established themselves on a long-term basis. Many, such as Hungary's National Pensioners' Party or Slovakia's two short-lived pensioner groupings, appear effectively defunct, while others have merged, either temporarily or permanently, with larger electoral groupings. In general, however, pensioner parties appeared to perform somewhat more successfully in the post-communist CEE than in West European democracies. Several grey groupings in the region performed as credible extra-parliamentary groupings in parliamentary elections in the Czech Republic (1992, 1996 and 1998), Estonia (1993), Poland (1997) often polling 2–3% – a level of support usually sufficient to access state funding and offer a realistic chance of crossing electoral thresholds. Pensioners' parties have entered national parliaments in four post-communist states (Russia, Slovenia, Croatia, and Serbia).

Of these, three have been represented in government, and the Democratic Party of Pensioners of Slovenia (DeSUS) has held government office as junior partner in coalitional governments of the Left and the Right for more than a decade. Having increased its vote from 4.04 to 7.47% in the 2008 parliamentary elections, DeSUS is currently a partner in Slovenia's centre-left coalition government and has two ministerial portfolios. Similarly, the Party of United Pensioners of Serbia (PUPS) also won parliamentary representation in Serbia's 2008 parliamentary elections as part of coalition led by the Socialist Party of Serbia and subsequently entered government when this bloc became a junior member of the pro-European administration of Prime Minister Mirko Cvetković. The party's leader Jovan Krkobabić is currently a Deputy Prime Minister and has responsibility for several social affairs

Table 12.2 Pensioners parties in Eastern Europe

Bosnia and Herzegovinia	1. Pensioners' Party of Bosnia and Herzegovina (*Stranka Penzionera Umirovljenika BiH)* Parliamentary elections 2002, 1.4%, 2 (of 140) in parliament of Federation of Bosnia and Herzegovina (Croat-Bosnian entity); 1 seat (of 42) in Bosnian parliament (both entities) Parliamentary elections 2006, 1.48%, no representation in parliament of Federation of Bosnia and Herzegovina or Bosnian parliament 2. Pensioners' Party of the Republika Srpska (*Penzionerska Stranka Republike Srpske*) Parliamentary elections 2002, 1 seat (of 83) in National Assembly of the Serb Republic within Bosnia Parliamentary elections 2006, 2.49% no seats in National Assembly of the Serb Republic within Bosnia
Bulgaria	Social Solidarity Movement Founded May 2007
Croatia	Croatian Pensioners' Party (*Hrvatska stranka umirovljenika,* HSU) Founded 1996 Parliamentary election 2003 – 4%, 3 seats (of 151) Parliamentary election 2007 – 4.1% 1 seat (of 153) Some sub-national (communal/municipal) representation
Czech Republic	Pensioners for a Secure Life (*Duchodci za źivotní´jistoty*, DŽJ)* Parliamentary election 1992**, 3.77% Parliamentary election 1996, 3.09% Parliamentary election 1998, 3.06% Parliamentary election 2002, 0.86% Some sub-national (communal/municipal) representation Merged with Independent Democrats (ND) grouping 2006
Estonia	1. Estonian Pensioners' Union *(Eesti Pensionaride Liit)* Parliamentary elections 1992, 3.71% Some sub-national (communal/municipal) representation 2. Estonian Pensioners and Families Union (*Eesti Pensionäride ja Perede Liit*) Contested 1995 election as part of Coalition Party and Country People's Alliance (KMÜ). Later renamed the Estonian Pensioners and Families Party (*Eesti Pensionäride ja Perede Erakond*, EPPE) . Merged with the Estonia People's Party in 1999
Hungary	Pensioners' Party (*Nyugdijasok Partja*, NYUP) Parliamentary elections 1994, 0.02% (SMD) Parliamentary elections 2002, 0.00%**8 (SMD)
Poland	1. Legnica Association of Pensioners and Invalids (*Polski Zw. Emerytów, Rencistów i Inw. O/W Legnica*) Parliamentary elections 1991 – 0.04% 2. Disabled, Retired Persons and Pensioners (*"Niepelnosprawni, Emeryci i Rencisci")* Parliamentary elections 1991 – 0.04% 3. National Party of Pensioners and Retired Persons (*Krajowa Partia Emerytów I Rencistów*, KPEiR) Parliamentary elections 1997 – 2.18%

(*continued*)

Table 12.2 (continued)

	4. National Alliance of Pensioners and Retired Persons of the Polish Republic (*Krajowe Porozumienia Emerytów i Rencistów Rzeczypospolitej Polskiej*, KPPiRRP) Parliamentary elections 1997 – 1.63%
Romania	1. Party of Pensioners of Romania (*Partidul Pensionarilor din Romania, PPR*) Parliamentary election 2000 – 0.66% 2. Popular and Social Protection Party (*Partidul Popular şi al Protecţiei Sociale*) Parliamentary elections 2008 – 0.12%
Russia	Pensioners' Party**** (*Partiya pensionerov*, PP) Parliamentary elections 1999, 1.95% (national PR list), 0.71% (SMDs), 1 deputy elected in SMD Alliance of Pensioners' Party and Russian Social Justice Party 2003 Parliamentary elections 3.1% (national PR list), 0.5% (SMDs) Merged with Fair Russia bloc in 2006
Slovakia	1. Party of Pensioners and the Socially Dependent (*Strana dôchodcov a sociálne odkázaných*, SDSO) Founded May 1995 Did not contest national election Officially deregistered October 2005 2. Pensioners' Party of Slovakia (SDS - *Strana dôchodcov Slovenska*) Formed October 1995 Contested 2002 parliamentary elections on electoral list of Real Slovak National Party (PSNS). No deputies Officially deregistered October 2005
Slovenia	Democratic Party of Pensioners of Slovenia (*Demokratična stranka upokojencev Slovenije*, DeSUS) Parliamentary elections 1992, contested as part of United List of Social Democrats (ZLSD), 1 seat Parliamentary elections 1996 4.32% 5 seats (of 90) Parliamentary elections 2000, 5.17%, 4 seats Parliamentary elections 2004, 4.0%, 4 seats Parliamentary elections 2008, 7.47% , 7 seats Incumbent since 2000 2000-4 - coalition with Liberal Democrats (LDS), United Social Democrats (ZSLD) and Slovene People's Party. No ministerial portfolio, deputy speakership of parliament 2004- date, coalition with Slovenian Democratic Party (SDS), New Slovenia – Christian People's Party (NSi), Slovenian People's Party (SLS). One ministerial portfolio (defence)
Serbia	Party of United Pensioners of Serbia (*Partija ujedinenich pensionera Srbije*, PUPS) Founded 2005 2007 parliamentary elections - (in coalition with Social Democratic Party) 3.91% 5 seats (of 250)

(*continued*)

Table 12.2 (continued)

Ukraine	Bloc of the Party of Pensioners of Ukraine (*Blok Partii Pensioneriv Ukrainy* – BPPU) – coalition of Party of Pensioners of Ukraine and Party of Protection of Pensioners of Ukraine 2007 parliamentary elections 0.14%

*Later the Party for a Secure Life (*Strana za životní jistoty*)
** Figures for election to Czech parliament (Czech National Council)
*** 685 votes (1245 votes in 1994)
**** Subsequently merged with *Rodina* and other parties into Fair Russia bloc
Sources: Central Electoral Commission of Bosnia and Hercegovina http://www.izbori.ba; Czech Central Election Commission (www.volby.cz); Essex Election Archive (www.essex.ac.uk/elections); Russia Votes (www.russiavotes.org); Republic of Slovenia Electoral Commission (http://www.sigov.si/elections/rvk.html); Republic of Serbia Electoral Commission (http://www.rik.parlament.sr.gov.yu/index_e.htm); Slovak Ministry of the Interior as reported at http://www.civil.gov.sk/archiv/POLIT/zoz_psph_04072006.htm; 'Pensioners' Party Set Up in Bulgaria', Novinite news agency report, 12 May 2007, http://www.novinite.com/view_news.php?id=80585; Slovenian Government Communication Office, 'Slovenia Gets Its Sixth Government', December 2000 http://www.ukom.gov.si/eng/slovenia/background-information/elections 2000-government/; http://volitve.gov.si/dz2008/en/rezultati/rezultati_slo.html; *Central Europe Review*, 29 November 1999 http://www.ce-review.org/99/23/estonianews23.html; Permanent Electoral Authority of Romania (www.roaep.ro/en/index.php)

portfolios. The Croatian Pensioners' Party (HSU),which unexpectedly entered parliament in 2003 and retained one deputy in 2007 elections, has also exercised some influence on government acting as a 'support party' for successive administrations led by the reformed nationalist Croatian Democratic Union (HDZ).

12.2.1 Ideology and Impact

In both western and eastern European pensioners' parties articulate straightforward (usually short-term) material demands linked to distributional issues and represent themselves as a non-partisan voice for 'old folk' generally, in a way which gives them a degree of legitimacy and insulation from political attack. Their demands have centred on a series of essentially similar concerns: higher (and more regularly and effectively uprated) pensions; improvements in public services heavily used by older people such as health, social care and public transport; reductions in tax or reduced charges for public services for old people; and measures to combat age discrimination and change the social climate to give greater recognition and status to older people. Such demands have usually been expressed in short programmatic statements, which do not generally attempt to develop broader policy prescriptions or formulate detailed ideological standpoints.

At the same time, however, most pensioners' parties seek to represent themselves as something more than a sectional interest. Some project themselves as reformers contributing to the general debate about social cohesion and intergenerational solidarity. The slogan of Germany's *Die Grauen* 'Us today, you tomorrow', for example, sought to highlight that the party was defending the status of older people and the services and institutions they used on behalf of *all* citizens, who would inevitably pass through retirement and old age one day. German Greys have now described their party as a 'Party of Generations' (*Generationenpartei*).[2] Other grey interest parties have sought to identify themselves as part of broader movements for social justice or social welfare, making common cause with other groups dependent on transfers from the state, such as disabled people, carers or single parents. This trend is especially marked in CEE where such groups are often seen as among the hardest hit of 'transition losers'.

The political leverage that 'grey interest' parties have been able to exercise has been limited, but not non-existent. An unexpectedly high vote for a novel political formation like pensioners' party, even of a few percent, receives disproportionate publicity and can be taken as a signal by established parties already highly sensitised to the (largely erroneous) notion of a powerful 'grey vote' (Vincent et al. 2001; Goerres 2009; and Tepe and Vanhuysse 2009), that they should attend more closely to demands and interests of older and retired voters. In addition, there is the 'blackmail potential' derived by taking votes from other parties. 'Grey interest' parties which gain parliamentary representation can often enjoy quite significant 'coalition potential' with both the Left and the Right as potential junior partners in government: especially in finely balanced political systems, grey interest parties' smallness, lack of ideological profile and focus on specific (and hence, negotiable) redistributive demands generally make them *attractive* to both the Left and the Right as possible junior partners in government. Slovenia's DeSUS, for example, has participated in three successive coalition governments, of centre-left, centre- right and centre-left respectively.[3]

Once in office, pensioners' parties, although they lack wide political influence, are often able to extract specific or short-term concessions relating to the material or institutional support of older people. During its short tenure in government, Israel's GIL party, for example, used its control over the health and pensions ministries to help launch a new plan with a budget of seven million shekels to improve medical care for the elderly, centring on rehabilitation plans operating in and across hospitals, private homes and the wider community (Azoulay 2007). Similarly, in 2008, Serbia's PUPS blocked the rescinding of a 10% increase

---

[2]Founded as a party in 1989, *Die Grauen* formally dissolved in February 2008 in consequence of party funding scandal (*Kölnische Rundschau* 2007), but has been replaced by two successor pensioners' parties: the *Die Grauen – Generationspartei* and the *Allianz Graue Panther*. The former, whose leader is significantly younger than retirement age, is committed to the 'grey populist' strategy described later in this paper.

[3]Similarly, Italy's small *Partito dei Pensionati* has shuttled between the right-wing Pole of Liberty bloc with whom it was allied in the 2001 parliamentary elections and its centre-left rival the L'Unione/Olive Tree coalition, which the PP joined in February 2006 before leaving to rejoin the Pole of Liberty (later, People of Freedom (PDL) in November 2006. In the June 2009 European elections, the party formed part of the heterogeneous Pole of Autonomies coalition, but its MEP was not re-elected.

in pensions agreed as part of a package of spending cuts required for Serbia to obtain an IMF loan. Instead, public sector salaries were frozen to achieve the required spending reductions with pensions frozen in the subsequent year (Javno 2008).

12.3 Explaining Pensioners' Parties

How and why have pensioners' parties have formed? And why have some been more successful than others? The academic literature on new parties broadly agrees that three sets of conditions are important for the development of new types of party: (1) new or unmet demands for political representation generated by changes in underlying socio-economic, demographic and family structures; (2) political institutions and patterns of political competition that present a favourable set of 'opportunity structures' for new parties seeking to enter the political arena; and (3) the mobilization and co-ordination of sufficient material and human resources (Harmel and Robertson 1985; Willey 1998; Kitschelt 1989, 2007; Redding and Viterna 1999; Hug 2001; Sikk 2005; and Tavits 2006, 2008)

12.3.1 Population Ageing

The most basic social trend in post-industrial societies that might underlie the emergence of pensioners' parties is the growing number of older and retired people in European societies. This, it may be hypothesized, would generate both strong resource demands and demands for greater participation by older people leading to a new, more contested politics of old age (Walker 1998) At one level, demographic ageing seems a highly relevant factor. Certainly, the non-emergence of pensioners' parties in Ireland and Iceland, the two West European states with the lowest proportions of older and retired people, is perhaps not coincidental.

However, the development of pensioners' parties cannot be accounted for simply by raw demographic change. In some contexts, there is only very slight correlation between demographic ageing and the proportion of pensioners in the population. In some central and eastern European states in 1990s, for example, numbers of older people and numbers of retirees diverged significantly as a result of an artificially induced 'pensioner boom' stemming from the use of generous early retirement schemes to facilitate industrial restructuring and pre-empt social discontent following the fall of communism (Vanhuysse 2006). Similar less-marked divergence can also be found in many West European countries (Kubitza 2005). A change of focus to numbers of pensioners rather than older people, however, also offers only partial explanation. Israel, for example, presents an obvious anomaly: it is a case with a relatively low proportion of retired people compared to other Western democracies, which since 1980s has seen a succession of grey interest parties enter the political arena and on one occasion – that of the GIL party in 2006 – gain sufficient support to enter parliament and enter government. When assessing the drivers of political phenomena thrown up by the new politics of ageing such as pensioners' parties it is therefore important to consider demographic processes of ageing *as filtered* through political and institutional context(s).

12.3.2 The Politics of Pensions and Welfare

One such key context is that of the changing welfare state. From the 1980s, the focus of welfare politics in western Europe shifted from one centring on claiming resources and representation in an extensive, expanding welfare state to a 'new politics of welfare focused on their retrenchment and reform (Pierson 1996; Vanhuysse 2001; Green-Pedersen and Haverland 2002). Technological, socio-economic and demographic changes in western societies have also generated a range of New Social Risks (NSRs) to which welfare systems need to adapt and reconfigure such as the provision of care for elderly relatives and social protection in a labour market characterized by patterns of more intermittent employment and greater participation of women, (Bonoli 2004). Despite important differences of context, the politics of post-communist welfare and pensions in CEE have broadly mirrored those in western Europe. As in western Europe, CEE welfare states faced a politics of retrenchment and reform of pension and welfare system in the context of market-oriented liberal reforms and demographic change (Pop and Vanhuysse 2004).[4] However, post-communist societies are generally poorer than those in western Europe and thus enter the 'new politics of welfare' with fewer resources to manage political change as well as more complex tasks in reconfiguring welfare regimes largely inherited from the state socialist period (Mukesh et al. 2007).

The new politics of ageing, welfare and pensions have shaped the development of pensioners' parties in a number of ways. Firstly, age-specific controversies relating to social policy have often acted as trigger events for pensioner party formation, by providing a focus for mobilization and an outlet for a deeper sense of social and civic exclusion which some seniors feel (usually experienced as various forms of ageism and age discrimination). In some cases, these were widely publicised decisions or debates over policies specifically or

[4]As in Western democracies, post-communist welfare and pension systems in CEE proved resistant to reform efforts, although some states (Hungary 1997; Poland 1998; Latvia 2001; and Russia 2002) did introduce pension reforms on World Bank models by creating a second tier of (compulsory) individual accounts.

disproportionately affecting older people, often coming in a pre-election period. Examples of such trigger events have included proposed cuts to care allowances paid to those in retirement homes (Holland in 1994) or plans to raise retirement ages (misperceived as affecting those approaching retirement), which prompted the foundation of the Scottish Senior Citizens Unity Party (SSCUP).

At a deeper level, welfare states can be seen as a key shaper of socio-political interests and identities (Campbell 2003), which form the social backdrop to the emergence of pensioner parties. The new politics of welfare has been hypothesized as generating anti-(neo-)liberal distributional demands for the retention of post-war social democratic or social market status quo. Generationally-based conflicts are said to have emerged through the interaction and mutual reinforcement of established welfare and health institutions and a powerful 'grey lobby' able to outcompete other client groups such as families with children or the working poor in claiming health and welfare resources.

Such competition between beneficiaries of traditional welfare states and younger age groups facing NSR – and their different preferences regarding which risks should be prioritized – may, it has been suggested, be destabilising to existing party systems and party alignments. Kitschelt (2004, pp. 9–10), for example, foresees particular problems for Christian Democratic parties in core West European states where, he argues, the development of ageing post-industrial societies will tend to pull apart these parties' post-war electoral coalitions making it difficult to reconcile pressures from the older and retired people to maintain benefits from 'old' welfare state structures with pressures to liberalize the economy, curb welfare spending and offset the social risks that younger and middle-aged groups will face. One option, he speculates, might be to jettison social protectionist groups such as (current) pensioners from such coalitions. Such dynamics, if realized, could clearly open up political space for grey interest or other challenger parties. Such generational conflicts are echoed in the transitional politics of Central and Eastern Europe, where pensioners are generally disproportionately protected against the social consequences of market reform compared to other 'losers' in the reform process such as the unemployed and poorer families with children (Vanhuysse 2006).

12.3.3 Sectoral Divisions

Potential conflicts between generations are, however, often crosscut and inflected by sectoral divisions *within* generations. Pensioners in established Western democracies encompass diverse sub-groups – from prosperous retirees with generous occupational and private pensions to poor, marginalized older people dependent on state welfare guarantees. Such sectoral divisions seem particularly prominent in Bismarckian welfare states, which have historically offered generous pension benefits to certain sectorally – and gender-defined groups reflecting an organizing principle of maintaining occupational income and status differentials in retirement.[5]

Such sectoral divisions are usually seen as impeding the capacity of pensioners and older people to articulate their interests as a group or take collective action. Older people's interest groups, for example, are often highly fragmented in their agendas and activities, according to which particular strata of older people they focus on and the supporting or sponsoring groups that back them (Evers and Jürgen 1999; Viriot Durandal 2003). In the United Kingdom, for example, some campaign groups focus on the impact of property taxes on elderly homeowners, while trade union-affiliated groups focus on state pension indexation and NGOs with charitable status such as Help the Aged concentrate more on standards of social care and social services (Gynn and Sara 1999).

However, the intersection of generational and sectoral divisions can also act as a catalyst for socio-political mobilization. Goerres (2009, pp. 140–159), for example, notes the role of property taxes as focus for protest mobilization by older people in the South West of England. Moreover, the origins of Europe's most successful grey interest party, Luxembourg's ADR lie in precisely such a confluence of sectoral and generational grievances. The ADR has its origins as the 'Action Committee for 5/6 Pensions for Everyone', which co-ordinated protests in March 1987 by private sector employees (approaching retirement age), trade unions representing the self-employed and private sector pensioners against the more favourable pension regime enjoyed by state employees (Fehlen and Porier 2000, pp. 91–98).

12.3.4 Opportunity Structures

However, the shift from lobbying or protest to party-electoral politics and the subsequent limited success of some grey interest grouping also requires explanation in terms of the broader political institutions and sets of opportunity structures facing (prospective) new parties. There is broad consensus in the literature that the proportional electoral system which set low effective thresholds for parliamentary representation opens up opportunities for new parties to enter the political arena. Less fixed and formal institutions such as patterns of party competition or party-society relations are also important. Volatile or fragmented party systems and relatively large numbers of available, weakly committed and/or discontented voters also favour the formation and success of new parties (Willey 1998; Hug 2001; Sikk 2005, 2006). Forms of interest representation represent a further aspect of the

[5]Conversely, where pension provision is more universal and state-centred, retirees may form a more homogenous and cohesive group in terms of income, lifestyle and interests. This seems most marked in central and eastern Europe, reflecting the lower levels of differentiation of incomes and pension provision under state socialism, the role of the state as the main pension provider and post-transition income maintenance strategies after the fall of communism (Večerník 2006; Vanhuysse 2006).

political opportunity structure which may affect the prospects of emergent new parties. Kitschelt (1989), for example, suggests that strong patterns of corporatism privileging producer groups encourage the development of new parties because new interests struggle to find a voice through existing representation structures.[6]

The opportunities offered to 'grey' parties by varying national political institutions such as electoral and party systems seem, at first sight, to differ little from those faced by other small new emergent parties. The success of 'grey' parties in countries with PR systems, very low thresholds, fragmented and changeable party systems and long traditions of minor party formation such as Holland and Israel comes as no surprise. Similarly, the greater prevalence and success of pensioners' parties in eastern Europe seems closely related to the fluid and changeable nature of party politics in new democracies, especially during their early development (Sikk 2005; Tavits 2008). The initially somewhat blurred distinction between the role and nature of interest organizations and political parties in the region during 1990s (Waller 1993; Lewis 2000) also offered a favourable environment for the development of small interest parties.

However, on closer examination, a slightly more complex picture emerges. Many West European states have electoral systems which set relatively low thresholds for representation but have rarely seen new parties emerge from the political fringe. Conversely, while party organizations and systems in CEE are in many cases more fluid than in the longer established party systems of western Europe, the high formal electoral thresholds common across the region should represent a substantial obstacle to the development of small niche groupings such as pensioners' parties – and a disincentive to their formation (Birch 2001; Sikk 2005).

Available evidence suggests that corporatist interest intermediation structures (or their absence) may be of limited relevance to the development of grey interest parties. Feltenius (2007) finds that in Sweden, a country with relatively strong corporatist structures, pensioners' interest organizations were effective in lobbying despite lacking formal representation on tripartite bodies. In neighbouring Slovenia, one of the few Central and East European countries with corporatist arrangements, the Slovene pensioners' federation ZDUS has likewise had little difficulty accessing Slovenia's national tripartite body, the Economic and Social Council.[7] In Slovenia, moreover, the existence of strong, mass interest organization for older people has not precluded the development of a successful pensioners' party, DeSUS.

Taken together, this evidence suggests that in western Europe, the key impediment to the emergence of relatively successful pensioner parties is the stability of existing parties and, by implication, their ability to appeal to older voters, rather than more formal institutional barriers such as electoral or interest representation

[6]Others come to opposite conclusions suggesting that the corporatist-style devolution of power to social partners impedes the development of new parties and makes interest group politics more attractive (Tavits 2006).

[7]Author's telephone interview with the President of ZDUS, Dr Mateja Kozuh-Novak. 19 February 2009.

systems. In central and eastern Europe, by contrast, grey interest parties may have been constrained more by their inability to break through formal electoral thresholds. Here, it is perhaps telling that most electorally successful and durable grey interest party in the region, DeSUS, first independently entered the country's parliament in 1996 when the electoral threshold for representation was set at 3.33% (Fink-Hafner 2008).

12.3.5 Mobilizing Resources

Strong social demand and broad institutional opportunities are, however, in themselves insufficient for new parties to emerge. New parties also need access and organize sufficient money, media and human resources and offer policies for which there is electoral demand or a relevant political project (Lucardie 2000). Political entrepreneurs founding new parties also need to effectively *coordinate* their resources to overcome the collective action problems that all newly organizing groups face.

Older people in European societies have historically lacked both significant organizational resources and a distinct socio-political identity, which is a crucial prerequisite for collective action (Dunleavy 1991). Although levels of pension provision vary significantly both cross-nationally and by occupation, older people experience significant reductions in income on retirement and greater levels of ill health than citizens generally. Although modern welfare and pension systems have helped define the identity of 'senior citizen' or 'elderly person' (Wang 1999), in doing so they have constructed older citizens as passive and needy claimants on the state and society, rather than active political participants. In post-communist CEE, moreover, the status of older people has arguably declined for other reasons. Whereas youth in CEE is seen as a repository of liberal values and a crucial factor in bringing about change, older people are typically seen as an obstacle to change: apart from being a significant economic 'loser' group, they are seen as less flexible and as having a psychological stake in the institutions and practices of the communist past.

However, the resources required to found a new small party can be modest requiring a relatively low critical mass of activists, finance and organization, especially in those states where extra-parliamentary parties which meet minimum conditions regarding registration, membership or votes can easily obtain state funding. In Germany, for example, the qualifying threshold for state funding of 0.5% of the vote in national or European parliamentary elections, proved attainable for that country's electorally very marginal pensioners' party, *Die Grauen*.

There are, moreover, a number of trends mitigating the resource constraints on grey interest mobilization. Current cohorts of older and retired people in most European countries are, however, healthier, wealthier and better-educated than their equivalents in previous decades (Eberstadt and Groth 2007; Goerres 2009). Retired people in Western democracies also have often accumulated sets of experience of civic engagement and professional skills, as well as higher levels of free time, which may offset their lower financial and other resources. An established infrastructure of older people's interest and campaign groups can also provide a potential resource base for the formation of grey interest parties. Such interest groups, although they are unusually indifferent or hostile to the notion of grey interest parties, can generate individual political entrepreneurs and networks of activists who can act as the founders of such groupings.

This pattern is exemplified in the formation of early West European grey interest parties such as Germany's *Die Grauen*, Italy's Pensioners' Party or Slovenia's DeSUS, which has its origins in a local electoral list fielded in 1988 by frustrated members of the long-established Slovenian pensioners' federation. In a variation on this pattern, older people who had previously been prominent in established parties and social organizations have sometimes acted as early supporters of newly formed grey parties as a means of continuing in public life after retiring from mainstream politics. This pattern can be detected in, for example, the role played in the creation of Israeli pensioners' parties of 1980s by former trade union leaders (Iecovich 2002) or in the early momentum gained by the Scottish Senior Citizens Unity Party through the backing of retired local politicians once prominent in the Labour Party (Vincent 2003).

Only in some newer democracies in CEE where the civic infrastructure for older people – and civil and political society generally – is seriously under-developed does lack of resources seem to have been a crucial obstacle impeding the development of grey interest parties. This seems, for example, to have been the case in Bulgaria where regular protest movements against the financial and social position of the large older and retired population since 2007 have yet to produce a grey interest party capable of contesting national elections.

Media publicity can represent an important start-up resource for overcoming the collective action problems which face small new parties. Given the dominant discourse of 'compassionate ageism' in most European societies, which sees defence of older people's interests an uncontentious non-partisan issue, newly established grey-interest parties can also benefit early media interest and support. Pensioners' parties often have news value as a novelty or serve as a focus for populist media campaigning – in South–West England, for example, the activities of the tiny Senior Citizens Party founded in January 2004 were supported and sympathetically reported by the regional *Western Daily Press* newspaper as part of a campaign to highlight the neglected interests of the elderly (*Western Daily Press* 2004). However, case studies suggest, sympathetic early media coverage can quickly become hostile if grey interest parties gather political momentum and gain a real prospect of political representation (Vincent 2003).

12.4 The Political Prospects of Pensioners' Parties

Do pensioners' parties have any real prospect of emerging as significant political actors? Although the notion of a coherent and powerful 'grey vote' has been shown to be largely erroneous (Vincent et al. 2001; Goerres 2009), the growing numbers of older and retired voters in most European electorates and the increased salience of issues related to population ageing suggest that, all other things being equal, grey interest parties will have potential for further growth, especially in political systems that offer favourable institutional environment for new parties. Although political entrepreneurs seeking to establish grey interest parties are likely to face the additional barrier of established party loyalties among older voters developed over a political lifetime, there is some evidence of a nascent 'grey' political consciousness among some older voters. Opinion polling in western Europe in the late 1990s (Walker 1998) – as well as more recently in Scotland (Help the Aged in Scotland 2005, pp. 34–37) – suggests that large minorities of senior citizens in Europe have at certain points, in principle, been willing to consider supporting a pensioners' party.[8] Moreover, many current retirees in western Europe belong to age cohorts socialized in the more participatory, less deferential culture of 1960s when many West European party systems were undergoing dealignment, and may be more open to new political appeals. Similarly, in the new EU member states of central and eastern Europe, although older cohorts have undergone different patterns of political socialization to younger voters – and some may have a degree of identification with former ruling communist parties or 'historic' parties with roots in the pre-communist period – the absence of competitive party systems before 1989 has left voter-party linkages across the region comparatively loose.

However, even if they are likely to become more a frequent phenomenon in European politics, grey interest parties seem unlikely to advance beyond minor party status. There are a number of reasons for this. Firstly, although less constraining than sometimes argued, class, sectoral and social divisions among older people; established political identities and loyalties; and competition from established parties clearly set limits on the ability of grey interest parties to win the support of their chosen constituency. Available case study evidence suggests that grey parties' inroads into the elderly and retired electorate have rarely exceeded 20%. Slovenia's DeSUS, for example, has estimated that it gains about 15% support among older and retired voters (DeSUS 2006).[9] This suggests that even in ageing democracies where retired and older people form a high and growing proportion of the population – and typically – make up a still higher proportion of the electorate due to higher rates of turnout (Goerres 2007) – the *total* potential vote for grey interest parties lies in the region of

[8]Eurobarometer polling date for western Europe from 1992 cited by Walker (1998) finds that between 14% (Germany) and 42% (Portugal) of those aged over 60 would consider joining anage-based party promoting their interests. The average across the (then) EU12 was 22%.

[9]Similarly, evidence for the Czech Republic suggests that the Czech Pensioners for a Secure Life (DŽJ) party gained no more than13% of pensioners' voters during its best national election performance in 1992 (Kopeček 2005; Večerník 2006, p. 6) and was favoured by one-in-five Czech voters aged 60 or above during a short surge in popularity in the run-up to elections in 1998 (Hartl, Huk and Haberlová 1999).

5–15%. Even allowing for doubling or trebling of grey parties' ability to convert sympathy into electoral backing that might come with additional finance, better organization or greater professionalism, this implies electoral scores of between 2 and 7%.[10]

12.4.1 Towards a Grey Populism?

Some pensioners' parties seem content to play the role of niche minor party groupings representing sub-constituencies of older voters attracted by 'grey' politics. In some cases, this is because their activity is focused on goals such as winning publicity, rather than challenging for electoral representation. For other more successful groupings such as Slovenia's DeSUS, it reflects caution about changing a formula that has already brought a degree of political success.[11] Other grey parties, however, have sought to broaden their appeal beyond the claim to be a special representative for older people. Such efforts reflect both the electoral need to boost low levels of voter support and the fact that overtly representing sectional interests in the party political arena is widely seen as less legitimate than general programmatic appeals.

One such strategy for broadening the base of grey interest parties is to link demands on behalf of pensioners and older people with anti-establishment or anti-political protest positions, which are likely to appeal to unaffiliated and disaffected voters from other age groups. Some grey interest groups have effected this by simply merging with populist groupings, effectively becoming the 'seniors' platforms' of such protest parties.[12] Other pensioners' parties have fused grey interest politics and populism in more creative ways. One such example can be found in the GIL party's successful campaign in Israel's 2006 parliamentary elections, which saw it unexpectedly enter the Knesset. Although GIL polled well in population centres with large retired populations (Izenberg 2006), the party also gained the support of young professional voters in metropolitan districts in Tel Aviv, who reportedly saw GIL as a novel but safe form of protest voting, justifiable as a charitable gesture of solidarity with their grandparents' generation. Indeed, GIL's election strategy consciously sought to combine appeals for justice and empowerment

---

[10]As Mair (2001) notes, on aggregate, in West European democracies, even large, well-established parties such as Christian Democrats and Social Democrats only manage to garner the electoral support of around 40% of those who say that they are potentially sympathetic to these parties.

[11]Interview with the General Secretary of DeSUS Pavel Brglez, Ljubljana, 9 December 2008.

[12]For example, in 2005, significant elements of the Antwerp-based Flemish pensioners party WOW joined far-right Vlaams Blok (now *Vlaams Belang*) party contributing to the organization of VB's Seniors' Forum in that city. Similarly, in 2006, Russian Pensioners' Partymerged into theleft-wing nationalist Fair Russia (SR) bloc and the Czech Pensioners for a Secure Life (DŽJ) was absorbed by the populist, eurosceptic Independent Democrats party (NEZ).

for older people with an irreverent campaign targeted at young voters calling for anti-establishment protest voting (Urquhart 2006; Derfner 2006).[13]

The 3.8% unexpectedly polled by Germany's *Die Grauen* in the 2006 regional elections in Berlin stemmed from a very similar hybrid strategy combining demands for material improvements for older people; appeals to vote against the corruption and inertia of established parties; and a deliberately controversial poster campaign urging older voters to 'Screw for a Secure Retirement' (McKay 2007; Bekler 2008). A more advanced fusion of populism and 'grey' politics can be found in Luxembourg's ADR, which has shifted from demands for 'pension justice' for those employed outside the state sector towards a more general anti-establishment stance critical of corruption, wasteful public spending and elite projects such as European integration (Fehlen and Porier 2000, pp. 95–99).

12.5 Conclusions

Over the past two decades, pensioners' parties have been a widespread and recurrent minor party phenomenon in both western Europe and eastern Europe. Although in most cases they have remained fringe groupings – albeit sometimes of considerable longevity – in a smaller number of cases, they have enjoyed a degree of electoral success, gaining national parliamentary representation and exercised some political influence. 'Grey interest' parties operating at the margins of European party systems, this paper suggests, should be taken seriously and analysed using the broader comparative frameworks for new party formation.

Although there are considerable – and probably insurmountable – barriers blocking their development into major political actors, given the right institutional and political opportunities grey interest parties can draw on sufficient socio-political demands to establish themselves as minor parties. In this regard, the ability of some grey parties to link age-based demands with sectoral or populist discontent with the political systems of ageing democracies may be of particular significance.

References

Azoulay Y (2007) New plan aimed at helping infirm elderly regain independence, Haaretz.com. Online at http://www.haaretz.com/hasen/spages/923554.html (accessed 1 May 2009)

Bekler S (2008) Die Grauen machen weiter, *Tagesspiegel*, 29 February. Online at http://www.tagesspiegel.de/berlin/art270,2485741 (accessed 3 January 2009)

---

[13]GIL's success in 2006 was also facilitated by the charismatic appeal of its leader, the retired intelligence officer Rafi Eitan, well known as the commander of the covert operation in 1960 which abducted Nazi war criminal Adolf Eichmann for trial in to Jerusalem.

Birch S (2001) Electoral systems and party systems in Europe East and West. Perspect Eur Polit Soc 2(3):355–77

Bonoli G (2004) The politics of new social risks and policies, paper prepared for the International Sociological RC, 19th meeting, Paris, 2–4 September

Campbell AL (2003) How policies make citizens: senior political activism in the American welfare state. Harvard University Press, Princeton, NJ

Derfner L (2006) The grand old party, Jerusalem Post, 6 April (online edition)

DeSUS (2006) Izkušnje, poštenost, strpnost, modrost, odprtost, http://www.desus.si/?nav=90&blog=29&m=1# (accessed 1 October 2007)

Dunleavy P (1991) Democracy, bureaucracy and public choice: economic explanations in political science. Prentice Hall, London

Eberstadt N, Groth H (2007) Healthy old Europe, Foreign affairs, May/June 2007

Evers A, Jürgen W (1999) Political organization and participation of older people: traditions and changes in five European countries. In: Alan W, Gerhard N (eds) The Politics of Old Age in Europe. Open University Press, Buckingham, pp 42–61

Feltenius D (2007) Client organizations in a corporatist country: pensioners' organizations and pensions policy in Sweden. J Eur Soc Policy 17(2):139–151

Fehlen F, Porier P (2000) Les élections au Grand-Duché de Luxembourg, Rapport sur les élections législatives du 13 juin 1999, Luxembourg: Chambre des deputés.Online at http://www.chd.lu/fr/organisation/documentation/espTele.jsp (accessed 1 July 2007)

Fink-Hafner D (2008) Electoral reform in Slovenia: Much ado about nothing, Paper presented at the EPOP conference, Manchester, 12–14 September 2008

Goerres A (2007) Why are older people more likely to vote? The impact of ageing on electoral turnout across Europe. Br J Polit Int Relat 9(1):90–121

Goerres A (2009) The political participation of older people in Europe: the greying of our democracies. Macmillan, Basingstoke

Green-Pedersen C, Haverland M (2002) Review essay: the new politics and scholarship of the welfare state. J Eur Soc Policy 12(1):43–51

Gynn J, Sara A (1999) The politics of old age in the UK. In: Alan W, Gerhard N (eds) The politics of old age in Europe. Open University Press, Buckingham, pp 152–167

Hanley S (2001) Towards breakthrough or breakdown? The consolidation of the KSČM as a neo-communist successor party in the Czech Republic. J Commun Stud Transit Polit 17(3):96–116

Harmel R, Robertson JD (1985) Formation and success of new parties: a cross national analysis. Int Polit Sci Rev 6(4):501–23

Hartl J, Jaroslav H, Haberlová V (1999) Česká společnost 1998. Management Press, Prague

Help the Aged (2005) Council tax: a path to poverty? Help the aged. Online at http://www.scottish.parliament.uk/business/committees/lg/inquiries/ctax/Help_the_Aged.pdf (accessed 25 October 2007)

Herzog H (1987) Minor parties: the relevancy perspective. Comp Polit 19(3):317–29

Hug S (2001) Altering party systems: strategic behavior and the emergence of new political parties in western democracies. University of Michigan Press, Ann Arbor, MI

Henn M, W Mark, W Dominic (2002) A generation apart? Youth and political participation in Britain. Br J Polit Int Relat 4(2):167–92

Iecovich E (2002) Pensioners political parties: the Israeli case. In: Jean-Philippe VD (ed) Cahiers du FIAPA, vol 1, Grey power? political power and influence. FIAPA, Paris, pp 118–32

Izenberg D (2006) The nuances behind the numbers, *Jerusalem Post*, 6 April

Javno (2008) 'Serbia Agrees 15-Month IMF Stand-By Deal', 13 November. Online at http://www.javno.com/en-economy/serbia-agrees-15-month-imf-stand-by-deal_203534 (accessed 3 January 2009)

Kitschelt H (1989) The logics of party formation: ecological politics in Belgium and West Germany. Cornell University Press, Ithaca, NY

Kitschelt H (2004) Diversification and reconfiguration of party systems in postindustrial democracies. International Policy Analysis Unit, Friedrich Ebert Stiftung. Online at http://www.fes.de/europolity/finalversionkitsch.PDF (accessed 11 January 2008)

Kitschelt H (2007) Growth and persistence of the radical right in postindustrial democracies: advances and challenges in comparative research. W Eur Polit 30(5):1176–1206

Kölnische R (2007) Spendenaffäre bei den Grauen, 10 October

Kopeček L (2005) Strana za životní jistoty. In: Malíř J, Marek P et al (eds) Politické strany: vývoj politických stran a hnutí včeských zemích a Československu, II díl 1938–2004. Doplněk, Brno, pp 1633–43

Kubitza A (2005) Pensions in Europe 2002: pension beneficiaries, Statistics in focus 11/2005, European Commission. Online at http://www.eds-destatis.de/en/downloads/sif/nk_05_11.pdf (accessed 1 June 2009)

Lewis P (2000) Political parties in post-communist Eastern Europe. Routledge, London

Lucardie P (2000) Prophets, purifiers and prolocutors: towards a theory on the emergence of new parties. Party Polit 6(2):175–85

McKay J (2007) The Berlin land election of 2006. Ger Polit 16(4):518–25

Mair P (2001) The green challenge and political competition: how typical is the German experience? Ger Polit 10(2):99–116

Mukesh C, Betcherman G, Banerji A (2007) From red to gray: the third transition of ageing populations in Eastern Europe and the former Soviet Union. World Bank, Washington, DC. Online at http://siteresources.worldbank.org/ECAEXT/Resources/publications/454763-1181939083693/full_report.pdf (accessed 10 July 2007)

Novinite news agency (2007) 'Pensioners' Party Set Up In Bulgaria', 12 May. Online at http://www.novinite.com/view_news.php?id=80585 (accessed 11 October 2007)

Pierson P (1996) The new politics of the welfare state. World Polit 48(2):143–79

Phelps E (2006) Young adults and electoral turnout in Britain: towards a generational model of political participation. Sussex European Institute working paper No. 92

Pop L, Vanhuysse P (2004) Review article: varieties of capitalism, varieties of theory? Conceptualizing paths of change and patterns of economic interaction across models of market democracy. J Eur Publ Pol 11(1):167–177

Redding K, Viterna JS (1999) Political demands, political opportunity structures and the differential success of green parties. Soc Forces 78(2):491–510

Robertson F (2009) Youth political participation in Poland and Romania. Unpublished PhD thesis, University College London

Sikk A (2005) How unstable? Volatility and the genuinely new parties in Eastern Europe. Eur J Polit Res 44(1):391–412

Sikk A (2006) Highways to power: new party success in three young democracies. Tartu University Press, Tartu

Susser B (2007) The retirees' (Gimla'im) party: an "escapist" phenomenon? Israel Aff 13(1):187–92

Tavits M (2006) Party system change: testing a model of new party entry. Party Polit 12(1):99–119

Tavits M (2008) Party systems in the making: the emergence and success of new parties in new democracies. Br J Polit Sci 38(1):113–133

Tepe M, Vanhuysse P (2009) Are aging welfare states on the path to gerontocracy? evidence from 18 OECD democracies, 1980–2002. J Publ Pol 29(1):1–28

Thornton G (1995) Pillars of society shaken by political earthquake: the Dutch election – May 1994. Representation 33(3):106–110

Time (1972) Symptoms of malaise, 20 March. Online at http://www.time.com/magazine/article0,9171,942501,00.html (accessed 1 May 2009)

Urquhart C (2006) Youth contribute to success of group promoting rights of the elderly, The Guardian, 30 March

van Stipdonk VP, van Holsteyn JJM (1995) Wat Ouderen Verbond, Verklaringen van het ontstaan en succes van een nieuwe partij, *Jaarboek DNPP*. Online at www.rug.nl/dnpp/jaarboeken/jaarboek1995 (accessed 1 July 2007)

Vanhuysse P (2001) Review article: the political economy of pensions: western theories, eastern facts. J Eur Publ Pol 8(5):853–861
Vanhuysse P (2006) Divide and pacify: strategic social policies and political protests in post-communist democracies. Central European University Press, Budapest
Večerník J (2006) Changing Social Status of Pensioners and Prospects of Pension Reform in the Czech Republic, Institute of Economic Studies, Charles University, Occasional Paper 2/2006
Vincent JA, Patterson G, Wale K (2001) Politics and old age: older citizens and political processes in Britain. Ashgate, Basingstoke
Vincent JA (2003) Demography, politics and old age, paper presented at the British Society for Gerontology Annual Conference, Newcastle upon Tyne, 4–6 September. Online at http://www.people.ex.ac.uk/JVincent/Conference%20papers/BSG%20Newcastle/Newcastle%20Paper.doc (accessed 1 July 2007)
Viriot Durandal J-P (2003) Le pouvoir gris. Presse universitaires de France, Paris
Walker A (1998) Speaking for themselves: the new politics of old age in Europe. Educ Ageing 13(1):13–36
Waller M (1993) Political actors and political roles in East-Central Europe. J Communist Stud Transit Polit 9(4):21–36
Wang FTY (1999) Resistance and old age: the subject behind the American seniors movement. In: Adrienne SC, Allan I, Laura E (eds) Reading Foucault for social work. New York, Columbia University Press, pp 189–218
Whiteley P, Seyd P, Richardson JJ (1994) True blues: the politics of conservative party membership. Oxford University Press, Oxford
Willey J (1998) Institutional arrangements and the success of new parties in old democracies. Polit Stud 33:125–64
Western Daily Press (2004), Grey power aiming to shake up politics, 15 April Online at http://westpress.co.uk/new/util/content.jsp?id=9602626 (accessed 7 September 2007)

Kolibri 360 GmbH
Ferdinand-Jühlke-Straße 7
99095 Erfurt, Deutschland
produktsicherheit@kolibri360.de